DEDICATION

This book is dedicated to all personnel who served with or supported 51 Squadron and in memory of those members who gave their lives In the service of their country.

Squadron Autographs

[signature] D.F.C. (Pilot) — SQUADRON ASSOCIATION CHAIRMAN

Keith S Ford — AUTHOR

[signature] — SQUADRON ASSOCIATION SECRETARY

[signature] (NAV)

David Hearn DFC (Pilot

Alan Gaskell (Navigator)   *[signature]* Engineer

Tom Bayfield DFC. (Gunnery Leader)

p.p. William Morton DFC (Navigator)
Alan Morton

D. P. Storey D.F.C. (Navigator)

[signature] George DFC. (Pilot)

Wallace A. *[signature]* DFM (Engineer)

Wallie Stocker DFC. (Engineer)

A. S. *[signature]* AE (WOP/AG) POW

Bill *[signature]* (Eng)

[signature] Fitter II A.

[signature] Palmer A/G.

John Brewster (Pilot)

[signature] (Dixie)
BOMBING LEADER

Shuburton nee Poole
Sgt (W.A.A.F.)

P. I. Radford

Leo Sharp D.F.C (AG)

J.J.H. Huddfield. (PILOT)

N. Val Hood. (AG)

Harrison DFM

J. R. Georges

Reginald Levy D.F.C.

H. Johnson (WOP)

C.A. Clifford (NAV)

Ian Nelson (NAV)

(PILOT)

H.A. Cocestell DFC

Betty King (OTT)

Don Jevons (WAG)

Ernie Herrald

Phil Barens.

Arthur E. Ellis
(PTI)

Typeset using Ventura Publisher Version 3

Fonts used, Courier and Times

Published in the United Kingdom by Compaid Graphics
T'otherside, Drumacre Lane East, Longton, Preston. PR4 4SD. Lancashire
www.compaidgraphics.co.uk

COPYRIGHT All rights reserved. No part of this publication may be reproduced, or transmitted in any form without the permission of Compaid Graphics (Publishers) and the Author.

Crown copyright material included in this book is reproduced with permission received on behalf of The Controller Of Her Majesty's Stationery Office.

ISBN 0 9517965 1 8
Library Cataloguing Data

RAF SQUADRON HISTORY

358.430 942

Rev 3 August 93

SNAITH DAYS

Life With 51 Squadron 1942/45

by

KEITH S FORD BSc
1992

51 SQUADRON ASSOCIATION HISTORIAN

Compiled for the 51 Squadron Association

LIST OF MAPS AND ILLUSTRATIONS

Map 1 RAF Snaith
Map 2 RAF Snaith Technical Site
Map 3 RAF Snaith Site 4 and Communal Site
Map 4 RAF Snaith Sites 1 and 3
Map 5 RAF Snaith Site 5
Map 6 RAF Snaith Site 2 and WAAF 1
Map 7 Navigator's plotting map.
Map 8 Route map for Krefeld operation.
Map 9 Route map for Nuremberg operation.
Map 10 Mine laying in Frisians.
Map 11 Route map for Hamburg operation.
Map 12 1944 Strategic targets.
Map 13 Layout of V1 site.
Map 14 Kiel 'Mandrel' screen.
Map 15 RAF Snaith bomb dump.

Fig. 1 Krefeld Order of Battle
Fig. 2 Meteorological report
Fig. 3 Navigator's 'Flimsy'
Fig. 4 Goldfish Club certificate
Fig. 5 Operations board.
Fig. 6 'Drem' Mk II lighting system.
Fig. 7 'D' Type landing circuit.
Fig. 8 Angle of Glide Indicator.
Fig. 9 Snaith lighting at night.
Fig. 10 Layout of Halifax Navigator's station.
Fig. 11 Flight Engineer's Log.
Fig. 12 Layout of Halifax W/Ops. station.
Fig. 13 Wireless Operator's Log.
Fig. 14 'Gee' Hyperbolic chart.
Fig. 15 'Gee' displays.
Fig. 16 Layout of Air Bomber's station.
Fig. 17 Sterkrade Order of Battle.
Fig. 18 Telegrams to next of kin.
Fig. 19 Letter to next of kin.

Fig. 20 Caterpillar Club certificate.
Fig. 21 H2S Plotting chart.
Fig. 22 Bombing Plot for Krefeld operation.
Fig. 23 Compass corrector card.
Fig. 24 Bomb-Sight Calibration Card.
Fig. 25 'Fishpond' Indicator Unit.
Fig. 26 'Fishpond' display.
Fig. 27 H2S Scanner.
Fig. 28 H.E. Bomb.
Fig. 29 T.M.H.D.O.O.T.I.F.
Fig. 30 Mains operated 'Gee' set.
Fig. 31 Navigator's Assessment Form.
Fig. 32 H2S Indicator Unit.

Fig. 33 H2S Trainer.
Fig. 34 Map for H2S Trainer.
Fig. 35 AML Bombing Trainer.
Fig. 36 'Q' Type dinghy.
Fig. 37 'Seven Deadly Sins of A.G.s'
Fig. 38 'Seven Deadly Sins of W/Ops.'
Fig. 39 IFF Control Unit.
Fig. 40 Flight Engineer's Petrol Log.
Fig. 41 Key to Navigator's Log Sheets
Fig. 42 Navigator's Log 1944 (5 pages)
Fig. 43 Propaganda leaflet.
Fig. 44 F24 Camera
Fig. 45 Menu and Entertainments
Fig. 46 Gun Harmonisation
Fig. 47 'Gee' transmissions
Fig. 48 Aerial system on a Halifax
Fig. 49 Nose art 'D' Dopey.
Fig. 50 Cartoon
Fig. 51 Christmas card.
Fig. 52 Nose Art Photos.
Fig 53. Winners Cup
Fig 54. Bomber Command Night Photography report
Fig 55. Landing Control board

In addition there are 77 photographs included in the book. A total of 158 photos and illustrations.

VI

TABLE OF CONTENTS

List of Maps and Illustrations	VI
Table of Contents	VII
Forewords	IX
Acknowledgements	XI
Introduction	XIII
Chapter 1 A Tour Around The Station	1
Chapter 2 Administering The Station	7
Chapter 3 Organising The Operations	19
Chapter 4 Flying Control	31
Chapter 5 Facets of A Squadron Operation	43
Chapter 6 Post-Operations and Losses	73
Chapter 7 Analysis Of Operations 1943 - 1945	95
Chapter 8 Technical Support	124
Chapter 9 Training and Practice	148
Chapter 10 Mishaps, Achievements and Anecdotes	164
Appendix A 51 Squadron Aircraft Losses	180
Appendix B Halifax Aircraft Serving With 51 Squadron	184
Appendix C 51 Squadron Operations Between Jan 1943 and May 1945	186
Appendix D Roll Of Honour	194
Appendix E Commanders and Awards	208
Bibliography	210
Glossary	212
Photo Album: Centre Pages	

FOREWORDS

Foreword by Wing Commander Mike Blee, Officer Commanding No 51 Squadron, RAF Wyton.

At first sight this may appear to be just another collection of wartime stories, but Keith Ford's meticulously researched book gives a fascinating insight into the day to day running of an operational heavy bomber squadron and the station on which it was based. From Keith's narrative, full of human interest, the serious historian can trace the development of equipment and tactics on heavy bomber squadrons in the RAF from 1943 to 1945. The author has drawn heavily on his personal experiences and those of the squadron's wartime members in the 51 Squadron Association, of which he is an active member.

The detail of Keith Ford's personal memories and the inclusion of hitherto unpublished personal anecdotes of past members of 51 Squadron make compulsive reading for anyone with an interest in the Royal Air Force and its history, but the humour, courage and comradeship brought out in its pages make the book a good read for anyone.

Keith Ford served on No 51 Squadron at Snaith from 1943 to 1945 as Groundcrew, Instruments-today known as Flight Systems, Avionics. He is a voluntary helper at the Yorkshire Air Museum as a specialist on Avionics and is also a member of the RAF Amateur Radio Society.

Foreword by Jim Feaver, DFC, Chairman of 51 Squadron Association and Officer Commanding C Flight, 51 Squadron, at RAF Snaith 1944.

Take the A645 road East from the A1 and cross the M62 at Eggborough, Pass through Heck and you will see on your left just before you approach Pollington Village a disused airfield. The hangars are still standing but like so many other similar airfields it is now only a ghost of what it once was- RAF Snaith. This was the wartime home of over 2,000 mainly young men and women perhaps better described as lads and lasses-'youth in its prime'.

Keith Ford has given rebirth to the life and times of that era in this book 'Snaith Days', life with 51 Squadron 1942-45. It will recall many happy and not so happy memories for those lads and lasses of that era. They will, I am sure, give thanks to Keith for writing up this production telling the story of a Yorkshire airfield from where 51 Squadron flew Halifax bombers which joined the Armadas of those years, en-route to Germany and the occupied territories.

Keith, who served with the squadron from 1943 to 1945 in the Instrument Section, became a specialist in Flight Systems and Bombsights and was in an ideal position to observe the workings of the squadron. This must have sparked off his enthusiasm and dedication to give so much of his time to researching and producing this book.

In the book Keith has covered a whole range of the life of an operational squadron from the moment of passing through the guardroom at the main gate, to life in the various mess halls, the preparation of operations, the debriefing at their conclusion and the maintenance of the aircraft. It is detailed with interesting and authentic accuracy.

In addition to his writing Keith has given much of his time as a voluntary helper at the Yorkshire Air Museum, Elvington, in the capacity of a specialist in Avionics. He is also a part-time lecturer in navigation at his local college.

In conclusion, this book proves to be an excellent record of a Halifax bomber squadron - No 51.

"TIME MAY BE SWIFT BUT MEMORIES ARE SURE"

Acknowledgements

I must acknowledge the help and support received from the 51 Squadron Association Committee and the numerous members of the association who provided materials and photographs for inclusion in the book. Many of these members are mentioned in the text. Thanks to mrs Paddy Reed of 76 Squadron Association for information on 4 Group operations procedure. Wing Commander Blee and Squadron Leader Mason, serving members of 51 Squadron, assisted by supplying information and photographs from the squadron archives.

Thanks are dure to the Keeper of Aviation Records, RAF Museum, and the Public Records Office Kew who on behalf of HMSO have authorised publication of information from their archives. The Imperial War Museum have kindly allowed me permission to publish copyright photos from their collection. Crown copyright information from the RAF Museum, PSA, Ordnance Survey, PRO Kew, and RCHME Swindon helped in the production of some of the sketch maps.

I am grateful to Marie and John Jackson for information on Pollington Village and a civilians experience of 51 Squadron sojourn at Snaith. Also their son Neal Jackson LRPS of Appolo Photography for providing photographs.

Thanks to Mike Mansfield, with hisprofessional experience in computers and software, whose support was necessary for a successful DTP exercise.

I am also indebted to my wife, Margaret, for encouragement and the help she gave me in the production of the text by employing her word processing and keyboard experience.

INTRODUCTION

In researching the history of the squadron it became clear that there was sufficient material available to fill more than one volume. However the 50th Anniversary of the squadron's arrival at Snaith, to commence operations with the Halifax aircraft, occurred in Oct 1992. This book was therefore compiled on behalf of the Squadron Association to mark the event and record this era of the unit's history. An endeavour has been made to cover in detail all aspects of life and operations at Snaith so that the book should have an appeal to all members of the Association

Previous efforts to produce a book on the squadron's history have not come to fruition. This is possibly because there can be difficulties in finding publishers interested in squadron histories, since they may not be sure about the demand for such a publication. Publishing problems have been compounded by the current recession, which has affected the industry. To overcome this problem Snaith Days has been produced by Desk Top Publishing and stored on magnetic media. This means that it is possible to publish on demand and overcome any problems of a limited edition. A thermal binding process with soft back has been employed in order to fit in with this publishing system. To ensure the clarity of a number of maps and diagrams, most of which have not been reproduced before, an A4 size format has been chosen.

Chapter 1

A TOUR AROUND THE STATION

It was on a winters day in October 1942 that the 51 Squadron 'Chiv. and Dish.' boys arrived at Snaith following a tour of duty with Coastal Command. The squadron had returned to the Yorkshire based number Four Group of Bomber Command to exchange its Whitley aircraft for the newer four engined Mk II Halifax bomber, which had come into service with the Group in 1941. The majority of the squadron arrived by rail on a special train, the carriages being shunted into the sidings at Heck station and during the unloading process a problem occurred when one of the carriages ran back onto the main line causing a blockage. Heck station, which was located near the airfield, is now closed but remnants of it can still be seen. Being located on the main LNER railway line it was regularly used by RAF personnel travelling to and from Snaith.

RAF Snaith was a World War 2 airfield which opened in July 1941, and although it was located near the village of Pollington the name Snaith was chosen to avoid confusion with RAF Pocklington, also in Yorkshire. The layout of the airfield as shown in Map 1 was typical of many Bomber Command airfields constructed in World War 2. A Yorkshire location being a convenient take off point for raids on Germany.

The airfield had three runways set at approximately 60 degrees to each other to cope with changes in wind direction. This facility was very important since pilots could encounter problems taking off or landing a Halifax with a strong crosswind. Two of the runways were of concrete construction, and the third and main runway which had been extended to cope with four engined bombers, was Tarmac. On the same site as the runways there was a Control Tower, three hangars and the Technical Site. Unlike the pre World War 2 designs, this was a dispersed airfield with several Domestic Sites containing sleeping quarters, located at strategic distances from the main airfield in order to reduce casualties in the event of an air attack.

Since it was a dispersed airfield, bicycles were widely used as a form of personal transport. There was however a limited supply of RAF issue bicycles available from the Cycle Store, so many of the personnel brought their own bicycles to the station. These private bicycles had to be registered with the Guardroom and the registration number along with the owners name and section painted on the crossbar or down tube of the frame. Another item which had to be registered but also deposited with the Guardroom was a camera, since it was an offence to use a camera on the station without official permission. This is one of the reasons for the limited number of war time photographs available.

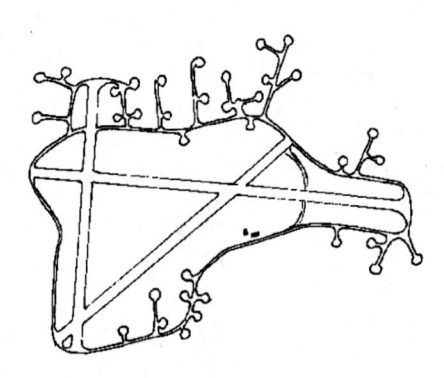

The domestic accommodation was able to cater for over 2,000 personnel and in 1944 the establishment was for 164 RAF Officers, 8 WAAF Officers, 375 Senior NCO's, 8 WAAF Senior NCO's, 1,477 RAF other ranks, and 378 WAAF other ranks. On the Technical Site there were a few wooden barrack huts mainly for Officers and Senior NCOs but the majority of the personnel were accommodated on the Dispersed Sites in wooden barrack huts or Nissen huts, the latter being the major form of accommodation for other ranks. These Nissen huts were semi-circular corrugated iron constructions with doors and windows at the ends and were rather spartan affairs. Being largely metal they were cold in winter, and in summer could be oppressively hot and suffered from condensation under conditions of high humidity. Other Ranks occupied huts which were not partitioned, with a circular iron stove in the centre. This was not very effective for heating the hut even when the fuel (coke or coal), which was generally in short supply, was available. On cold nights the occupants of the huts would gather round the stove to try and obtain some warmth from it. The beds were typical RAF issue metal utilitarian affairs provided with hard mattresses supplied in the form of three squares and hence known as 'biscuits', plus the ubiquitous military blankets and hard pillows.

For Officers and some NCO's the huts were partitioned into rooms and the Officers were able to

1

A TOUR AROUND THE STATION

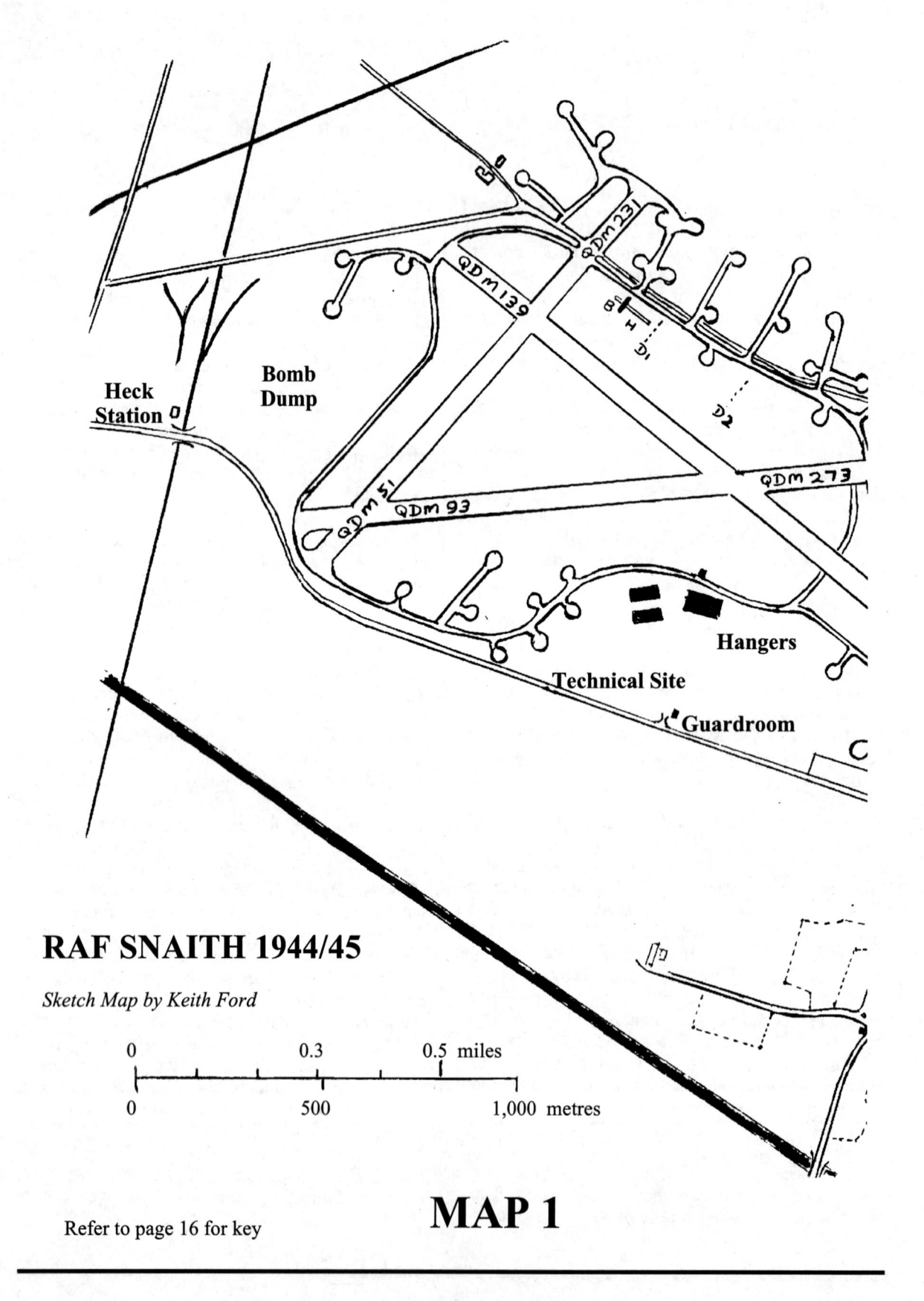

RAF SNAITH 1944/45

Sketch Map by Keith Ford

MAP 1

Refer to page 16 for key

A TOUR AROUND THE STATION

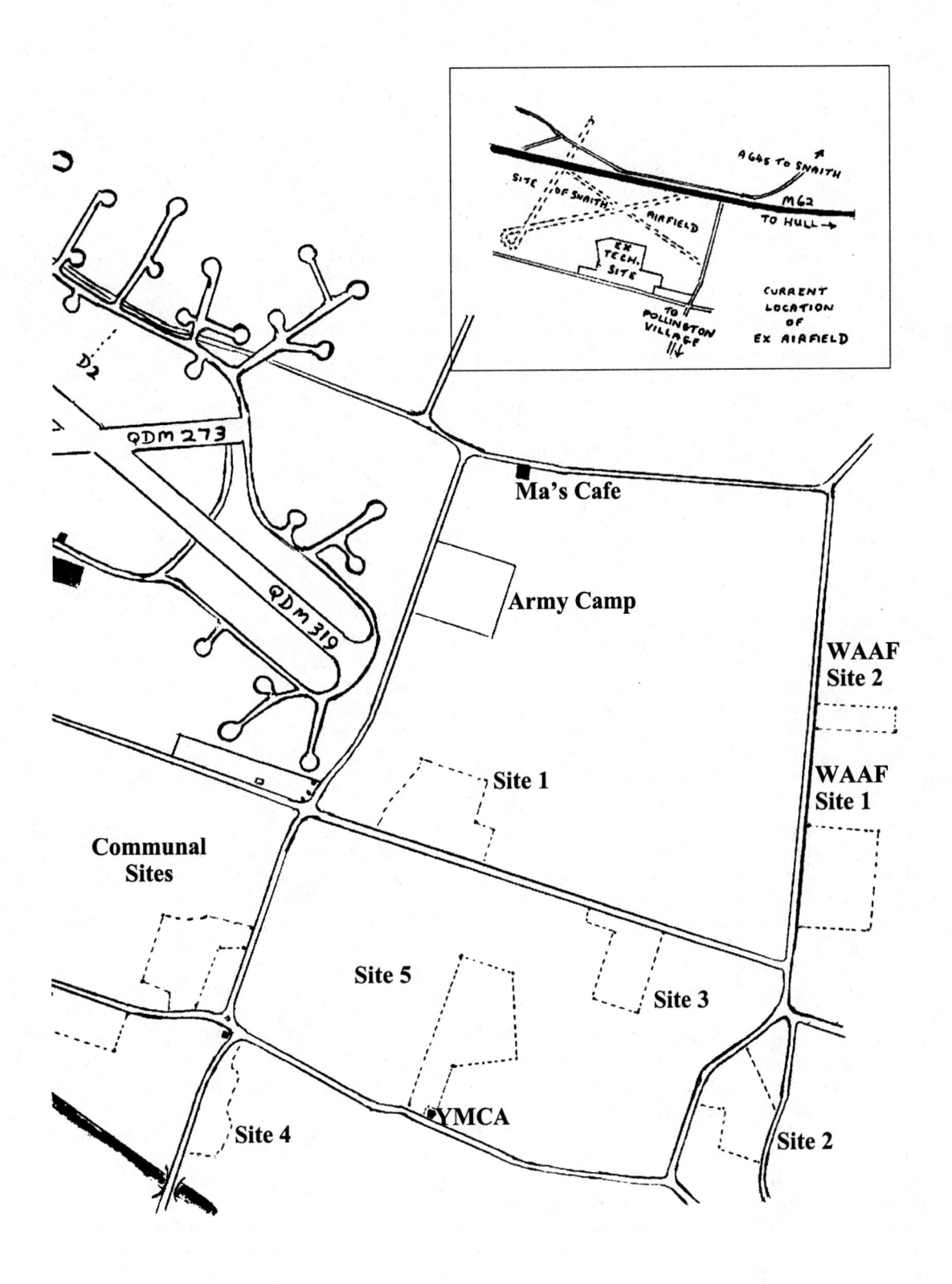

A TOUR AROUND THE STATION

avail themselves of the domestic services provided by WAAF batwomen. The huts on the domestic sites were accompanied by ablutions accommodated in small 'Maycrete' buildings. On a winters morning airmen and airwomen would tumble out of bed and having dressed in a cold hut would run across to the ablutions to wash and shave in water which was regularly cold. A general problem with RAF ablutions was the absence of sink plugs, so it was a common practice for airmen to keep a sink plug with their toilet gear. Shower or bath blocks were available on the Technical Site, Communal Site and WAAF site.

For breakfast, personnel cycled or walked to the appropriate mess then afterwards the airmen made up their bedspace to the satisfaction of the Admin. personnel and cycled off to work leaving the duty hut orderly behind during the morning to finish off tidying up the hut and carrying out other chores. Officers of course could leave domestic duties in the hands of their Batwomen.

Airmen's hut furnishings were very spartan, the beds being ranged alongside one another down both sides of the hut, with a single shelf above the beds running the full length of the hut, on which to keep folded items like greatcoats and 'best blue' uniform, plus webbing haversacks. The rest of the kit being stored in a locked kitbag alongside the bed. Very little furniture was issued apart from the odd table and wooden chairs. however many airmen and women after getting established on the station would obtain further storage facilities such as wooden boxes. Armourers could acquire empty ammunition and bomb boxes, members of the Instrument Section had access to wooden suitcase style boxes used for transporting Astrographs, the instrument having been installed in an aircraft lost on operation. They also had some useful mouse traps made from portable oxygen bottle transit boxes. Some Wireless mechanics built radios for their huts using redundant valve storage boxes and available radio components.

There were five Domestic Sites, primarily providing living accommodation for Airmen and Officers and a Communal Site containing buildings which included the Number Two Officers, Sergeant's and Airman's Messes, a NAAFI Club, Education block and ablution blocks containing showers and baths. Originally No 1 WAAF Site was the only domestic location for the WAAFs, but as the war progressed the number of WAAFs on the station increased since they were now involved in nearly all the sections on the station, including Administration, M.T, Sick Quarters, Messes, Signals, I/O, and Engineering trades. Hence because of this increase a second (No.2) WAAF site was opened. This consisted of Nissen huts and an ablution block in a field. There were no baths, so to get a bath the WAAFs had to cycle down to No 1 site in pyjamas and greatcoat. Fortunately they did not have to pass any of the airmen's sites on the way. Generally Airwomen who were not on shift work and did not need 'early calls' were moved to No 2 site. The layout of these sites is shown in Maps 3 to 6.

On Domestic site No 1 there was a building originally built as a gymnasium, but in order to improve the entertainment facilities for the personnel it was converted into the Station Cinema called the 'Astra', by the addition of a projection room and the installation of a sloping floor and seats. An example of this type of building is shown in photo No 15. The 'Astra' became very popular with all ranks, but in winter it suffered from a lack of adequate heating even with the presence of a WAAF companion to cuddle up to keep an airman warm. It was therefore a common practice in winter for cinemagoers to take one of their blankets to wrap around themselves. The WAAF clerks from Accounts had to collect the entrance money, and there was a degree of unfairness here, since for the WAAFs this counted as an extra duty, whereas the volunteer projectionists were paid two shillings and six pence for their services. Seats cost 4d, 6d and one shilling (the shilling seats were the first six rows, reserved for Officers). and when asked 'how many' at the ticket office a joking reply by some other ranks was "a fourpenny one and a blanket". In common with other wartime RAF cinemas, when the film tended to lack entertainment value the audience provided their own by virtue of the humorous remarks shouted out. On occasions these comments were guaranteed to make the WAAFs blush. Often propaganda war films, particularly American ones, were divorced from the realities of service life and these would raise some ribald comments from the audience. Of all the domestic sites used by 51 Squadron the only one still in existence today is WAAF Site No 1, most of the buildings are still in existance but have been converted for use as an animal farm.

The layout of the main airfield was designed to facilitate the take-off, landing and dispersal of the Squadron aircraft. A tarmac and concrete perimeter track circled the airfield connecting the ends of the various runways and at various points around the peri. track were circular hardstandings connected to it by an access track. Because of their shape these were colloquially known as 'frying pan' style hardstandings. Air Ministry regulations decreed that unless required to go into hangars for servicing or repair all aircraft should be dispersed around the airfield. The Squadron aircraft were allocated to the two and subsequently three flights designated A, B and C with up to 10 aircraft per flight. These were parked on the permanent hardstandings at which daily servicing, refuelling and bombing up were carried out. There were huts on the flights for use as Flight Offices etc and numerous dugouts. In early 1944, particularly during maximum effort raids, taxiing problems were observed so in June 1944 an Air Ministry Works Dept. representative from 4 Group came to discuss the problem and suggest possible alterations to the airfield layout. The layout shown in Map 1 was the modified peri-track in existence at the end of 1944.

Initially all the aircraft at Snaith carried the squadron code letters MH, but later on in 1943 some of the aircraft, particularly those of C Flight were given the code letters LK. However, in January 1944 when 578 Squadron was formed from C Flight, the code letters LK were allocated to it, and code C6 was allocated to 51 Squadron to replace LK.

RAF Snaith like most wartime airfields contained a Technical site which is shown in Map 2 and was located on the main airfield. It included two T2 type hangars, manufactured by the Teeside Bridge and Engineering Company, The 'T' standing for transportable, and the approximate size was 113 ft x 239 ft. There was also the larger main hangar a 'J' type size 150 ft x 300 ft, designed in 1939 by Sir William Arrol and Co. Ltd. Attached to this hangar were lean-to buildings housing various Engineering sections including Instruments, Electrical, Armoury, Wireless, Engine Bay and Servicing Adminstration. When the squadron's engineering personnel first moved into the Technical Site they found a glider in one of the T2 hangars. For the record, in 1942 glider towing experiments were carried out at Snaith and the General Aircraft 'Hamilcar' tank carrying glider made its first flight from this airfield on 27th March 1942.

Other buildings on the site included various sizes of wartime concrete buildings, Nissen huts and wooden huts to accommodate both Administrative and Technical activities along with a limited amount of domestic accommodation and ablu-tions. The hangars, along with some of the Technical Site wartime 'Maycrete' and 'Orbit' buildings, are still in existence today and can be readily viewed from the Heck to Pollington road. These concrete buildings are the few remaining signs in various parts of Yorkshire and other counties that an airfield once stood there. They were built around reinforced concrete posts and had roofs of either boards and roofing felt or corrugated precast asbestos cement. There were also a number of air raid shelters and EWS tanks for use in the case of fire.

Some of the sections accommodated in the Technical Site buildings, the locations of which are shown in the plan of the site (Map No 2), included Maintenance Workshops, Safety Equipment and Parachute Section, Photographic Section, Station Armoury, Radar and Link Trainers, Main Store, Gas and Decontamination Centre, Flying Control, Bombing Trainer, Motor Transport Section, Station Sick Quarters and various Messes.

Engine fuel was an important storage item at Snaith and the M.T. Section had a storage facility for motor engine fuel convenient for their garage. However, the major petrol storage facilities were those necessitated by the consumption of 100 octane petrol by the four engines on each Halifax aircraft, since a raid well into Germany could require a fuel load of over 2,000 gallons per aircraft. This was provided by 72,000 gallon bulk storage units located at two points on the Technical Site, each with six 12,000 underground tanks and separate hard standings for the RAF tankers and the vehicles bringing in petrol supplies from a Petroleum Company. At each unit there were facilities for pumping the fuel into Refuelling Tankers of 2,500 gallons capacity and 900 gallon trailable Petrol Bowsers.

Water, being an essential commodity on the station, was pumped to an elevated water tank to provide water under pressure for distribution to various buildings on the site. This was a standard Braithwaite tank on a high scaffold, located on the Technical Site. Along with water supplies the disposal of sewage was important. This was dealt with by a Sewage Plant located to the East of No 1 WAAF site. In the early days of Snaith there were problems with the sewage leaking into the irrigation systems of the local farmers. The influx of a large RAF population was making its presence felt by the local community in more ways than one.

A TOUR AROUND THE STATION

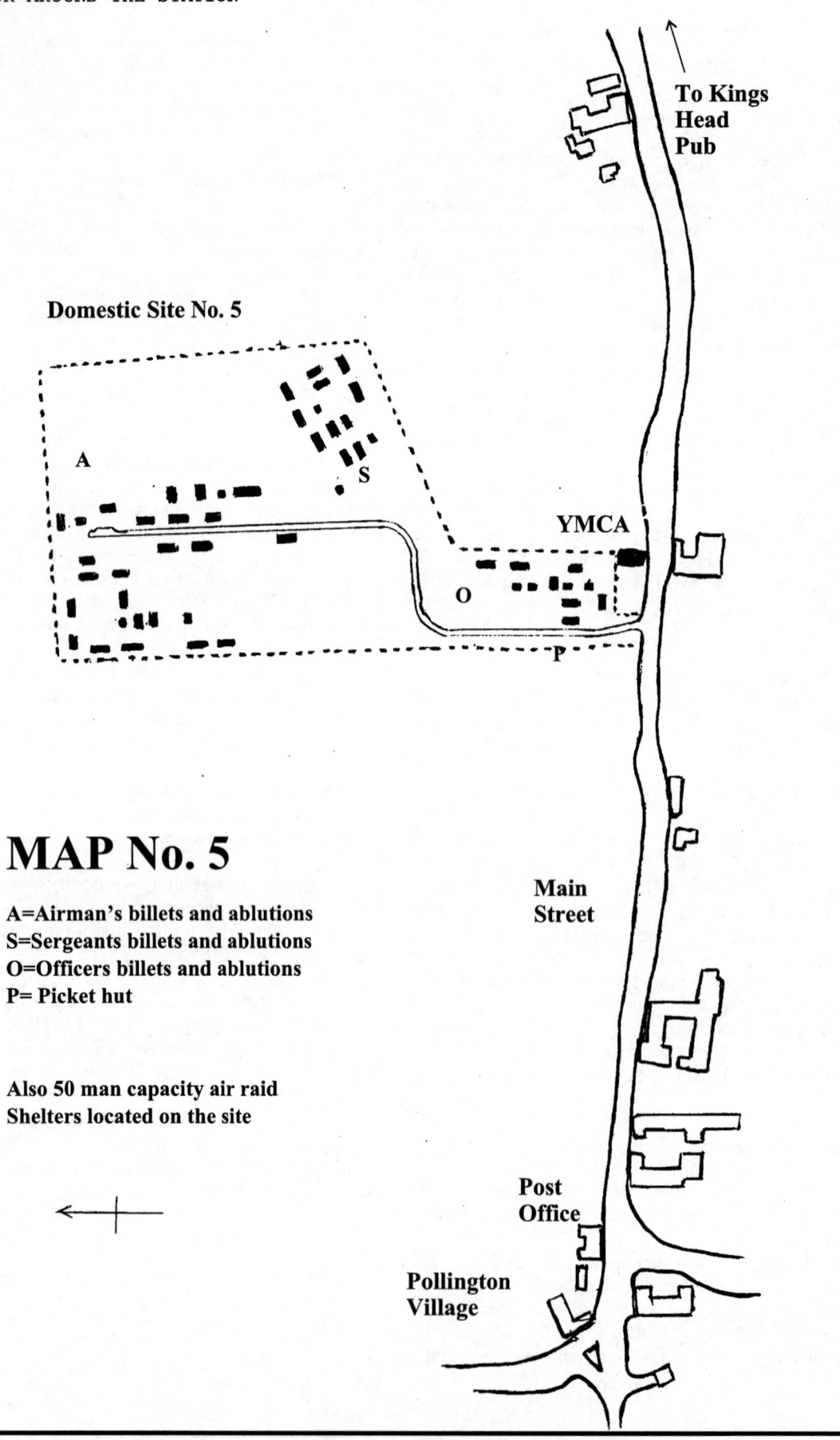

To Kings Head Pub

Domestic Site No. 5

A

S

YMCA

O

P

MAP No. 5

A=Airman's billets and ablutions
S=Sergeants billets and ablutions
O=Officers billets and ablutions
P= Picket hut

Also 50 man capacity air raid Shelters located on the site

Main Street

Post Office

Pollington Village

Chapter 2

ADMINISTERING THE STATION

Newcomers arriving at Heck station to join the squadron, unless they were senior enough to request transport, would have to trek from the station, with loaded webbing equipment and a heavy kitbag, to the Technical Site. At the main gate they met the S.P. on duty and passed the inevitable lifting barrier across the road to book in at the Guardroom. From the Guardroom the next port of call for a daytime arrival was the Orderly Room in SHQ, where they would be allocated a billet, generally on one of the Domestic Sites. After settling in they had to carry out a 'booking in' procedure with a New Arrival Chit which had to be completed by reporting to the various sections listed on the form and obtaining the appropriate signature. These sections included the Squadron Orderly Room, Station Sick Quarters, Pay Accounts, Padre, Sports Store, Catering Officer and several others. The time it took for new arrivals to find the various sections and obtain the necessary signatures could take a day or two depending on how enthusiastic the airmen were to start active duty. It was however a useful exercise in helping newcomers to the squadron find their way around the station. Having obtained all the necessary signatures, the new arrival then returned the form to the Orderly Room and reported for duty to his section.

In the HQ block, located on the main drive from the Guard Room to the hangars, was housed the C.O's Office, Adjutant, Equipment Accounts, WAAF Admin Office, Station Discip. Office, Orderly Room, Accounts Officer's Room, and the Pay Accounts Office. Much of the clerical work was done by WAAFs. SHQ was divided by two corridors. The one to the right led to the offices of the CO, the Adjutant, and Equipment Accounts. The staff of the latter waded through masses of vouchers and paper work, all items on the station (apart from Catering) had to be accounted for through them. On the left was the corridor containing entrances to the other offices, the SWO's Office was the first, often entered with something approaching terror by young airmen. WO '303' Browning was the Station Warrant Officer, a regular and a disciplinarian, who could make his presence felt on the station, particularly through the Discip. Office, which was under his control. The WAAF Admin Office was opposite, F/O Dent being the 'Queen Bee' who was considered to be strict, but very fair.

In the Orderly Room, the DROs and PORs were compiled, and typed on to wax stencils, from which copies were produced on a duplicating machine and issued to the appropriate sections and notice boards. There was also the Central Registry where many of the other administrative duties were carried out. The Commanding Officer's shorthand typist also had her desk in the Orderly Room, which was a hive of activity, with personnel coming and going all day.

The Pay Accounts Office was opposite the Orderly Room with the Accounts Officer's room next to it. The pay ledgers employed in the accounting system comprised large hand written loose sheets, which were subsequently fastened together. All accounting was done mentally as there were no adding machines (the fore-runner of modern calculators) issued, and every 3 months these ledgers were re-written. The old ones were balanced, compiled into a Summary and sent to the Air Ministry. The Summary had to balance and the clerks spent many late evenings on these quarterly returns, all this being very time consuming compared with the modern computer assisted information technology era. The Accounts Officer held all officers' accounts, their pay being paid direct into accounts in London banks such as Cox & Kings. Warrant Officers came into the office for their pay. For the airmen and NCOs there was a fortnightly Pay Parade which was one of the highlights of their lives. Personnel on essential duties, such as Sick Quarters, M.T., Signals, Sergeants and Officers Mess staff etc were paid in situ by Nominal Roll.

Pay was calculated to the nearest two shillings, the amounts worked out the day before, and entered in pencil in the ledgers, being inked in, as the cash was

ADMINISTERING THE STATION

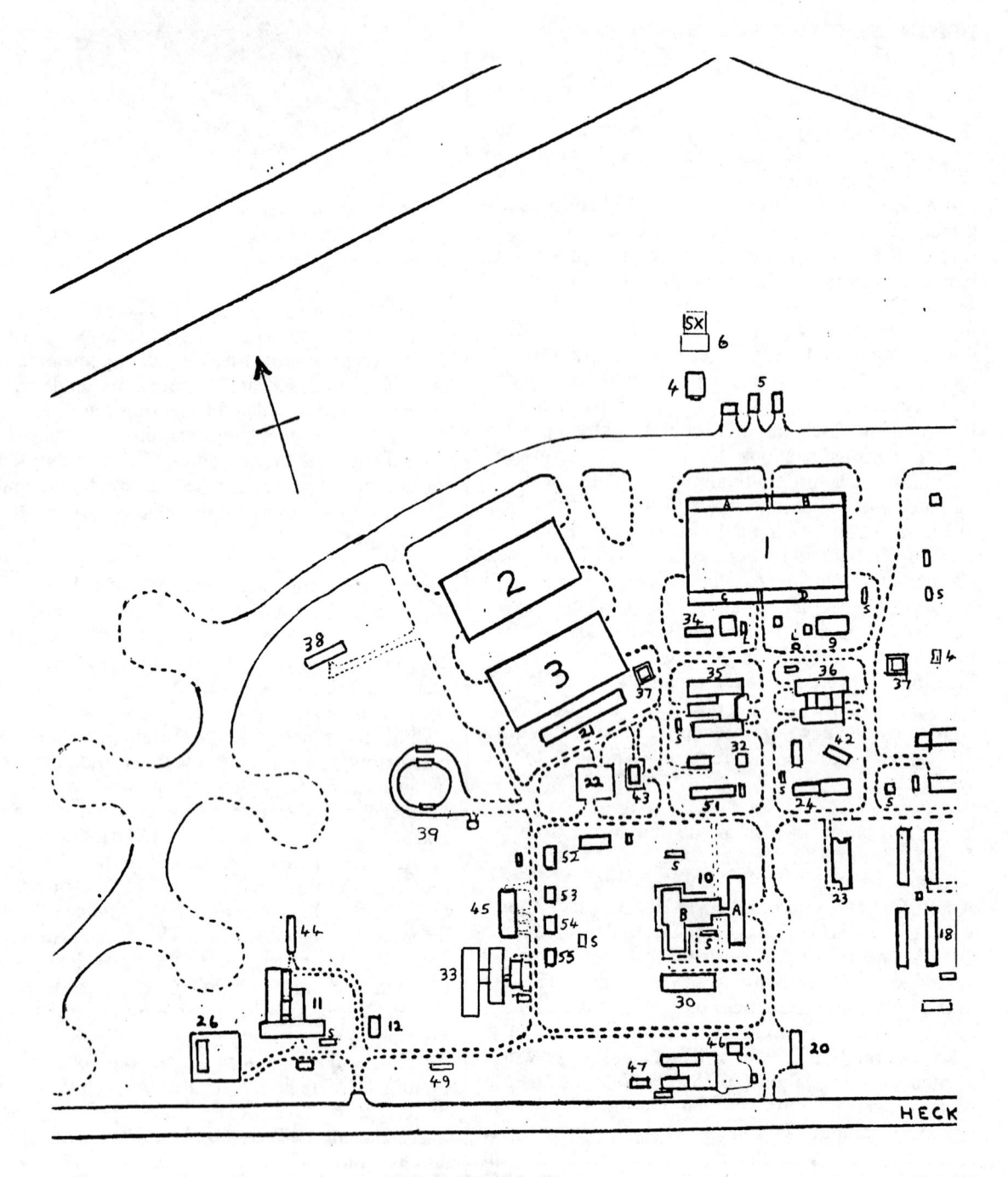

MAP 2

RAF SNAITH 1944/45

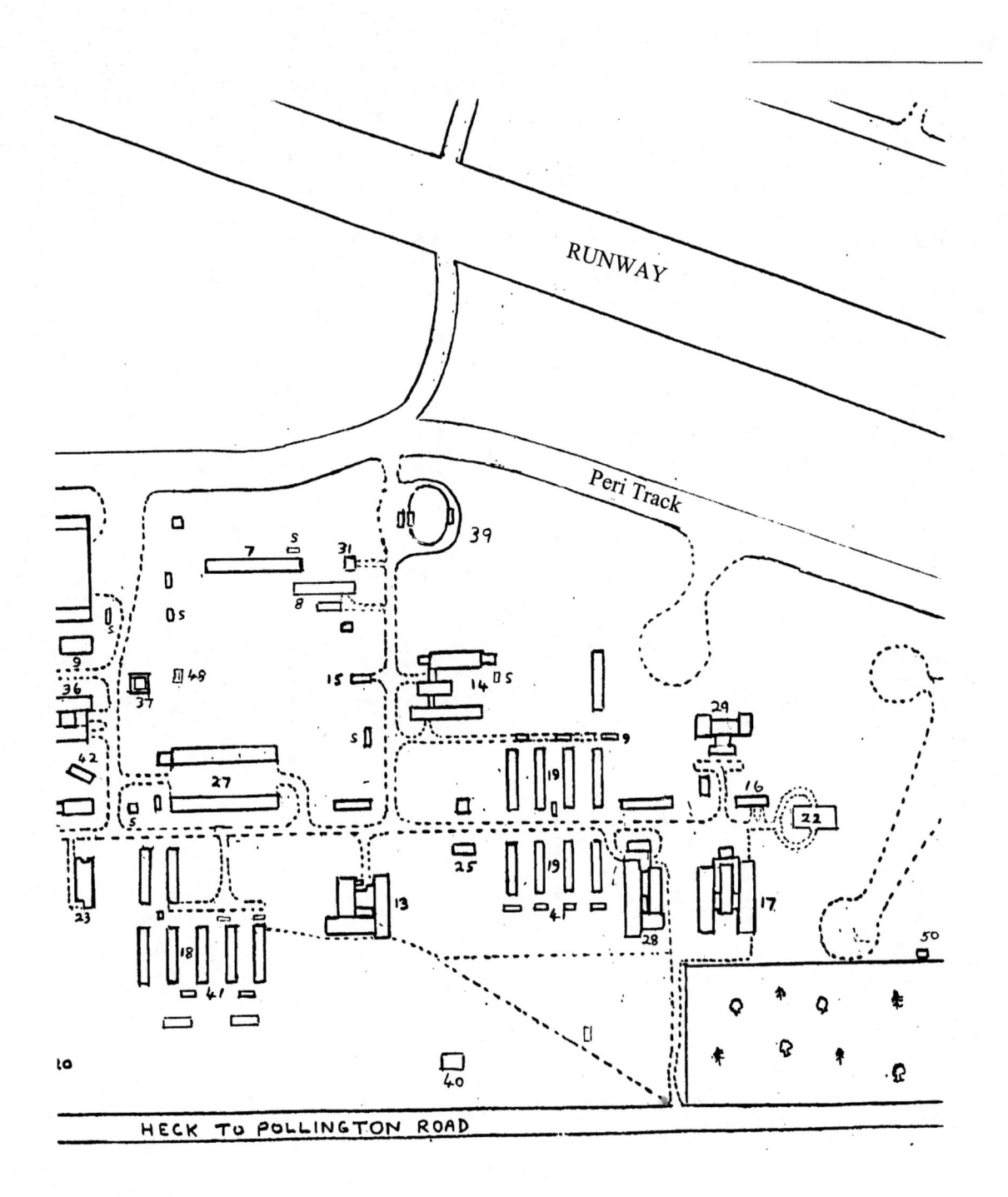

Technical Site
Sketch Map by Keith Ford
(See Key For Identification of Buildings)

ADMINISTERING THE STATION

Key To Snaith Maps

Technical Site

1 Hangar No 1
2 Hangar No 2
3 Hangar No 3
4 Control tower
5 Ambulance & crash tender garages
6 Signal square
7 Squadron H.Q.
8 Crew room
9 Station armoury
10A Station H.Q.
10B Operations block
11 Officers mess
12 Squash court
13 Sergeants mess
14 Station sick quarters
15 Ambulance garage
16 Grocery stores
17 Airmans mess & concert hall
18 Billets
19 Billets
20 Guardroom
21 Workshops
22 Fuel compound
23 Gas defence/radar trainer
24 Photographic section
25 Tailors/hairdressers/boot repairs
26 Station CO's dwelling
27 M.T. garages & office
28 Naafi
29 Shower & bath block
30 Briefing room
31 Gunnery trainer
32 Bombing trainer
33 Aircrew sections (bombing etc)
34 Parachute building
35 Workshops
36 Main stores
37 E.W.S. For fire fighting
38 Radar maintenance
39 Aviation fuel storage
40 Water storage tank
41 Toilets & ablutions
42 Link trainers
43 Gas station
44 Bath house
45 Maintenance
46 Fire tender garage
47 A.M. Works dept.
48 Gas chamber
49 Pigeon loft (approx. Location)
50 Sandra searchlight (approx. Location)
51 Gas clothing store
52/55 Varipis buildings see photo 4
S Air raid shelter
L Latrines

Main Map
B Firing butts
H Harmonising range
D Harmonising datums
S Sandra light

paid out on the parade. Pay Parade day was hectic, in the morning the Accounts Officer (with escort) collected the cash from the local bank, several thousands of pounds in notes and coins (two-bob pieces). On his return this cash had to be counted and checked. The Pay Parade took place in the Airmens' Mess on the Technical Site and the drill was for NCOs and Airmen to parade with Senior NCOs in the front ranks, facing a table covered with a blanket. The Accounts Officer sat at the table with the large quantity of money he had collected from the bank, accompanied by a WAAF Pay Clerk one such being LACW Eileen Poole. In front of the WAAF Clerk was the opened Pay Accounts Ledger and naturally the SWO or one of his NCOs was on hand to oversee the Discip. side of the operation.

The pay parade procedure was for the Pay Clerk to read out the airmens' names in alphabetical order from the ledger and when called an airman would shout out "Sir" followed by the last three digits of his RAF number and march up to the table. The WAAF read out the amount due and the Officer counted out the money. This would be picked up smartly by the airman who saluted and then marched away under the eagle eye of the SWO. As they walked away from the parade, some airmen looked in disgust at the amount received, possibly because of unexpected deductions from their pay. If he wished to query the deductions then he had to attend a designated pay query session at the Pay Accounts Office. On return to the Pay Accounts Office after the parade the balance of cash left was calculated and the accounts staff waited anxiously to see if this agreed with the A.O's cash in hand.

There was also a daily Casual Pay Parade, held in the Accounts Offices, this was for crews going on leave, postings, people who had been unable to attend P/P because of night shift duties, and various similar reasons. As the war progressed more and more airman were posted overseas, or on special courses for updating technical skills. At these Casual Pay Parades there was often a bunch of aircrew NCOs going on one of the periodic leaves they were granted during a tour of Ops. Obviously feeling very happy and relieved to be having a rest from Ops. they were generally in bouyant mood and very noisy waiting to be paid. The Accounts Officer was likely to pop his head out of the office and ask the WAAF in charge of the Pay Parade to try and keep the noise down.

The Equipment Officers and Assistants located in the Main Store were responsible for a large stock of equipment necessary to keep the squadron and station operational. Items of aircraft equipment which became u/s and were repairable could be exchanged for a new item from the stores. Stocks of clothing were carried so that when airmen considered that items of clothing were worn out they could attend one of the clothing parades which were held at regular intervals. At these parades an Equipment Officer inspected any items of equipment produced and if he considered them to be worn out would authorise exchange for a new issue. There were cases when an airman who considered he was due for a new item of uniform, such as a pair of trousers, could accelerate the wear process by the judicious use of a file. When uniform jackets were being issued with black plastic buttons, to conserve the use of brass, these became popular because it removed the chore of having to polish buttons. If an airman lost any personal equipment he would pay for a replacement by filling in a Form 664B FOR CLOTHING REIMBURSEMENT which would then be authorised by the Accounts Section, so that the cost could be deducted from his pay.

At the rear of SHQ, located partly below ground level with an earth covering to afford protection in the case of an air raid, were offices housing the Intelligence/Operations (I/O) and HQ Signals Sections. In view of the confidential nature of their activities access was restricted to authorised personnel.

As mentioned the Guardroom was the first point of contact for arrivals but it could have more poignant memories for any airmen who had a brush with Kings Rules & Regulations by being caught out on a misdemeanor. This could result in them being put on a charge, known by the airmen as a 'Fizzer', the offence being recorded on a Form 252 Charge Sheet. Subsequently the offender would be marched in before the Commanding Officer or his deputy, accompanied by the SWO, or in his absence a Discip. NCO, in a smart airman-like manner. The CO having read out the Charge Sheet and listened to any mitigating statements would ask, "Are you willing to accept my punishment or do you prefer to be tried by court martial?", before passing sentence. For minor offences this was a number of days confined to camp on a punishment generally known as 'Jankers'.

Airmen on 'Jankers' had to carry on with their normal duties but the punishment meant they were confined to camp for a specific number of days during which time life was made as difficult as possible for them. They had to parade at the Guardroom twice a day with all their kit for an inspection and any spare time was occupied by fatigues. Serious offences could involve detention in the Guardroom cells or worse still a period at a Detention Barracks. There were also Technical Charges against the personnel involved with negligence in the servicing or use of aircraft or equipment. In 1943 disciplinary action was taken against three NCOs in connection with an aircraft which had to make an emergency landing whilst on air test.

The Guardroom was located on the Technical Site, but in order to keep a watching brief on the dispersed sites there was a 'Maycrete' building, designated as a Picket Hut, near the entrance to each site. This was manned by a representative of the Discip. Section or a picket orderly. Its function as well as looking after discip. matters was to organise and supervise mundane domestic arrangements such as fuel stocks, laundry, accommodation and check the site housekeeping, including toilets. For the occupants of the WAAF site there was a nightly bed check by a WAAF Discip. Officer or NCO, looking for WAAFs absent without permission. Sometimes the absence of a WAAF could be spotted by the fact that her bicycle was missing.

The health of the personnel on an Operational Station like Snaith was of prime importance, hence there was a well-appointed Sick Quarters with wards to accommodate all ranks (Photo 16). When 51 Squadron arrived in October 1942 one wing of the WAAF Officers Mess was turned into a WAAF Sick Quarters and replaced in December 1943 by an extension to the SSQ. The SSQ was run by the SMO (S/L Rhys-Jones) supported by other officers in the Medical Branch including a Dental Officer and various ORs in medical trades such as Nursing Orderly and Dental Orderly. Daily Sick Parades were held and any personnel wishing to attend had to report sick to a representative of the Discip. Office or an Orderly NCO. A rule not always complied with was that all kit should be packed away in kit bags and haversacks so that if a person on sick parade was admitted to a ward or hospital then his kit could be taken into storage for safe-keeping.

At the Sick Parade the majority of those attending were for minor ailments, consequently they were given a chit stating 'Medicine and Duties' implying that they were fit for work but should attend SSQ for medicines or treatment. One common medication was Mist. Expect (A mixture of Ammonia and Ipecacuanha). It was a standing joke that malingerers were recorded as suffering from 'Plumbus Penduli' (lead swinging).

As would be expected the wards were kept spick-and-span and patients nearing the end of their hospitalisation and who were considered fit enough were expected to engage in the pastime of 'Bumpering'. A 'Bumper' was a heavy wooden block fitted with a hinged handle and covered with an old blanket. The procedure was to put wax polish on the lino and polish it by pushing the heavy 'Bumper' back and forth along the floor.

For new arrivals, who had to include the signature from SSQ on their arrival form, there was a procedure known as FFI, ie a freedom from infections check, particularly VD. This inspection of the genitals could be rather embarrassing and at one period applied to all personnel returning from leave.

The SMO was concerned about the general health and welfare of the personnel at Snaith. In November 1943 there was a mild 'flu epidemic and therefore certain precautions were recommended including gargles at SSQ for persons with respiratory infections. During the winter he advised that aircrew should report sick as soon as they contracted a cold, because he was concerned that flying at high altitudes with a severe cold could produce Otitis Barotrauma, (known to us laypeople as a perforated eardrum). In 1944 the MO instigated a system for the daily issue of vitamin tablets by detailing some WAAF personnel to hand them out to aircrew entering the messes. Also, in order to improve aircrew fitness sun lamp treatment was available for them. They generally attended the Sick Bay as a crew. Stripped to the waist to get the benefit of the treatment and wearing special goggles to protect their eyes, they sat for up to half an hour under the lamps. This treatment was particularly acceptable in winter.

Other problems occurring with aircrew were frostbite in the fingers due to the removal of gloves at high altitudes in cold conditions, and aircrew becoming unconcious, caused by moving around the aircraft without a portable oxygen bottle. This latter problem became important in early 1944 when the squadron converted to the Halifax Mk III. With the Mk II aircraft the normal ceiling was 18-20,000 ft, whereas the Mk III had a ceiling of 21-25,000 ft and aircrew used to flying in Mk II aircraft tended to take the same liberties in the Mk III aircraft at high altitudes, namely not using a portable oxygen bottle, without realising the consequences. The SMO recommended that the HCUs should warn ex OTU aircrews of these dangers.

ADMINISTERING THE STATION

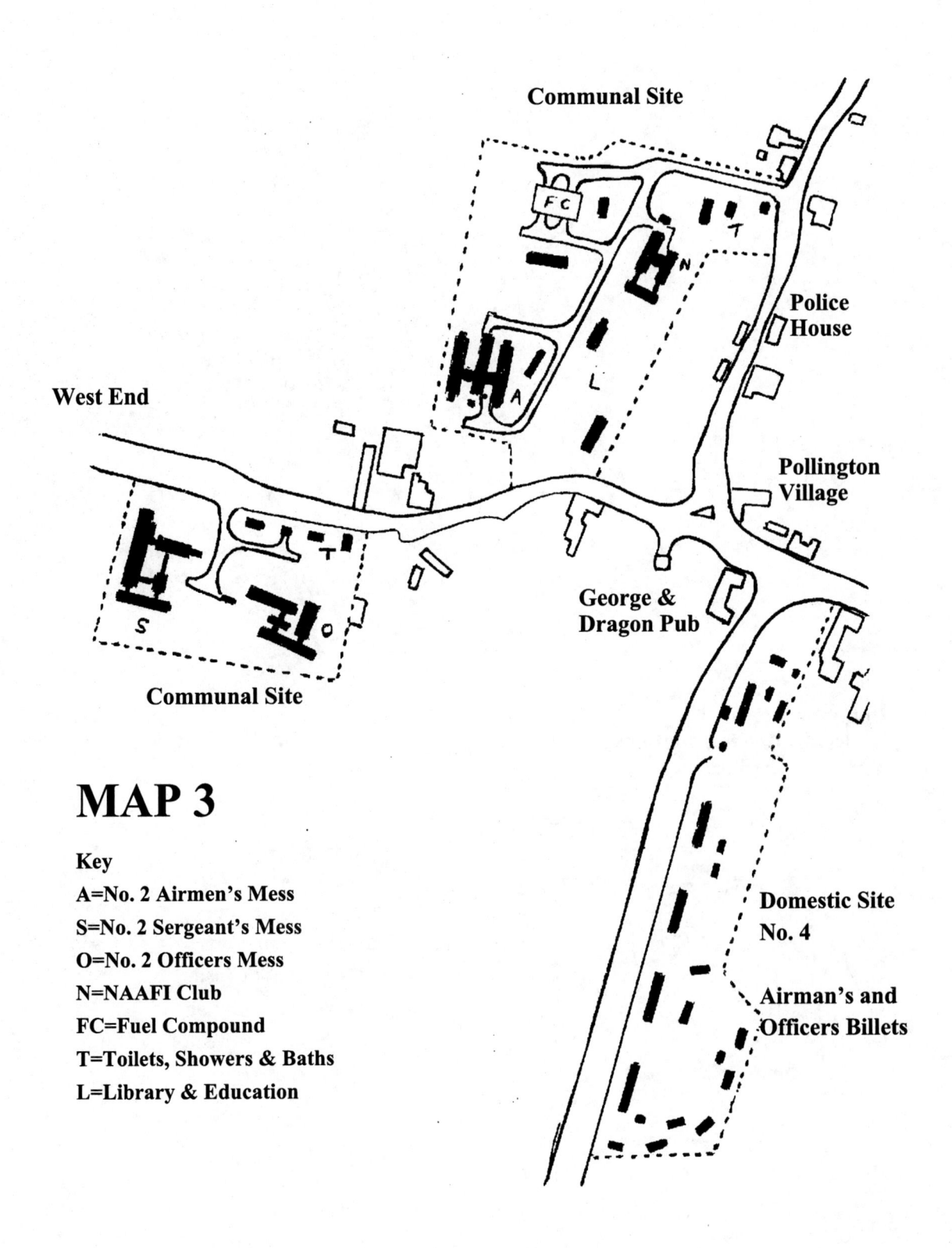

Communal Site

West End

Police House

Pollington Village

George & Dragon Pub

Communal Site

Domestic Site No. 4

Airman's and Officers Billets

MAP 3

Key
A=No. 2 Airmen's Mess
S=No. 2 Sergeant's Mess
O=No. 2 Officers Mess
N=NAAFI Club
FC=Fuel Compound
T=Toilets, Showers & Baths
L=Library & Education

ADMINISTERING THE STATION

PH

**Domestic Site No. 3
All Ranks Billet,
Ablutions and Air
Raid Shelters**

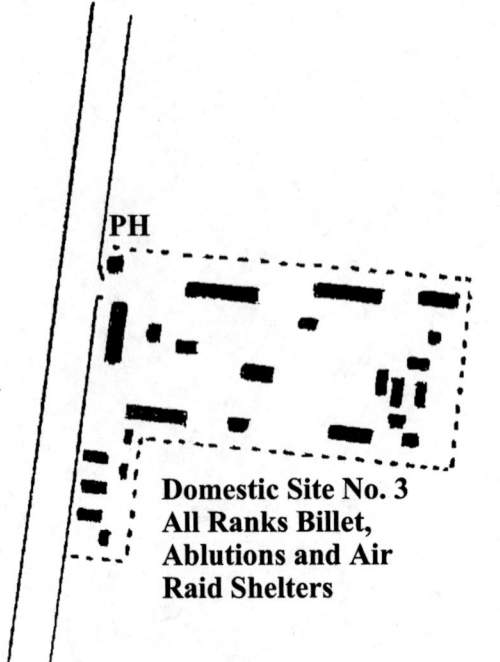

**Domestic Site No. 1
All Ranks Billets, Ablutions
and Air Raid Shelters**

MAP 4

Key
FC=Fuel Compound
C=Gymnasium/Cinema
G=Generator Building

Consideration was also given to the problems of the ground crew working out on the Flights in winter. It was recommended that they should be well clothed and hot showers or baths made available when coming off duty. Many ground crews built dugouts on the flights as shelters, particularly for use during a night vigil in bad weather when waiting for the return of their aircraft from a raid. In 1944 Penicillin, which was then known as the new wonder drug, had become available at Snaith.

The saying "An army marches on its stomach" is an old cliche but nevertheless it could be true to say that "51 Squadron flew on its stomach", so the mess staff, which included cooks and waitresses, fulfilled an important function at Snaith. In the Officers Mess the staff worked shifts, with 2 or 3 sittings per meal and up to 80 officers per sitting (Photo 18). Polished cutlery was laid out by the waitresses who ticked off the names of the officers as they came in for a meal. Even after the mess staff had gone off duty they could expect to be called out in the middle of the night to serve an operational meal. These meals included the 'operational egg' often served with carrots in the belief that the high beta carotene content could improve night vision. The RAF used this idea as a cover story for the successful use of AI radar in nightfighters by stating that John Cunningham, the night fighter ace, had exceptional night vision due to carrots. As a result of this he was dubbed 'Cats Eye's Cunningham' by the press.

In the Officers Mess there was an ante room with a piano. WAAF Joyce Wilton, one of the waitresses, liked to see the officers gather around it for a sing song, including the 51 Squadron ballad. This song was sung to the tune of 'All the King's horses and all the King's men', one verse of which went "51 Squadron, 51 men, Flew over Germany and flew back again, 51 Squadron, 51 men". The bar in the mess was located in a small annex attached to the mess with a serving hatch in the wall and given the name 'The Ha in the Wa' (Photo 17). When aircrew were on stand down they often took part in high spirited activities to relieve their tensions. One of these was mess rugby, when the squadron CO's team played the station CO's team, all the players being stripped to the waist using a cushion as a rugby ball. Possibly because of his experience in organising games on a troop night for Scouts, 'Skip' Seymour (who would have this nickname as a Scout Leader pre-war), was one of the prime movers in boisterous activities. One rather hairy competition he revelled in, involved jumping over a line of armchairs in the ante room. The doors into the dining room were opened up to give the competitors a good run up for the take off, and they landed on a pile of cushions at the far end. The winner was the person who could clear the largest number of chairs, fortunately no broken necks resulted from this activity.

Most officers appreciated the domestic services of their batwomen, generally shared by several officers, and these WAAFs often took a great interest in the welfare of their charges. Lets take the example of Jim Feaver, one of the 'C' Flight Commanders. He shared a batwoman called Nancy Benson with Jeff Flak and Jack Ripper and being appreciably older than her charges she tended to take a matron-like approach towards them. One of her self imposed duties was to eye her officers up and down before they left the billet to ensure they were properly turned out and tell them if they were not tidy enough. Like many other batwomen she looked after their creature comforts as for example a cup of tea in bed. The WAAFs had a busy day attending to all the necessary chores since the rule was that they should leave the officers billets by 1600 hrs.

The Sergeants Mess was also located on the Technical Site and provided a comfortable off duty venue for Senior NCOs. In order to improve the decor one aircrew Sergeant who was a brick layer in 'Civvy Street' built a brick fireplace around which, in winter, the NCOs gathered with their drinks. If there was something to celebrate there could be some very enjoyable mess parties. The aircrew got up to all sorts of pranks such as that carried out by Jack Musson DFM, a Navigator and one of the 'Chiv and Dish' contingent who came to Snaith with the Whitleys. He completed his tour of 42 ops in mid 1943 and in order to celebrate before departing he climbed up onto the roof supports in the mess and wrote "Poor Muss 42" on the ceiling.

The Airmen's Mess which was located at the east end of the Technical site near the NAAFI building, consisted of two long buildings joined by a kitchen and services. The WAAFs and Corporals also used this mess, eating in a section of the dining hall allocated to them. At breakfast a queue would form in front of the servery, and a query would be passed down the line "whats on the menu"? A typical reply would be "cowboy's breakfast", which implied beans and something else, possibly bacon. When kippers were on the breakfast menu, these were not so popular with the airmen, but a few erks who really enjoyed them would benefit by staying behind for second helpings. All airmen had to bring their own personal issue of knife, fork and spoon with them to meals, commonly referred to as a set of 'eating irons'. After breakfast as they left the mess they would pass a steam heated washing trough which was usually so hot that the best they could do for cleaning their 'irons' was to swish them through the water up to the handles. With ground crew working long hours and shifts there was a system of early or late meals for airmen or women and many sections had permanent chits signed by the Adjutant to be presented by the duty crews. Some sections glued their chits to a substantial wooden block to preserve it and make it easy to locate. It was quite amusing to see a duty crew member walk into the mess and plonk a heavy wooden chit on the counter.

There was a sports store on the Technical Site manned by the PTIs, which supplied a wide range of gear for use on the various pitches in the sports area. The Sports Officer also organised the use of sports facilities, both on and off the airfield, one area of the airfield to the east of the Technical Site being used for these activities. An important service on the station was provided by the Fire Section, which supplied the airfield crash tender and a fire engine to attend fires anywhere on the station, using the emergency water supply tanks provided for use in the case of a fire. In the event of an air raid there were numerous surface shelters located at strategic points.

One possible danger during the war was the use of chemical warfare by the enemy. The main war gases which were available to the enemy were 'Tabun', 'Sarin', and 'Soman' nerve gases, 'Arsine' blood gas, Phosgene choking gas and Mustard blister gas. Special clothing was needed for protection from some gases, in particular Mustard gas which was a toxic liquid thickened up with a polymer such as chlorinated rubber. The station therefore had a store of gas defence equipment which included gas masks, moisture resistant protective clothing such as oilskins, ointments, and decontamination chemicals. For example bleaching powder to be used with Mustard gas. There were also Gas Decontamination Centres on the Technical Site and No 1 WAAF site, to wash toxic materials off skin and clothes if blistering gases were used. The Decontamination Centres contained showers, a means of disposing of contaminated clothes and spare clothing. These centres had ventilation and filtration systems installed with a tall chimney to draw in fresh air from above the gas level. Boards painted with gas detection paint which changed colour in the event of a gas attack, were located at various points around the station, one of which can be seen in photo No 1.

As a general service to all ranks there was a block of shops consisting of a Tailor's shop, Hairdressers and a Boot or Shoe Repair shop (Photo 8). Finally there was the Squadron Headquarters building, the nerve centre of 51 Squadron, where the Commanding Officer, Adjutant, Flight Commanders, Flight Offices, Orderly Room, Squadron Warrant Officer, and at varying periods some of the aircrew sections were located. This building was located to the east of the main hangar and near the peri track (Photo 7).

ADMINISTERING THE STATION

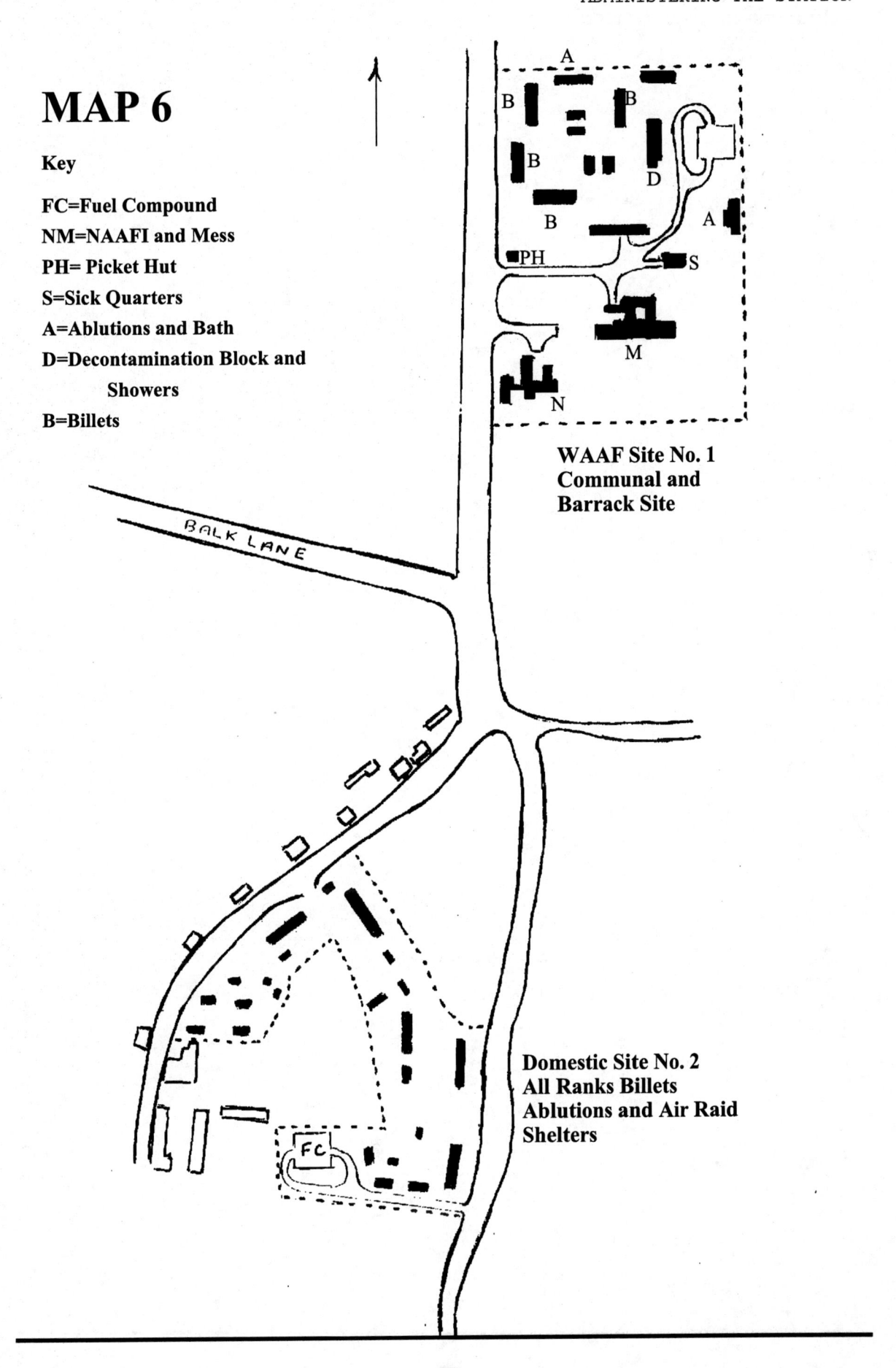

MAP 6

Key

FC=Fuel Compound
NM=NAAFI and Mess
PH= Picket Hut
S=Sick Quarters
A=Ablutions and Bath
D=Decontamination Block and
   Showers
B=Billets

**WAAF Site No. 1
Communal and
Barrack Site**

BALK LANE

**Domestic Site No. 2
All Ranks Billets
Ablutions and Air Raid
Shelters**

ADMINISTERING THE STATION

Chapter 3

ORGANISING THE OPERATIONS

The "Raison d'etre" of a Bomber airfield like Snaith was to act as a base for squadron operations against the enemy in Europe, and it is important to examine the mechanics of planning and organising 51 Squadron's operations from Snaith with particular reference to one significant operation.

The I/O. (Intelligence/Operations) section which played an important part in the planning of an operation was located along with Station Signals in a building partly below ground level at the rear of Station Headquarters and covered by a grass mound, see photo No 14. It was accessed from SHQ by a sloping corridor which was guarded to prevent access by unauthorised personnel. The I/O. Section was managed by the Senior Intelligence Officer, Squadron Leader 'Skip' Seymour, assisted by several Intelligence Officers, Watch Leaders and Clerks both RAF and WAAF. The section worked in co-operation with the Signals Section and Station Navigation Officer (S/Ldr Paul Jousse).

A typical days work for the I/O. Section would start in the morning for the duty Intelligence Officer when an operation was expected. The information from a previous operation which had been chalked in on the the Operations Board would be cleaned off ready for the day's operations, and outstanding paperwork cleared up. This would include ensuring returns had been made to Group HQ including Form 'Y' which gave details of the previous day's operation. If an operation was planned for that day, members of the I/O section would be alerted by a phone call from 4 Group HQ, about 10 am or earlier for a 'Broadcast' to all stations where operational squadrons were based. Initial contact would be on an 'open' telephone line and the first order was "Stand by for Broadcast". Then when all stations were 'plugged in' an order would come through to "Scramble", since the 'Broadcast' which gave full details of the operation was then transmitted via a telephone line which was made secure by a GPO 'Scrambler' known as a Privacy System. The 'Scrambler' was also used for daily tactical discussions between the AOC of 4 Group and the Commanding Officers of the various squadrons under his command. The Watchkeeper would write down the whole broadcast and later on in he day this was confirmed by a teleprinter message which included any fresh information. Watchkeepers were WAAF Clerk/SDs with the rank of Sergeant who had been chosen via a Selection Board at Group HQ and undertaken a training course. Watchkeepers' duties included the task of broadcasting 'Tannoy' messages which could contain information such as briefing, meal and blackout times, and messages about social events (eg films on at the cinema).

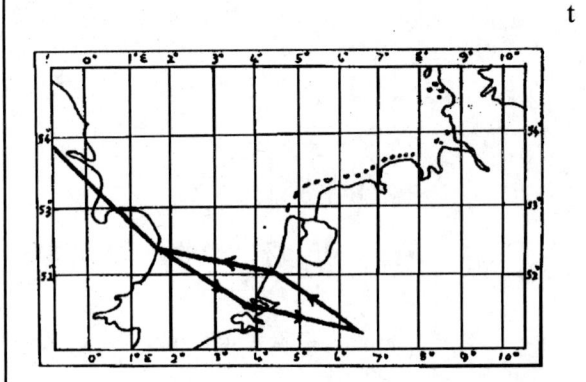

The type of operational information received at Snaith can be exemplified by some of the data which would have been sent for one of the operations during the Battle of the Ruhr in 1943. In addition to the data for this specific operation there

Photo 48 via B. Gazeley

Operations Room Staff in 1943

('Skip' Seymour 2nd from left at rear)

are comments on it plus notes about how operational information varied over the years 1943-45.

4 GROUP OPERATIONAL ORDER
DATE AND OPERATIONAL No:- 21 JUNE 1943
SNAITH OPERATIONAL ORDER No 55
4 GROUP FORM 'B' No 131

INTENTION:- TO CAUSE MAXIMUM DAMAGE AT AIMING POINT IN KREFELD.

In the case of "Gardening" it would state -Sow mines in required locations.

SIZE OF FORCE OPERATING AGAINST TARGET:- 705 AIRCRAFT

DATE OF OPERATIONS:- NIGHT OF 21/22 JUNE 1943

EFFORT REQUIRED FROM 51 SQUADRON:- 19 AIRCRAFT

This would be based on daily returns of aircraft available to 51 Squadron

TARGET AND AIMING POINT:- TARGET KREFELD. AIMING POINT DESIGNATED BY BEARING AND DISTANCE FROM GIVEN POINT ON TARGET MAP.

SECONDARY TARGET:- NONE DESIGNATED.

ROUTE TO TARGET AND RETURN:-
OUT:—BASE A-COTTESMORE LIGHT B-SOUTHWOLD C-51.48N 03.50E D-TARGET
RETURN: D-TARGET TURN LEFT E-NOORDWIJK F-SOUTHWOLD-BASE

TIME OF ATTACK:-ZERO HOUR 0130 HOURS, 51 SQUADRON TO BOMB DURING THE PERIOD 0157 TO 0211

REPORTING PROCEDURE:- PILOT'S REPORTS AND AERIAL PHOTOS OF TARGET BY PHOTOFLASH TO BE SENT TO 4 GROUP HQ ON FORM "Y".

MINIMUM FUEL LOAD:- 1390 GALLONS.

BOMB LOAD:- 6 x 1,000 lb HE, 2 x 500 lb HE.
BOMB SETTING:-NORMALLY TIMES TO SET ON DELAYED ACTION FUSES WAS SPECIFIED, SUCH AS LOADS=0.25 SECS.

No special bombs were carried by the Squadron on this operation because of the lack of normal bomb preparation facilities.

SECURITY:- INFORMATI0N ON RADIO AND SIGNALS DISCIPLINE SUCH AS DURATION OF RADIO SILENCE, TIME OF GROUP W/T BROADCASTS, RADIO CALL SIGNS, AND USE OF IFF.

In later raids when H2S was fitted, information on its use was detailed.

TACTICS:-RENDEZVOUS POINT WITH BOMBER STREAM GIVEN AND HEIGHTS TO MAINTAIN IN STREAM SPECIFIED, SUCH AS 18,000 Ft. OVER TARGET. PHASING OF THE VARIOUS WAVES OF AIRCRAFT DETAILED AS FOLLOWS:

1ST WAVE, LANCASTERS (SELECTED CREWS) (0132-0141HRS)
2nd WAVE, WELLINGTONS (0141-0149HRS)
3rd WAVE, STIRLINGS (0149-0157HRS)
4th WAVE, HALIFAXES (4 GROUP) (0157-0204HRS)
5th WAVE, HALIFAXES (6 GROUP) (0204-0211HRS)
6th WAVE, REMAINDER OF LANCASTERS (0211-0220HRS)
RADIO COUNTERMEASURES:
INFORMATION ON THEIR USE GIVEN.
THE USE OF 'TINSEL' AUTHORISED.

'Window' was not issued, still on the secret list.

TARGET MARKING:- CLEAR SKY EXPECTED OVER TARGET, SO AIMING POINT TO BE MARKED BY 'OBOE' MOSQUITOES WITH RED TI's IN SALVO BETWEEN 0127 & 0229HRS. IF MOSQUITOES FAIL TO MARK, 'Y' AIRCRAFT OF PFF WILL BLIND MARK WITH YELLOW TI's USING H2S. 37 PFF BACKERS-UP AIRCRAFT WILL AIM GREEN TI'S AT THE RED'S (OR YELLOW TI'S IF NO REDS DROPPED).

Some of the foregoing operational data requires amplification as follows: Re target marking, in this raid the new 'K Oboe' was used operationally for the first time. Later on in 1943 when Master Bomber techniques were used, Master Bomber and Main Force call signs and R/T frequencies would be given (e.g. 5154 kc/s.).

Bomber Command had code names for their targets which were published in a Secret Document issued to I/O Officers and kept locked in a safe.

For major towns and cities they used the names of fishes.

eg. Trout=Cologne, Grayling=Nuremberg, Catfish=Munich.

The use of fish's names was devised by AM Sir Robert Saundby, Deputy C in C of Bomber Command, who was an enthusiastic angler.

Mine laying operations were given the code name 'Gardening' and the mines they sowed were known as 'Vegetables' The code names for mining locations were fruits or vegetables.

eg. Artichokes=Lorient, Nectarines=Freisian Islands.

When a mine laying operation was detailed the information from Group would include High Water and Low Water times (since tidal movements would affect the appearance of the coast line), dropping positions, and dropping intervals. The technique used in 1943 was to start from a fixed point on land and fly a steady course at a speed of about 180 mph. Initially, in order to ensure the parachutes operated correctly heights of 1,000 to 1,500ft were specified, but later on these heights were raised to about 5,000 ft. The mines would be dropped at specific intervals, such as 3 secs apart. For mine laying operations various types of mines were carried. These included Acoustic, Magnetic and Delay type mines.

Bomb Load. A typical bomb load for the Squadron during the Battle of the Ruhr was, two 1,000 lb GP HE bombs, 810 of 4 lb incendiaries, and 32 of 30 lb incendiaries in SBC's, including a percentage of Type 'X' explosive incendiaries. However this type of load could not be provided due to the bomb dump explosion (see Chapter 10) so an emergency load was carried.

Bomb Settings. When delayed action bombs were required then the delay times would be set on the bomb fuses by the Armourers in the bomb dump. Loads = 0.25, meant a delay of 0.25 secs after impact so that the bombs would explode in the basement of buildings.

Information on 'Tinsel' and 'Window' is given in Chapters 5 & 7. After Nov 1943 at a briefing the squadron was given information on 100 Group activities such as diversionary operations or spoof raids using 'Window'.

The squadron having been detailed for the operation, it would be required to give a return to I/O Section of the number of serviceable aircraft (based on information from the Engineering Officer) with crews available for the operation and the following actions would take place before the squadron took off. Over the period the squadron was at Snaith, procedures would vary, but times and some of the specific details given in this chapter are for the Krefeld operation of the 21.6.43. Based on time over target (TOT) the time for the aircrew briefing could be set and in the case of the Krefeld raid this was about 1800 hrs. The Station Navigation Officer would provide a plot of route to target with ground track distances and times for each leg calculated, from which information a take-off time could be set.

In preparation for the briefing the I/O staff would be kept busy assembling as much information as possible on the target and the route to the target. This would include maps, photos, areas of flak concentrations, details of previous attacks, and information provided via teleprinter from Group Headquarters. Confidential information such as colours of the day, call signs, Pundit codes, 'Gee' corrections etc were typed by Operations and Signals clerks on rice paper 'Flimsies'. The object of using these 'Flimsies' was so that they could be swallowed or dissolved in the coffee flask to prevent them falling into the hands of the enemy. Escape kits containing a silk map, compass, Horlicks tablets, water purifying tablets, European currency and a hacksaw blade which stowed away inside its handle, would be prepared ready for issue to the aircrews. These items were stored in a small metal or plastic box which just fitted into the pocket of the aircrew's battle dress.

The Operations Board in the I/O Room would be filled in based on information received from the clerks in Squadron HQ, listing aircraft serial numbers, code letters and pilots names. An Order of Battle would be produced, listing crews and aircraft detailed for the operation and this would be posted up for the benefit of the aircrews (Fig 1). Having seen the Order, aircrews involved would book in at the Crew Room to indicate their availability. When no ops. were planned a notice stating "Stand Down Till————" would be displayed, indicating the possibility of a night in the Pubs. All the sections involved in support of the operation would need to be notified, so a copy of

ORGANISING THE OPERATIONS

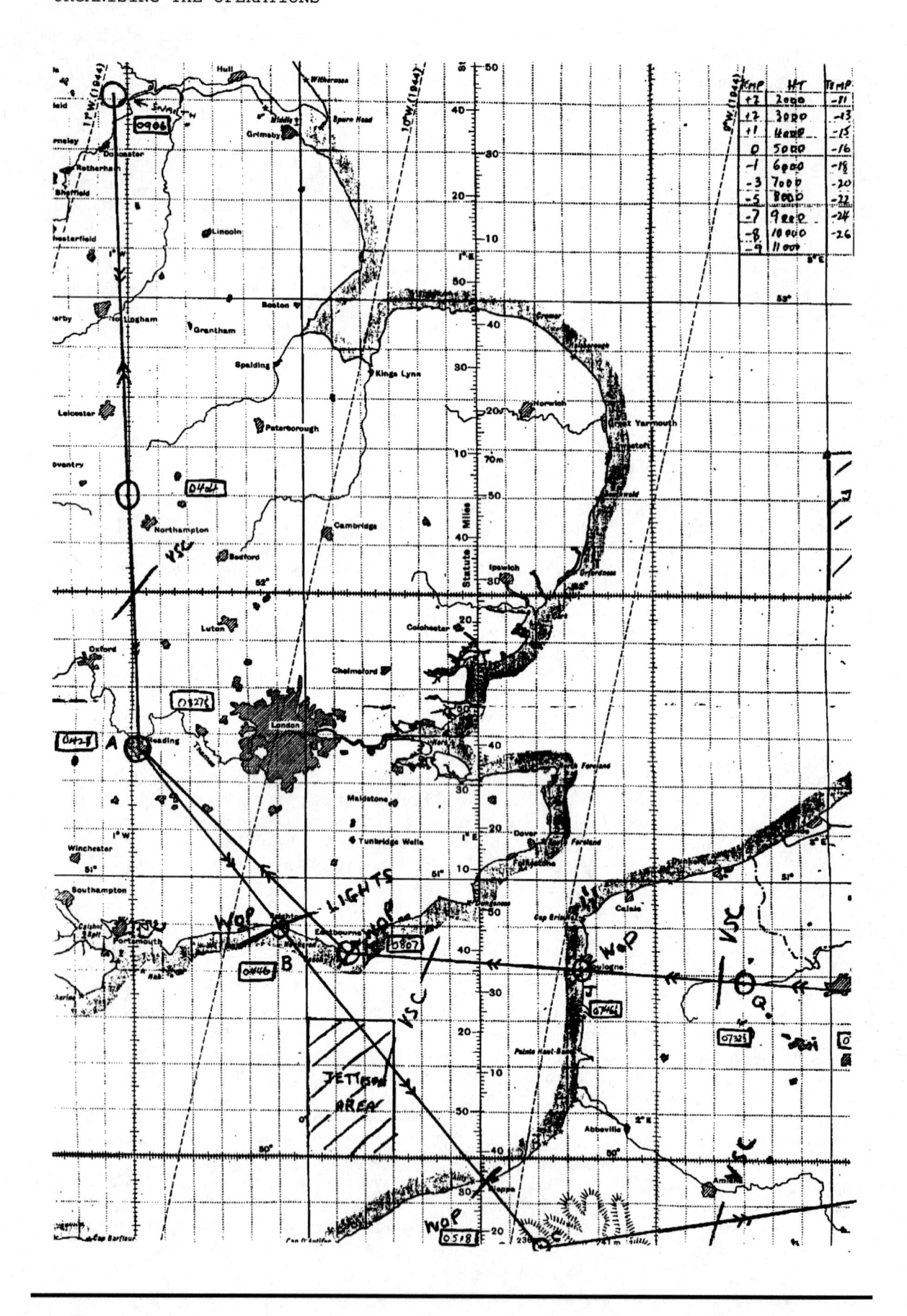

Map 7

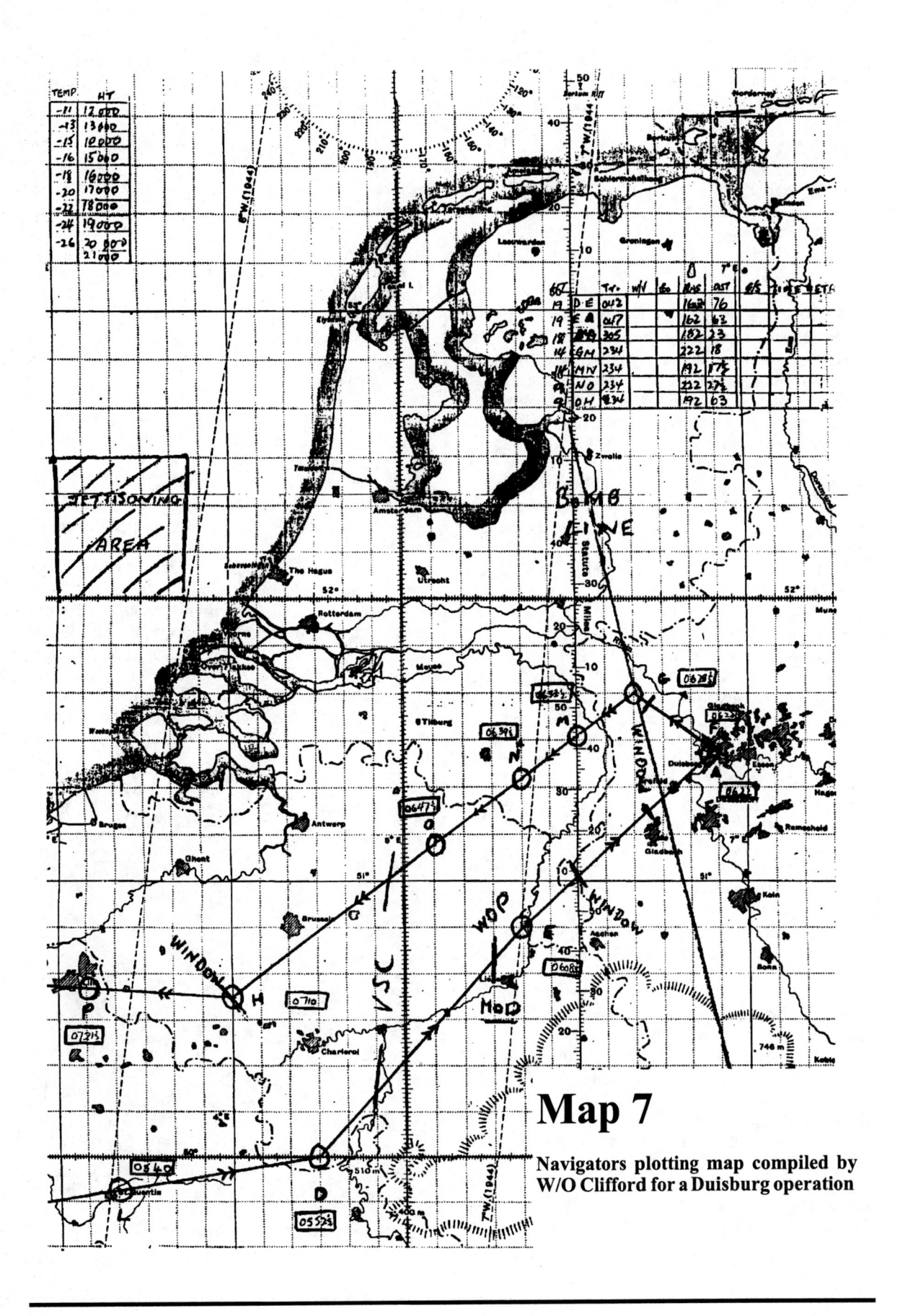

Navigators plotting map compiled by W/O Clifford for a Duisburg operation

ORGANISING THE OPERATIONS

the order would be sent to them. This would include the Station CO, Squadron CO, OC 'A' Flt, OC 'B' Flt, OC 'C' Flt, I/O Section, Navigation Officer, Flying Control, Station Medical Officer, Officer's Mess, Sergeant's Mess, Transport Officer, Signals Officer, Engineering Officer, Electrical & Instrument Officer, Radar Officer, Meteorological Officer, Station and Squadron Armouries, Photographic Section, Section Leaders (Navigation, Bombing, Wireless, Flight Engineers, and Gunnery), Guard Room and NCO I/C Locker Room.

As an example of what could take place with the various aircrew sections before a raid we can consider the Navigation Section. In this section there was a black board carrying the state of readiness, with aircraft code letters and pilots flying them. When the 'buzz' went round that ops were on, Navigators would examine the board to see if there was an 'O' against their Pilot's name, indicating that the crew was required for ops. Also displayed would be times for ops meal, pre-briefing, main briefing, and transport time. Navigators could leave the section provided they wrote on the blackboard where they could be found as for example Intelligence Library, Messes, NAAFI, Hairdressers etc.

Ground crews from all trades in the Daily Servicing Flights would carry out DIs (Daily Inspections) on all the aircraft involved. It would then be up to the various aircrew involved to decide if they needed to carry out air test. In many cases the Flight Engineer would carry out a ground check on behalf of his crew. In the case of the Krefeld raid air tests had to take place before 1230 hrs. Aircrew would check if their aircraft were satisfactory on the air test and report any problems to the Squadron or Engineering Wing. The Engineering trades would be kept busy before take-off curing any snags which had been found on the aircraft and entered in the Form 700 Servicing Record. There were also numerous pre-flight preparations to be carried out. The in-situ bottles of Oxygen and Nitrogen (if installed) had to be topped up by the Instrument Section. A 'milk run' would deliver a fresh stock of charged portable oxygen bottles, often accompanied by a stock of propaganda leaflets ('Nickels') and 'Window' strips (if these were used) to each of the aircraft. The Electricians would check that the accumulators were fully charged and sometimes stored the connecting leads in their workshop so that their accumulators could not be used without permission. If the Electricians spotted a short to earth on any of the ancilliary equipment, eg Radar sets, they would notify the appropriate tradesman, who would then rectify the fault. With regard to the Radar equipment, at the appropriate time the detonators would be installed so that the equipment could be destroyed if likely to fall into enemy hands.

If all went well the arming and refuelling of the aircraft would go ahead. Armed with details of the required fuel content, which had been calculated allowing a safety reserve, tankers and bowsers, having been filled up at one of the two bulk petrol installations, would trundle around the flights to carry out their refuelling tasks on the dispersals. One important rule in refuelling was the earthing of the tanker, by means of a ground stake, since static build up on an aircraft could discharge and unless earthed correctly, produce a spark, with disastrous consequences.

Information on the bomb load required having been passed to the Station Armourers in the bomb dump it was then the task of the NCO in charge to ensure that the correct bombs were selected and fused as per their instructions. In the case of the Krefeld operation the bomb dump was out of action so bombs had to be prepared on the eastern end of the airfield, where Station Armourers sweated in the warm June sun to fuse the bombs and load them onto trolleys which were then hauled by tractors around the peri track to the various aircraft. When the bomb loads arrived at the dispersals, the hard work would start for the Squadron Armourers, since they would have to winch the HE bombs and also small bomb containers (when incendiaries were carried), into the fuselage and wing bomb

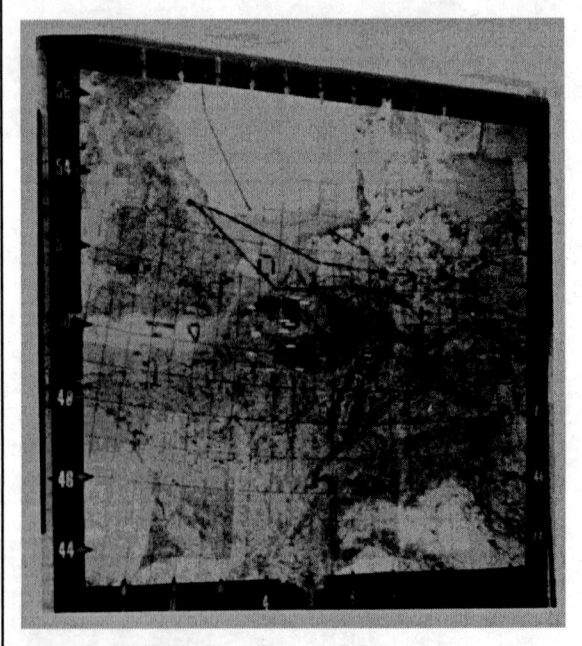

Photo 49 Briefing Room Map

ORGANISING THE OPERATIONS

S E C R E T

51 SQUADRON, R.A.F. STATION, SNAITH
Battle Order - Operational Number 55. 21/6/1943
Officer I/C Flying S/Ldr RUSSELL

AIRCRAFT	CAPTAIN	NAVIGATOR	BOMB AIMER	WIRELESS OPERATOR	FLIGHT ENGINEER	M.U. GUNNER	REAR GUNNER
HR843 (MH-A)	Sgt Solomon	Sgt White	Sgt Archer	Sgt McKier	Sgt Pickup	Sgt Stephen	Sgt Davis
HR852 (MH-D)	Sgt McPherson	Sgt Ellis	Sgt Payne	Sgt Silvester	Sgt Moore	P/O Grudzein	P/O Clow
JD252 (MH-T)	P/O Haley	Sgt Wright	F/Sgt Bramfit	F/Sgt Dodgson	Sgt Marks	Sgt Baldwin	P/O Price
HR732 (MH-Y)	Sgt Richards	Sgt Barnicotes	Sgt Moore	Sgt Holland	Sgt Stow	Sgt Tidmarsh	Sgt Grisdale
JD253 (LK-A)	Sgt Lander	Sgt Palmer	Sgt Collier	Sgt Wickersham	Sgt Thompson	Sgt Bonner	Sgt Swain
HR726 (MH-B)	Sgt Thompson	Sgt Russell	Sgt Sharp	Sgt Godden	Sgt Harris	Sgt Murray	Sgt Jones
HR870 (MH-HI)	Sgt Cates	Sgt Nelson	Sgt Robinson	Sgt Manning	Sgt Mitchell	Sgt Watson	Sgt Brondgeest
HR839 (LK-L)	P/O Tay	F/O Popley	S/Ldr Porter	F/Lt Heaton	Sgt Smith	Sgt Butler	Sgt Widal
HR868 (LK-B)	Sgt Lambert	Sgt Wilkins	P/O Howse	Sgt Newland	Sgt Watson	Sgt Johnson	Sgt Warren
HR834 (MH-V)	Sgt Gregory	Sgt Gardiner	Sgt Rowbotham	Sgt Passey	Sgt Pitt	Sgt Brownless	Sgt Crozier
W1224 (MH-E)	Sgt Foulston	Sgt McDonald	F/O Adams	Sgt Spalding	Sgt Knight	Sgt Cooper	Sgt Colling
JD244 (MH-K)	Sgt Heathfield	F/O Dothie	Sgt Poulton	Sgt Beresford	Sgt Keane	Sgt Masters	Sgt Cooper
JD250 (MH-R)	F/O Mackenzie	P/O Fitchett	P/O Johnson	Sgt Stevenson	Sgt Blackie	Sgt Alexander	Sgt Murdock
JD248 (MH-S)	Sgt Bishop	Sgt Neve	Sgt Isaac	Sgt Boulter	Sgt Wales	Sgt Turnham	Sgt Halden
HR731 (MH-C)	Sgt Osmond	Sgt Mortimer	Sgt Barton	Sgt Blundell	Sgt Huggan	Sgt Emerson	Sgt Rorison
HR838 (MH-Q)	F/Sgt George	Sgt McLaughlin	Sgt Chadwick	Sgt Malmsbury	Sgt Farr	Sgt Cook	Sgt Limond
HR869 (MH-Z)	F/O Dobson	Sgt Merricks	Sgt McGregor	Sgt Meugham	Sgt Kemp	F/Sgt Camerson	F/Sgt Carrington
HR728 (LK-D)	F/O Irwin	P/O Dawkins	P/O Watkinson	Sgt Lang	Sgt Watson	Sgt Dixon	Sgt Gordon
JH118 (LK-K)	Sgt Morris	Sgt Storey	P/O Binham	F/O Hebblewaith	Sgt Russell	Sgt Finn	Sgt Boyd

Signed : F/Lt G Roundtree, Adjutant - For : Wing Commander A D Franks, C/O 51 Sqdn.

FIG. 1 Order Of Battle For Krefeld Operation 21/22 June 1943

ORGANISING THE OPERATIONS

bays. The time taken for preparing the bombs, delivering them and loading them into the aircraft could take over five hours. The Armourers would hope the operation would not be cancelled since this would involve them in the unenviable task of debombing again. A change of target could cause quite a few problems to ground crew because in addition to changing the bomb load it could mean altering the fuel load. If the new target was of shorter range with a larger bomb load this could mean removal of fuel, an unpopular task.

In the 51 Squadron song mentioned in Chapter 1 there were lines particularly relevant to the armourers. These went "51 Squadron, 51 men, bombed up the kites and debombed again, 51 Squadron, 51 men." Another line of a song was a dig at the 'bull' which could be imposed on the ground trades with the effect of reducing in their operational efficiency. This line went, "We are not here to fight the foe, we're only here for the Lord Mayor's Show".

For mine laying operations, mines instead of bombs had to be winched into the aircraft but since mines came under the jurisdiction of the Admiralty there was a lot of red tape involved. The I/O Officer would want full details of all the mines installed for his returns to the Admiralty via Group and Bomber Command HQs. These returns would include a tracing of the positions of the mines on an Admiralty chart along with details of the mines dropped.

Meanwhile, final preparations for the aircrew briefing were being carried out with all the necessary information for the briefing collected and the briefing room prepared. The Ops. board was filled in with details of the pilots, aircraft, take off times etc and on the 1:500,000 scale briefing map strips of red tape would indicate the routes to and from the target. Cellophane could be pinned over the maps and used to mark specific items, such as heavily defended areas, by hatching with Chinagraph pencils. In the Met. Office the latest weather forecast on conditions at bases and target had been obtained and the Met. assistants were busy producing synoptic charts and visual aids of expected weather over the target for the Met Officer to use at the briefing session. An indication of how the forecast for the Krefeld raid could have been presented on Form 2330 is shown in Fig 2.

An announcement over the 'Tannoy' system would inform the aircrew of the time of the briefing, which

Fig 3 NAVIGATOR'S FLIMSIE

FB 1	54 34 N 01 01 W	EMERGENCY RUNWAYS	QDM of R/way
FB 2	52 22 N 01 08 W	1 CARNABY 5404N 0016W	259 M
FB 3	53 22 N 00 02 W	2 WOODBRIDGE 5205N 0124E	270 M
FB 4	51 57 N 02 31 W	3 MANSTON 5121N 0121E	290 M
FB 5	50 31 N 04 59 W		
FB 6	57 32 N 02 01 W	GEE LINE OF APPROACH	approx QDM of "C" line
FB 7	54 40 N 05 36 W	1 N.E. Series VI (C = 36.99)	240 M
FB 8	51 19 N 01 24 W	2 E. Series II (C = 38.92)	266 M
FB 9	55 52 N 02 13 W	3 E. Series II (C = 35.88)	292 M
FB 10	50 46 N 03 18 W		
FB II			
FB 12	55 33 N 04 33 W		
FB 13	54 22 N 04 31 W		
FB 14	54 27 N 08 08 W		

Form 2330	ROUTE FORECAST (for Period 2200 hours to 0600 hours) :		Date 21 June 43
	Time of Origin 15.00 hours.		

Synoptic situation (Fronts, etc.) at _____ hours	SECRET.		
Stage From / To	OUTWARD AND HOMEWARD	TARGET	BASE ON RETURN.
Weather	Fine. Cold Front 62°N 12°E to 57°N 15°E. Warm Front approaching from West Ireland.	Fine	Fine
Cloud	Well broken cloud along NW Coast of Germany. Thence residual thundery cloud with thunderstorm near Cold Front.	Very thin layer of medium cloud between 15,000 and 20,000 ft probably clearing by 01.00 hours.	Small amount of Sc at 2-3,000 ft.
Freezing Level (above M.S.L.)			
Visibility	Moderate/Good — S of 53°N	Moderate/Good — 02°E to Ruhr	Good — Base to 04°E
		Moderate/Good — Target	
Wind Surface	Direction m.p.h.	Direction m.p.h.	Direction m.p.h.	Direction m.p.h.
8,000 ft	280° 10	300° 10/15	– –	– –
18,000 ft	270° 15	300° 20/25	240° 25/30	– –
26,000 ft	– –	– –	200° 50/55	280° 25/30
Pressure at M.S.L. at ___ hours	At° ___ mb. Rising/Falling	At° ___ mb. Rising/Falling	At° ___ mb.	At° ___ mb.
Place	Sunrise: Sunset: Moonrise: Moonset:	Place Target — Sunrise: Sunset: Moonrise: 00.30 hrs Moonset:	Phase of moon 75% of full

All times are according to the ordinary standard time in use at the Station of issue, e.g., in Britain, Summer Time during its currency
Issued by Met. Office at Snaith at 15.15 hours

* insert name of place.

FIG 2

Representation Of How Meteorological Information For Krefeld Raid Could Have Been Compiled On Form 2330

for the Krefeld raid took place round about 1800 hrs. Aircrew would file into the briefing room, with armed SPs on duty at the door, and sit down at the tables (Photo 33). The CO would open the briefing, when the curtains would be drawn back to reveal the operations map with the red tapes indicating the target and the route to and from it. When the location of the target was observed the murmer among the crews would indicate their reaction to it, particularly if it was a dicey target. There were very rare occasions when the crews considered the operation to be a "piece of cake". Various officers would stand up in front of the assembled company of aircrews to brief them with information considered essential for the success of the operation. These would include the Station CO, Squadron CO, and the Intelligence Officer who would discuss the target, bomb loads, routes, times, spoof raids, any night fighter support, information on target marking and diversion airfields. The Meteorological Officer would discuss weather expected on route and other briefings would come from the Flying Control Officer and the various Section Leaders (Navigation, Bombing, Signals, Gunnery, and Engineers). An Episcope was available as a visual aid and could be used to project photos, maps or diagrams onto a screen. During the briefing the Navigation officer would give the Navigators additional 'gen' for their flight planning and any special points to watch and after the main briefing they would stay behind to complete their flight plan on information read out by the Navigation Officer.

In addition to the general briefing some aircrew attended a specialist briefing, before or after it, with the appropriate Section Leader. They may have to collect equipment required for the operation. For example the Wireless Operators would collect their 'Goodies Bags' from one of the WAAF clerks in the Signals Section. This bag held a screwdriver, pliers, Q codes, log, torch and secret signals codes on rice paper 'flimsies'. Air Bombers could get special instructions from the Bombing Leader at their briefing such as information about PFF support and target marking. The Navigators attended a flight planning briefing before the main briefing, held by the Station Navigation Officer or his deputy, which normally took about an hour. The Navigation Officer would read out the Lat & Long of each turning point, with reference letters allocated to them, and tracks and distances for each leg. The Navigators would then draw these tracks on their charts with coloured pencils, as for example blue out and green for return tracks, denoting each turning point by the code letter given to them. A check would be made on the 'Gee' charts as to which chains could be used and information provided on 'Gee' frequencies. Plots would be made of diversion airfields and beacons close to the tracks which could be used for emergency fixes. For aircraft fitted with H2S, the charts would be examined for landmarks which could give a clear, possibly unambiguous display and these would be given a code letter for identification purposes.

The Navigators would put various information on their charts such as points at which 'Window' dropping should occur and coast was being crossed so that they could notify the Wireless Operator. Also noted positions at which Navigation lights and IFF were switched on and off, when the VSC on DRC needed to be altered, and the location of bomb jettison areas. Possible hazards such as flak locations and shipping convoys were noted. Any secret information was marked on the chart in code so that if it came into the hands of the enemy it would not mean anything to them. Also on the chart the Navigator would include a small plotting table of turning points, heights to fly at, true course, air speed and distance between turning points plus a table of Adiabatic Lapse Rate information provided by the Met. Officer. The latter showed how the predicted rate of change of temperature differed from the ICAN law so that the correct altitude could be calculated from the altimeter reading. Later on in the war when Allied troops were advancing across Europe a Bomb Line had to be marked on the chart so that the bombs were not dropped on territory held by the allies. An example of a Navigator's Chart as prepared at Navigators' briefing by W/O Clifford for a raid in 1945 is shown in Map No 7.

Turning points are indicated by letters A to K and letters L to Q indicate positions of special significance to the Navigator such as unambiguous radar targets which would give a good fix. As mentioned earlier if any additional information became available this would be presented at the main briefing. At the end of the flight planning session the Navigators would fold up their charts and leave them on the tables in the Briefing Room, which was then locked up and left with an SP on guard at the door. Before the operation the Navigator had to collect his large canvas bag from the Navigation Section. This contained various items such as log sheets (Form 441), navigation tables, flight plans, Dalton Computer and all the necessary charts. The Navigators were also issued with rice paper flimsies containing secret information, an example of one being shown in Fig 4. In 1943 when some Navigators still used Astro navigation, a bubble sextant and sight reduction and astro tables were carried.

Pilots, by virtue of their task of flying the aircraft, may find themselves restricted in the use of the Elsan toilet at the rear of the aircraft, particularly if 'George' the automatic pilot was inoperative. Therefore some Pilots could be issued with a special receptacle like a hot water bottle fitted with a funnel, for use while sitting in the pilot's seat. All aircrew were issued with rations which could include chocolate, sweets, chewing gum, Horlicks tablets and vacuum flasks containing a hot beverage. They were also given what they called 'wakey wakey' tablets i.e. Benzedrine stimulant tablets to be used only in an emergency and an escape kit. Before the operation they would be given their traditional pre op. supper, typically bacon and eggs or egg and chips. When the time came the aircrew proceeded to the locker room to be kitted out and collect their parachutes. In addition, during 1943, the Wireless Operator collected the aircraft pigeons in their containers. The purpose of these pigeons was for release with a message on their legs if the aircraft ditched in the sea. In the locker room the aircrew donned their flying gear and checked their oxygen masks on a test rig with oxygen economisers, which had been installed by the Instrument Section. Later on in the war Air Gunners wore electrically heated suits and other members of the crew generally wore a thick white roll neck pullover under their battledress. Crews also had silk, woollen and gauntlet gloves, a belt to carry a revolver, 6 rounds of ammunition, a 'Mae West', parachute harness and flying boots. They could also test their microphones and headphones if they wished. There was a final briefing when the crews could hand over for safe keeping personal effects or items which should not be taken on a raid. Having left the locker room, strapped up with flying gear the crews congregated in the assembly area to await their transport. Crews were required to be at their aircraft well before take-off. The crew buses, generally driven by WAAFs, would pull up (at approx. 2200 hrs in the case of the Krefeld raid) and the crew scrambled aboard passing their accoutrements to one another as they got in. Driving around the dark peri. track the buses dropped the crews off at the various dispersals, where they were greeted by the ground crews in charge of the aircraft.

At the dispersal, after a chat with the ground crew the Pilot and Flight Engineer walked around the aircraft for a visual check up which included ensuring that the pitot head cover and static vent plugs were removed, if the protective items were left in place the air speed indicator and altimeter would not read correctly. On entering the aircraft the the crew ensured that all loose equipment was stowed, this could mean putting the fresh supply of portable oxygen bottles in their carriers and if 'Window' strips and 'Nickel' leaflets were provided, locate them in a convenient place for the Wireless Operator who also stowed his pigeons in the rest position. The Air Gunners would check that their turrets were centralised and engaged. The Pilot and Flight Engineer ensured that the flying controls were unlocked and if not would remove the aileron parking gear from the control column and the locking lever for locking the elevator and rudder control rods together (the purpose of these locks was to stop strong winds damaging the controls). The electrical system Ground/Flight switch would be set to Flight so that the lights and indicators could be checked. The pressures in the air pressure accumulators for the tailwheel, flaps, and bomb doors were checked. The flap isolating cock was unscrewed, up lock disengaged and clips secured. The Flight Engineer ensured that the cross feed fuel cock was in the OFF position and the fuel contents checked by means of fuel contents gauges in the Flight Engineer's position.

The rest of the crew also had to carry out various checks and when they were all satisfied with their equipment, and the pilot considered that the aircraft was serviceable, Form 700 was signed and they would then be in the hands of Flying Control. The crews then hung around either inside or outside their aircraft waiting for the start-up time signal from the Control Tower. Pilots could be given an approximate time to start taxiing from the dispersal, based on the distance from the dispersal to the Marshalling Point and the take off time. A red Very light curling across the sky meant operation cancelled but the normal signal was a green cartridge to indicate that the operation was due to commence. Since engines could overheat if ground run for too long then it was advisable not to start them up too soon. In the case of the Krefeld operation, the first aircraft started to taxi at about 2345 hrs and took off at 2351 hrs. All the aircraft were airborne by 0021 using the main runway and the aircrews could see the fires in the bomb dump still burning as they flew over it.

ORGANISING THE OPERATIONS

Chapter 4

FLYING CONTROL

Station and Squadron support operations having prepared the aircrew and their aircraft for the operation and with the aircrew standing by their aircraft as mentioned in previous chapter, it was then the resposibility of Flying Control to get the aircraft airborne. Flying Control personnel under the leadership of the Senior Flying Control Officer, Squadron Leader Frank ('Basher') Varey were housed in the large Type 518/40 Control Tower situated in front of the main hangar.

R/T radio communication with the aircraft on the 50 metre band was provided in 1942 by TR9 single channel transceivers, which were later on replaced by the more efficient TR1196 transceivers. These radios, which had a limited range of about 10 miles or so, were located in the Aircraft Control Room and used by Radio Operators who were frequently WAAFs. The operators, as well as talking to the aircraft, had to keep a precise log of all calls made. A Form 68 Watch Log was kept in both the Control Tower and the ACP's Caravan. Also in this room was a desk for use by the Station or Squadron CO during an operation, so that they could keep track of what was happening. Located next to the Control Tower were buildings to house the fire crash tender, an ambulance (nicknamed "The Blood Wagon" by the airmen) and the Landmark Beacon or Pundit

Supervision of the airfield was the responsibility of the Sergeant Airfield Controllers, known as the ACPs, whose centre of operations was the Airfield Control Caravan, with a transparent observation roof extension on top of it. The caravan was parked at the beginning of the runway in use and could also be used by Flare Path Party whose job was to support the ACP. To control the aircraft taking off the duty ACP had two Aldis lamps fitted with red and green filters, a Very pistol with a selection of coloured cartridges and a field telephone for communication with the Control Tower. This can be seen at the bottom of the steps in photo No 36. For transportation between the Tower and the Airfield Caravan the SFCO's Humber staff car was available and this can also be seen in the photgraph.

As previously described Snaith had the typical three runway layout of a wartime airfield, each runway being designated by a QDM. QDM was the radio Q code for the magnetic course on which a pilot would have to fly when landing on the runway in use. Since there were three runways and two possible landing directions for each, this meant six QDM's and these were reduced to two significant figures, eg QDM 319 was designated runway 32. Whatever runway was in use was indicated by its two numbers displayed on large boards on top of the Control Tower as shown in photo No 2. In front of the Control Tower was the signal square used to display RAF ground signal codes plus another square displaying the airfield code letters, SX.

The Meteorological Section was located in the Control Tower and it was classified as an RAF Type III Met. Office, with staff qualified to explain forecasts and brief aircrew on expected weather for

Photo 50 Via B. Gazeley
Flare Path Party

operations. The section received forecasts from Type I stations at Bomber Command and 4 Group Headquarters, which was the highest grade of Met. Office and able to provide forecasts at all times. Snaith's Met. Officer's duties, with the help of the Met. Assistants under his control, was to make weather observations, supply routine weather forecasts, provide forecasts for operations and other flights and give weather reports at pre-operations briefings for aircrews. It was not the responsibility of the Met. Officer to say whether aircraft could fly or not, this was the duty of a GD Officer, such as the Officer I/C flying who would make the decision after consultation with the Met. Officer. AMO's stated that aircraft Captains who intended to make a trip of more than 100 miles were entitled to obtain a route forecast from the Met. Office on Form 2330.

Outside flying control was a white louvred box known as a Stevenson Screen containing instruments from which Met. Assistants took readings every hour of air temperature, humidity, rainfall (by means of a rain gauge), and barometric pressure. For wind speed there was an anemometer in the tower and they also carried out a subjective assessment of visibility by checking how far they could see across the airfield and reported on the height of the cloud base and cloud coverage in tenths. At night the Sandra cloud searchlight could be used to estimate height. This information was sent to a Type I Met. Station by telex identifying the sender with Snaith's three figure code number. The Met. Assistants would also be involved in preparing Synoptic Charts and other information for the Met. Officer. The Type 1 Met. Offices obtained information from a variety of sources including civilian meteorological observers. For example sub Post Office personnel in rural areas who rang in met. information to the major Met. Offices every 6 hours.

When Operations were due to take place a green Very flare would curl up into the sky from the Control Tower indicating to the expectant aircrews waiting out on the dispersal that the Operation was on and aircrew could prepare to taxi. When the aircraft were due to leave the dispersals, their engine would have to be started, but prior to this it was necessary to carry out a pre start-up procedure. There were some differences in the procedures for the Mk II Merlin engined aircraft and the Mk III Hercules engined ones. For the Mk III aircraft the procedure was flap position checked, landing lamp retarded, undercarriage, flap and bomb door levers set in correct position and brake pressure checked.

The flying controls were tested for freedom of movement. As mentioned previously, on first entering the aircraft the Pilot would have ensured that the Control locks were removed, but there were cases of foreign objects such as tools, still causing restrictions in the use of the controls. In modern aircraft, legislation against FOD (foreign object damage) is of prime importance. The current RAF procedure is for service personnel to use shadow boards (which indicate missing items) during servicing to ensure all tools are returned and items removed during servicing must be accounted for. However, during WW2 there were no facilities for niceties such as shadow boards, tools were very scarce and tradesmen were lucky to have a full tool kit.

The oxygen capacity and flow rate were checked with the master oxygen regulator on the pilots panel. Finally communication with the crew via the intercom was checked using the call light system and the A1134 intercom amplifier.

With these checks completed satisfactorily the engine could then be started up. The Flight Engineer was responsible for the engine starter and boost coil switches, gill controls (on Mk III aircraft) and checking temperature and pressure gauges and indicators. The engines were started up in turn, one of the ground crew plugged the trolley acc. into the socket on the leading edge of the starboard wing and the Flight Engineer switched the electrics Air/Ground switch to Ground.

When a Mk III Halifax with a radial engine had been standing oil and fuel could drain into the bottom cylinder and cause damage by 'hydraulicing'. In such a case the engine would have to be turned over by hand using the prop before starting in order to get the oil moving. The Flight Engineer turned on the master cock and tanks one and three and opened the cowling gills, with the Pilot setting the engine controls. Throttles were set just off the rear stop, the mixture control down, the propeller control fully up and the super charger control 'M' ratio selected. The engines were started up one at a time in sequence, with a ground crew member standing under the engine to access the priming pump. The Pilot switched the ignition on and signalled the ground crew to press the button on the starter acc. trolley to supply 24 Volts power to the aircraft. The Flight Engineer then pressed the starter and boost coil switches, whilst the ground crew 'erk' worked the priming pump as the engines were turning over. Starting recommendations were that the turning period should not exceed 20 seconds with a 30 second wait before turning engine over again if it had not started. Even when the engine started there were occasions when the ground crew mechanic may have found it necessary to continue priming until the engine had picked up on the carburettor. When the engine was running satisfactorily the Flight Engineer removed his finger from the booster coil switch and the ground crew screwed down the priming pump and turned off the priming cock for the engine in question.

A check on satisfactory running of the engines was the mag. drop test. Each engine had two plugs with a magneto for each plug and the procedure was to switch off a magneto in turn whilst the engine was running. A large drop in speed as indicated by the rev. counter was considered unsatisfactory and could mean that the aircraft would not be available for the operation if the fault could not be rectified quickly. If the engines were running satisfactorily and it was time to start taxiing, the Pilot called over the intercom "OK for taxiing" and having received satisfactory replies gave the chocks away signal to the ground crew. Two 'erks' then ran under the wings avoiding the whirling propeller blades and bracing themselves against the slipstream from the props, grabbed the ropes attached to the heavy wooden chocks. With the knack born of experience they pulled them away from under the wheels. Running an engine for an appreciable length of time for warming up or taxiing was not recommended since it could burn up a lot of valuable fuel before take-off.

One of the ground crew took on the task of marshalling the aircraft out of its dispersal onto the perimeter track. The pilot released his brakes and with suitable revs. of the engine moved the Halifax forward, following the marshalling ground crew walking backwards in front of it with his hands above his head to give come on or change of direction signals. When turning a Halifax it was recommended that the aircraft should execute an arc of a circle since turning it with one wheel locked could put an unnecessary strain on the stationary wheel and undercarriage.

Once the Halifax was safely on the peri. track and heading in the correct direction the marshaller leapt smartly onto the grass at the side of the peri. track to avoid the whirling propellor blades. The pilot then negotiated the narrow peri. track, guided by the blue taxi way lights. Depending on the location of the dispersal, the pilot could have up to a mile or more to taxi to the Marshalling Point at the start of the runway. Taxiing along the peri. track at a slow speed could be quite a difficult problem for the pilot, steering by revving the appropriate outer engine if not on course and keeping his hand on the brake lever.

The Halifax eventually joined a queue of aircraft heading towards the Marshalling Point. On reaching the latter the pilot carried out his prior to take-off Vital Actions checks which were, Trim, Mixture, Pitch, Fuel, Flaps, Gills (Mk3 only), Gyro and Hydraulics. Aircrew not required during take-off occupied the rest position. When a flashing green was received from the ACP the Halifax moved from the Marshalling Point and lined up on the take-off point on the runway. Then at the sight of a steady green from the Airfield Controller's Aldis lamp the engines were opened up with a roar, the brakes released and the straining aircraft would surge forward down the runway. At this point the Bomb Aimer came into action as a temporary 'Second Dicky', sitting on the fold down seat next to the Pilot. The Pilot controlled the throttles with his right hand, assisted by the Bomb Aimer who had placed his left hand behind the Pilot's hand on the throttle. When the throttle gate was reached the Pilot called "lift" and the throttle levers were lifted through the gate with the Bomb Aimer taking over their control to give maximum power for take off. The Pilot's right hand was then free to operate the undercarriage lever and the Bomb Aimer locked the throttles with his right hand. The Flight Engineer frequently stood behind the Pilot and Air Bomber to give assistance if necessary.

With its full bomb load the heavily laden Halifax would roar down the runway, the crew waiting apprehensively for the moment when the aircraft having passed the point of no return was safely

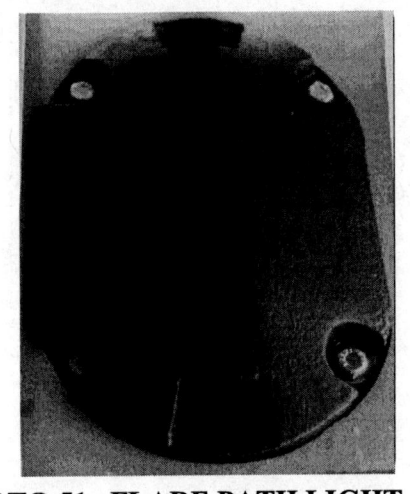

PHOTO 51   FLARE PATH LIGHT

FLYING CONTROL

OP C/S	M H YANKEE 0SA	BEACON SITE 1	UI	ETD	2355 (1) 0005 (2)
	LK ORCLE DG8				
STN C/S	LADY	RUNWAY	14	ETA	0406 (1) 0413 (2)

21/22-6-43 51 SQUADRON KREFELD

A/C LETTER	A/C NUMBER	CAPTAIN	TIME OFF	ON R/T	PAN	TIME DOWN	REMARKS
MH-A	HR843	SGT SOLOMON	0004	0406	0442	0446	
" D	HR852	SGT MACPHERSON	2357	0355	0355	0401	NO NOSE LIGHT ACKNOWLEDGEMENT
" T	JD252	P/O HALEY	0007	0359	0406	0408	TURNED AND TAXIED ALONG RUNWAY
" Y	HR732	SGT RICHARDS	0010	0403	0439	0441	CANCELLED (BRAKE PRESSURE TROUBLE)
LK-A	JD253	SGT LANDER					HEAVY OXYGEN LEAKAGE
MH-B	HR726	SGT THOMPSON	0003	0205	0210	0216	LANDED AT POCKLINGTON AS INSTRUCTED
" H	HR870	SGT CATES	0008	0421	0501	0525	
LK-L	HR839	P/O TAY	0015	0358	0404	0405	NO NOSE LIGHT ACKNOWLEDGEMENT
" B	HR868	SGT LAMBERT	0001	0401	0413? 0429?	0437	SHORTEST CASE
MH-V	HR834	SGT GREGORY	0016	0402	0416	0421	B/A SICK
" E	W1224	SGT FOULSTON	0014	0256	0257	0301	
" K	JD244	SGT HEATHFIELD	0011				MISSING
" R	JD250	F/O MACKENZIE	0009	0419	0456	0500	NO NOSE LIGHT ACKNOWLEDGEMENT
" S	JD248	SGT BISHOP	0020	0407	0441	0455	LANDED AT POCKLINGTON AS INSTRUCTED
" C	HR731	SGT OSMOND	0005	0425	0505	0536	
" Q	HR838	F/S GEORGE	0017	0337	0347	0352	NO NOSE LIGHT ACKNOWLEDGEMENT
" Z	HR869	F/W DOBSON	0018	0359	0409	0412	
LK-P	HR728	F/O IRWIN	0012	0420	0423	0427	HYDRAULICS SHOT UP PRIORITY LANDING
" K	JD118	SGT MORRIS	0021	0436		0552	LANDED AT POCKLINGTON AS INSTRUCTED

FIG 5 Flying Control Operations Board For Krefeld Raid

FLYING CONTROL

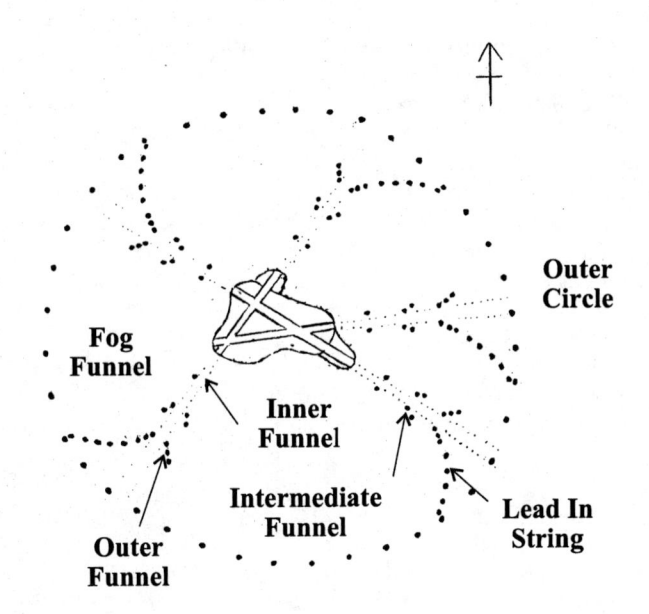

FIG 6.

'Drem' Mk2 Lighting System At Snaith

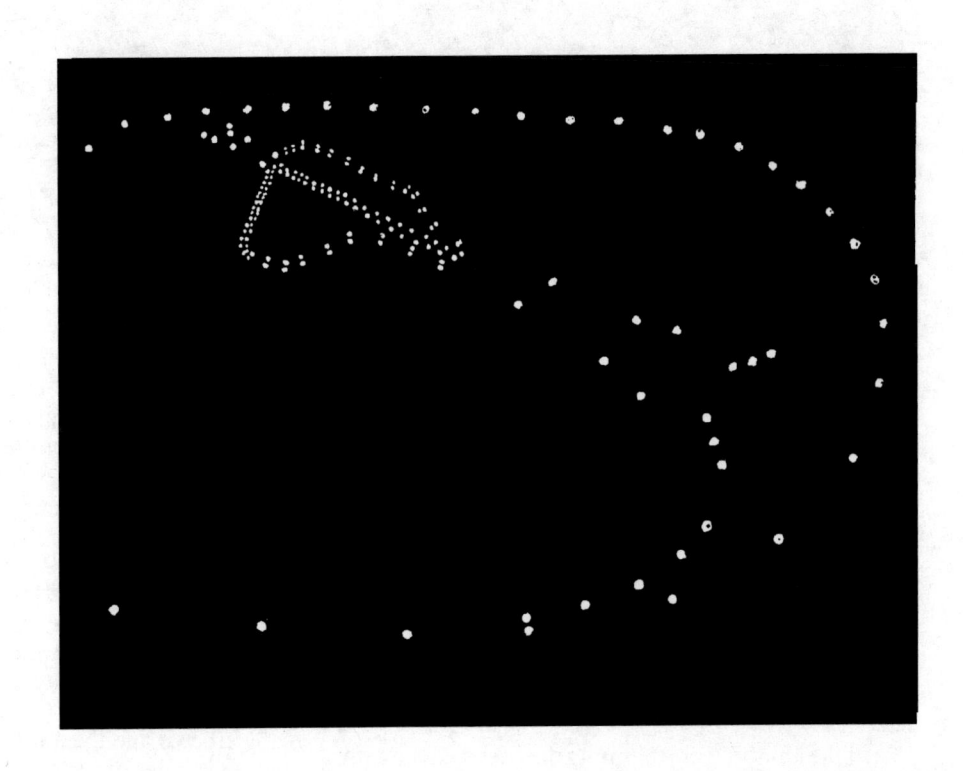

FIG 9

Snaith Lighting System at Night

35

clear of the 'deck'. To many pilots the Halifax appeared reluctant to get airborne, but when airborne was a solid, stable and dependable aircraft after initial problems associated with fin and rudder design were overcome. With a satisfactory take-off the Pilot concentrated on attaining the required altitude. The time between each aircraft taking off could be as short as one minute so that in the case of the Krefeld raid the whole squadron was airborne in 24 minutes. With all the operating aircraft of the squadron airborne, members of Flying Control and other supporting services could now only wait for the return of the squadron at the end of the operation, hopefully with as few Halifax losses and casualties as possible.

As an aid to the control of the aircraft once they were airborne there was an Operations Board and a Landing Control Board (Fig 55) located in the Aircraft Control Room in the Tower, and an example of the former being given in Fig No 5. This was a

PHOTO 52   TAXI TRACK LIGHT

record of the aircraft operating whereas the Landing Control Board was used to control the movement of aircraft during landing and take-off, by keeping a check on the movements of the Halifax. The Landing Control Board was divided into sections showing the height of aircraft which were in landing circuits above the airfield and also aircraft which had called in, but were not yet in a circuit. There were lettered tokens for each aircraft which could be placed on the board so that the duty Flying Control Officer and the R/T Operator could see the situation at a glance.

When the aircraft were returning the first contact with them would normally be via the R/T Operator. If not already in operation the 'Drem' Mk 2 lighting system installed at Snaith would be switched on and the appropriate runway illuminated. This system would normally only be switched on when in use, since it could act as a marker for German intruder aircraft. The lighting system installed at Snaith was a vast improvement on the system the Squadron had to operate with when using a grass landing ground at Dishforth early on in the war. The Snaith flare path lighting system known colloquially as 'Drem' Mk 2 was far more efficient than the goose neck flares, Money flares and glim lamps used at Dishforth.

The 'Drem' Mk 2 system comprised three parts,

PHOTO 53   AIRFIELD LIGHTING CONTROL CONSOLE (YAM)

namely outer circle, lead in and funnels, and runway and perimeter track lighting as shown in Fig No 6. For the outer circle the lights were laid out in the rough form of a circle around the airfield, and consisted of fittings which contained two unscreened 60 Watt metal filament lamps mounted on poles and shining upwards. The height of the poles varied between 20 foot and 60 foot, the height chosen being such that they were not screened by any obstructions such as trees, buildings, etc around the airfield. When the lighting system was being installed at Snaith, many of the locals looked on in surprise at the number of high poles with lights on being erected and the amount of electric cable both over and under ground which had to be laid. The majority of cable was erected overhead and in order to save rubber, a scarce wartime commodity, bare wire was used. This outer circle of lighting was fed

FIG 7 'D' TYPE LANDING CIRCUIT

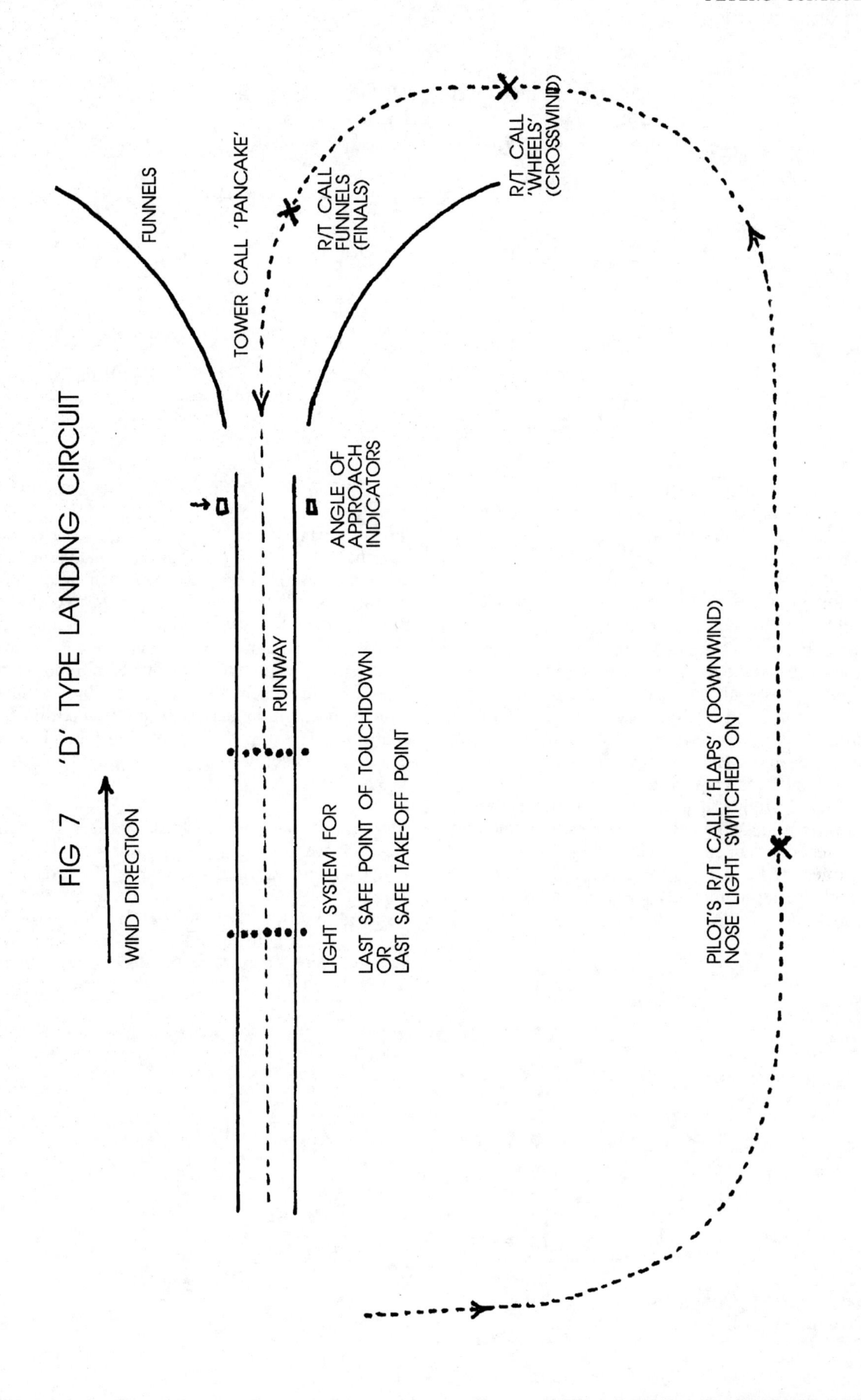

FLYING CONTROL

Pilots Observations Of Angle Of Approach Indicators

Angle of approach (degrees)	Indication given by A of A LHS Indicator	Indication given by A of A RHS Indicator	Position Of Halifax
Under 3	Red	Red	Too Low
3 to 4	Green	Red	Slightly Low
4 to 5	Green	Green	Perfect
5 to 6	Amber	Green	Slightly High
Over 6	Amber	Amber	Too High

from a transformer in the Control Tower, switched by a contactor in the transformer circuit and controlled by a switch on the control panel in the Aircraft Control Room.

From the outer circle lighting there was a lead in set of lights to the end of the runway, known as the the approach lighting system. There were six of these one for each end of the runway and arranged for left hand circuits of the airfield by the Squadron aircraft. Because left hand, anti-clockwise, circuits were the norm, the Pilot's seat was situated on the port side of the Squadron's Halifax aircraft. These approach lighting systems employed the same fittings as the outer circle lights, and as far as possible were all mounted at the same height. They were divided into four sections named Lead in String, Outer Funnel, Intermediate Funnel and Inner Funnel, the latter two funnels being commonly referred to as the Fog Funnel.

The Lead in String indicated to the Pilot at which point he should turn from the outer circle towards the runway in use and was also intended to give him an indication of the type of turn to make in order to enter the centre line of the approach path when landing. The Outer Funnel comprised two sets of three lights in the shape of a `V', this was followed by the Centre Funnel comprising two sets of two lights either side of and equidistant from the centre line of the approach path and finally by the Inner Funnel of single lamps also equidistant from the centre line (see Fig No 6). The Fog Funnel lights could also assist Pilots taking off at night by acting as a horizon.

After transversing the various approach Funnels, the Pilot was then guided by the runway marker lights. The marker lights were set 100 yards apart longitudinally either side of the runway and installed in cast iron fittings set in the runway so that they did not project more than 1.1/4" above the level of the tarmac or concrete comprising the

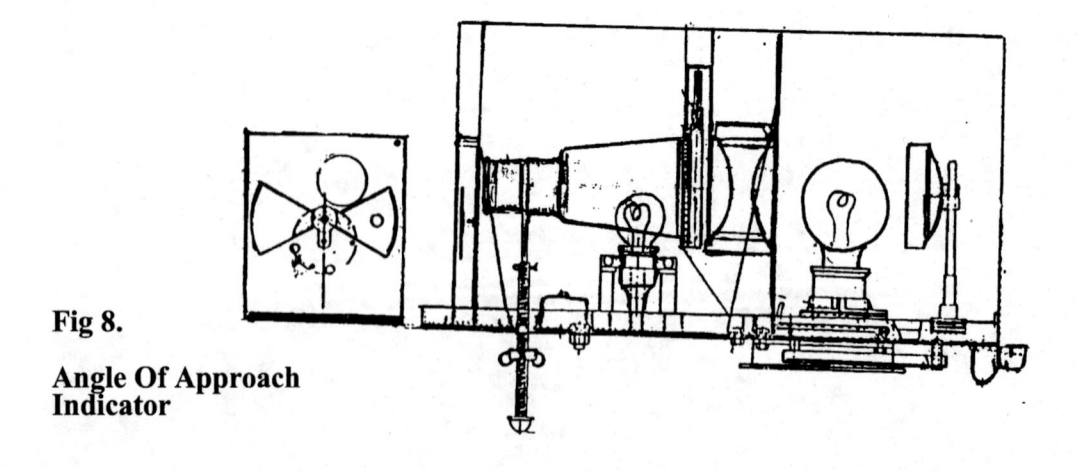

Fig 8.

Angle Of Approach Indicator

runway. These fittings were strong enough to be run over by a Halifax aircraft and contoured so that there were no sharp edges which could damage the tyres. Inside these fittings were two 15 Watt metal filament pygmy lamps, shining out through slits facing in the two Runway directions, but only one direction being lit at any one time so as to avoid a Halifax landing in the wrong direction.

At right angles across the runway, 800 yards from each end were crossbars of seven unidirectional blue lights to warn the Pilot of the last safe point of touch down and the amount of runway left at the end. Selecting the appropriate runway flare path circuit was affected by operating the six position Runway Master Switch to select the runway lights required and closing the main flare path switch, both of which were located on the Control Console in the Aircraft Control Room. The runway lights in use were indicated by the lights on the mimic diagram above the Control Board. The Control Console also had facilities to adjust the lighting intensity from 25 to 100% brilliance and there was a Diesel electric generator available as an emergency standby for lighting. At the end of runway 32 there were trip wires which could be activated by any aircraft which overshot the runway. The purpose of these wires was to activate the railway signalling system, so as to warn the railway authorities that there was the possibility of an aircraft having landed on the railway line.

As a guide to the Pilot in order to achieve the correct angle of approach when landing there were Angle of Approach indicators (subsequently called Glide Path Indicators), either side of the start of the runway (see Fig No 7). The angle of Approach indicators comprised an optical projection lantern with three coloured slides which in a vertical plane gave 6 degree, 2 degree and 8 degree angle beams of red, green and amber respectively. A spirit level was included to permit correct setting up of the equipment. The indicator on the left hand side of the runway had a 5 degree inclination and the one on the right hand side a 4 degree inclination, the purpose of the difference being to help Pilots obtain a close estimate of the approach angle. There was also a rotating iris to produce an intermittent beam and hence help in the identification of the indicator. A guide to the indication that the Pilot received from these landing aids is given in the Table on the previous page.

Another aid to Pilots returning from an operation was the Pundit landmark beacon to help the Pilots identify the airfield. This was a red Chance light mounted on a trailer (see photo No 2), flashing two morse code letters. Initially the code letters were changed daily by altering the operating cams in the beacon but towards the end of the war the Snaith code letters SX were flashed. For an operation the beacon could be located on the airfield or towed out to a designated site near the flight path of the runway in use. For the Krefeld raid which has been described in detail, the Pundit was located at site No 1, near the flight path for runway 14, about 4 miles from the airfield, and flashing code letters UI.

The Pundit was operated by a crew which could include a driver for the vehicle, a signals person and a tradesman normally an Electrician, whose job it was to set the appropriate operating cams in the Pundit in order to flash the required code letters. The crew could connect a portable hand set into the GPO phone system to enable them to make contact with Flying Control and for the Krefeld raid the extension number was Whitley Bridge 21. They were supervised by the duty Pundit officer, a job which rotated amongst all officers including aircrew. One aircrew officer, F/Lt Bill Allen, who had to do this duty found the crew well organised, they produced an appetizing fry-up of sausage, bacon and beans washed down with lashings of hot tea. This was very acceptable during the Pundit watch on a cold winters night.

The returning 51 Squadron pilots normally achieved radio contact via their TR1196 transceivers at a range of about 10 miles from the airfield. After a gruelling operation the view of the outer circle lights glistening like a string of pearls in the dark (Fig 9), were a welcoming sight, with the Pundit flashing the airfield identification letters and in certain cases the Sandra searchlights would be coned over the airfield to identify it to returning aircrews. Also the friendly voice of a Snaith WAAF R/T operator was a great boost to a tired crew. The base and the aircraft were allocated operational call signs for both R/T (voice) and C/W (morse) communication which were changed daily in order not to help the enemy, examples for the Krefeld raid are shown in the Operations Board reproduction in Fig No 1. Near the end of the war the same call signs were used for a period, as for example when aircraft were given the call sign "Graceless" and the base call sign was "Agnola".

There were occasions when aircraft had to land away from Snaith for various reasons, which included the airfield being fog bound, a shortage of fuel or the aircraft was too badly damaged to be able to make base. Diversion instructions could be

FLYING CONTROL

received either by the W/Op. by means of his R1155 receiver or by the Pilot via the TR1196 transceiver, depending on the distance from base. Landing away at a strange airfield could cause problems for the aircrew. Navigator Dave Storey reported that difficulties could be encountered in landing at an American Air Force base at night since American airfields were not used to landing aircraft in the dark. On one occasion he recounts that they were told to land at Andrews Field near Gt Soling in Essex, which was the first airfield to be built in England by the U.S. Pioneer Corp and was occupied by B26 Marauders of the 322nd Bomb Group. When the squadron aircraft landed they found that the American Flying Controllers did not have a satisfactory system for marshalling aircraft at night.

The result was that when the squadron aircraft taxied off the runway after landing they all finished up in a pile near the end of the runway. In 1943 American aircrews could not take off and assemble in formation in the dark and were not trained in night landings. The debriefing they received at the station was the briefest one the squadron had ever experienced. "Did you find the target", "Did you drop your bombs"? The Debriefing Officer could not at first believe the tonnage of bombs carried by a Halifax, since it appeared large compared with that carried by a Flying Fortress. One aircraft captained by Bill Addison had engine trouble and spent three days at the airfield whilst ground crew flown down from Snaith carried out repairs.

When the squadron was returning from a raid on Sterkrade on 21/22 November 1944 Snaith became fog bound so they were directed to land at Hutton Cranswick a few miles south of Driffield, since this was one of the few Yorkshire airfields which were clear of fog that night. This was a smaller airfield than Snaith and came under the control of 12 Group. It was the home of various fighter squadrons and 291 Anti Aircraft Co- operation Squadron, which flew Hurricanes and Martlets for target towing duties, so it normally dealt with daylight operations. Because of their inexperience of night flying Flying Control seemed to have problems in bringing in the Halifax aircraft.

When F/Lt Bill Allen came in to land he found aircraft making their approaches from different directions so that whilst he was making a landing approach another aircraft suddenly shot in front of him with the result that he had to overshoot and go around again for another landing. After the squadron had landed they found the controller in high state of tension after having to deal with the sudden convergence of 13 heavy bombers at night, without the experience of the Bomber Command procedure which could land 13 aircraft in as many minutes. After landing the squadron finished up parked against a fence on the airfield, awaiting the light of day.

When the squadron returned to Snaith the arrival times of some aircraft could be within minutes of each other, and so some form of stacking was necessary. It was normal to stack at 500 ft intervals upwards hence the use of the `Landing Control Board'(Fig 55), using the movable tokens to indicate aircraft heights. When an aircraft was allocated the next circuit 500 feet up, this was indicated by placing the tokens at at the appropriate height level on the board. The standard procedure was for aircraft to approach at 2,000 ft or below cloud, whichever was the lowest and on reaching the circuit would be showing navigation lights. When approaching Snaith the airfield could be identified by the letters flashed by the Pundit and radio contact would be made with Flying Control on R/T, giving station and aircraft call signs and petrol endurance to the nearest 15 minutes.

Taking the example of `D' Dog with 75 minutes endurance, being stacked and given a height to fly at.

Aircaft: "Hello Agnola, this is Graceless D Dog, 75, Over."

Flying Control: "Hello Graceless D Dog, Agnola answering, height to fly 1,500, QFE 1,000 Over."

(QFE 1,000 meant set your altimeter to airfield barometric pressure of 1,000 millibars so that it would indicate zero altitude on landing).

The aircraft would acknowledge by repeating height to fly and join the circuit at 1,500 ft, having listened for the broadcast of the aircraft ahead of it to ascertain its code letter and call sign (in 1943 LK aircraft had different call signs from MH aircraft) so that the Pilot could keep a check on its position whilst in circuit and when landing.

Aircraft on arrival would make left hand circuits of the airfield at the height allocated to them over R/T by Flying Control. There was often a problem with post operational circuits due to the proximity of Snaith's satellite airfield Burn only 5 miles to the North of Snaith, since aircraft from both squadrons could be arriving back at the same time. Liaison between flying controls at the two airfields was therefore essential. On the occasions when the wind directions meant that the runways in use could produce a risk of accidents with aircraft from both stations executing left hand circuits, arrangements were made for Burn to execute right hand circuits. Despite these precautions, on the night of the 18th of November 1944 when aircraft from both squadrons were returning from a raid on Munster, Halifax MZ559 from 578 Squadron collided with Halifax NR241 from 51 Squadron, all the aircrew were killed.

Aircraft were expected to execute 'D' shaped circuits as shown in Fig No 7, and the landing circuit was generally established at 1000 ft, though it could vary according to weather conditions. When an aircraft had landed the aircraft in the next higher circuit would be called into land eg: Flying Control: "Hello Graceless D Dog, this is Agnola, prepare to land, Over."

PHOTO 54 HALIFAX MK II SERIES 1A LANDING

'D Dog' switched on upward and downward identity lights, acknowledged by repeating instructions over R/T and lost height to come down to landing circuit, taking up the correct position in the circuit behind the aircraft in front already preparing to land. In the landing circuit, on the downwind leg and opposite the middle of the runway, 'D Dog' would call "Flaps" and switch on the nose light, then when it had entered the crosswind leg the Pilot called "Wheels".

Broadcasting positions of "Flaps", "Wheels", and "Funnels" enabled other aircraft to check on the landing aircraft's position so that when the landing aircraft was in the downwind position, the aircraft behind should be in the upwind position. It was important for aircraft to use the correct R/T procedure and phonetic alphabet. The standard version of the latter, introduced in 1943, was given in AP 1970 as follows: A Able, B Baker, C Charlie, D Dog, E Easy, F Fox, G George, H How, I Item, J Jig or Johnny, K King, L Love, M Mike, N Nan, O Oboe, P Peter, Q Queen, R Roger, S Sugar, T Tare, U Uncle, V Victor, W William, X X-ray, Y Yoke, Z Zebra.

'D Dog' would lose height around the circuit so as to arrive at the Funnels at about 800 ft and then, on its final approach with trim all ready for landing 'D Dog', broadcast "Funnels" on the R/T. If the runway was clear of preceeding aircraft, the Tower gave the order to "Pancake". If for any reason the Pilot could not land during his final aproach then the R/T call was "overshoot", the landing was aborted and the circuit rejoined. However if the Pilot did decide to land he would approach above the stalling speed, which for a Halifax was 100-120 mph or slightly less with flaps and wheels down, observing the Angle of Approach Indicators for a correct angle of descent. The wheels would touch down with a bump, with the runway lights flashing past until the aircraft slowed down at the end of the runway. Having landed safely and cleared the runway the Pilot broadcast as soon as possible the message "End Clear". It was a rule that when landing one member of the crew should have a Very pistol loaded with a red flare ready for use in case the Pilot could not clear the runway.

Having landed and cleared the runway, the Pilot finally taxied the aircraft to its dispersal and the tired crew, thankful for a successful operation, would probably light up a fag ready to became involved in all the post operational procedures which will be discussed in a later chapter.

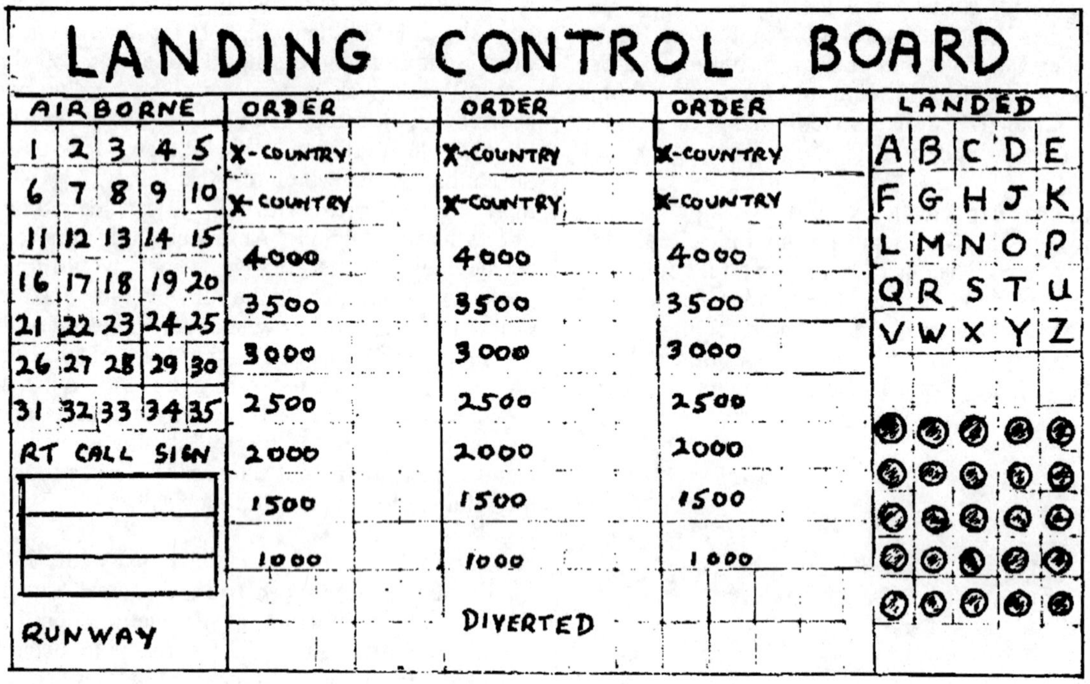

FLYING CONTROL

AIRBORNE	ORDER	ORDER	ORDER	LANDED
1 2 3 4 5	X-COUNTRY	X-COUNTRY	X-COUNTRY	A B C D E
6 7 8 9 10	X-COUNTRY	X-COUNTRY	X-COUNTRY	F G H J K
11 12 13 14 15	4000	4000	4000	L M N O P
16 17 18 19 20	3500	3500	3500	Q R S T U
21 22 23 24 25	3000	3000	3000	V W X Y Z
26 27 28 29 30	2500	2500	2500	
31 32 33 34 35	2000	2000	2000	⊛⊛⊛⊛⊛
RT CALL SIGN	1500	1500	1500	⊛⊛⊛⊛⊛
	1000	1000	1000	⊛⊛⊛⊛⊛
		DIVERTED		⊛⊛⊛⊛⊛
RUNWAY				⊛⊛⊛⊛⊛

LANDING CONTROL BOARD

Fig 55 Layout of Landing Control Board at Snaith

Tokens hung in appropriate locations on board in order to display information on aircraft movements. Location marked 1000ft is for aircraft in landing circuit.

Chapter 5

FACETS OF A SQUADRON OPERATION

The object of this chapter is to give a general picture of a squadron operation and the activities of the various crew members. However it must be recognised that over the period January 1943 to April 1945 the operational procedures could vary considerably and in addition there would be differences between the ways the various crews operated, so an endeavour has been made to incorporate these in the text. During a squadron operation one member of the crew was designated as the Captain and the person ultimately responsible for the safety of the aircraft and anything within his control that occurred during a flight. The Pilot was normally designated as the Captain but by KRR's any crew member could be appointed to the post by the C.O. and he had absolute authority over the rest of the crew regardless of rank.

Once airborne as described in the previous chapter the undercarriage was retracted and at a safe height the flaps were withdrawn, the aircraft levelled out, and the aircrew took up their operational stations. With engine revolutions and boost set, the Flight Engineer withdrew to the rest position and engaged mechanical locks for the undercarriage and isolated flaps. The Bomb Aimer then left the co-pilot's seat to help the Navigator. All the post take off actions having been carried out the Pilot could start to settle himself down for the op. and as Captain checked on his crew by calling over the intercom. "crew check". If everything was OK he would get a reply from each of the crew in turn, for example "Rear Gunner, OK Skip". A good Captain instilled a sense of discipline in the crew, such as insisting on strict intercom procedure with no unnecessary chatter over the intercom. Some skippers strongly enforced other rules such as no smoking in the aircraft. There was a case with F/Lt Bill Allen's crew where the Rear Gunner, without the knowledge of the skipper, used to carry cigarettes and matches for the rest of the crew. When they wanted a smoke crew members would go back to the rear turret and the gunner would hand them a cig. and matches. However on one occasion the skipper went back to the rear turret to see the gunner, who not realising in the dark it was the skipper, passed him a cigarette and matches. Next day after the operation the skipper assembled the crew in the crew room and gave them a dressing down for smoking in the aircraft. This crew survived the war and one school of thought was that good aircrew discipline could be a factor in completing a tour safely.

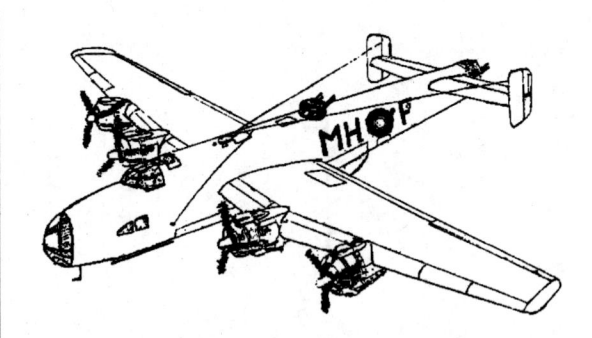

Having reached the required altitude, if there was time available the Navigator may want to get the Pilot to carry out a radius of action circuit. It was up to the Pilot and Navigator as to what course they flew and with Navigator 'Cliff' Cliffords's crew, if their take off was early, they flew west and then returned to Snaith at setting off time. On one occasion when they were first off they had almost reached the Lake District before returning. If it was a crew where the Bomb Aimer helped the Navigator, then the former would take fixes and compasses could be checked whilst the Navigator sitting in his station (Fig 10) was getting himself sorted out for the trip. A recognised procedure when the Navigator was organised was to give the pilot a heading to reach the red 'B' lattice line on the Eastern 'Gee' chain which passed through Snaith running NW to SE. From this point the Navigator would set a course from base and give the Pilot a course to steer to join the rest of the aircraft comprising the bomber stream. If the coastal crossing point for the bomber stream was on the south coast, Reading beacon was often used as a turning point. Navigator Ken Staple recalled that the bearing of this beacon from Snaith was 185 degrees True. It was important for the Navigator to check that all his navigation instruments were fully serviceable and he could do this by asking the Pilot to steer a steady course for a period. Whilst the Pilot was steering this steady course, the Air Gunners could help by centralising their turrets and the Navigator would check the D.R.Compass repeaters with the help of the Flight Engineer who reported the master unit readings whilst the Navigator was checking the repeaters. During this period some Bomb Aimers helped their Navigator by taking 'Gee' fixes

FLIGHT ENGINEER'S LOG (HALIFAX). BC/F6

Captain F/Lt FEAVER Engineer P/O STOCKER

Airframe No. and Letter LW 496 C6A Total Petrol 1438 Galls. Bomb Load 11,500 lbs. A.U.W. at T.O. 64,316 lbs.

Pressure Head Cover OFF Rad. Shutter GILLS 1/3 OPEN Air Intakes COLD Supercharger M Auto Controls ON Controls unlocked YES D.R. Compass ON

Target * LE MANS Track Miles .... Squadron No. * 51 Date 7.3.44

To be filled in every 20 minutes and whenever flight or engine conditions are changed.

Time	Height in Feet	Air Temp. °C.	I.A.S.	Altitude C.L. or D.	R.P.M.	Boost lbs./in.	Oil Temp. °C.				Oil Press. lbs./in.				CYL. Coolant Temp. °C.				Supercharger M. or S.	Air Intake H. or C.	Auto Controls	Oxygen Time		Remarks
							S.O.	S.I.	P.I.	P.O.	S.O.	S.I.	P.I.	P.O.	S.O.	S.I.	P.I.	P.O.				On	Off	
	— TA	KE	OFF	→	2,800	+8	30	50	40	45	95	100	90	90	200	210	210	220	M	C			OFF	

* INFORMATION TO BE ENTERED ON RETURN TO BASE

FIG 11 'Specimen Copy' Of The Type Of Entries In A Flight Engineers Log On Take-Off

With all his preliminary checks carried out, the Navigator then gave the Pilot a course to steer. They would eventually join the bomber stream, which was an air armada the like of which the world will never see again. Night after night hundreds of four engined bombers set off from bases in Yorkshire and elsewhere to attack targets in Germany and occupied Europe. Over 55,000 aircrew died and more than 9,000 aircraft were lost. The aircrew had to cope with mechanical problems, radio communication difficulties and bad weather including fog, ice, electric storms, and sub zero conditions. They endured the incessant throbbing of aero engines for hours on end, with the possibility of mid air collisions, and the stress of being on the alert from take-off to touch-down.

On course the Pilot would decide when he considered it was time to inform the rest of the crew that the use of oxygen was necessary and switch on the oxygen regulator. The rule was that oxygen had to be used at heights over 10,000 ft. Later on in the war, crews used to fly the first part of the trip at about 2,000 ft to keep below German E.W. radar and then when approaching the enemy coast they made a rapid climb to operational height and plugged into oxygen. As soon as possible after setting course and then at 6 minute intervals, fixes would be determined by means of 'Gee.' A fix was marked on the chart so that the Navigator could plot a ground track on his chart along with air positions and with this information a check could be made on the Air Position Indicator readings. If diverging from track the Pilot was given a course correction. A six minute fix routine was recommended because 6 minutes is a tenth of an hour and hence speeds were easier to work out. It could be difficult for the Navigators to maintain the 6 minute routine without interruption so it was advantageous if the Bomb Aimer could assist the Navigator by providing help when needed in order to obtain regular fixes throughout the trip. As the trip proceeded the Navigator would have several fixes and air positions marked on the chart, this made it possible to determine the wind vectors. During the rest of the trip the Navigator would be involved in ETA and timing checks and determining wind vectors at intervals of about 18 minutes. The API could be regularly checked and reset when necessary.

A Navigator's slogan was 'Keep on time-Keep on track-Keep on operating'. During an operation timing was very important and it was easier to lose time than to gain it since the Pilot could not markedly increase speed without greatly increasing fuel consumption. The normal procedure for losing time was to 'dog leg' whereby the Pilot turned 60 degrees to port or starboard, flew for the length of time he needed to lose, turned 120 degrees and flew for the same length of time as before, and finally turned 60 degrees to resume the required track. On later operations when a lot of France was safer to fly over alternative tracks were given out at the Navigator's briefing, so that the crews could gain or lose time. Throughout the operation the Navigator would up date his log, keep the Pilot fed with course information and alert the Bomb Aimer when nearing the target.

Photo 56

Air Position Indicator

The air position indicator received information on compass heading from the DRC and air speed from the pitot head via an elastic metal diaphragm

The data was continuously fed in so that the API could clock the aircraft's air position. By applying wind vectors the navigatior could obtain an estimated position.

FACETS OF A SQUADRON OPERATION

Time		Details of Calls, Messages, &c.	REMARKS	Time of Origin of Message
20 18		EQUIPMENT CHECKED	OK	
		R 3003 ON		
		TAKE OFF		
		ON WATCH		
		R3003 24V 1.3 mA		
		GENS 29v 30A		
21 00	B09 v JF3	NR1 -F- GRS = SG RQ KZLY		2100 īmī
		CAPT. INFORMED – ACTION TAKEN		
10		6 - VVV - X 445 -	2111 ∴ V̄Ā	
25		GENS 29v 30 A		
26		R3003 24V 1·1 mA		
		INTERFERENCE – 4		
35		TR AE OUT		
57	SP10	8 2° 1ST CLASS QE	APP	
22 00	JF3	-7- VVVV - X 445	2203 īmī	V̄Ā
14		ENGLISH COAST		
17	SP 8	170° 1ST CLASS QE	APP	
22		R 3003 OFF		
23		GENS 29V 2A CHARGE		
		Mmmm ON		
24		SHsss ON		
30		ENEMY COAST		
31	JF3	-5- VVVV - X 445 -	2233 īmī	V̄Ā
		BAD INT - RECEPTION	OK ON LOOP	
32		SEARCHING TINSEL		
42		5300 - OTHER A/C	JAMMING	
43		LOUD ENGLISH R/T -	JAMMED	
53		5250 - OTHER A/C	JAMMING	

FIG 13 Extract From A 1943 Wireless Operators Log Compiled During The Battle Of The Ruhr

(provided by ex. 4 Group H.Q. Signals Officer)

FACETS OF A SQUADRON OPERATION

Time	Details of Calls, Messages, &c.	REMARKS	Time of Origin of Message
23 00	JF3 - 8 - vvv - x445 -2	303 - IMI	VA
10	TINSELLATING		
14	5590 JERRY R/T	JAMMED	
16	OTHERS JAMMING		
20	INTERMITTENT - SEEMING	EFFECTIVE	
24	FIGHTER REPORTED	- EVADING	
	PROVING PERSISTANT		
30	FIGHTER ENGAGING	- HIT US	
	UNDERNEATH - EVADING		
	JF3 - RECEIVED THRU	INTERFERENCE	
34	FIGHTER AGAIN -	GUNNER	
	WORKING ON GUNS -	PACKED UP	!!
36	STILL WITH US - MANUEVERING		
	FOR ATTACK EVADING		
	- CLOUD - SEEMS WE'VE LOST HIM		
	FLAK AHEAD		
47	GENS 29 V 2 A		
	SEARCHING TINSEL	BAND	
00 00	JF3 - 5 - vvvw - x445 -	0003 IMI	
	5 - vvv - x445 -	0003 VA	
10	TINSEL		
11	5325 - R/T JAMMING		
	WITH OTHER A/C		
30	JF3 4 - vvv - x445 -	0033 IMI VA	
55	GENS 29 V 1 A		
01 00	JF3 - 9 - vvv - x445 -	0103 IMI VA	
	SEARCHING TINSEL 5900	- R/T JAMMED	
	UNSUCCESSFULLY		
01 30	JF3 - 5 - vvv - x445 -	0133 VA	

FACETS OF A SQUADRON OPERATION

TANK	TANK CONTENTS	TAKE OFF 1 & 3 USE 90 GALLS	CLOSE 1 & 3 OPEN 5 & 6	USE 22b GALLS	CLOSE 5/6 OPEN 1 & 2 USE 80 GALLS	CLOSE 1 OPEN W.B.C USE FD GALLS	CLOSE 4 OPEN 2 & 5/6	DRAW 5/6 OPEN 4	DRAW 2 OPEN 1	CLOSE 4 OPEN 3
1	247	167	167	167	167	107	107	107	107	107
2	63	63	63	63	63	63	63	38		
3	188	108	108	108	108	108	108	108	108	108
4	161	161	161	161	161	101	51	51	13	13
5/6	245	245	245	25	25	25	25			
WING BALANCE COCK	OFF	OFF	ON	ON	ON	ON	OFF	OFF	OFF	OFF
MAIN BALANCE COCK	OFF	OFF	OFF	OFF	OFF	OFF	OFF	OFF	OFF	OFF

FIG 40   Example Of Typical Entries In A Flight Engineer's Petrol Log, Compiled By F/Sgt Arthur Ashton

FACETS OF A SQUADRON OPERATION

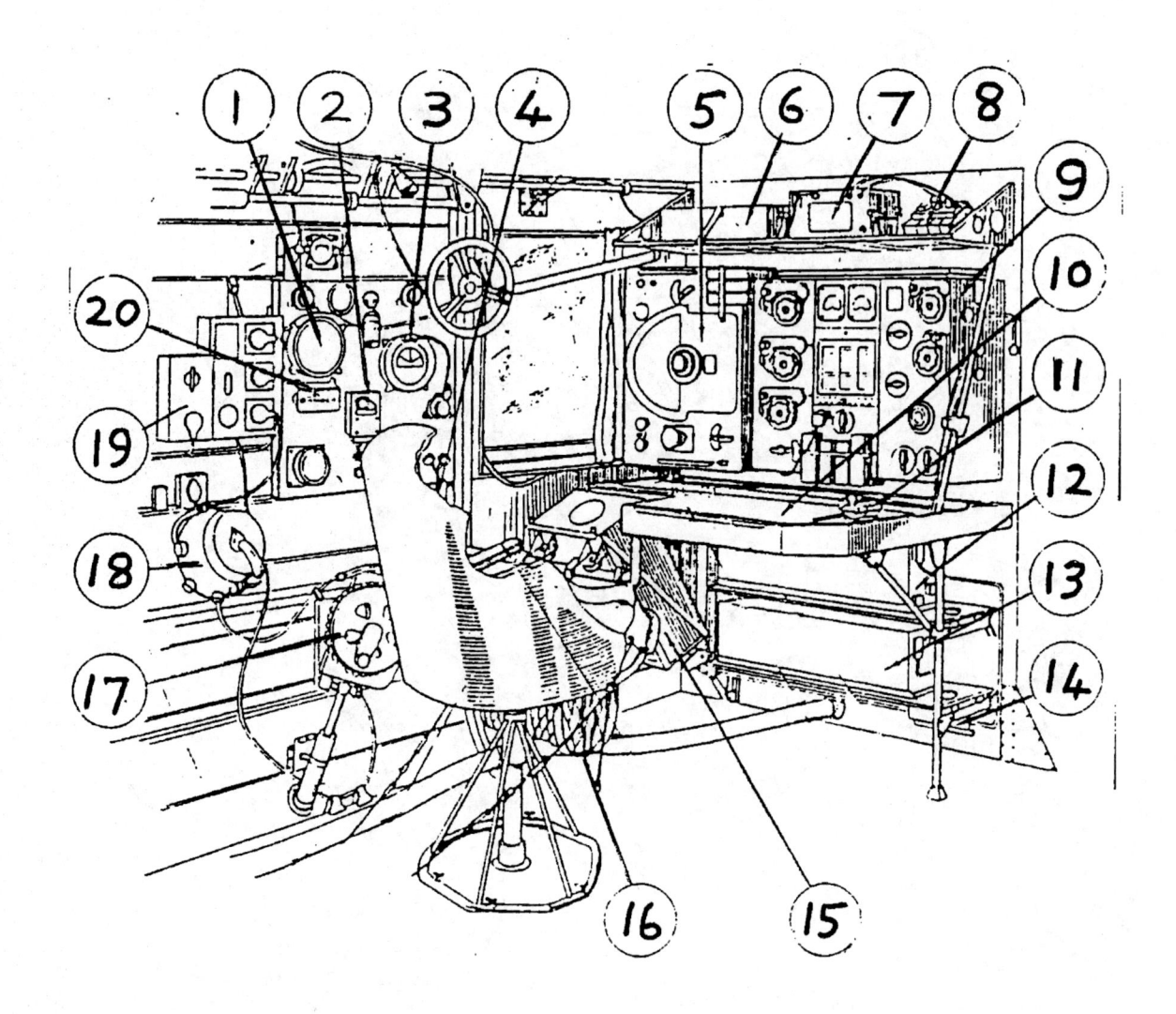

Key To Diagram Of Wireless Operator's Station

1 DF Loop Indicator
2 Intercom. Call Lamp
3 DF Visual Indicator
4 Intercom. Socket
5 R1155 Receiver
6 H.T. Dry Battery
7 A 1134 Intercom. Amplifier
8. Intercom. Distribution Panel
9 T1154 Transmitter
10 W/Op's Table
11 Morse Key
12 H.T. Power Unit
13 L.T. Power Unit
14 H.T. & L.T. Sockets
15 'Fishpond' Indicator Unit
16 Emergency Oxygen Bottle Stowage
17 Trailing Aerial Winch
18 Aerial Switch Unit Type 'J'
19 IFF Control Panel
20 Radar Demolition Buttons

FIG 12 Layout Of Halifax Wireless Operator's Station
Crown Copyright

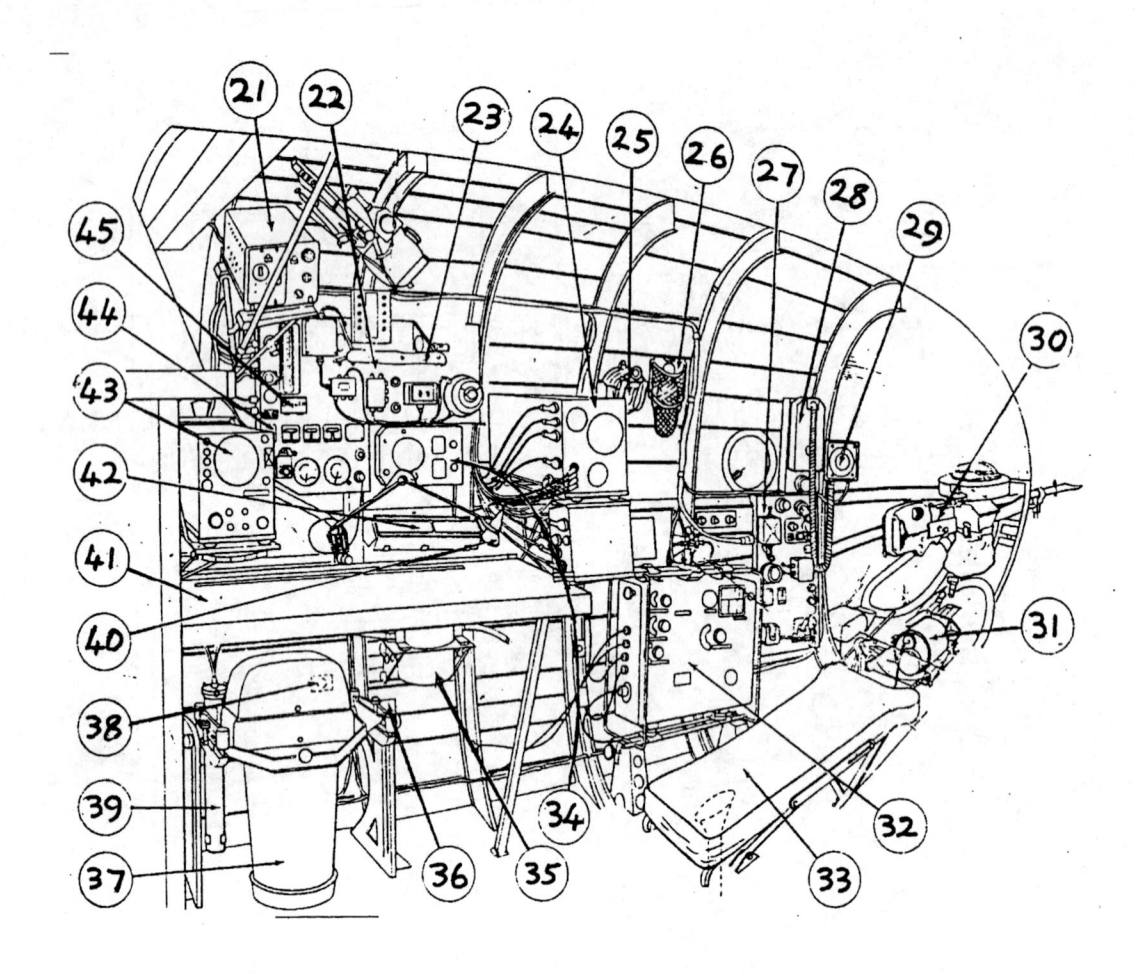

FACETS OF A SQUADRON OPERATION

Key To Diagram Of Navigator's Station

21 'Gee' Receiver Unit
22 Navigator's Instrument Panel
23 Astrograph Mounting
24 H2SIndicator Unit
25 Signalling Lamp
26 Emergency Oxygen Bottle
27 Port Air Bomber's Panel
28 Oxygen Economiser
29 D.R. Compass Repeater
30 Vickers G.O. Gun
31 Bombsight Sighting Head
32 Mk XIV Bombsight Computer
33 Air Bombers Couch
34 Air Position Indicator
35 Air Mileage Unit (if fitted)
36 Gravity Impact Switches
37 F24 Camera
38 Camera Magazine
39 Air Drier
40 Adjustable Lamp
41 Navigator's Table
42 Navigator Instruments Stowage
43 'Gee' Indicator Units
44 Navigator's Crash Switch
45 Radar Demolition Switches

FIG 10 Layout Of Halifax Navigators Station
Crown Copyright

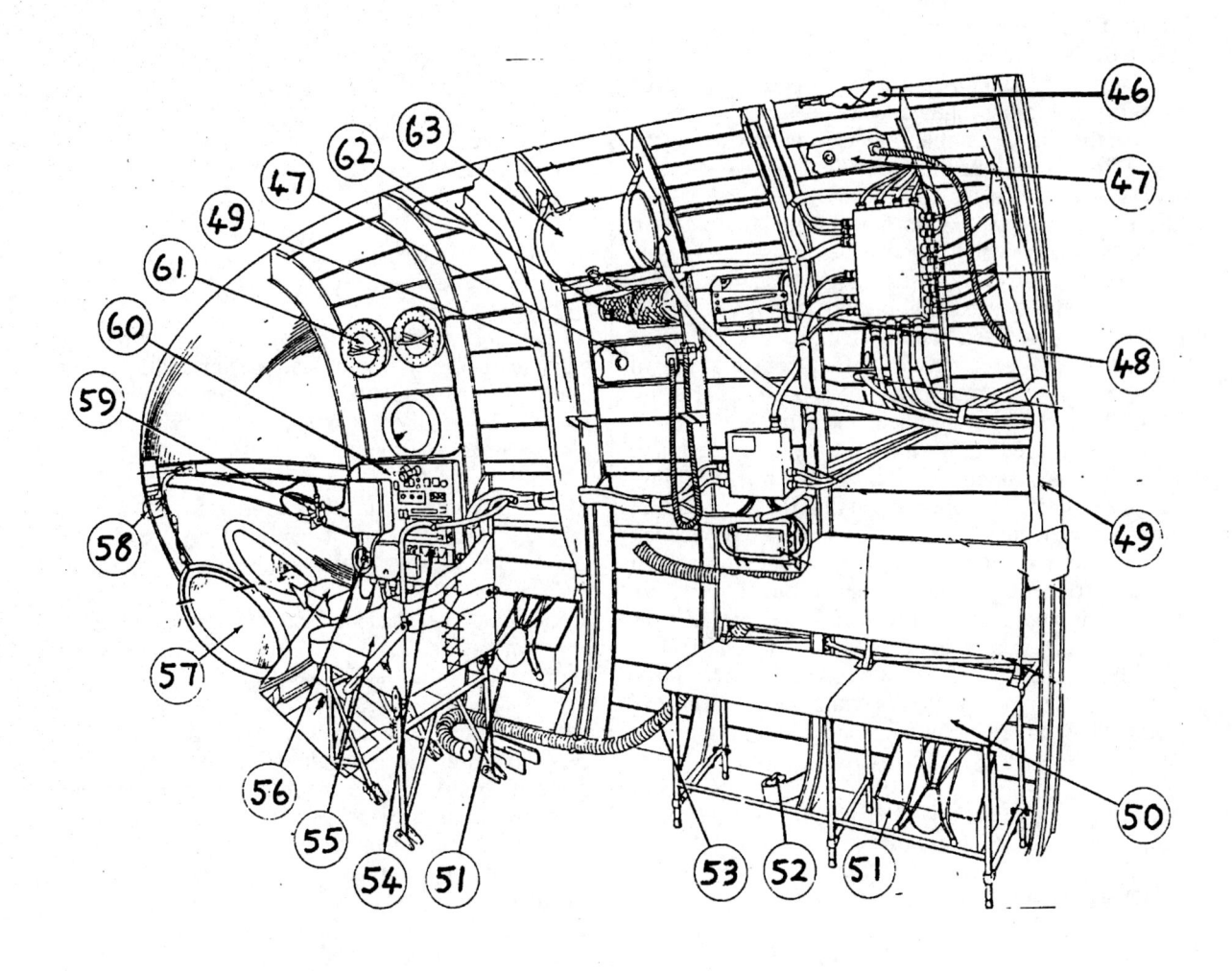

FACETS OF A SQUADRON OPERATION

Key To Diagram Of Air Bomber's Station

46 Fire Extinguisher
47 Oxygen Economiser
48 First Aid Stowage
49 Black Out Curtains
50 Navigator's Duel Seat
51 Parachute Stowage
52 'Gee' Whip Aerial
53 Heater Duct
54 Multiple Flare Switch
55 Air Bomber's Seat/Couch
56 Bomb Release and Stowage
57 Air Bomber's Observation Window
58 Head Lamp
59 De-ice Pump
60 Starboard Air Bombers Panel
61 Ammunition Drum Stowage
62 Emergency Oxygen Bottle
63 De-icing Fluid Tank

FIG 16 Starboard Side Layout Of Halifax Air Bombers Station
Crown Copyright

FACETS OF A SQUADRON OPERATION

The task of the Flight Engineer was to help the Pilot by taking care of fuel and engines, juggling with fuel contents and engine revolutions, thus relieving the Pilot of these duties. During take-off, landing and whilst over the target Nos 1 and 3 petrol tanks, the ones nearest to the engines, were used but having set course the Flight Engineer would switch over to the wing tip tanks. These needed to be used first because flapping of the wings could cause fuel surges from these tanks and the possibility of an engine cut-out. The Engineer would check the boost and agree settings with the Pilot. A maximum speed was quoted in the Halifax specification but this was not a practical proposition for any length of time, since flying at max speed boosted fuel consumption to double or even treble that at economic cruising revolutions. The economical cruising boost for a Halifax III used 42 gallons per hour per engine, which could go up to 50 gallons, and it was the Flight Engineer's responsibility to see that there was a fuel safety margin during the trip. In order to keep a check on his fuel consumption and various actions which were carried out during an operation, the Halifax Flight Engineer's log, Form BC/F6 (See Fig 11) was filled in at 20 minute intervals or whenever flight or engine conditions changed, along with the petrol log. If there was a loss of fuel as for example due to enemy action then the Flight Engineer had to inform the Pilot of the amount of flying time left.

The Flight Engineer's fuel management procedures can be summarised as follows:-

1 All the balance cocks were closed at take-off and over the target area.

2 Engineer only opened the main balance cock in an emergency with the captain's permission.

3 Engineer did not allow an engine to draw fuel from more than one tank at a time.

4 Whenever the Engineer made a tank change he always closed the tank in use before opening the next one.

5 All tank changes were carried out in collaboration with the captain.

6 The Engineer never drained a tank completely when carrying a bomb load because this could allow air to be sucked into the fuel system and produce an engine cut out, probably with serious consequences.

7 The Engineer controlled the distribution of the fuel so that there was no danger of having to change tanks in the vicinity of the target area.

8 The Pilot was warned when one hour's supply of fuel remained and subsequently when only half an hour's supply was left in the tanks.

After the Pilot had completed the steady course run the Air Gunners could unlock their turrets and check their movements, switch guns from 'safe' to 'fire' and adjust the illumination of the sighting ring in the Mk 3a reflector gunsight. At a suitable opportunity after permission from the Pilot, usually when over the sea, Gunners would fire off a few rounds to check that the guns were working. They would then have to settle down for a long, tense and lonely vigil, particularly 'Tail End Charlie' in the rear turret feeling the most isolated, with only the hiss of the oxygen economiser and the sound of the engines for company. The Rear Gunner would continually rotate his turret to scan the dark sky, with his hand in a convenient position to activate the firing mechanism for his 4 Browning guns fired by an electric solenoid, with a mixture of Ball, Tracer, Incendiary and Armour Piercing

Halifax Load Calculation

Operation -- Le Mans - - 7.3.44

Tare Weight of Aircraft	38,322lbs
Service Load (Ammunition, Guns etc.)	2,500lbs
Fuel 1438 Gallons at 7.2 lbs per gal	10,354lbs
8x 1,000lb MC bombs (8 x 1,020 lbs)	8,160lbs
7x 500 lb GP bombs (7 x 530 lbs)	3,710lbs
15 Bomb carriers at 18 lbs each	270lbs
Oil approx.	1,000lbs
	64,316lbs

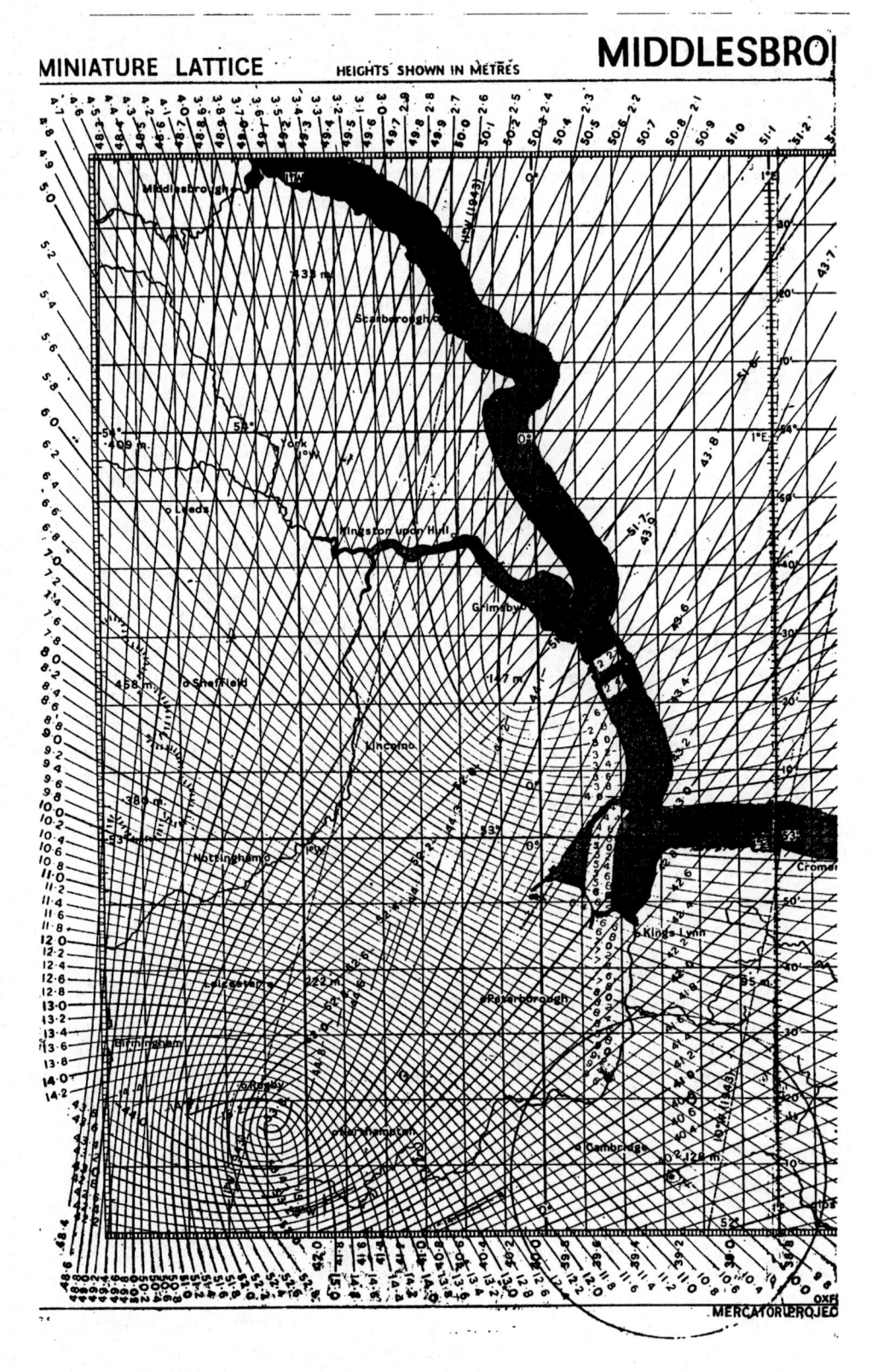

FIG 14   Portion Of 'Gee' Hyperbolic Chart
Crown Copyright

ammunition for the guns. The Rear Gunner had a BP Type E turret and the Mid Upper a Type A Mk 8 turret. During his vigil in the cold conditions which could be encountered in the rear turret, with air temperatures well below freezing point, saliva running down the tube connecting the mask to the oxygen economiser tended to freeze and it would be necessary for the Air Gunner to regularly squeeze the tube to break up the ice and prevent it blocking the tube. Latterly Air Gunners wore electrically heated overalls under their Irvin flying suits. Once over enemy territory the Gunner's prime responsibility was to keep a sharp look out for the dark shapes of aircraft, trying to distinguish between enemy night fighters and friendly aircraft in the bomber stream and if necessary give the Pilot orders for suitable evasive action.

The Wireless Operator's station (see Fig 12) was located below the Pilot's cockpit and one of his tasks was to keep a listening watch with his R1155 for the 4 Group coded call sign (one example in 1944 was 7FP) This was sent out at regular intervals and could help the W/Op to keep netted onto Group broadcasts. Half hourly broadcasts from Group HQ, which took about five minutes, could include important information such as wind vectors compiled from information sent back to Britain by wind finder aircraft in the bomber stream or a recall in cases when an operation was cancelled. An example of a Wireless Operator's log compiled early in 1943 is given in Fig 13. During 1943 the W/Op. had the task of carrying out 'Tinsel' radio counter measures and then after the use of 'Window' commenced it was their task to drop the 'Window' strips. Initially they were dropped from the flare chute but when the use of 'Window' became well established, chutes were built into the floor of the aircraft on the starboard side near to the W/Op's position. In this case the W/Op could move over from his station and open up a small hatch to drop the bundles through the chute. When the nose chute was installed crew members found it more convenient to use this to relieve themselves, rather than walk back to the Elsan near the tail. The crew derived great satisfaction when they used it over Germany. However, a problem occurred when a Wireless Operator found that the 'Window' packets he was putting down the chute had blocked it. He then had to remove soggy, unsavoury strips from the chute and his language had to be heard to be appreciated. After an experience like this the W/Op provided himself with a stick with which to clear blockages. Sometimes the aircrew would use the 'George' plate cover as a 'Potty', a practice which became obvious to members of the Instrument Section when they came to service the autopilot.

When visual 'Monica' was installed in a limited number of aircraft then it became the W/Op's responsibility to monitor the indicator unit in his station. Then in 1944 when the 'Fishpond' night fighter warning device replaced it the operation of this was also the W/Op's responsibility. With this equipment he would keep a sharp look out for indications of enemy night fighters underneath his aircraft. These could be armed with a 'Schrage Musik' cannon.

The bomber stream headed for the English coast along an allocated corridor and crossed at a designated point; typical crossing points were Flamborough Head, Mablethorpe, Cromer and Southwold. If an aircraft did not cross at the recognised crossing points it was liable to be shot at. On occasions the stream would navigate to a beacon such as Reading before heading for the coast. After crossing the coast the navigation lights had to be switched off and on again when returning. On a night operation over Europe the squadron's aircraft were dispersed amongst the bomber stream which was not a true formation since the Pilots did not use visual contacts to keep in the stream. In 1944/5 when daylight operations were carried out with a fighter escort, one of the squadron's aircraft with an experienced crew, which could be distinguished by checkered or striped fins, was nominated as a lead aircraft. The other aircraft would follow in formation. The course followed during an operation was dictated by the Navigator who had been given a route and turning points as exemplified by Maps 8 and 9 for the Krefeld and Nuremburg raids.

Aerial navigation in World War 2 with navigators often having to rely on DR plots, could not achieve the precision possible with the sophisticated electronic navigation aids available in the 1990s. All the squadron aircraft were fitted with the 'Gee' electronic hyperbolic navigation aid, which could enable a Navigator to fix a position in the region bordered by an arc extending from Britain to the Elbe, Hannover, Cassel and Mannheim, but this could be negated by the effects of enemy jamming over Europe. The H2S navigation aid which came into use from 1943 onwards had the advantage that it was not affected by jamming. From early 1944 onwards the number of squadron aircraft fitted with H2S increased and initially 'A' & 'C' Flights were given priority for this equipment, although the policy was that eventually all squadron aircraft would be fitted with H2S.

When using 'Gee', which had a range of about 400 miles, the Navigator would decide on which chain to use and in order to set his equipment to the required frequency would fit the appropriate RF unit (Type 24, 25 or 27) in the receiver and select the chain frequency. The principle of 'Gee' was the use of a Master transmitter plus two or three Slave transmitters, the ground transmitters being designated Type 7,000 stations. The Master transmitter sent out a pulsed signal which activated a Slave transmitter. The Halifax received the signals from both the Master and Slave transmitters (see Fig 47) and the 'Gee' equipment measured the time interval between the receipt of the Master and Slave signals, a time difference which was very small, being measured in microseconds (a millionth of a second), so special equipment was required. For a given time difference with one Slave station there were a variety of positions in which the aircraft could be located, so a line could be drawn on a chart for all positions having the same time difference. The shape of such a line is known as a hyperbola (hence the term hyperbolic navigation) and a series of these lines were overprinted on Navigators charts, using different colours for the different Slave stations (See Fig 14). The Master station was designated A and the Slave stations B, C, and D, with transmissions taking place in the order ABACAD. The B line was printed in red, C line in green and the D line, if a third station was employed, was printed in purple. Since the time difference was so small, a system employing a cathode ray tube display was used for their measurement and details of the operating procedure are given in Chapter 9. It could take an average of four and a half minutes for the Navigator to adjust the signal on the screen, find co-ordinates on the 'Gee' chart, note Latitude and Longitude, work the fix on a plotting chart, put in air position and work out wind speed and direction. If the aircraft was off track then it was necessary to give the Pilot a course correction.

When jamming occurred the anti-jamming selector switch would be set to the appropriate position. The 'Gee' signals would look like little green stalks on the screen and when jamming commenced they were joined by dozens of similar 'stalks' alongside the genuine signals, hence they were given the nickname of 'grass'. If a Navigator or Air Bomber could keep their eye on the position of the genuine signals then they may be able to distinguish them from the spurious signals. There were small differences between true signals and jamming signals, but in order to pick out the differences continuous monitoring was important, which is where assistance from the Air Bomber could be invaluable. In the early use of 'Gee' any fixes obtained by this equipment, when logged, were not identified as such for security purposes in case the Navigator's log fell into the hands of the enemy.

When H2S was fitted this could be used to obtain fixes if the terrain was suitable for giving an unambiguous display. The bright areas on the screen did not always indicate the correct relative sizes of towns and villages since the strength of a signal depended on the lie of the land. A village on a slope facing the approaching aircraft could give a stronger signal than one on a slope facing away. It was therefore important when using H2S to keep an accurate DR plot so that there was not much doubt about the Radar target. The primary use of H2S was for target location, hence 'Gee' was used as long as possible in order to get an accurate DR plot which could be carried on when 'Gee' was not available. Forecast winds broadcast by Group and received by the W/Op. on his R1155 were known as 'P' winds as against an 'F' wind found by the Navigator from his own plots. With a good Navigator his 'F' winds could be more accurate than the 'P' winds, particularly when 'Gee' plots were used. However the broadcast wind system was devised for two reasons. Firstly for use by aircraft outside 'Gee' range which where not fitted with H2S and secondly it was considered that if all aircraft found their DR position from 'P' winds and steered courses found by 'F' winds, then even if broadcast winds were inaccurate the main force concentration would be maintained even if it was flying along a track parallel to the planned one. There were situations when 'Gee' fixes were not available because the aircraft was out of range or the enemy jamming was very effective. In addition H2S may not be available or if fitted its use was restricted because of radio security, and in such a situation at night there was little chance of obtaining visual fixes from ground features. In this case the Navigator's skill in carrying out DR plots using 'P' & 'F' winds came to the fore. On occasions some help could be obtained from 'Loop' fixes provided by the Wireless Operator using his R1155 and the DF loop to take a radio bearing on MF beacons.

To get an impression of the bomber stream then a mid 1943 Ruhr operation could be considered when the aircraft involved would number over 700. The aircraft could be spread over a volume of the sky which approximated to a rectangle 150 miles long, 6 miles wide and over 2,000 ft in depth, with numerous aircraft having strayed out of the main stream due to navigation problems. Later on in the war the bomber stream densities increased considerably with a greater chance of collision or

FACETS OF A SQUADRON OPERATION

KAMMHUBER LINE

▬▬▬ Original Helle NachtJagd Zones
••••• Ultimateley part of Dunkel Nachtjagd

- - - - Some of the E.W. radar coverage for
'Himmelbett' controlled zones

←——→ Krefeld raid track

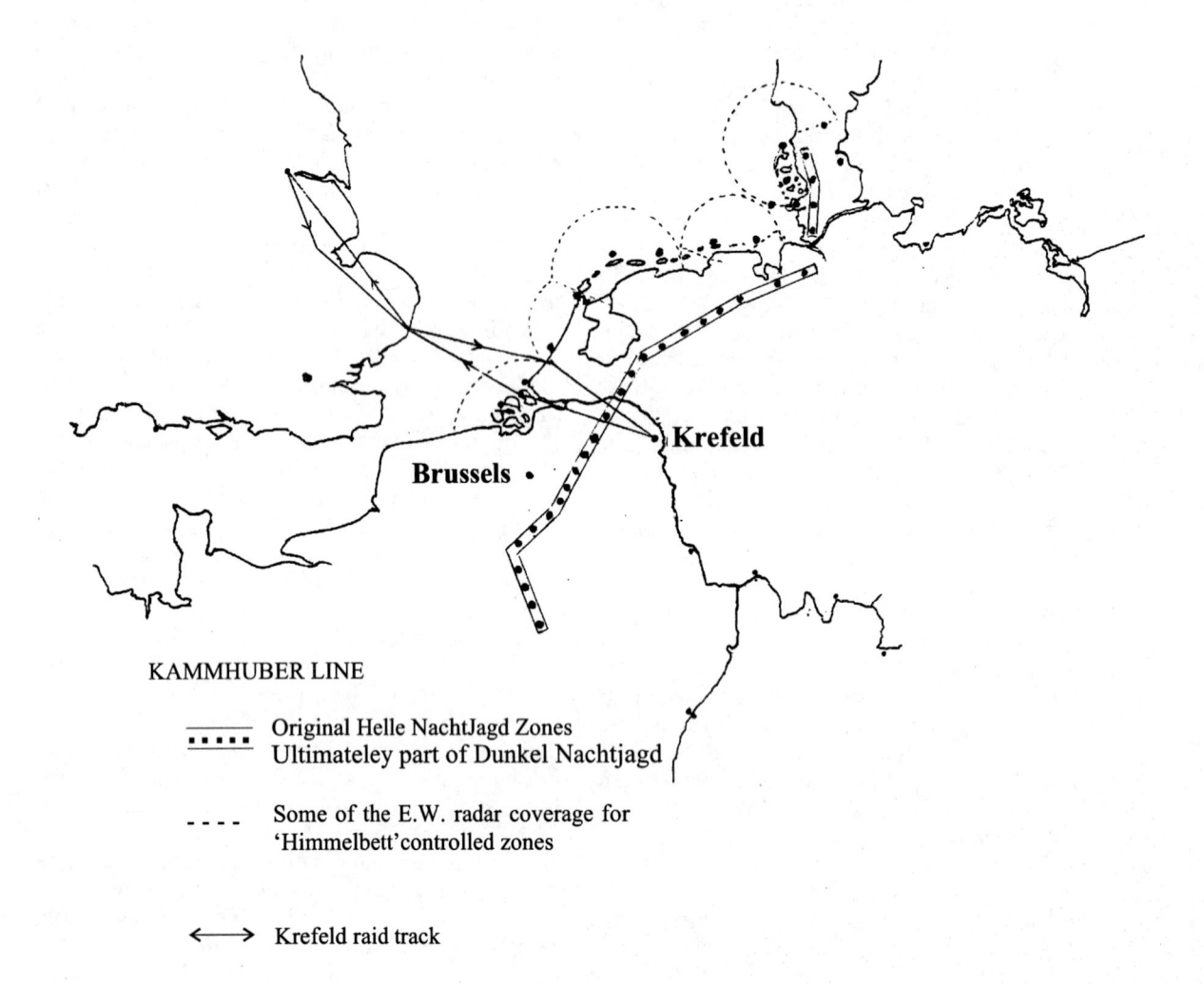

MAP 8

**Route Map For Krefeld Raid Of 21/22 June 1943.
Showing Part Of German Defence Systems**

being hit by a bomb dropped by an aircraft at a higher altitude. The question can be asked, what was the advantage to the squadron in participating in such a stream with the possibility of the aforementioned hazards? The answer lay in the German defence system.

The Luftwaffe night fighter system goes back to late 1940, when 51 like other squadrons sent aircraft off on a raid individually, so in June 1940 a system was developed to cope with the interception of individual aircraft. A defensive belt of searchlights was set up in front of the expected target areas known as 'Helle Gurtel' (Iluminated or Searchlight Belt), with fighter patrols behind the searchlight belt, hoping to spot the RAF bomber, without ground control. In July 1940 ground control for the fighters was set up and given the title of 'Helle Nacht Jagd' (Illuminated Nightfighting). About this time General Josef Kammhuber became head of all the night defence units and Inspector of Night Fighters so with Radar equipment becoming available he incorporated this in the night fighter system. Sixteen areas were set up containing 'Freya' EW Radar and 'Wurzburg, close support Radar. Subsequently the 'Wurzburg' Radar was used for night fighter control as well as monitoring enemy aircraft for position and height, this system being given the name 'Dunkel Nachtjag' (Dark Night Interception).

The network of night fighter defence boxes was known officially as 'Himmelbett' (Four poster bed), each box contained a GCI station linked to 'Freya' radar for early warning and two 'Wurzburg' tracking radar stations, a 'Red' one to track the RAF bombers and a 'Blue' one to track the night fighters attached to the box. The 'Freya' radar which operated on a frequency of 125 MHz had a range of 60 miles at 10,000 ft and the 'Wurtzburg' operating on a frequency of 560 MHz had a range of about 25 miles and this was superseded by the 'Wurzburg-Riese' (Giant Wurzburg) with a 24 inch dish and a range of 36-42 miles. As the war progressed the German early warning radar facilities were upgraded by the use of 'Mammut' (frequency 125 MHz and with a range of about 150 miles at 19,000 ft) and 'Wasserman'(frequency 125 MHz with a range of about 110 miles at 19,000 ft). The night fighters were eventually fitted with AI radar to aid interception. The total organisation was known colloquially by the RAF as the 'Kammhuber Line' and worked well with the early operational techniques of the RAF since single aircraft could be initially detected by the 'Freya' EW Radar of a 'Himmelbett' box and the information passed on to the two 'Wurzburg' radars. The 'Red' radar would track the bomber and the information could be plotted on a frosted glass 'Seeborg Table' for the benefit of the controllers. The 'Blue' radar would track any night fighters sent in to intercept. This system was originally devised to cope with a small number of aircraft, so the RAF devised the bomber streams system to saturate the German defence control system of the box they were passing through, but aircraft which strayed out of the bomber stream were vulnerable to individual detection and interception. An outline of the 'Kammhuber Line' layout is shown in Map 8. Later on in the war the German's defence system was modified as discussed in Chapter 7.

Once under the surveillance of the German defence system the bomber stream could expect interception by night fighters and the gunners would need to be fully alert for the appearance of the dark shape of an enemy night fighter. As an aid to the detection of enemy aircraft a tail warning device called 'Monica' was installed in the squadron aircraft from mid 1943. The transmitter in this system sent out radar pulses which on reflection from an aircraft within range activated the receiver and fed an audio signal into the intercom system in the form of bleeps. The rapidity at which these bleeps occurred increased as the aircraft detected got closer. Unfortunately this system could not distinguish between enemy and friendly aircraft, and in fact the larger RAF bombers provided a better radar reflector than the smaller night fighters. The result of this was a lot of false alarms in view of which the aircrew accused the system of 'crying wolf' and tended to ignore it. It could also have the unfortunate consequence of increasing tension amongst the aircrews. As a result many Air Gunners considered their 'Mk 1 Eyeballs' to be more reliable than the black boxes. As an alternative to 'Audible Monica' a 'Visual Monica' device was fitted to a limited number of squadron aircraft.

The bomber stream having reached the German defence system, the Luftwaffe night fighters would be orbiting radio beacons ready to be vectored onto the bomber by the GCI controller on R/T. This was where the Wireless Operator's 'Tinsel' operation could be valuable by helping to jam the German R/T transmissions and the Pilot would be on the alert for a call for evasive action in the event of a night fighter contact. Based on information from German night fighter reports, the following was a typical tactic used in 1943 to attack a bomber. The Bf 110 night fighter, with a speed of up to twice that of a Halifax, would be vectored towards the bomber stream by the 'Himmelbett' controller, whilst the

FACETS OF A SQUADRON OPERATION

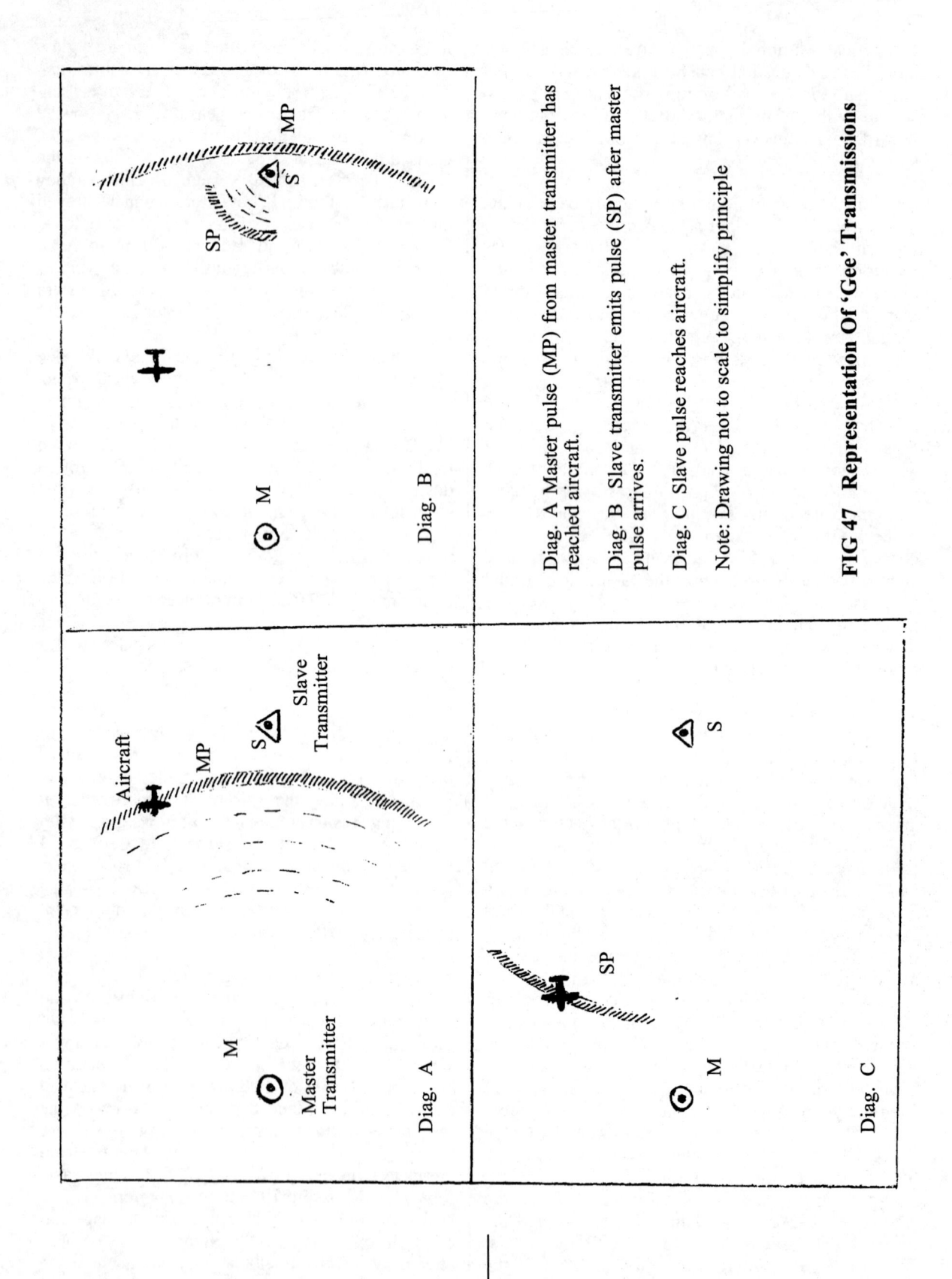

Diag. A Master pulse (MP) from master transmitter has reached aircraft.

Diag. B Slave transmitter emits pulse (SP) after master pulse arrives.

Diag. C Slave pulse reaches aircraft.

Note: Drawing not to scale to simplify principle

FIG 47 Representation Of 'Gee' Transmissions

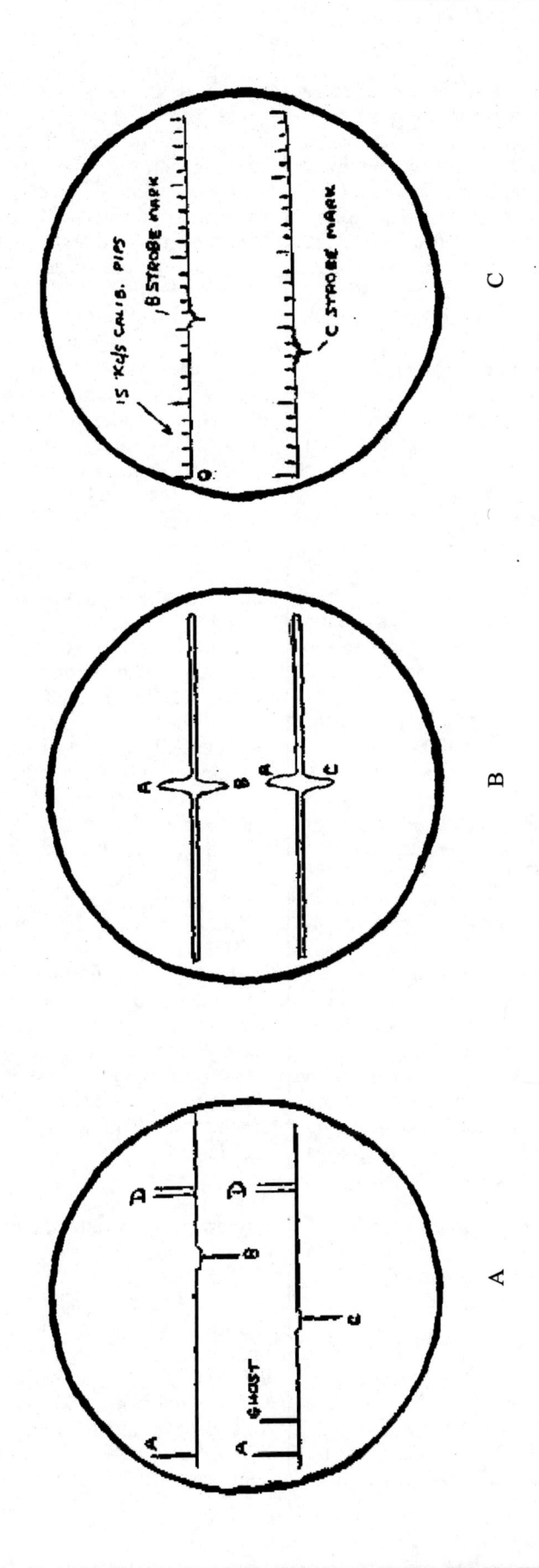

FIG 15 Displays On 'Gee' Indicator Unit

FACETS OF A SQUADRON OPERATION

radio operator was scanning the three cathode ray tubes of the FuG 202 A1 radar in front of him, looking for traces indicating the azimuth, elevation and range of a contact. When a contact was achieved a trace, which could be a 51 Squadron 'Halifax', would suddenly appear on the tubes. The Radio Operator would report the height and range of the contact. With this system the max. range was about 2 miles. The azimuth position of the bomber would be within the 70 degree search angle of the antennae system, so the Radio Operator would give course correction information to the Pilot in order to centre the trace on the screen. When the Radio Operator reported that the night fighter was now directly on track for interception of the the bomber the Pilot would open the throttles, whilst the operator would watch the range screen indicating that the contact distance was closing. With the displays from the other two screens he would help the Pilot to keep on track for the target, by giving course corrections as necessary. As the night fighter closed up on the target, the Pilot's first view of it was likely to be the glow from the exhaust pipes and depending on the light available would eventually spot the dark shadow of a Halifax. For Bf 110's fitted with front firing 20mm cannons he would position himself for what was known as the 'Von unter hinden' position behind and below the rear turret of the aircraft.

The RAF heavy bombers had powerful gun turrets for which the night fighters had a healthy respect, unfortunately the turrets suffered from the limitations of using rifle calibre ammunition. Consequently one technique was for the night fighter to stand off to 400-600 yards and use their longer range cannons. The Rear Gunner would obviously reply, some of whom had extra tracer put in their ammunition feed, hoping that the psychological effect of vivid tracer streams hosing towards him would deter the night fighter Pilot. Rapid notification of such an attack to the Pilot was important to enable him to carry out evasive action, so the Rear Gunner normally being the first to see a rearward attack could give a command to the Pilot such as "Corkscrew port, go".

In response to this call the Pilot would carry out a corkscrew action which involved a steep diving turn of about 30 degrees to port for a few hundred feet, to be followed by a steep climbing turn of 30 degrees back to the original height in a starboard direction. For maximum effect this manoeuvre should be as violent as possible to confuse the night fighter's aim. However, with the Halifax Mk II, fitted with the original rudder system with small triangular fins, there was a problem of rudder balance. This meant that in this manoeuvre the rudder could go hard over to one side and the pressure necessary on the rudder pedal then became excessive. Experienced Pilots could react to this problem by actions such as banking into the turn by application of ailerons, allowing them to achieve rudder control. Inexperienced Pilots may not be able to cope with the problem of rudder overbalance, which could be the cause of loss of control. Early in 1943, Ken Dean, who subsequently became Bombing Leader during his second tour with the squadron in 1944, had a bitter experience of the problems of assymetric flying. When returning from a raid the captain of the aircraft, S/Ldr 'Dinty' Moore the 'B' Flight Commander, found it necessary to pay a visit to the Elsan toilet at the rear of the aircraft. Ken therefore took over the controls but without warning the Flight Engineer shut down both engines on one side of the aircraft, which caught Ken unawares. This meant that he was not prepared for the problem of rudder balance which occurs under these conditions, with the result that the aircraft took a sudden dive and Ken had to wrestle with the controls to get the aircraft back on an even keel. When he had got himself sorted out he found that he was flying back towards Germany so he had to turn the aircraft round. Shortly afterwards the captain reappeared in a rather aggrieved mood, not smelling of roses, since he was covered with the contents of the Elsan. What particularly upset him was the fact that he was wearing his best uniform ready to go on leave next day.

As a consequence of the handling problems a rudder modification incorporating a larger fin was introduced. There was a trade-off for this increase in stability since aircraft with the modified rudder were slower to react when executing the corkscrew evasion technique. However, on balance it was considered that the modified fin and rudder system was an advantage since it could overcome the problem of assymetric flying (engines out of commission) experienced with the earlier marks of the Halifax.

There was a school of thought amongst some aircrews that a better tactic when attacked from astern was to turn to port or starboard at same altitude and come up alongside the fighter with the Gunners getting a shot in as the came abreast. Against this tactic was the fact that after turning, the bomber was flying against the bomber stream with the possibility of a collision. A very successful defence operation by 51 Squadron Air Gunners took place during the Munchen Gladbach operation of the 30/31.8.43. On the way to the target P/O Johnny Morris's aircraft was attacked by an Me110 but thanks to the efforts of two first class Air Gunners the night fighter was shot down before it could open fire.

When the night fighter was manoeuvering to attack the Halifax the rear gunner Allan Massey quietly informed the Pilot that a fighter was closing in on them dead astern and stated that he would give a count down on the range, advising Johnny to start weaving when he gave the word. Allan started counting off the range in yards, 1,000, 900, 800, 600, 500, 400, then "Start weaving", which the Pilot did immediately and quite violently. By this time the the mid upper gunner had also spotted the fighter. Both gunners had their guns trained on the enemy and as soon as Johnny started to weave, Alan Massey opened fire hitting the fighter with his first burst closely followed by Bob Kennedy whose fire was just as accurate and went straight home. Within seconds the Bf109 burst into flames with the combined fire power of two turrets pouring into the aircraft. The fire was so bright and the action so close that the gunners could see the German Pilot slide back his canopy and jump, by which time they had ceased firing. The whole action was over in minutes and the German hadn't fired a shot, possibly due to a case of over confidence on his part, believing that the Halifax was a sitting duck. The coolness of the two Air Gunners and the Pilot was magnificent and reinforced the confidence the rest of the crew had in them. There was boundless elation amongst the crew who after cheering like mad and congratulating the victors completed the trip in very high spirits. As reported in Chapter 10, this was one of the few early 1943 crews which managed to complete a tour of operations.

In the case where the Pilot was not able to take evasive action in time, taking for example the situation where cannon shells started a fire in the wings, then the aircraft with flames licking out of it would act as a beacon for the night fighter. The night fighter Pilot may stand off for a short period to watch the stricken bomber and see if another attack was necessary to finish off the bomber, or if he could save his ammunition for another contact. If the bomber Pilot realised that his aircraft was doomed he would warn his crew to collect their 'chutes and prepare to abandon the aircraft. When he called "Jump, Jump" over the intercom, the Rear Gunner could rotate his turret, open the rear door and bale out and the rest of the crew would then go to the appropriate escape hatch, grateful that they were in a 'Halibag'. The crew survival statistics for escape by parachute when shot down were a 29% chance of survival from a Halifax against only 11% for a Lancaster crew. The stricken bomber would then spiral down to earth, finishing up as a bright flash on the ground and the night fighter could fly off in search of other quarry.

In 1944 as a more effective alternative to the 'Unter von Hinten' method the Luftwaffe came up with a very effective weapon for their twin-engined night fighters, namely an upward firing cannon code named 'Schrage Musik'. The technique was to fire at the blind spot underneath the aircraft without using incendiary bullets so as not to reveal the presence of the night fighter.

All the way to and from the target the squadron aircraft had the constant risk of being attacked by night fighters. When the squadron first started operating from Snaith all the night fighters, which were mainly Bf 110s and Ju 88s, were operated by the GCI Controllers in the 'Himmelbett' boxes and normally orbited radio beacons ready to be vectored onto a target. However early in 1943 a new night fighter force was set up, the original unit being called 'Kommando Herrman' employing single seater FW 190 and Bf 109 fighters manned by ex night bomber pilots with experience of night flying and given the name 'Wilde Sau'.

The story of 'Wilde Sau' has been well explained by a 51 Squadron Association member, Peter Hinchliffe. His comments are that 'Wilde Sau', literally Wild Sow, is normally translated as Wild Boar by British authors but the confusion goes back to usage in the German language that cannot be translated directly into English. In Germany, hunting the wild boar (as we would say) was very popular amongst the aristocracy and landowners and to hunt wild boar is 'Wilde sau jagen'. The story of how the name 'Wilde Sau' was adapted for the free ranging night fighters is an interesting one and in this context the term 'Sich wie eine Wilde Sau benehmen' which means behaving crazily like a bull in a china shop should be considered.

Hajo Herrman put forward his proposals at a General Staff meeting, for a single engined night fighter force to join the night battle against Bomber Command and suggested that the flak could restrict their height of operation so that the single seater fighters could operate above the Flak zone. He received a hostile reception from Generaloberst Weise who commanded the Berlin Flak and had 700 heavy guns under his control. The Generaloberst was at a loss to find words to describe what he saw as a crazy idea by Herrman, so a colleague of Herrman, Boehm-Tettlebach, supplied an adjective 'Wilde Sau'. Herrman particularly liked this in view of its connection with hunting since the wild sow is in fact more ferocious than the wild boar, particularly when defending her young - the female of the species is more deadly than the male. So when Herrman's unit JG300 was formed they called their method of night fighting 'Wilde Sau. Co-operation between 'Wilde Sau' aircraft and flak batteries over various cities, was known as 'Kombinierte Nachtjagd' (combined nightfighting)

'Wilde Sau' were free ranging and most effective over illuminated areas. Illumination could be provided by searchlights on a low cloud base when the bombers would show up in silhouette, also by TIs over the target and incendiary fires on the ground. In some cases aircraft were coned in searchlights. Additional assistance from the 31 August 1943 was the use of night fighter flares dropped from above to illuminate the bomber stream. Herrman managed to reach agreement with the Flak Batteries to restrict their gunfire to a specific height, above which the 'Wilde Sau' could operate. Then after the Hamburg attack in 1943 when the first use of 'Window ' upset the 'Himmelbett' night fighter control system, Oberst von Lossberg conceived a new method of freelancing the twin engined night fighters into the bomber stream on the basis of broadcast commentaries. For the twin engined night fighters the name wild was changed to tame and hence they were called 'Zahme Sau'.

As the Squadron's bombers pressed on towards the target the crew could be in a high state of tension as exemplified by the fact that there were numerous reports of 4 Group aircraft having been fired on by friendly aircraft in a case of mistaken identity. As mentioned earlier, the Wireless Operator would receive half hourly reports of broadcast winds sent out particularly to help Navigators who did not have access to H2S fixes and when 'Gee' fixes were unavailable. There was also a period when because of the necessity for radio silence the use of H2S was restricted until approaching the target. Some aircraft fitted with H2S were designated as 'Windfinder' aircraft and were required to send out wind vectors determined from accurate fixes. The Wireless Operators in these aircraft were required to transmit the information as close as possible to the time when the vectors were determined and it was essential that the information was not more than 15 minutes old when 4 Group received it.

The signals sent out by the Wireless Operator consisted of an eleven figure group followed by a four figure group. The eleven figure group comprised three figures indicating wind direction followed by two figures for wind speed, and then figures to denote aircraft height and latitude or longitude to nearest ten minutes between which wind was found. The four figure group denoted the time of the fix which produced the vectors.

Example - Wind vectors of 230 degrees at 25 knots found between 48.40N and 48.50N at a height of 15,000 Ft (with a datum height as specified to all navigators of say 45,000 ft). Time 0105. Hence eleven figure group would be 230 & 25 plus, 45-15 = 30 (Code for height), plus 84 and 85 (second and third figures of latitude) ie 23025308485. The four figure group would be 0105 (time).

Somewhere along the route, possibly during a quiet period the crew often had a secondary task to carry out. At the outbreak of war 51 Squadron was one of the first units to carry out an operation against Germany. This was the 'phoney war' period when the RAF was not allowed to drop bombs over Germany, so the squadron had to be content with bombarding the enemy with 'Nickels' as propaganda leaflets were code named. During the bombing campaign in 1943/44 leaflets were still being dropped but this time it was to the accompaniment of a bombing raid. The banner headline of one of the leaflets dropped in September 1943 is shown in Fig 43.

In addition to propaganda leaflets an operation was carried out which it was hoped would affect the German economy. This involved dropping counterfeit German bank notes and ration coupons (Photo 58). The bank notes had been treated to give them an aged appearance since crisp new bank notes would have been a give-away. The purpose of the

FIG 55 Bomb Selector Switch Unit

counterfeit ration coupons was to upset the rationing system. It was considered that many hungry members of the population picking them up would still try and use them to obtain extra rations even if they knew that they had been dropped by the RAF.

From August 1943 onwards a radio counter measures operation would take place. This was because at some point on the track towards the target the Navigator had to notify the Wireless Operator when he was required to start dropping 'Window', which was an effective radio countermeasure. Then when nearing the target the Navigator gave the crew an ETA so that the Air Bomber could check his equipment and maps. For an operation 1:100,000 scale target maps were issued and in addition if the aircraft was fitted with H2S a 1:63,360 scale target map was issued to indicate likely target returns. The latter had concentric circles 1 mile apart radiating out from the aiming point.

Nearing the target the Bomb Aimer would be lying on his couch in the nose ready for the run-in, with the Flight Engineer preparing to switch over to Nos 1 & 3 tanks. On the run-in the crews could expect a warm reception, especially if the target was in the Ruhr. When the raids on towns and cities intensified Hitler withdrew guns and searchlights from the 'Kammhuber Line' to protect the populated areas and boost the morale of its citizens. Each searchlight battery had a blue radar controlled marker searchlight and Flak Batteries used 'Wurzberg' radar for gun laying. Whilst the Bomb Aimer could be too involved in his task to worry about the defences the rest of the crew were in a state of apprehension until the bombs had been released. They could expect attention from searchlights and flak.

The squadron could encounter two types of flak during an operation, namely light and heavy. Light flak which comprised 20mm and 30mm was generally not effective above 10,000 ft and normally employed percussion fused shells and tracer ammunition. If an aircraft was caught in a searchlight the light flak could fire coloured tracers up the beam in a manner known as 'hosepiping'. Heavy flak included 88mm, 105mm and 150mm guns. The 88mm guns could fire 20 lb shells at a rate of 12 rpm up to 25,000 ft and 105mm fired 32

Photo 58 (above)

Counterfeit German money and ration coupons dropped by Squadron aircraft

FIG 43 (Left)

Heading of propaganda leaflet (Nickel) dropped during an operation in 1943

lb shells at 10 rpm up to 30,000 ft These heavy shells contained barometric or proximity fuses and a near miss could badly damage or wreck an aircraft.

The searchlight normally used over industrial targets was the 150mm type. It could be rather traumatic for an air crew to be illuminated by the blinding glare of searchlights with the security of the veil of night lifted. All the defences could appear to be focused on them, putting them at the mercy of infuriated ground gunners. Caught by a single beam the aircraft may have some chance of escaping it but if coned by several searchlights evasion became more difficult. Having escaped one beam it could soon be caught by another.

On the approach to the target on a specified heading, the Bomb Aimer, would ready himself to drop his bomb load by setting the controls on his panel (See Fig 16), including the bomb selector unit (Photo 55). He would then keep a sharp look out for the PFF target markers and listening out for instructions from the Master Bomber. Over the target many aircrew appreciated the welcoming voice of the Master Bomber after the long slog to the target.

With a clear sky over the target, the PFF special aircraft would accurately drop primary ground markers, generally with the help of radar, to be followed by PFF 'backers-up' dropping TIs of a different colour to the primary markers. In later raids the Master Bomber (or Master of Ceremonies) would stay over the target to advise mainstream crews by R/T if any of the markers were incorrectly placed or the enemy were using decoy markers. There were occasions when a raid on a particular target had to be aborted and in these cases the Master Bomber could give the bomber crews authority to go and look for opportunity targets for which he may have used the R/T code "Freehand". An example was the Wesel raid in Feb 1945. On clear nights Steady Ground Markers were used which burst on impact and burned with a red, green or white flame. In 1945 non-illuminated ground markers were available which comprised a 250 lb marker in red, blue, green or yellow versions which burned for about 8 minutes and remained visible until dispersed by the wind. The primary Target Indicator Markers were 250 lb and 500 lb marker bombs which by means of a barometric fuse burst at set heights from 3,000 to 10,000 ft from which numerous small brilliant magnesium cartridge 'candles' cascaded to fall to the ground. There they would burn like small coloured balls of red, green. yellow or white light in a circular pattern up to 100 yards diameter for about 3 minutes.

There were also longer burning versions which could last up to 7 minutes.

For obscured targets sky marking was carried out, code named 'Wanganui' by the PFF, this was a close pattern of flares of a given colour marking the aiming point on which the Air Bomber had to bomb whilst flying on an exact magnetic heading as detailed at aircrew briefing. For a sky marking situation the Mk XlV bomb sight computer was set for true heights, true air speeds and zero wind if allowance for wind drift had already been made. If the sky markers appeared widespread, then the Bomb Aimer had to estimate the centre of the flares and bomb on this. Sky marking was inaccurate since the flares drifted down wind as they descended so re-marking was required at five minute intervals. Various types of sky markers were used, their casings ejecting different types of flares which included steady red or green, red with green stars, green with red stars, and flares dripping white. At the aircrew briefing the Air Bombers were briefed as to which colours to aim at in order of preference.

For aircraft which were not 'windfinders' the W/Op would receive a transmission just before reaching the target giving the wind vectors which would be passed on to the Bomb Aimer. The Air Bomber having spotted the target markers and identified his aiming point, would take charge for the run-in and ask the Pilot to head in to the target on a specific compass heading, which was particularly important with sky marking. At the appropriate moment he would call for bomb doors open and give the Pilot instructions such as "Left, left, steady, now go right a shade, okay, steady". A convention used by some crews was to repeat left twice and say right once to try and ensure that the Pilot made the correct turn. Staring intently at the Aiming Point the Bomb Aimer watched as it came up to the illuminated graticule on the gyroscopic stabilised glass plate of the Mk XlV Sighting Head and ran along the illuminated line till it reached the 'crosswire'. At this point the bomb 'tit' was pressed and the call "Bombs Gone" went out to the Pilot. The crew breathed a sigh of relief when they felt the aircraft lift, relieved of its heavy bomb load. Having pushed over the jettison bar on the Bomb Selector Unit to ensure all the bombs had gone, there was however, still another 30 seconds straight and level run to enable the F24 camera to take the bombing photo. The camera indicator lamp having shown that the photograph had been taken, the Pilot reported camera operated and with bomb doors closed took the opportunity to get out of the target area as soon as possible. This was not a healthy place in which to linger any longer than necessary and a sharp look out needed to be kept for the bluish coloured radar controlled searchlights and the possibility of 'Wilde Sau' aircraft.

Having left the target area the Navigator then designated a course for home and the Pilot checked with his crew to see if they were all OK. The Flight Engineer could check if the bombs had all gone and if there were any hang ups he could remove the inspection covers above the bomb bay with a screwdriver and press the test plunger to release the bomb. He then gave the Pilot a report on the fuel safety margin for the return trip eg "X hours duration at base" and switch off Nos 1 & 3 tanks. The Navigator could call through with a report on ETA at base and any microphones left switched on inadvertently would be indicated by a buzzing in the intercom. During the return journey the squadron's aircraft still had to face the hazards of night fighters and heavy flak concentrations. On reaching the coast of Europe a crew who had survived the operation intact would probably want to relax and open their thermos flasks and rations. But even crossing the Channel a crew had to be on the alert since aircraft which did not identify themselves correctly with the colours of the day when flying over a convoy, took the risk of being shot at by the Royal Navy.

Many aircraft became badly damaged during the raid and often crashed whilst still over Europe, some reached the coast only to crash in the sea, and others crashed on the U.K. mainland. To cope with the latter, from Nov. 1943 onwards three emergency landing fields were constructed along the coasts so that crippled bombers could land as soon as they reached the mainland. These airfields were situated at Carnaby near Bridlington in Yorkshire, Manston near Ramsgate in Kent and Woodbridge near Bentwaters in Suffolk. These emergency airfields were designed to cope with aircraft which were damaged, short of fuel, or suffering from undercarriage problems. These aircraft normally called in for assistance using the call "Darky, Darky" on the frequency of 6440 Kcs, usually Stud 'D' on the TR1196 Selector Box. Each airfield had a runway 3,000 yards long and 250 yards wide, with a 500 yard grass undershoot and overshoot at each end of the runway. This runway was divided into three lanes which were illuminated by lines of lights. The southern lane, which was marked out by green lights, was the emergency lane into which any aircraft could land without first contacting Flying Control. A bulldozer was always on hand so that any aircraft crash landing on this runway could, after the crew had evacuated it, be pushed onto the grass alongside the runway. There was also a 'Fido' installation comprising a line of petroleum jets along the end of the runway to be ignited when fog reduced visibility for landing aircraft.

When within one hours flying time from base the Wireless Operator had to maintain a listening watch for every full 10 minute period until the aircraft was in R/T contact with base. Messages received concerning the Squadron, could include one diverting them to other airfields for various reasons, for example the possibility of Snaith being fog bound, as happened in the case of the Krefeld raid reported in Chapter 7. The Flight Engineer, who had been keeping a regular log, making entries every 20 minutes including recording all engine and oil temperatures, checked on fuel reserves so that when approaching base the Pilot could report to Flying Control the amount of flying time left. Approaching base Air Gunners would still be keeping a look out for the possibility of German intruder aircraft and the Flight Engineer could switch to tank numbers 1 and 3 ready for landing.

In the final circuit, when ready for landing the Flight Engineer pulled out the mechanical locks on the undercarriage and when the Pilot was ready for flaps he unlocked the flap isolation cock, the purpose of this cock being to ensure that the flaps would not be lowered unnecessarily if the hydraulic pipes were damaged. If there was a possibility of damage to the hydraulics the Flight Engineer would check on this by turning the cock one quarter. If the Pilot reported flaps were not descending the Engineer then turned it to one half, and if there was still no movement, he turned it full on. If flaps had still not descended the Flight Engineer could control with the isolation cock until required amount of flap obtained. The Pilot then went through the landing procedure described in Chapter 4, thankful that another operation had been successfully concluded counting towards the number required to complete a tour.

When an operation was planned the aircrew were generally involved from as early as 1000 hrs with all the pre-operation activities necessary until take off, a period which could be longer than that of the actual operation. This would mean that with pre-op. activites plus the actual operation the aircrew could be involved for as long as 24 hrs. Consequently at the end of this period the aircrew would thankfully retire to their beds for a well earned rest.

FIG 41 Key To Navigator's Log Sheets

A log produced by P/O Ken Staples during an operation in 1944 is reproduced in the following pages and a key to the entries in the log is given below:-

First page:

Target = Opladen
R of A = Radius of Action after takeoff to ensure that all the squadron aircraft set off from Snaith together. In the case of this operation Navigators had to plan a course which allowed their aircraft to arrive over Snaith at about 0356 hrs. See entry s/c 0356.
H = 0630 is 'H' hour, start of raid over target.
0610 = Wind, this meant that MH-Z was a Wind-finder aircraft which had to send forecast winds back to base
Windows 2PM = Dropping rate of 2 bundles per minute
Reading, B & C .06 & coast .04 were 'Gee' coordinates.
Reims = 34.255 & C = 37.62 were 'Gee' coordinates.
Letters A,B,C etc indicated turning points
Figure 7 at top of page was the 'Score' on a 1 to 10 scale allocated to the log by the Station Navigation Officer.

Second page:

Z = IFF on
API = Air Position Indicator
DR on Syn meant DR Compass switched on and synchronised.
X tested = 'Gee' tested.
VP Loaded = Very pistol loaded with the colours of the day.
A/c "A", A/c "B" etc were wind directions and velocities calculated by the Navigator.

Other pages:

RF27 = 'Gee' RF unit
No "B" pulse indicated 'Gee' being jammed.
"Duff" indicated unreliable 'Gee' fix.
No "B" pulse on Eastern, indicated no 'Gee' pulse on the Eastern chain.
Final entry is Navigation Officer's report on the log.

For comparison some of the entries in a 1943 log by F/O Keeling are given below:

'Benetnasch' - indicated compass check by Astro Compass.
'Met W/V' - Meant using forecast winds
'SP 9 Bore 211 - meant straight and level run for navigator to take sextant shot.
'Polaris' - indicated sextant bearing on the Pole Star for a latitude determination.

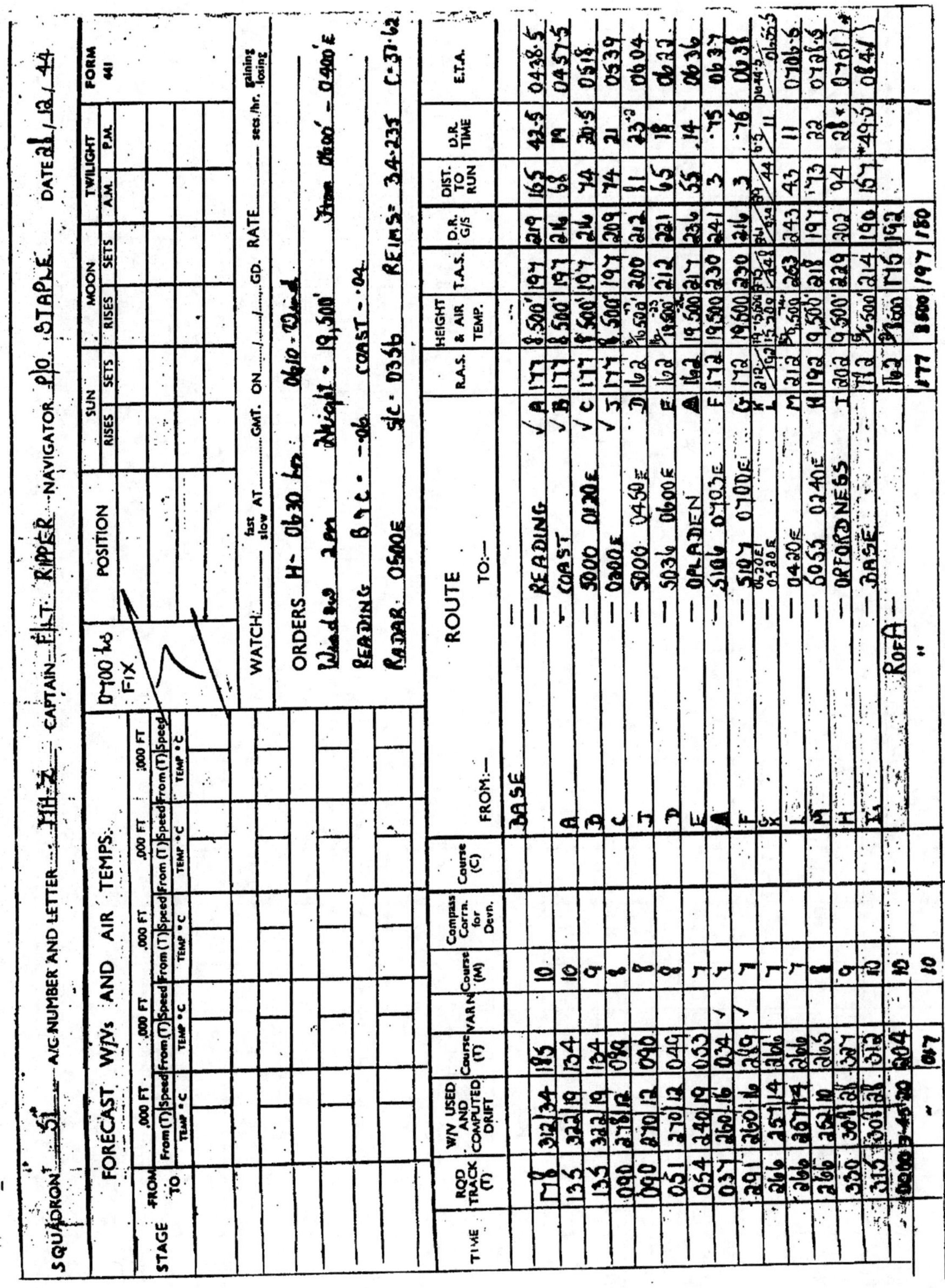

FACETS OF A SQUADRON OPERATION

FIG 42 Navigator's Log Sheets Via Ken Staple (51 Squadron Navigator 1944/45)

FACETS OF A SQUADRON OPERATION

FACETS OF A SQUADRON OPERATION

TIME	RQD TRACK (T)	W/V USED AND COMPUTED DRIFT	Course (T)	VARN	Course (M)	Compass Corrn. for Devn.	Course (C)	NAVIGATIONAL OBSERVATIONS (Pin Points, Fixes, Position Lines, Actual T.M.G. Actual Drift, G/S and W/V Manoeuvres, etc.)	GENERAL (Met. Conditions, Bombing, Intell., Enemy Action)	R.A.S.	HEIGHT & AIR TEMP.	T.A.S.	D.R. G/S	DIST. TO RUN	D.R. TIME	E.T.A.
0459						5041	0016	X	W/V = 005 / 21				220	125	17	0516
0506						5031	0034	X	W/V = 300 / 20							
0511						5121	0059	X	W/V = 308 / 22				221	19	5	0516
0516	090	350/30 6°S	084			5013 -13	0117	□ A/c 'J' X	W/V = 300 / 22	174	8500	194	193	45	23	0539
0522						6001	0046	X	W/V = 351 / 35							
0529						5103	0217	X RF 27	Z OK W/V = 336 / 16				204	30	9	0538
0535						5004	9244	X "DUFF"	W/V = - / -				201	81	34	0602
0532 0535.5	090	4°S	036			5015	0302	□ 'J' A/c 'D' X	W/V = 340 / 14							
0544						5005	0336	X "aircraft off course"	W/V = 343 / 15				306	61	12	0602
0550						5026	0359	X	W/V = 335 / 11				209	40	11.6	0601.6
0556						5028	0428	X □ A/c 'E'	W/V = 335 / 16							
0601.5 0601.5	049	335/16 4°S	048			6029 -13	0444 +6	X	W/V = 344 / 22	162	9500	212	208	65	19	0620.5
0606						5009	0510	X	W/V = 365 / 50							
0612 0618	044		034					□ A/c X X	Z OK	162	9500	212	199	47	15	0627

FACETS OF A SQUADRON OPERATION

FACETS OF A SQUADRON OPERATION

					NAVIGATIONAL OBSERVATIONS (P/o Points, Fixes, Position Lines, Actual T.M.G. Actual Drift, G/S and W/V Manoeuvres, etc.) Watches Synchronised W/T Go.	GENERAL (Met. Conditions, Bombing, Intell., Enemy Action)				
0732	360	5°S	325		□ X Ai "I"		202	230	229	225	70	19	0751
0732				0109	0207 X	W/V= 225 19				
0740				6150	0246 X	W/V= 250 18				
				+6	+24	Z OK				
0146				5152	0252 X	W/V= 259 60 ?				
				-3	+11					
0752	313		308	5208	0235 □ A/C BASE		182 3000 196	184	169	55	0841
					X Skipped Bombing	NAV LIGHTS ON W/V= 333 20				
0800				5221	011.4 X					
0810				5233	0052 X	W/V= 315 10	190	119	37.5	09.43.5
0813				5241	0037 X	W/V= 227 17				
0821				5304	0002 X "DUFF"					
0827				5317	0020 X	W/V= 225 13	210	52	15	0842
0833				5327	0024 X Homing to BASE		225	20	4.5	0840.5
0840.5					BASE					
0841					Landed					

A very good trip plotting + cycle of fix / v.v. good. Handed in Cockpit chit

D.F.E.Cryer F/o   R Forbes
Signed   Navigator

FACETS OF A SQUADRON OPERATION

51 Squadron
PHOTOGRAPHIC ALBUM

KEY TO PHOTOGRAPHS OPPOSITE

VIEWS AROUND THE STATION

Photo No 1 via 51 Squadron

Technical Site
March past in front of
Station Headquarters.
Note gas detection board
in front of leader

Photo No 2 Via 51 Squadron

Technical Site
Control Tower. Note Pundit
beacon on left.

Photo No 3 E.Millet
Via J Feaver

Technical Site
View of Technical Site.
from road

Photo No 4 E.Millet
Via J Feaver

T2 Hangar, Building number 45,
in Map 2, on the left.

Photo No 5 E.Millet
Via J Feaver

Technical Site
View looking East from
the top of the Control
Tower.

Photo No 6 E.Millet
Via J Feaver

Technical Site
View looking West from
the top of the Control
Tower

Photo No 7 E.Millet
Via J Feaver

Technical Site
51 Squadron Headquarters
and Gunnery Trainer

Photo No 8 E.Millet
Via J Feaver

Technical Site
Tailors, Hairdressers and
Boot/Shoe Repair shops on
on right

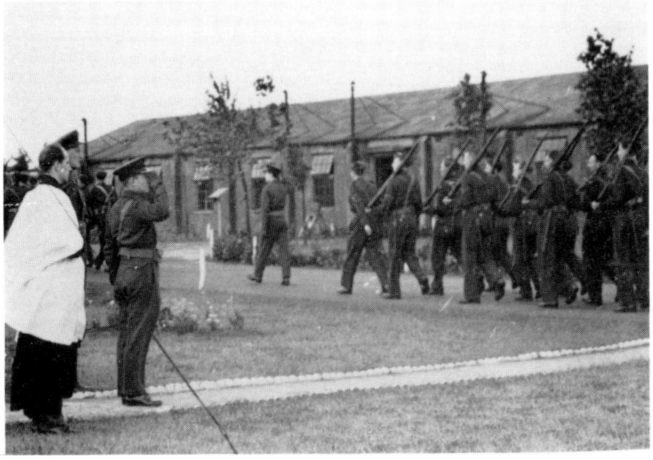
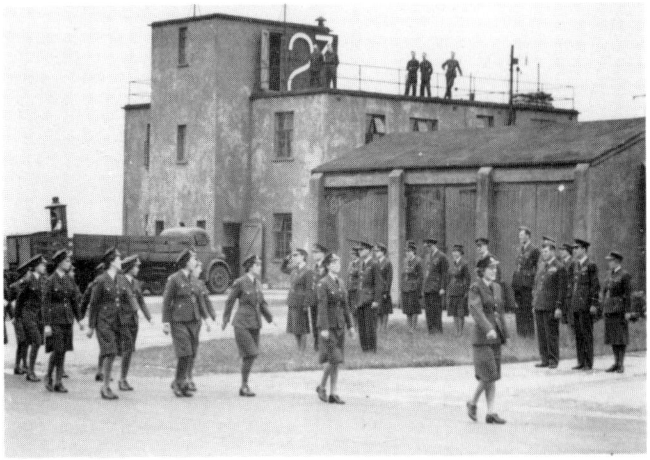
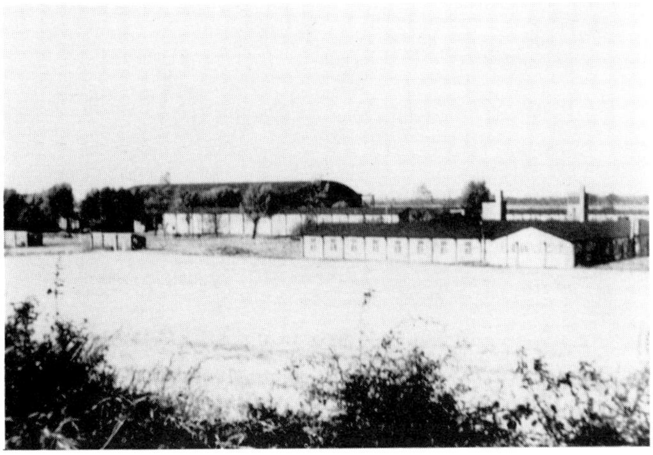
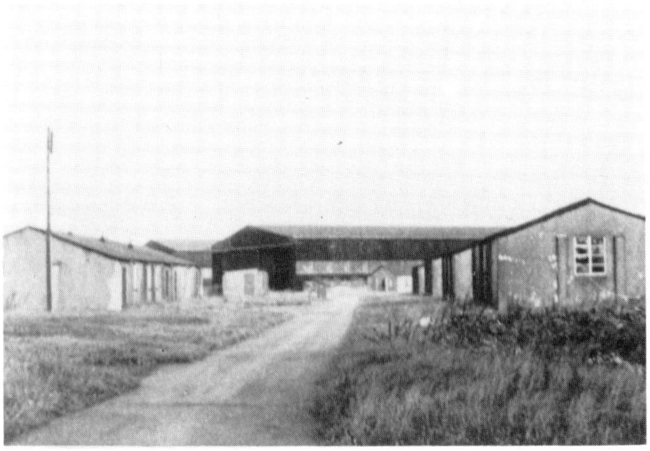
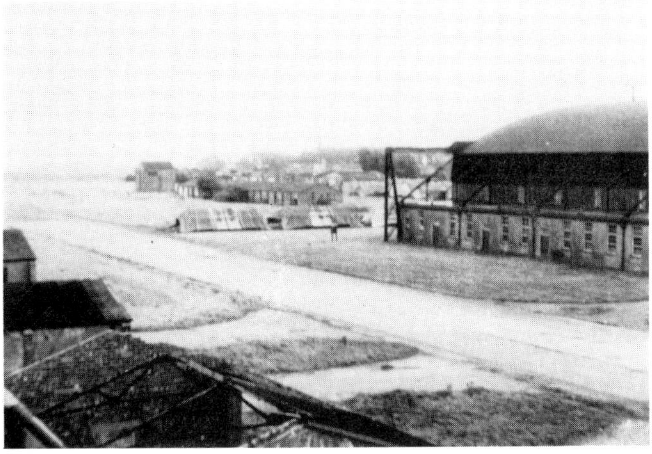
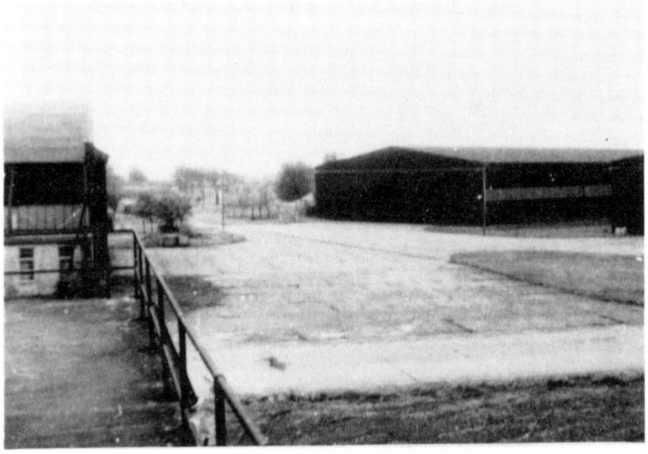
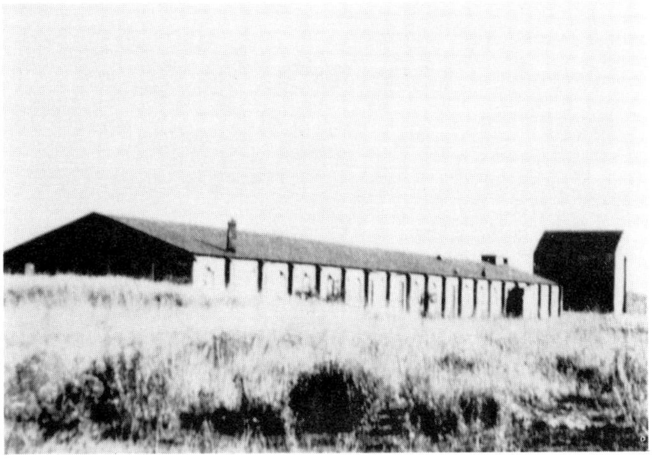
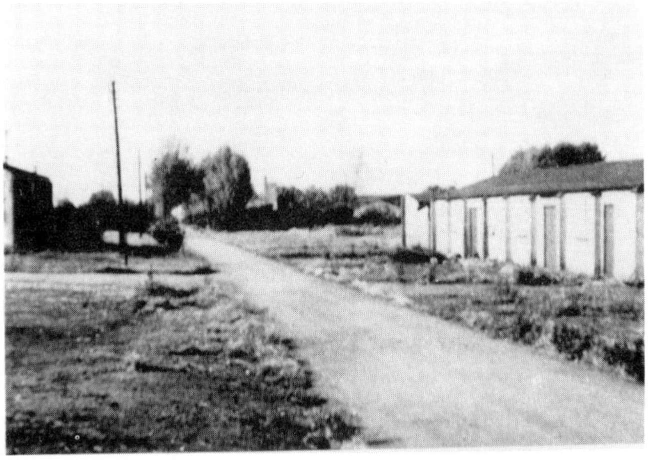

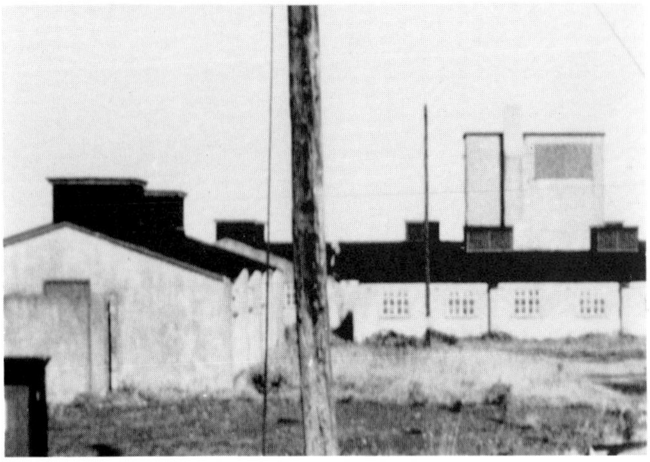

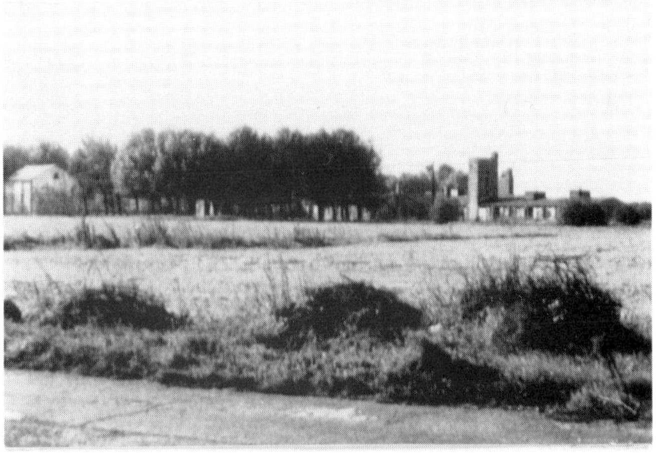

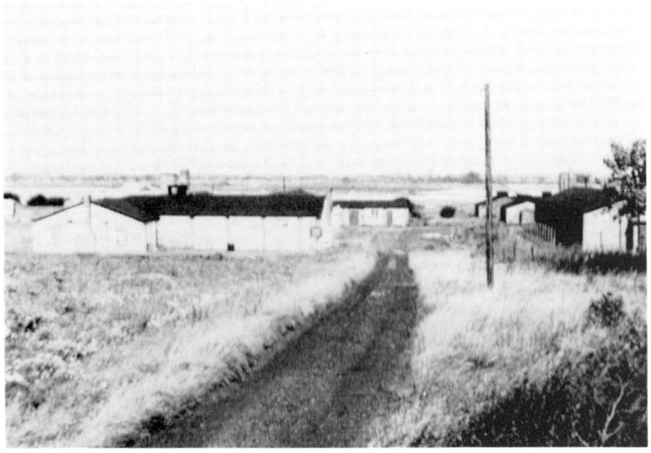

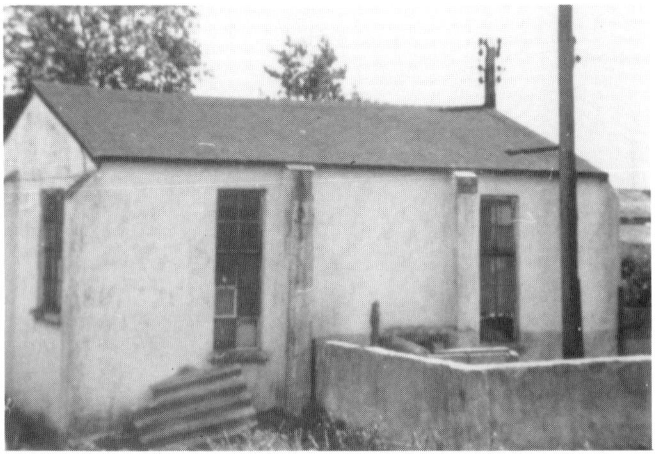

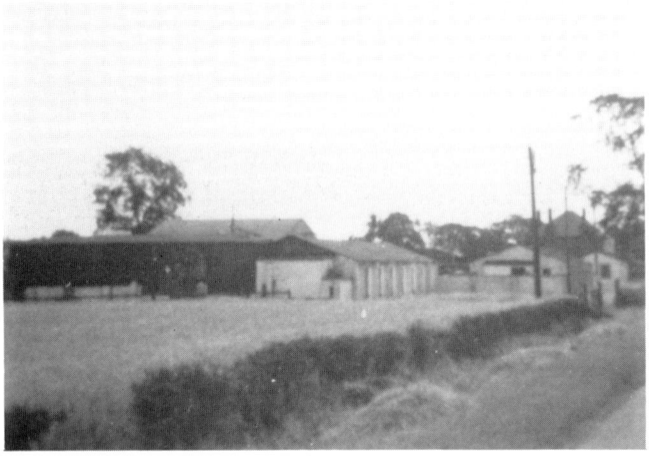

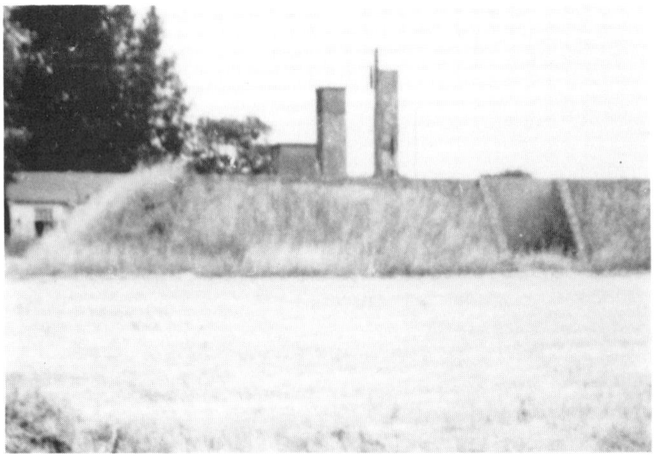

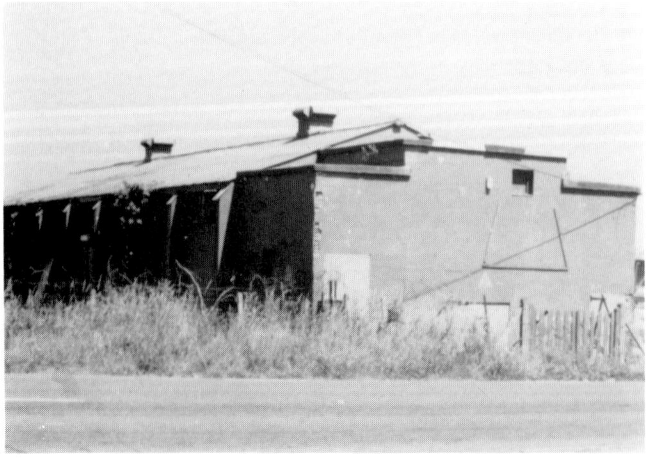

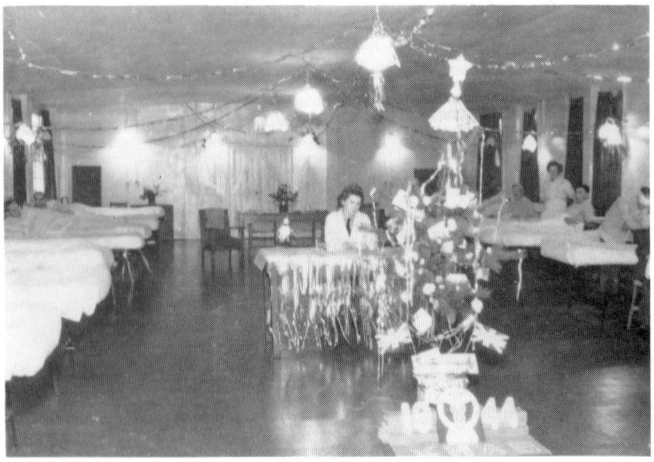

KEY TO PHOTOGRAPHS OPPOSITE

VIEWS AROUND THE SITE

Photo No 9 E.Millet
Via J Feaver

Technical Site
Sergeant's Mess

Photo No 10 E.Millet
Via J Feaver

Technical Site
Officer's Mess with
the Squash Court on the left
of the photo

Photo No 11 E.Millet
Via J Feaver

Technical Site
Airmen's Mess on right and
Naafi on the left

Photo No 12

No 1 WAAF site
Picket Post

Photo No 13 Via B.Gazely

No 1 WAAF site

Photo No 14 Via B.Gazely

Operations block

Photo No 15

Domestic Site
Cinema conversion from Gym.
similar to one at Snaith

Photo No 16 Via Mrs E.Morton

Technical Site
Station Sick Quarters

KEY TO PHOTOGRAPHS OPPOSITE

AROUND THE SITE

Photo No 17 Via 51 Squadron

The `Ha in the Wa' bar in the Officer's Mess.

Photo No 18 Via Mrs J.Wilds

Officer's Mess staff

ACTIVITIES

Photo No 19 Via 51 Squadron

Presentation of Sunderland Cup to WAAF section by Lady Welsh

Photo No 20 via A.Ellis

WAAF Handicraft display

Photo No 21 Via 51 Squadron

Concert Party

Photo No 22 Via 51 Squadron

Station Band

Photo No 23 Via A.Ellis

Station Sports

Photo No 24 Via 51 Squadron

F/O Jim Gill and Pilot F/Lt `Tex' McQuiston with guitar

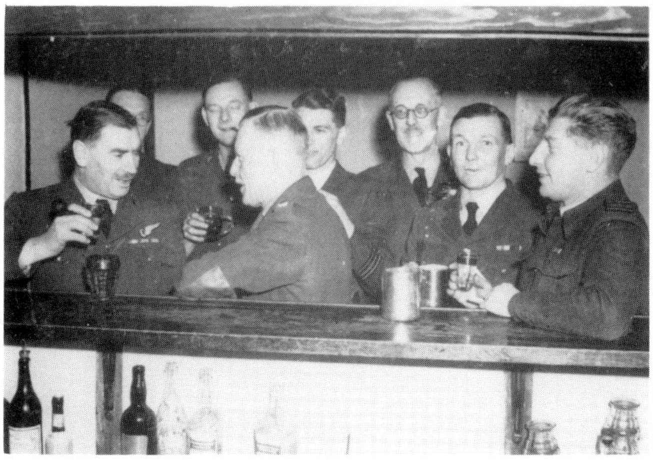

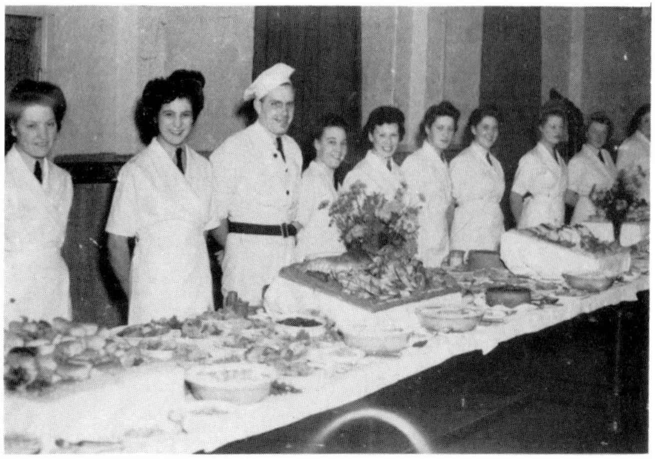

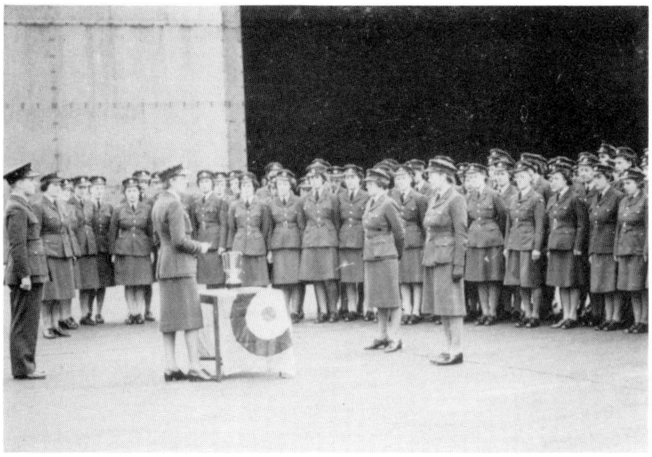

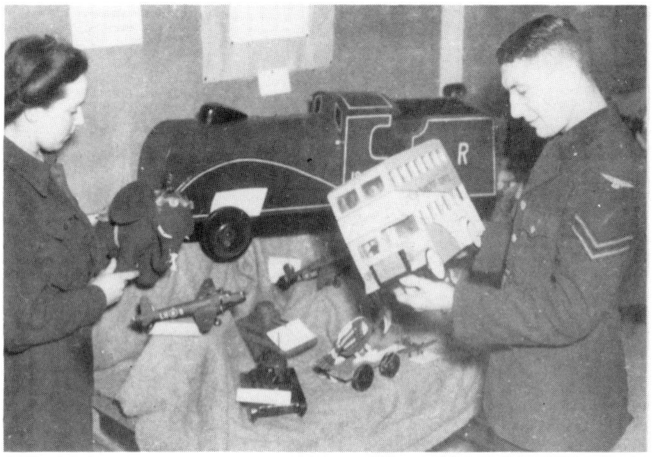
R

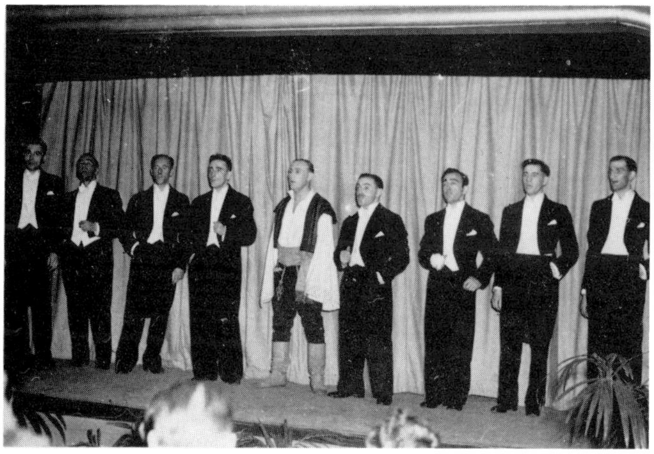

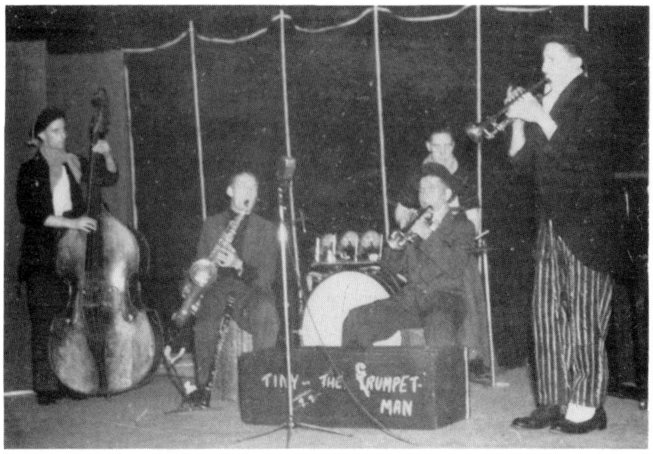
TINY - THE TRUMPET-
MAN

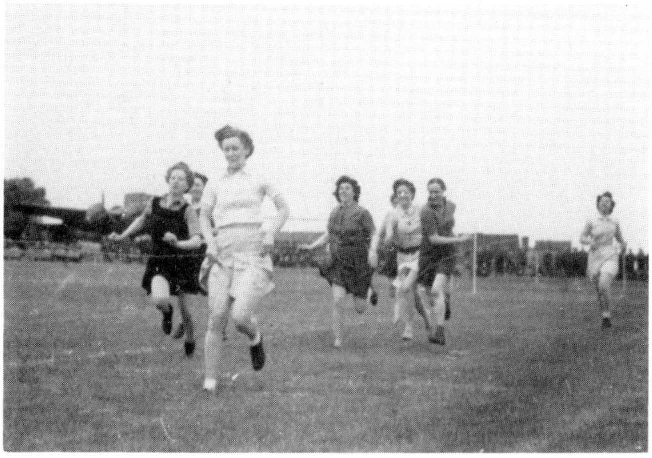

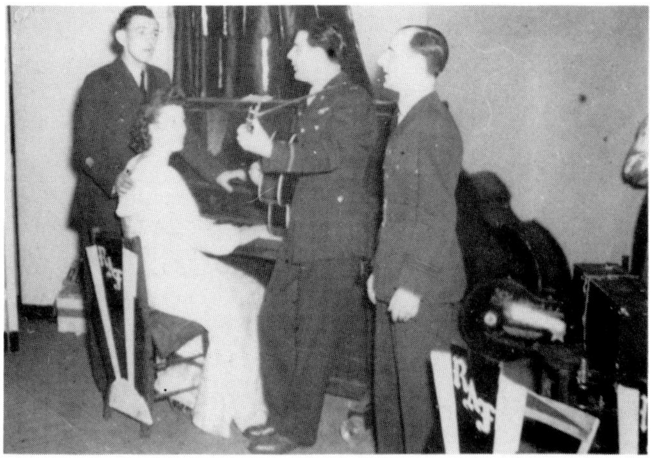
RAF

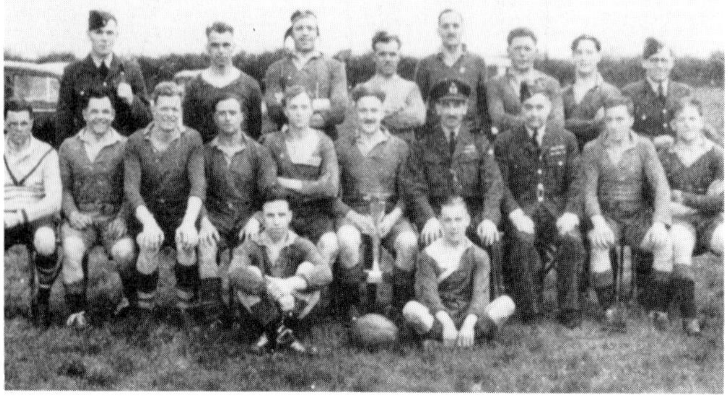
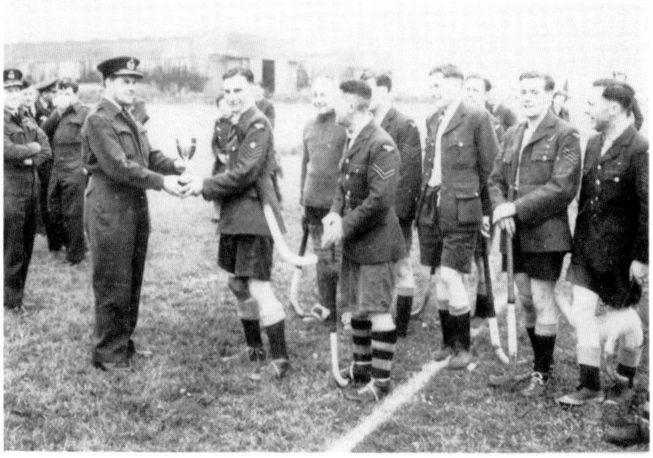
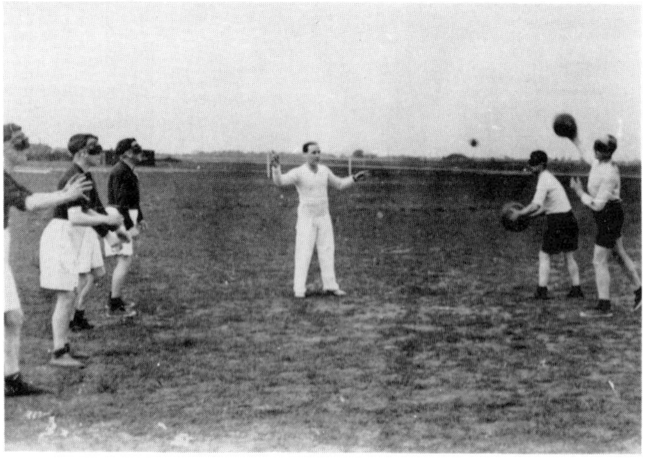
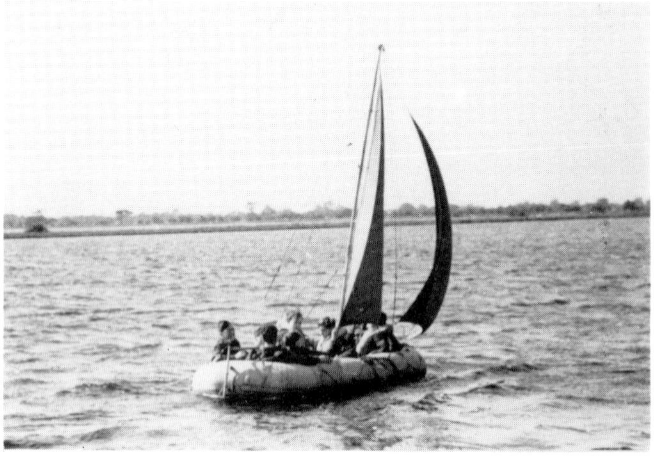
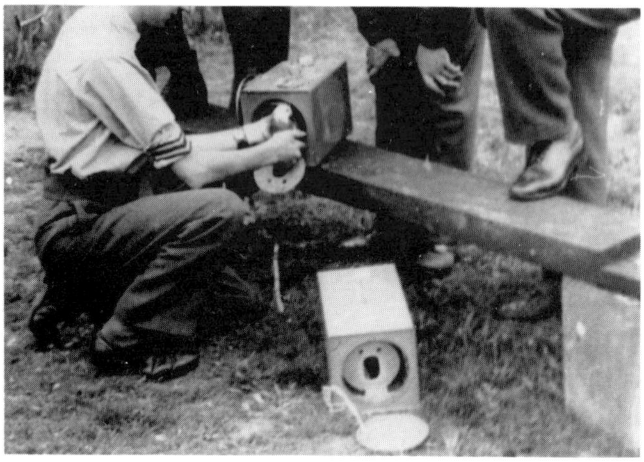
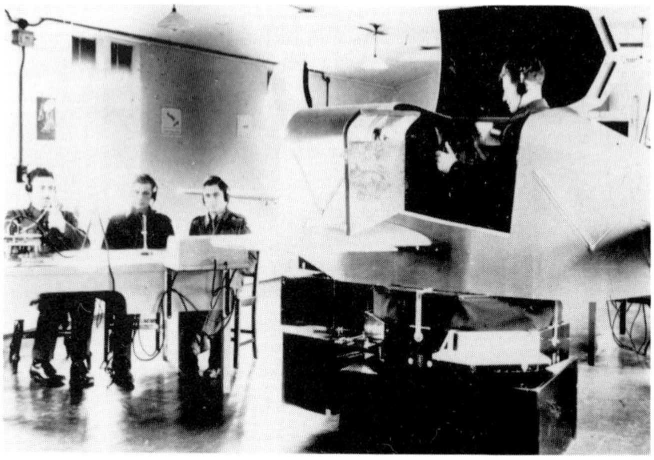
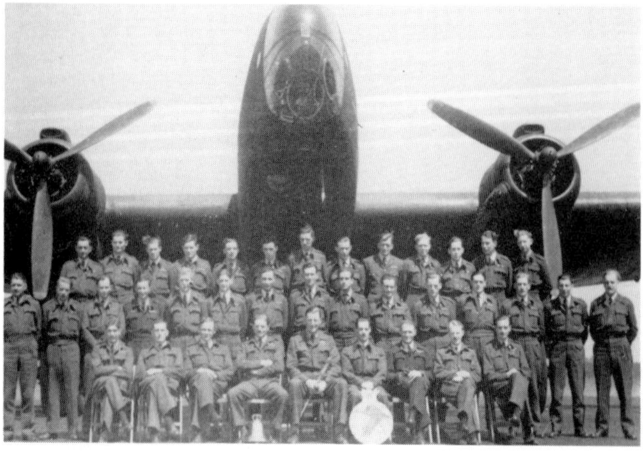
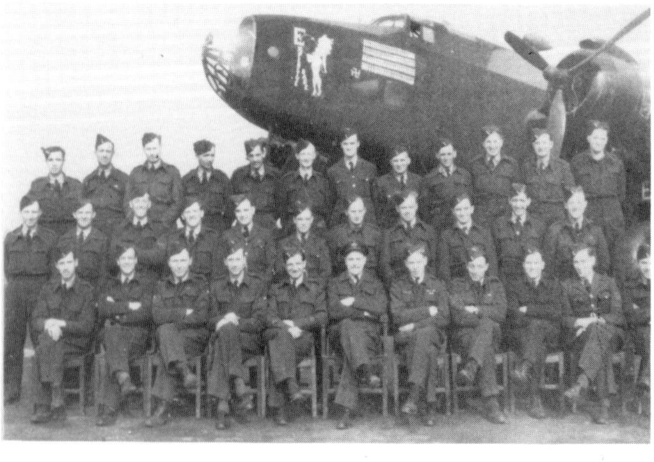

KEY TO PHOTOGRAPHS OPPOSITE

ACHIEVMENTS

Photo No 25 Via A.Ellis

Winners of 4 Group Rugby Cup

Photo No 26 Via A.Ellis

Presentation of 4 Group Hockey Cup.

TRAINING

Photo No 27 Via A.Ellis

Night vision training

Photo No 28 Via A.Ellis

`Q' Type dinghy training on Cowick Reservoir

Photo No 29 Via L.Davison

Demonstration of pigeon handling for aircrew.

Photo No 30 Via RAF St Athans

Link Trainer

SQUADRON PERSONNEL

Photo No 31 Via J.Feaver

51 Squadron Pilots and Leaders.

Photo No 32 Via Mrs E.Morton

Ground crew of `E' "Expensive Babe" after completion of 100 operations

KEY TO PHOTOGRAPHS OPPOSITE

OPERATIONS

Photo No 33 Via I.W.M.
Ref no CH12598
Squadron briefing for the
Nuremberg operation

Photo No 34 Via 51 Squadron

A squadron crew being
debriefed after an operation.

Photo No 35 I.W.M.
Airfield Caravan and a Mk II
Series 1 Special Halifax
taking off for the Ruhr
in mid 1943
(Ref No CH18505)

Photo No 36 via S/Ldr Varey
Halifax Mk III taking off for
first daylight raid in 1944

Photo No 37 I.W.M.
Ref no CH12599
S/Ldr Paul Jousse and sqdn.
Navigation Leader
Doug Rubery preparing flight
plan for Nuremberg raid.

Photo No 38 Via C.Pickard

Flak over the Frisians

Photo No 39 via 51 Squadron.

Start of main runway
Angle of Approach
indicator on the
left hand side

Photo No 40 Via 51 Squadron

Jack Paradise's crew, the W/OP
in this group did not take part
in the Rheine operation
reported in Chapter 6.

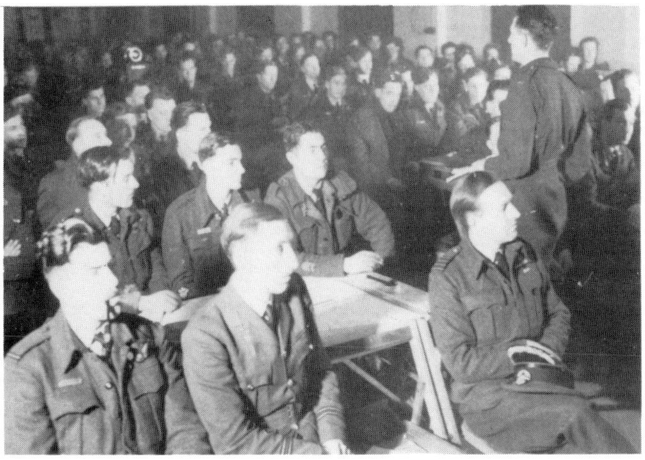

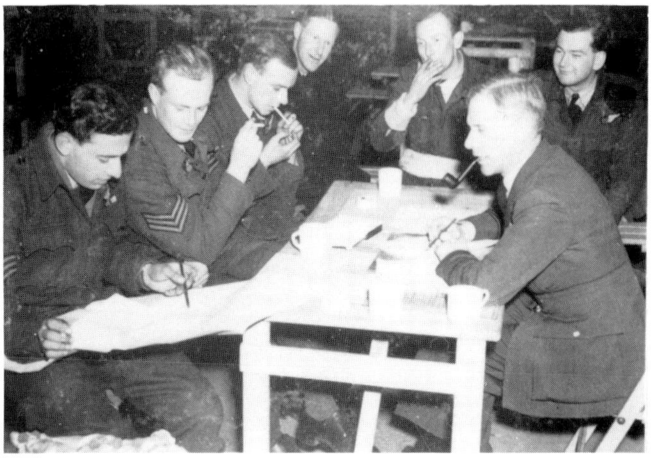

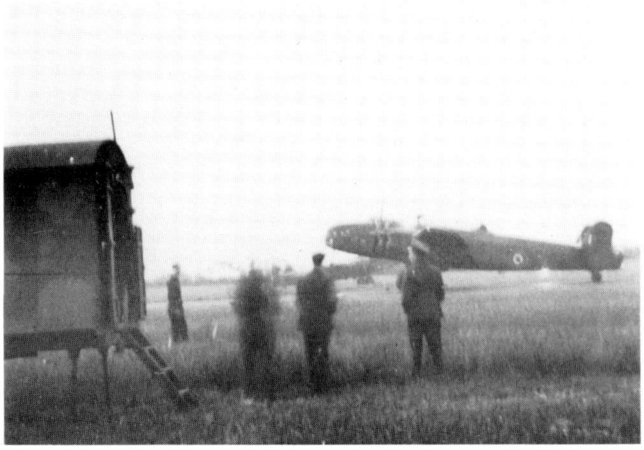

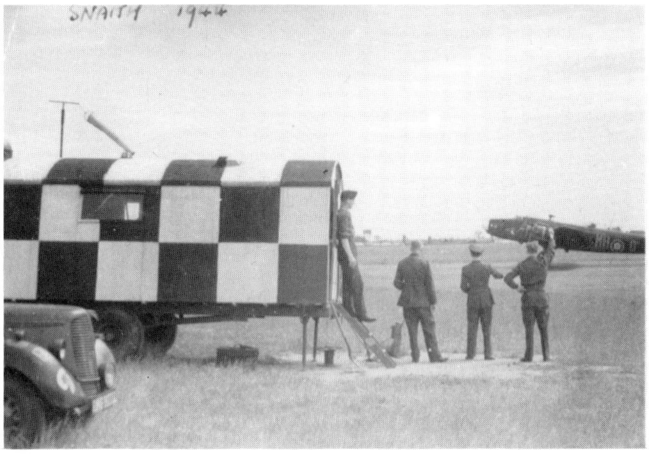
SNAITH 1944

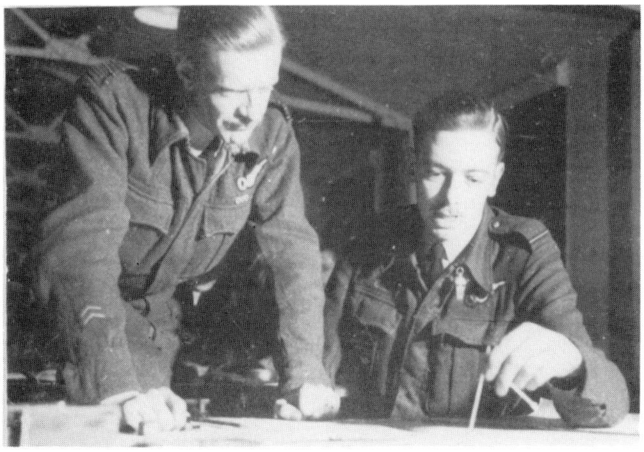

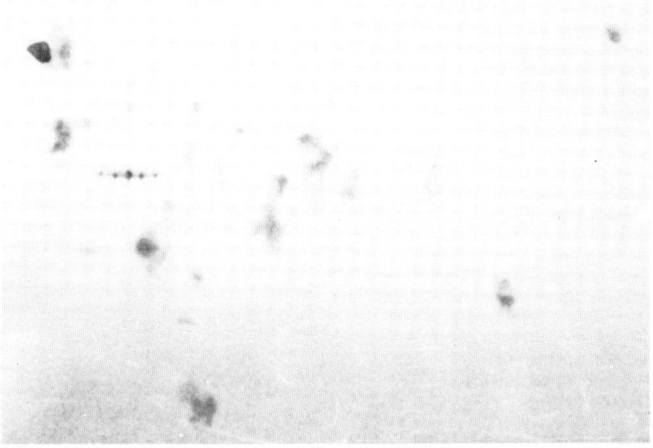

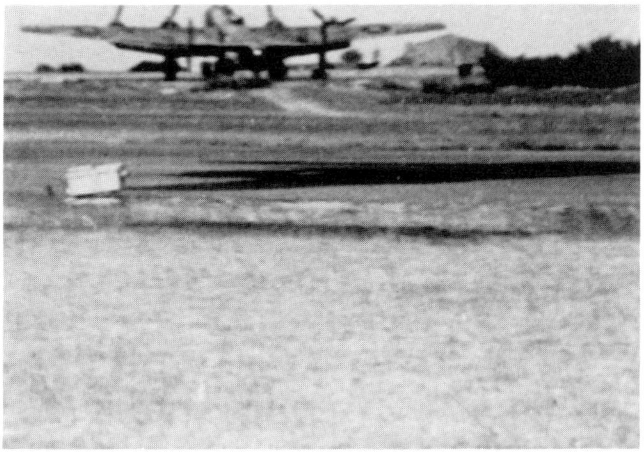

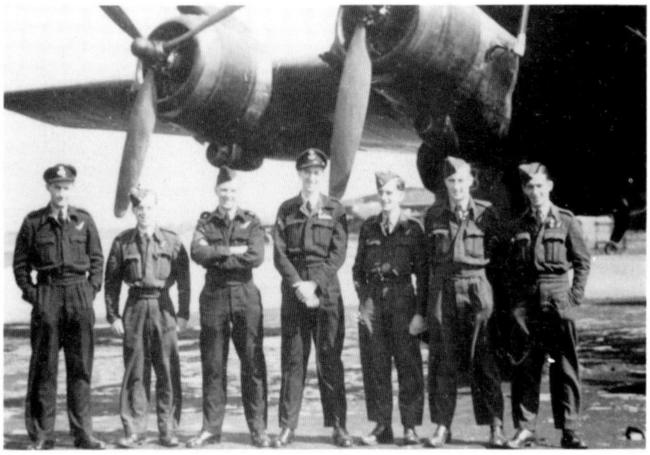

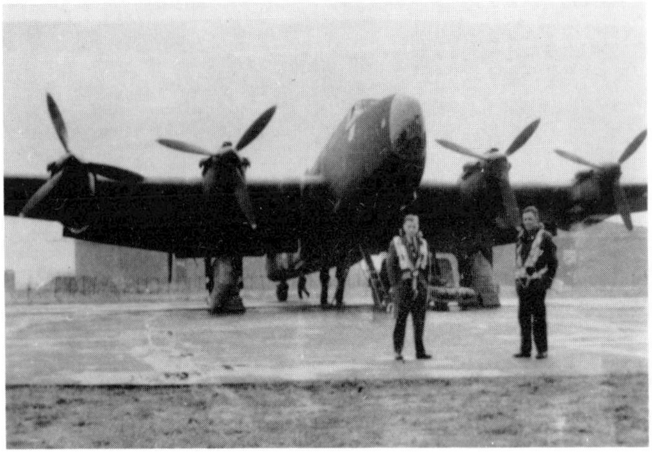

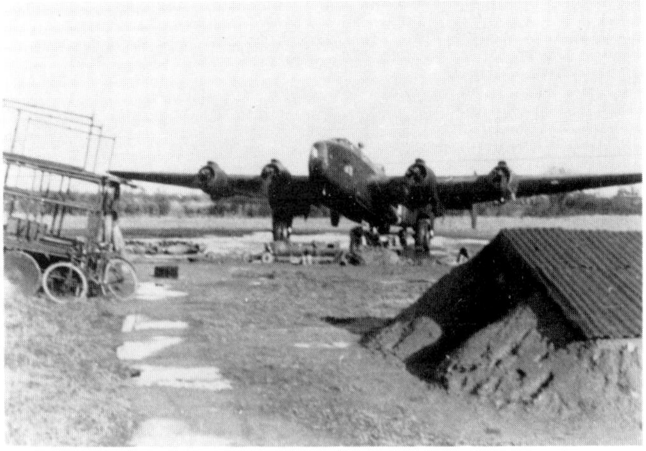

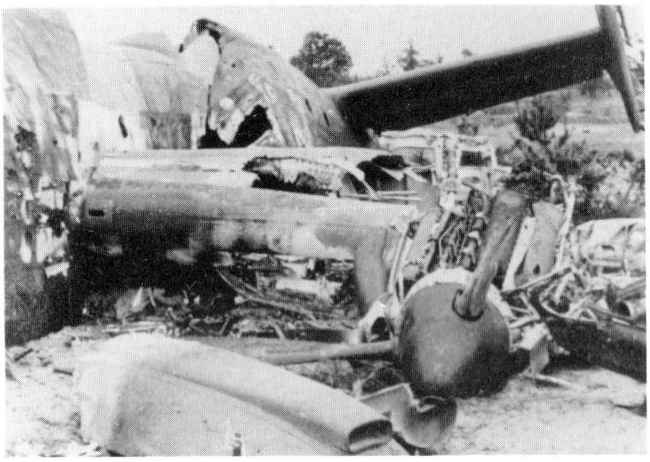

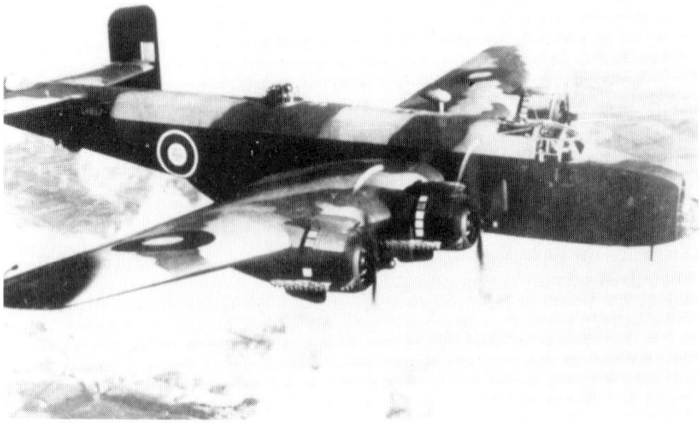

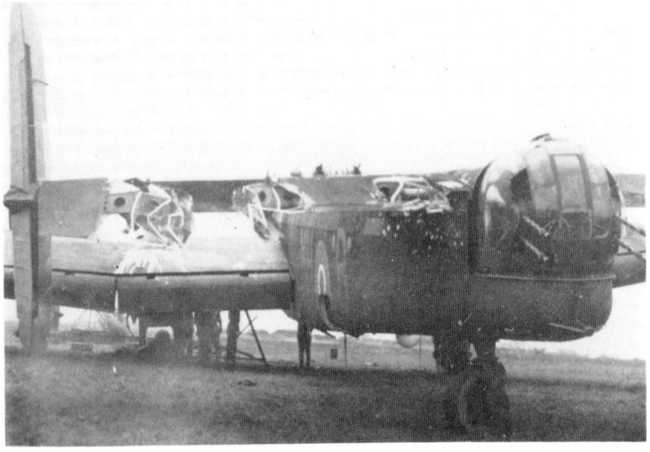

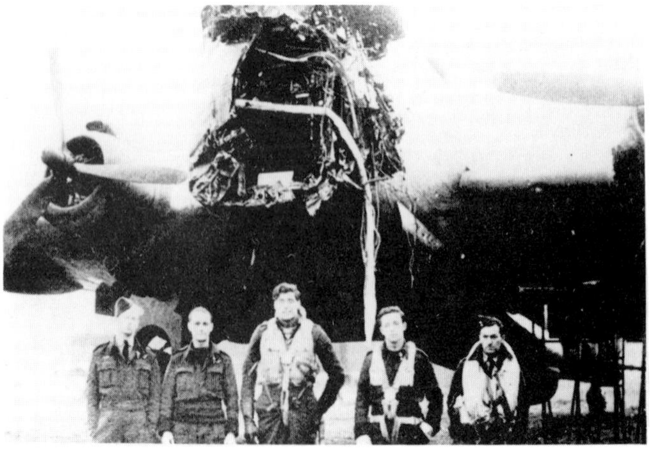

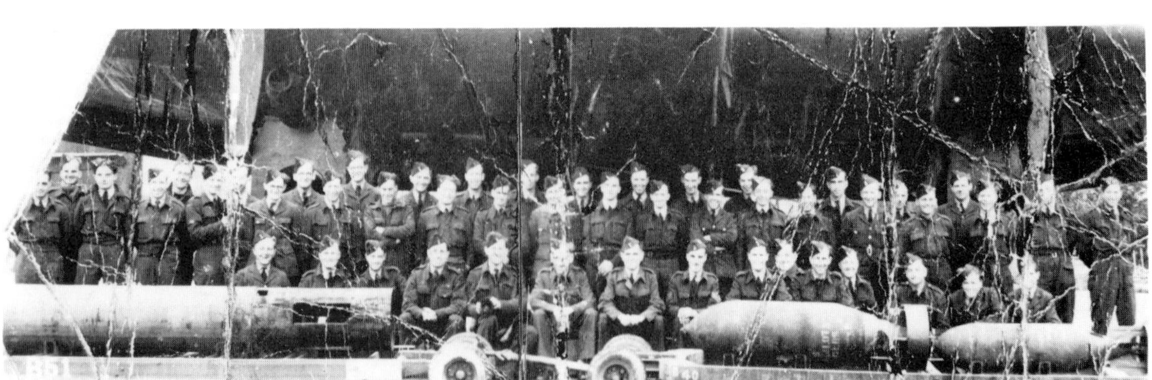

KEY TO PHOTOGRAPHS OPPOSITE

AIRCRAFT

Photo No 41 Via M.Foster

MH-D Halifax Mk II
Series 1a

Photo No 42 Via C.Pickard

Mk III Halifax on dispersal,
note dugout in foreground.

Photo No 43
Via Francois Webers

Crash photo of JD244 lost
on Krefeld raid of
21/22 June 1943

Photo No 44 Via 51 Squadron

Halifax III LV851
lost on Nuremberg operation
of 30/31 March 1944

Photo No 45 Via 51 Squadron

Halifax HR868 severely
damaged on Frankfurt raid.
See Chapter 6

Photo No 47 Via R.Holmes

Andy Wilson's aircraft
after the loss of its
nose, see Chapter 6

ARMOURERS

Photo No 47 Via R.Carter

51 Squadron Armourers and
the squadron's payload of
500 lb and 1,000 lb bombs
plus a 1,500 lb mine

Chapter 6

POST-OPERATIONS AND LOSSES

After returning from an operation the Pilots would taxi their aircraft to allocated dispersals, guided into place by the waiting ground crew, and run up the engines to about 800 rpm for a couple of minutes before cutting them. The Air Gunners cleared the rounds from the breech of each gun and set the safety catch to `Safe'. With all switches and petrol tanks turned off, the aircrew climbed out of the aircraft with an air of relief at another successful operation. The captain reported any problems or damage to the ground crew and unserviceable items would have to be entered in the Form 700. Duty Armourers arrived to check the aircraft to ensure there were no bombs still hung up, Radar Mechanics removed the detonators from the radar sets, and if everything was OK the ground crew could bed the aircraft down for the night, with cockpit and engine covers fitted. When a crew bus drew up the waiting aircrew jumped aboard, possibly to join some crews already picked up, to be driven to the locker room to divest themselves of their flying gear.

In 1943 a crew's next step was to attend the debriefing and on entering the building would probably find some of the crews who were back earlier already sitting at tables being debriefed by an Intelligence Officer (Photo 34). Possibly the first action for the new arrivals was to make for the urn to obtain a hot drink, usually cocoa, from the WAAF on duty who may proffer the question "With or without", meaning did they want rum in their drink. On occasions the Station Padre (S/L Watts) would be standing near the urn watching the crews come in, very sensitive to the fact that some may not return from the night's operation. This would involve him in certain sad tasks which he had to undertake on behalf of missing aircrew. When an Intelligence Officer was free a crew moved over to his table and sat down. At the table there may be packets of cigarettes for the crews. The officer after welcoming them and expressing his pleasure at their safe return, reached for another blank debriefing form from the pile in front of him and started his questioning. The debriefing could be a challenge for the Intelligence Officer with a crew in a state of fatigue and required skill and tact to acquire the necessary information. There was a recognised debriefing procedure so that the requisite information to prepare a night raid report could be obtained. Types of question asked were, "Did you find the target", "How did you know it was the correct target", "Did you get a photo", "Target Conditions", "Did they consider the bombing to be successful", "Any special observations". It was not advisable for aircrew to pass on information unless they were fairly sure it was correct since it was possible for the target photo to show up false claims.

Many interesting and amusing items of information came out during the briefing sessions. When the squadron participated in an operation against Milan in Aug. 1943, the aircrew reported that when approaching Milan they were overawed by the degree of illumination since the sky seemed to be full of searchlights. However when the first wave reached the target and started to bomb all the searchlights except four were extinguished, presumably because most of the Italian operators had fled to the shelters. This contrasted with the Ruhr targets where crews reported that the defences got hotter as a raid progressed. There were a number of light hearted moments in these debriefing sessions. After Dave Storey and his fellow crew members had been debriefed for the Milan raid and were passing one of the other tables they overheard the I/O Officer ask "Did you see any Italian night fighters?" The answer was "Yes, but he was going too fast for us to catch him", which highlights the RAF's opinion of the Italian Air Force. Another classic, this time referring to a well defended German target, was the reply to the question "Was the flak light?" The snappy catch answer being "It was so thick that we lowered our undercarriage and taxied in to bomb".

In addition to helping Bomber Command assess the efficiency of their bombing operations, the information could have another use which was not communicated to the aircrew. The Ministry of Information under Duff Cooper was operating `Black Propaganda' radio stations which transmitted from England. These purported to be

POST-OPERATIONS AND LOSSES

Telegram 1:

28   1.28* 1.1.49 SNAITH G.O. OHMS 37

PRIORITY MRS C H HEATHFIELD 31 HAZEL ROAD ROMFORD ESSEX =

DEEPLY REGRET TO INFORM YOU YOUR SON 1235550 SGT HEATHFIELD FAILED TO RETURN FROM OPERATIONS THIS MORNING LETTER FOLLOWS AUNT MISS TURNER HAS BEEN INFORMED = 51 SQDN

Telegram 2:

92   92 8.56 PM OHMS OF 29TH LONDON TELEX 64

C PRIORITY CC D MRS C H HEATHFIELD 31 HAZEL RISE ROMFORDESSEX =

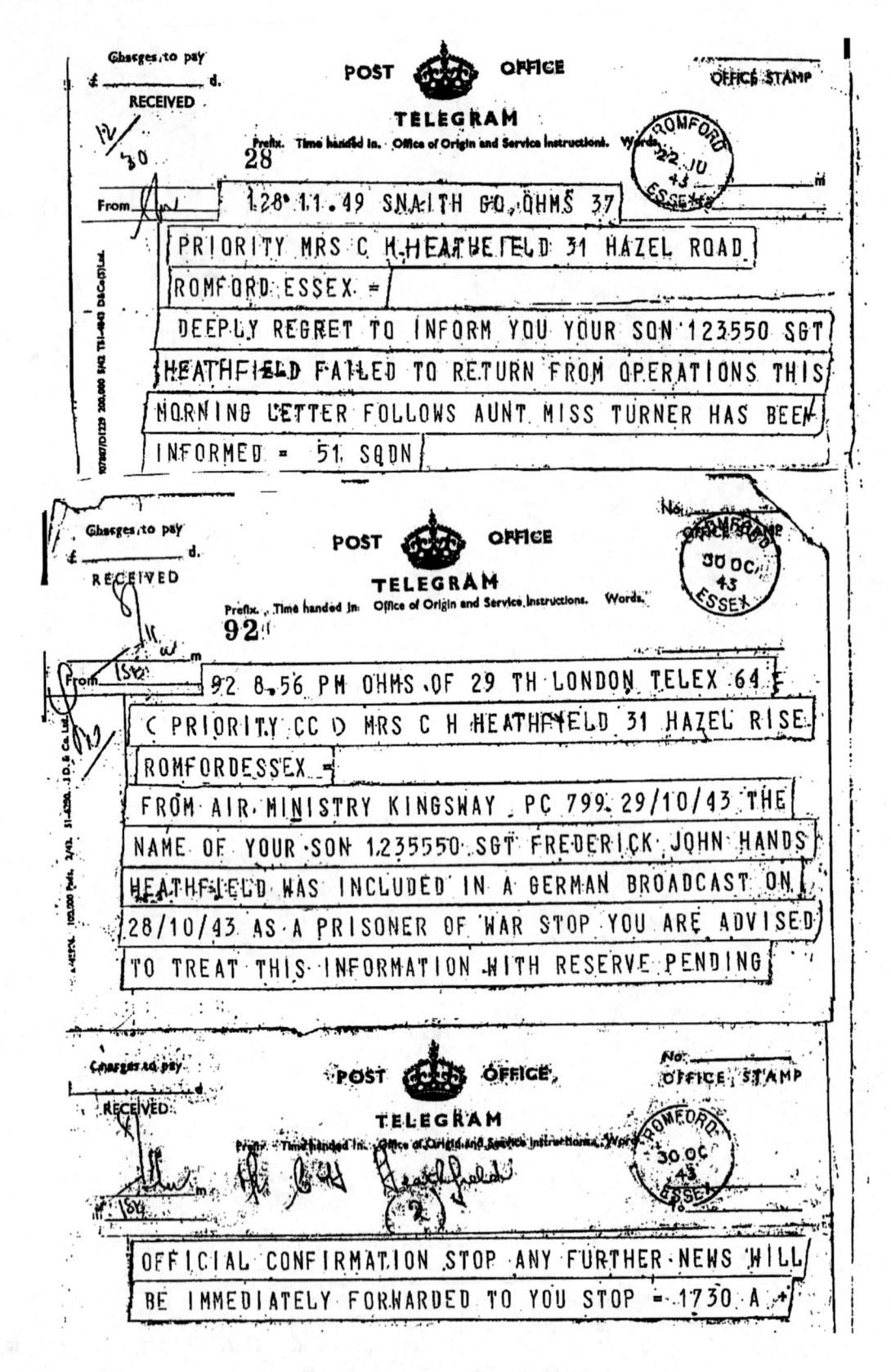

FROM AIR MINISTRY KINGSWAY PC 799 29/10/43 THE NAME OF YOUR SON 1235550 SGT FREDERICK JOHN HANDS HEATHFIELD WAS INCLUDED IN A GERMAN BROADCAST ON 28/10/43 AS A PRISONER OF WAR STOP YOU ARE ADVISED TO TREAT THIS INFORMATION WITH RESERVE PENDING

Telegram 3:

OFFICIAL CONFIRMATION STOP ANY FURTHER NEWS WILL BE IMMEDIATELY FORWARDED TO YOU STOP = 1730 A +

FIG 18 Telegrams Sent To Fred Heathfields Next Of Kin

POST-OPERATIONS AND LOSSES

---------- GERrard 9234

F. 405478/1/43/P.4.A.2.

Casualty Branch,
77, OXFORD STREET,
LONDON, W. 1.

6 July, 1943.

Madam,

I am commanded by the Air Council to express to you their great regret on learning that your son, Sergeant Frederick John Hands Heathfield, Royal Air Force, is missing as the result of air operations on the night of 21st/22nd June 1943, when a Halifax aircraft in which he was flying as captain set out to bomb Krefeld and was not heard from again.

This does not necessarily mean that he is killed or wounded, and if he is a prisoner of war he should be able to communicate with you in due course. Meanwhile enquiries are being made through the International Red Cross Committee, and as soon as any definite news is received you will be at once informed.

If any information regarding your son is received by you from any source you are requested to be kind enough to communicate it immediately to the Air Ministry.

The Air Council desire me to convey to you their sympathy in your present anxiety.

I am, Madam,
Your obedient Servant,

Mrs. C. H. Heathfield,
31, Hazel Rise,
Romford,
Essex.

FIG 19 Letter Sent To Fred Heathfields Next Of Kin

POST-OPERATIONS AND LOSSES

German stations such as the 'Atlantiksender' short wave station and the 'Soldatensender' in the medium wave band, but actually transmitting subtle Allied propaganda. This was achieved by incorporating selected items of subversive propaganda along with genuine German news information. The station gave out up to the minute news of damage resulting from air raids which were obtained from Bomber Command intelligence reports, bombing photos, and post raid PR photos, by comparison with street maps of the target. For example, for the Krefeld raid they could report on areas of the town damaged by fire or bombs, report on the fire storm and even give names of well known streets damaged. By guesswork based on experience with UK raids they could mention the problems of the rescue services.

As well as reporting to the I/O officer, some aircrew also had to to report to their various specialist officers such as Bombing Leader, Navigation Leader, etc. Navigators would have to hand in their charts, and along with other crews such as Flight Engineers and Wireless Operators hand in logs. If the Flight Engineer's log showed a fuel consumption of more than 0.9 air miles per gallon he had to give an explanation to the Engineering Leader. Next day, bombing photos were pinned up by the I/O Section and these would be examined with great interest by the aircrews. Aircrew needed to fill in their Log Books with details of the operation and every month the flying hours would be totalled up so that the log book could be signed by the Flight Commander or the CO.

A likely scenario for missing aircrew can be exemplified by the actions which could have taken place after the Krefeld raid. When the last crew had been debriefed one of the I/Os or the Adjutant would notify the Padre that one aircraft had not returned and was presumed missing. This was MH-K, JD244 captained by Sgt Fred Heathfield. The Padre having ascertained the names of the crew and the location of the billets, then collected a couple of SPs and piled them into a utility vehicle to drive out to the billets. At the billets all the crew's kit and and personal belongings would have to be collected and delivered to the Padre's office, so that he could go through them on behalf of the Committee of Adjustment. Any personal correspondence needed to be read through to see if it contained any sensitive items which meant they should not be passed on to the next of kin. RAF property was collected together for return to stores and personal items were deposited in a store near the chapel. Some large items such as bicycles were put on one side so that if the next of kin requested it they could be auctioned off by the Committee of Adjustment and the proceeds sent to the next of kin. Eventually all the personal belongings were put into special cardboard boxes and sent to the RAF Central Depository at Colnbrook.

A telegram was sent out to the next of kin of all missing aircrew, via one of the station Teleprinter Operators, and the one sent to Fred Heathfield's mother is shown in Fig 18. Telegrams were followed up by a letter from the Squadron CO, or in his absence a Flight Commander. When Tom Nelson went missing on a Berlin raid on 31st August 1943 his next of kin received a four page letter from W/C Franks, which showed his interest in and concern for his aircrew. The letter from the squadron was followed by a letter from the Air Ministry and the one received by Fred Heathfield's mother is shown in Fig 19.

In the records including PORs, missing aircrew were listed as 'Posted missing to No 1 Depot Uxbridge'. During World War 2 the distinctive voice of a collaborator named William Joyce was heard broadcasting in English from a German Radio Station in propaganda programmes designed for Britain. One of his preambles to the broadcast was "Germany Calling, Reich centre Bremen and Hamburg on the 31 metre band" and because of his distinctive voice was nicknamed 'Lord Haw Haw' by the British public. His broadcasts regularly included information which the listeners could definitely identify as being genuine, such as the names of POWs. These were included in order to give some credence to his propaganda and entice people to listen in. Consequently, in a broadcast on the 28 October 1943 the report of names of POWs included that of Fred Heathfield and subsequently Fred's mother received a telegram from the Air Ministry on the 30 October 1943, delivered from Romford Post Office. The contents of the telegram are shown in Fig 18.

The action which resulted in Fred Heathfield and his crew becoming POWs is a very interesting one and is described here in detail. For the Krefeld raid Halifax JD 244, MH-K was piloted by Sergeant Heathfield. This was a new aircraft which had been delivered early in June and they were the first crew to fly it on an air test, landing just before the bomb dump blew up at mid-day on Sat 19th June.

During the Krefeld raid JD 244 arrived at the target, and the maximum height they could reach was 17,000 ft, which meant they were in the flak zone. The target was burning well but the flak was very heavy, and on the run-up they saw signs of numerous air combats over the target with aircraft breaking up or going down in flames. Many of these would be due to night fighter action, possibly including 'Wilde Sau' operating above the flak zone. At the time with all the combats going on, Fred felt that flak may be the lesser of two evils. The Bomb Aimer lined up on the green indicators but a red TI indicated that 'creep back' was occurring so they bombed on the red. The Bomb Aimer called "bombs gone" and when the camera indicator light showed a bombing photo had been taken, Fred turned hard to Port, about 70 degrees, and dived about 400 ft. Then a flak explosion under the port wing turned the Halifax over onto its side with shrapnel rattling on the fuselage. The aircraft dropped for at least 5,000 ft before the Pilot was able to regain control and level out. During this traumatic period the Wireless Operator had his face slammed down onto the desk and suffered a tremendous pain due to the build up of pressure in his ears. Having levelled out Fred now realised that the port inner engine was over-revving and the port outer was blazing furiously, so he closed the port throttles, opened up the starboard ones, and feathered the port engines. With the fire extinguisher, which was located in the engine nacelle, he was able to put out the flames on the port outer. A crew check revealed that all the crew were OK but the Flight Engineer reported that petrol was leaking from the port tanks at a very fast rate. The starboard engines were starting to overheat because of excessive drag caused by the open bomb doors which could not be closed because there was no pressure in the hydraulic system. Fred was now encountering the problem of assymetric flying of a Halifax with the early fin and rudder system. The pressure required to control the rudder pedal was so excessive that Fred asked Bill Berresford the Wireless Op to slip his oxygen tube over the starboard rudder pedal and pull on it to take some of the pressure off his foot.

The engines continued to overheat and height was being steadily lost at the rate of several hundred feet a minute so the crew were asked to jettison excessive weight. The Navigator reported that the aircraft's present position was just past Eindhoven and doubted if they would reach the coast. The Pilot realised that ditching with bomb doors open would be a very risky business as the aircraft would sink very rapidly so it was agreed to turn towards Belgium and bale out. Heading for Belgium at about 4,000 ft the Pilot gave the order to bale out, but the Flight Engineer, Doug Keane, wanted to stay with Fred until he was ready to jump last, however Fred told him to jump in the proper order. The Flight Engineer and Mid Upper Gunner both realised that Fred had no hope of baling out. Fred noticed that all the crew had baled out except the Rear Gunner so he called out over the intercom and found out he was still in the turret and could not get out because he could not open the doors. He had been wounded in the back and arms but did not report this. However, a short while later he called out to say he had managed to get out of the turret and would jump in a few seconds.

With regard to the crew who baled out, the Navigator landed in the courtyard of an electricity station and next morning was taken prisoner along with the Wireless Operator, they were then joined by the Rear Gunner who needed medical treatment. The Air Bomber landed safely, was picked up by local Resistance workers and managed to stay free for six months until he was eventually captured in Antwerp. The Flight Engineer hid in a barn but the farmer discovered him and returned with German troops. The Mid Upper Gunner was lucky enough to find a friendly tavern and spent the day there drinking, until the local resistance workers contacted him and helped him to stay free for about six months. Unfortunately he was captured when trying to cross the frontier into Switzerland.

After a short period when he considered the last of his crew would have jumped, Fred tried to escape from the forward hatch but could not get out. He therefore returned to his seat, at which stage the aircraft was in a steep diving turn to port, so in order to level the aircraft out he opened up the engines and switched on the landing light in the starboard wing. Below him he observed tree tops and started to clip them at about 135 mph. The trees seemed to disappear and Fred said to himself "This is the end" as he pulled back the stick and cut the throttles, feeling for the ground. The tail touched, the port wing dropped and Fred was thrown sideways and forwards across the cockpit and knocked unconscious.

When Fred regained consciousness the first thing he noticed was an orange glow, which quickly alerted him because he thought it was a fire, but it turned out to be the lamp on the Navigator's desk. He climbed out of the hatch above the cockpit with pains in his face, head and legs, and walked around the wrecked aircraft (Photo 43). He could not find the Thermite bomb to fire the aircraft but did find the pigeon and a Very pistol. There was a pool of petrol which had seeped from the aircraft so Fred set this alight and flames started to spread which caused the ammunition to explode. He picked up the pigeon container and walked away from the aircraft planning to release it with a message.

POST-OPERATIONS AND LOSSES

Unfortunately he lost the message capsule in a ditch so he took a page from a small pocket book and wrote the message "Target bombed. Hit flak both ports. Crew baled out. Crash landed. Aircraft destroyed. Walking home. Heathfield 1235550" and tied the message with thread from his escape kit to the pigeon's leg. The pigeon was released and Fred waved goodbye to the last of his crew, W/C Pickard, an ex 51 Squadron CO had stated at an OTU that "Pigeons are members of a crew and must be saved". Fred presumes that the pigeon message reached the squadron because at a Dulag Luft he met 'Curly' Manning, a W/Op. with P/O Cates crew, who was shot down in September 1943. 'Curly's' first words to Fred were "Sgt Heathfield walking home", which was the information which he had seen pinned up on the crew room notice board. Jack Adams the Pigeon Corporal at Snaith reported that a pigeon returned to its loft in a very exhausted and distressed condition and when he picked it up from its civilian loft it still had black thread on its leg but the message had been collected, probably by Sgt Davidson from 4 Group HQ.

Fred managed to get a ride in the coal wagon of a train travelling to Brussels and subsequently after various other incidents he boarded a freight train to Louvain, where he was helped by Resistance workers. The Resistance people took him to Brussels where he spent time in an apartment being designated as 'A Package', awaiting contact by members of the Evasion Line. From Brussels he took a train to Paris with several other 'Packages' and thence to a small hotel. Unfortunately there was a traitor in the Resistance because they were arrested in the hotel and taken to a prison at Fresnes where they had a rough time. This included being interrogated by the Gestapo before being taken to a POW camp, where Fred spent the rest of the war. This was an unusual incident in that the Pilot managed to make a successful crash landing and survive, the only one to do so out of 27 who crash landed in the same forest.

THE SQUADRONS MILITARY CROSS AWARD

Fred Heathfield's normal Air Bomber F/O Harry 'Nick' Nock had a minor accident so was not able to accompany Fred on the Krefeld raid. However on the 3rd of July he flew with Sgt Garnham on an operation to Cologne and on the way back they were attacked by a Bf 110. The fighter was piloted by a night fighter ace, Oberleutnant Meister, whose final score was 42 victories. Three engines were set on fire and two members of the crew killed, so the captain ordered the crew to bale out. The Navigator, Sgt Grimble, jumped first followed by F/O Nock who knocked the parachute off his chest on the edge of the escape hatch. Then whilst pulling the parachute down to his chest, so that he could reach the rip cord, he fell about 5,000 ft. This mishap probably saved his life because when he looked up he saw that the canopy of the crewman jumping after him had been set on fire by the exploding Halifax and burnt out so that the body fell past him without the restraint of a 'chute.

F/O Nock landed safely and was picked up by a Resistance Group, Sgt Grimble was captured and when quizzed about the unrecognisable body without a 'chute reported that it must be F/O Nock who jumped after him. The remains of the four bodies destroyed with the aircraft were buried as five bodies. The Germans believed they had accounted for all seven crew members, the body without a 'chute being buried as F/O Nock who was officially declared 'Killed in action' and his father received a condolence letter from King George VI. 'Nick' Nock remained in the Ardennes area working as a farm labourer and fighting with the Resistance until 'liberated' by the Americans in Sept 1944. He dug up his RAF uniform which he had buried, added the armband of the Resistance and was flown back to Northolt, after which he was interrogated, given a railway warrant, and sent home in a very bedraggled uniform without a hat. He arrived home in Wolverhampton to the surprise of his parents, was awarded the Military Cross for his services to the Resistance and is believed to be the only member of 51 Squadron to receive this decoration in WW2.

Whilst the Squadron was operating from Snaith a lot of other aircraft were lost and sadly a lot of brave men. All the Halifax losses are listed in Appendix 1 but it is not possible to describe them all in detail. Hopefully an examination of a selection of various types of losses or severely damaged aircraft will give a general picture of what was involved in the loss of or severe damage to an aircraft.

THE SQUADRON'S EXPERIENCE OF GERMAN ATROCITIES

Dave Greenwood, was an Air Bomber with the Squadron, who after the war became ordained in the church, and latterly resided in America. At the 1990 Squadron Reunion he gave the sermon at the Sunday morning church service and mentioned his first operation at Snaith. He told the congregation how he and the rest of Les Byrne's crew were waiting apprehensively in the crew room when a tall pleasant mannered Pilot in dark blue RAAF uniform came over to them. He spoke to the new crew in a very supportive manner and finished by saying "Don't worry, you'll be OK on this operation". He was Flying Officer Jack Paradise. At 23 he seemed a very much older man than Dave.

During the Rheine Operation on the 21 March 1945, Les Byrne was Captain of a squadron Halifax over the target when he saw Jack Paradise's aircraft MH-D MZ 348 badly damaged by flak. Being a daylight raid a bombing photo taken by one of the squadron aircraft at a higher altitude showed a hole in the wing and fuselage of MZ 348. As Dave Greenwood watched from the Bomb Aimers position he saw parachutes emerge from the stricken bomber and thankfully counted seven of them. All seven crew landed safely. One of them, Air Gunner Val Hood, landed on a roof and rolled off so that his body got wrapped in his parachute, landing in the snow. He was apprehended by some Italian workers who handed him over to the authorities and along with his colleague Les Hart finished the war as a POW. The other five members of the crew, F/O Jack Paradise (RAAF), F/O Berwick (RAAF), P/O Greenwood (RAAF), F/Sgt Armstrong and F/Sgt Gunn both RAF, were all captured in a village near Dreierwalde Airfield. During the raid bombs had been dropped on the airfield, the home base of JG 27 Fighter Unit and 40 workers had been killed. After some ill treatment the five airmen were taken to the airfield and locked in a cell in the Guardroom.

On the 22 March arrangements were made for the five prisoners to be moved to Oberursel for dispatch to a POW Camp, so an escort was required to take them to the railway station. There was a Training Unit for Junior NCO's at Dreierwalde Airfield and its resident Sergeant Major was Oberfeldwebel Karl Ambeger who volunteered with two of his men to act as an escort. Ambeger was an ex airman who had been shot down during the Battle of Britain but had been repatriated to Germany as being medically unfit. The three escorts paraded the five airman to march them to the station, but not far from the airfield they turned off the road on to a rough track with woods on one side and fields on the other, where the prisoners were made to walk abreast. The Germans then opened fire with the Schmeisser machine pistols which they were carrying and four of the RAF men were killed. Berwick who had two bullet wounds in his left thigh managed to flee into the woods to the right hand side of the track and thus escape. He was on the run for two days and after being hunted by Germans with dogs and motor vehicles he surrendered on the 1st April and was treated in accordance with the Geneva Convention.

Apparently, this was not the only case of airmen being shot by Germans from Dreierwalde.

After the war at the War Crimes Trials evidence was provided by Berwick, he reported that he had heard a click from the Germans' weapons and turning round saw them ready to open fire, which gave him the signal to make a run for it. At his trial Oberfeldwebel Karl Ambeger was found guilty and executed by hanging in Hamelin Prison on 16 May 1946. This was particularly inexcusable behavior from a person who had been treated humanely by the British as a POW and repatriated.

"TWO OF OUR AIRCRAFT ARE MISSING FROM LAST NIGHT'S OPERATIONS".

This brief announcement over the radio on the morning of 8 March 1943, informed the country of the losses suffered by Bomber Command on the nights of 7/8 March due to operations against Germany. What had happened to the aircraft and their crews? The operations that night had involved a small number of aircraft engaged on minelaying tasks. One of the aircraft missing was despatched by 51 Squadron. This was Halifax Mk II Series 1 (Special) serial No DT567, MH-F, Captained by P/O A L Holmes. This crew was fairly new to the Squadron having been with it for only a month after arriving from an HCU Course at Riccall and it was only their second operation from Snaith. The take off time was 1826, ETA over target was to be 2011 and ETA back at Base 2201, but unfortunately they never returned.

Frequently the new crews were sent on minelaying ('gardening') operations on their own in order to give them experience before participating in a major raid with the whole Squadron. Bomber Command appeared to have the conception that minelaying was an easier trip than an operation over Germany (possibly because aircraft losses were lower at around 2%). However, the chances of a lone aircraft being intercepted were possibly greater than when included in a bomber stream since the 'Freya' EW Radar could pick up single aircraft over the sea and alert the night fighters in their zone. Mine dropping operations could be quite tricky and if the aircraft could not drop the mine accurately then it had to be brought back to Snaith.

In the first Operation by P/O Holmes' crew on the 2 March 1943, two aircraft from the Squadron were engaged in 'Gardening' and we can examine this operation to consider the problems of minelaying. For this operation both aircraft carried two B200 mines, which were the magnetic double contact GP type to be dropped from 5,000 ft. Because these were dropped by parachute there was a maximum dropping speed of 200 mph since at a faster speed the parachute could be pulled away from the mine when released. In order to drop the mine in the correct position, as detailed by the Royal Navy, a visual pin-point on land was specified from which the aircraft had to carry out a time and distance run before dropping the mines with a definite interval between them, typically about 3 seconds. In addition, so that the Germans could not pin-point the dropping position on Radar the aircraft was required to continue on the same course for a suitable period of time. The pin-point for P/O Holmes' aircraft, for this operation, DT730, was the SW tip of Vlieland as shown in Map 10, along with a hypothetical mine dropping course of the type which the squadron aircraft could have used to drop mines in the sea lanes. The other aircraft, DT582, could not obtain a visual pin-point so the mines were dropped by 'Gee'

MAP 10 (Below)

Mine Laying Area In Frisian Islands

Crosses indicate a post war plot of wrecks in the locality, many of which were due to mining operations.

Dotted line indicates likely mine dropping track from pin point on Vlieland

fix. Because it was important to drop the mine in the correct position if the pin-point could not be identified the Captain was ordered to bring the mine back. Aircraft could land with mines on board, since they had arming devices such as soluble plugs and hydrostatic detonators.

Up to the time of this operation in April 1943, over 20 thousand mines had been layed by the RAF in enemy waters, resulting in the sinking of or damage to 500 ships. By the end of the war Bomber Command had laid 47,307 sea mines, which had sunk 842 German ships with many more damaged. Map 10 shows a post war plot of the large number of wrecks in the vicinity of the Freisian Islands many due to mines laid during the war.

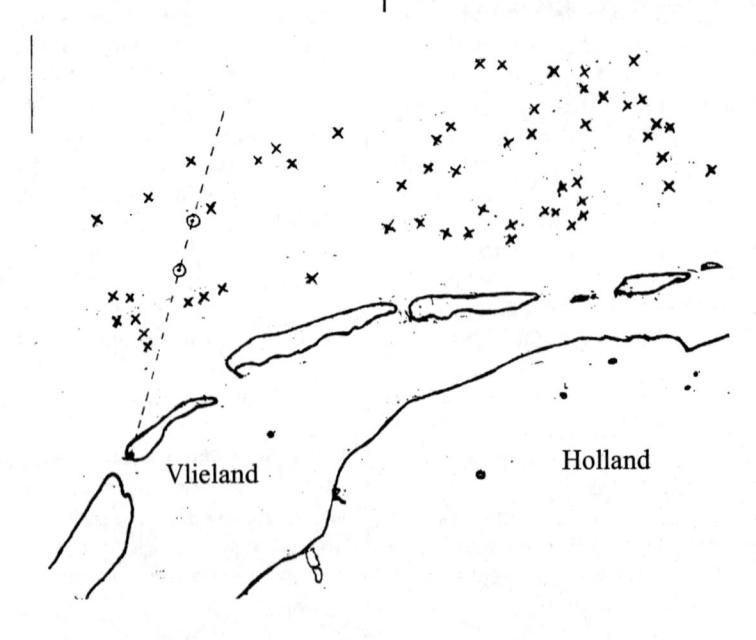

Another minelaying incident of interest occurred during the operation of the 28th April 1943 when 207 aircraft, of various types, took part in the largest 'Gardening' operation of the war in sea areas around Denmark. The squadron supplied 9 aircraft carrying a variety of mines including types B200 (magnetic double contact), G708 (acoustic trigger, single contact, magnetic firing) and A108 (magnetic). Aircraft HR789, MH-Z captained by Sgt Wilson was detailed to drop mines in the Kattegat area (code named 'Silverthorn'). They flew along the Skagerak and then turned south to fly down the Kattegat trying to avoid the Radar coverage. Low 10/10 cloud over the target area forced the aircraft to come down to a low level in order to be able to identify the mine dropping area and start their dropping run from a pin point on a spit of land called Sjaellands Odde, jutting out to the west from Sjaelland. As they were crossing the spit a flak battery suddenly opened up on them and Louis Wooldridge in the m.u.. turret fired back blindly at the location of the guns.

After dropping the mines the aircraft flew North West up the Kattegat towards Jutland and then back across the North Sea, landing safely at Snaith. There is an interesting sequel to this sortie since a Dane named Frank Weber, who had been writing a book on minelaying, made contact with Louis Wooldridge. The Dane reported that he had seen a German war diary in the Danish PRO which contained information on operations by the flak batteries in Denmark. The diary included a report on the flak battery which opened fire on HR789 on 28th April. This stated that when a four engined aircraft approached the battery at 820 ft they opened fire with 20mm and machine guns between 0052 and 0054 hrs, claiming a hit, which was incorrect. During the operations that night the battery recorded that it fired 229 rounds of 20mm shells and 320 rounds of machine gun ammunition.

Getting back to the loss of DT567 on 7/8 March, when operating over the Freisians this aircraft could have been detected by 'Freya' radar in the 'Tiger' night fighter box. It would have been able to alert Luftwaffe unit 11/NJG 2, on Leeuwarden airfield to the presence of an enemy aircraft. In addition there were flak batteries on the coast and islands along with flak ships on patrol.

The first news of the crew came on the 4.4.43 when the body of the Navigator Sgt.J.G.Ramshaw was washed ashore on the Dutch Frisian Island of Ameland. The body was found on the north side of the island by a German soldier on patrol near the 23 kilometre marker on the beach. The German Commander informed the local Dutch police who sent one of their members to investigate the sighting and identify the body. The local policeman, Johannes Monderman from the main village of Nes, carried out the identification and compiled a comprehensive report on his findings listing all the items of clothing with identity markings and service number, the identity discs verifying the markings on the clothes. The body was put in a coffin on the beach and transferred to the mortuary at the General Cemetery in Nes-Ameland by a local merchantman, Hendrick Nienhuis, using his horse drawn wagon. A German Doctor examined the body and estimated it had been dead about a month. After obtaining permission from the Dutch civil authorities and the German Commandant, Sgt Ramshaw was buried with Military Honours on the 7 April 1943 in the general cemetery at Nes Ameland.

The bodies of three other members of the crew were also washed up on the beaches. The next member of the crew to be found was Sgt.P.J.McAleese the Mid-Upper Gunner. His body was washed up on the west shore of the German island of Sylt on the 20 April 1943. The island being near the Danish border meant the body had been carried a considerable distance by the North Sea currents, which sweep along the Dutch and German coast in this area. Sgt McAleese was buried in Westerland Cemetery a few days later, after the same identification procedure had been carried out by the German authorities. The third member of the crew to be found was the Pilot and Captain, P/O A L Holmes, whose body was washed up on the Dutch island of Rottumerug on the 29 April 1943 and was buried in Borkum Cemetery a few days later. The fourth member of the crew to be washed ashore was Sgt G Tombe the Rear Gunner. His body was found on the 21 May 1943 on the shore of Norderney island in the German Frisian group, approximately eleven weeks after being shot down, a long time and a long journey before his final land fall. Sgt Tombe was buried in Norderney Military Cemetery,

The body of F/Sgt R E Dorman the Wireless Operator, was spotted in the sea by a patrol boat of the 12th Flotilla, B Group at position 53.30N, 5.27E, and buried at sea, the date of this find was not listed in the report, but this position is only about 20 miles from where the Navigator was found on the beach of Ameland. It was presumed this was probably near the spot where the aircraft was shot down into the sea.

The other two crew members were never found and therefore listed as lost at sea. They were Sgt A R Harding, the Flight Engineer and P/O J E Ulrich the Air Bomber.

When the war ended it was decided to bring all the bodies of the airmen buried in the outlying places to central cemeteries on the mainland of Germany, and in pursuance of this policy the crewmen buried on the German Frisnian islands were transferred to the mainland. The body of Sgt McAleese was reinterred in the main cemetery for the RAF at Kiel, the bodies of P/O Holmes and Sgt Tombe were reinterred in the main cemetery at Old Sage near Oldenburg. The grave of Sgt Ramshaw was the only one left undisturbed, his body is interred along with sixty other allied airmen, soldiers and sailors washed up on the shores of Ameland during the five years of the Second World War.

POST-OPERATIONS AND LOSSES

LOSS BY DITCHING

Since the squadron aircraft had to cross water to approach the European mainland, ditching in the sea was always a possibility. The crew mentioned in the previous loss report were no strangers to the hazards of operating over the sea because on an OTU course at St Eval, in Cornwall, five members had ditched in the atlantic in Nov 1942 due to an engine failure. They spent 50 hours in a `Q' type dinghy 300 miles out in the atlantic and after being located by one of the Unit's Whitleys were rescued by a Polish destroyer. This entitled them to membership of the Goldfish Club. The Goldfish Club was founded in 1942 by the Hon. Secretary of the club Mr Charles A Robertson, then the Chief Draughtsman of P B Cow & Co Ltd, one of the largest manufacturers of air sea rescue equipment. Membership was open to any member of the RAF who had escaped death from drowning by the use of an emergency inflatable dinghy. A copy of the certificate and badge awarded to S/Ldr Geoff Bond is shown in Fig 4.

"ANY CONVOYS EXPECTED"

This remark was shouted out by the assembled aircrew at a 51 Squadron briefing following the loss of aircraft DT742 piloted by F/Sgt Collins. The aircraft took off from Snaith on the 11.6.43 for an operation against Dusseldorf, flew south to cross the coast over East Anglia but ran into trouble with the port outer engine which went on fire. The Pilot therefore decided to abort the sortie and cross the coast to jettison his bombs in the English Channel. When they dropped their bombs they were unaware of the presence of convoy No FS 83 until the Merchant ships in the convoy opened fire on them. The Halifax crew fired off the colours of the day, but these were not recognised by the Merchant ships since they did not have copies of the recognition code. The aircraft was shot down in sea position 53.06N 01.10E, about 10 miles NE of Sheringham. The aircraft loss was blamed on the poor fire control organisation in the convoy. There was one casualty, Sgt P G Spreckley, the rest of the crew being saved by the Air Sea Rescue Organisation.

Two members of the crew were awarded the Air Force Medal for their part in this incident. The DFM was not applicable since they were shot down by 'Friendly Fire'.

There was a recognised ditching procedure in which the Flight Engineer had a key role. All crew members acknowledged the ditching order from the Captain and the Engineer opened the front ditching escape hatch. Then with the assistance of the mid-upper AG the rear ditching escape hatch was opened and the life line detached ready for an exit. When ditching was imminent all crew members would take up ditching positions, inflate `Mae Wests' and brace themselves. The Wireless Operator switched the IFF set to the distress position and sent out a message with the T1154 giving the aircraft's position based on information received from the Navigator, which normally included course, height, airspeed, position and time (C.H.A.P.T.). If it was only possible to send a short message then the position could be sent as `Gee' co-ordinates. Take the hypothetical example of a squadron aircraft due east of Snaith, which is having to ditch 50 miles off the coast. The `Gee' fix of B2.4 and C43.2 in the Eastern chain (EA) could have been sent as two 7 figure groups as follows; B0240EA C4320EA.

There was also a technique which some Wireless Operators were prepared to carry out in order to warn the crew of the instant of impact. This involved transmitting on a distress frequency with the morse key clamped down and the trailing aerial out. The instant the trailing aerial touched the water the Aerial Current and RF meters would indicate a dip so that the W/Op. could call out a warning over the intercom. After the aircraft had ditched and come to a rest the Engineer pulled the manual dinghy release and holding the lifeline climbed out onto the port mainplane through the rear ditching hatch. In 1943 when pigeons were carried, the W/Op. and another member of the aircrew would collect a pigeon carrier each to take it into the dinghy. Finally when every crew member had made an exit and boarded the dinghy the painter would be cut and the dinghy cast off.

In the dinghy a message would be written out and attached to the pigeon's leg before releasing it. During 1944 when an emergency radio transmitter had replaced the pigeons it was the W/Op's.

FIG 4. Via S/Ldr G. Bond
Goldfish Club Certificate And Badge

responsibility to collect this from the port side of the fuselage and take it into the dinghy. On board the dinghy the W/Op. would fly a kite to elevate the aerial wire. By rotating the generator handle a signal on the distress frequency of 500 K/cs would be produced. It was possible to send either a keyed or a continuous distress signal. There were also facilities for operating a signal lamp. The signal could be picked up at a range of 200 miles by an aircraft flying at 2,000 ft.

SOME OF THE MANY CANDIDATES FOR CATER- PILLAR CLUB MEMBERSHIP

The two main types of parachute used by the RAF in WW2 were the seat pack which the wearer sat on and the two point detachable pack for aircrew who needed to move around the aircraft, when the seat type would be too cumbersome. With the detachable pack squadron aircrew were fitted out with a harness by the Parachute Section, which they wore over their flying gear. In the Halifax there were special storage points for the parachutes belonging to the various crew members. When the aircrew needed to evacuate the aircraft, they grabbed their 'chutes and clipped them onto the front of their harnesses with snap hooks. Then after leaving the aircraft they opened the 'chute by pulling the rip cord.

In 1922 Leslie Irvin, of the Irvin Airchute Company, formed the Caterpillar Club, the name being derived from the silk worm, since silk was used in parachutes before the advent of synthetic polymers. Any airman whose life had been saved by the use of a parachute could apply for membership of the club, which issued them with a membership certificate and a small gold caterpillar lapel badge. An example of one of the certificates is shown in Fig 20. The first airmen to gain membership were Americans since the RAF did not start issuing parachutes till 1926. Their use by the RAF was occasioned by the death of a number of airmen in 1924, a scathing editorial in the 'Aeroplane' and public opinion. A Parachute Development Unit at Hendon carried out tests jumping from aircraft.

In WW2 34,000 airmen were enrolled as members of the club, thankful for the availability of a

**FIG 20 (above) via W. Powell
Caterpillar Club**

parachute. A fair number of 51 Squadron aircrew are included in the foregoing. The following is a personal report by Sgt Ken Goodchild, W/Op. on how the crew of an aircraft, named 'Yehudi Menuhin', escaped by parachute

**FIG 36 via A. Ashton
Drawing Of A 'Q' Type Dinghy**

83

POST-OPERATIONS AND LOSSES

during the Duisburg raid on the night of 12/13.5.43.

"Regarding my Duisburg raid, four 51s were lost that night, 13.5.43. Yours truly was flying in MH-J which included in the crew Sgt Bev Brown Pilot RAAF, Sgt Navigator "Chick" Henderson RAF, Sgt Johnny Rae Bomb Aimer RAF, Sgt A.L.G. Knight RAF Engineer, Sgt North-Lewis Mid Upper RAF and Sgt Philip De Bourbon Rear Gunner RCAF. I seem to remember we took off around 2200 hours from Snaith on the 12 May and flew north toward Stirling in Scotland to gain height and then south again crossing the coast over Scarborough. Somewhere over the North Sea we listened to the Ivy Benson band from the BBC (highly illegal) and heard that Jerry in North Africa had surrendered bringing the war in that theatre to an end that day and that thousands of prisoners had been captured. Imagine how elated we all were. Shortly after this a large explosion in front removed most of the front turret and it became rather windy in the aircraft - a near miss from Ack Ack. Next, standing on the staircase alongside the pilot, I watched a Lanc, caught in searchlights suddenly evaporate as a shell hit his bomb bay, this was followed by another blast close by and the Navigator slumped over his desk - he had shrapnel in his back. We took him aft to the bunk and administered morphine - 'blood' was oozing from his mouth so we thought he'd caught it in the lungs. I wiped his 'blood' from his mouth only to realise it wasn't blood but chocolate he'd been eating - in the green cabin light it was hard to tell the difference.

It was by now time for the Group broadcast from Base so I returned to my set and listened to the transmission from home - nothing of interest so I tuned in to the Jerry broadcasts vectoring their aircraft onto us. We used to do this then retune the transmitter to their frequency. We had a carbon mike fitted to the cylinder head of the starboard inner engine and with the transmitter on full power, blocked Jerry signals by transmitting our engine noise at about 50 watts on M.C.W. It must have blown their heads off and was great fun - they used to get so exasperated and swear at us in English. The system was called 'tinselling', why I don't know. A short while later there was a whooshing sound by my right elbow (bear in mind the W/Op's. position was directly below the pilot and the staircase alongside both). A large hole appeared in the top step and all the fuses blew on one generator. The Skipper said he had a draught from the roof. A shell had gone right through us from bottom to top and not exploded missing both me and the Skipper by about 18 inches. We now lined up for our run on the oil refinery and bombed the target with no further excitement.

We set course for home and put the aircraft into a shallow dive to reduce height to 15,000 ft, our return altitude. Over Holland we were attacked by a FW.190 and a JU.88 who made a converging attack. We avoided two passes but on the third they riddled the tail plane and the controls jammed leaving us without rudder and elevators in a nose down attitude. Also the starboard wing caught fire from loose petrol from a damaged tank, probably from the flak. The Skipper, Flight Engineer and myself tried to haul the stick back to no avail so the Skipper ordered everyone out - then the fun began. The centre section was ablaze so we hauled the Navigator out, attached his 'chute to a static line and slung him out of the forward hatch, closely followed by the Bomb Aimer. The Gunners went out of the rear and next out was the Flight Engineer who sat on the hatch for ages with me waiting behind him. I thought he had funked the jump so I kicked him out, only to learn later he had been caught up in the airframe by his intercom cord and when I kicked him out I nearly hung him. By now we had parted company with the starboard outer which had gone careering off on its own somewhere howling like a Banshee, so I jumped fast followed by the Skipper. I'm glad to record we all survived. The Nav's wound missed his lung by an eighth of an inch and he left hospital six weeks later as did the Rear Gunner, who hit the tail plane on the way out. The Bomb Aimer broke an ankle and I landed in a haystack with only a minor face scratch - we were very lucky. Of thirty-odd aircraft lost that night each with a crew of 7, only 16 men survived and we were 7 of them."

WAS IT "GREMLINS" OR THE "MURPHY FACTOR" WITH A NEW AIRCRAFT

This is a personal report by Air Bomber Rex Payne of the loss of a new aircraft the first time a crew took it on an operation. New aircraft could arrive with 'Bugs' in them, often due to the urgency with which new aircraft were produced. As mentioned in Chapter 8, because of the pressure on the Engineering Services, at the beginning of 1944 the newly formed Major Servicing Section was given the task of 'De-bugging' new aircraft. In 1943 with the best will in the world the overstretched squadron ground crews were not always able to spot 'Bugs' in new aircraft, as exemplified by the Bomb Selector Unit problem described in Chapter 10.

Rex reports: "On Tuesday 10th August 1943, we took off on a trip to Nurnburg but when we were airborne, discovered that the flaps would not come up and that the starboard wheel was still most of the way down. Owing to this the aircraft would only climb very slowly, with the engines fully opened up. We managed to hand pump the flaps up but the wheel would not budge. Eventually we managed to climb to three thousand feet and decided to set course for the coast so as to drop the bombs. A few seconds later, however, the constant speed unit of the starboard outer engine went, and with a terrific roar the engine registered 4,000 revs. It was impossible to feather it in this condition, so we cut off the switches and the petrol. By this time though smoke was pouring from it and soon after it burst into flames. The aircraft began to lose height rapidly and Mac decided to drop the bombs in a suitable field, so I went down the nose and looked around. We ran into more trouble, however, as

apart from a few of the incendiaries, the bombs all hung up, including the thousand pounder. Not a comforting thought.
Mac next ordered us back into our crash positions, so I left the nose. We were down to a thousand feet by this time and Mac had decided to belly land her in the fields. At five hundred feet, the fire which had been spreading along the wing, reached the inner engine and this also cut. In spite of this, Mac put her down nicely and everything was going fine when the only house for miles around loomed up in the gloom and we struck it with our starboard wing. A gaping hole was ripped in the starboard side of the fuselage and within seconds the plane was a mass of flames from end to end. I decided to try the rear hatch and, after clearing away a lot of wreckage, managed to get it open. Yelling to the others to follow, I scrambled through with nothing worse than a slightly burnt hand. Tony and Dinty soon followed, both badly burnt about the face and hands. Joe came out through one of the top hatches, after the ladder he was climbing had broken and suffered rather badly from the flames sweeping across the plane. Ralph came out of his rear turret with only a shaking but Mac, who had to jump down from his cockpit, arrived on the ground via an outhouse, with his clothes a mass of flames, and was only saved by Ralph rolling him over in the grass until the flames were out. Nothing at all was heard of Silvo who must gave been killed instantly by wreckage coming through the starboard side of the plane.
As the bombs were on the plane, we hurried away tearing the smouldering clothes off Mac as we ran. We managed to reach a labourer's cottage, and leaving the four burnt members there, Ralph and I went off in opposite directions to bring help. After half an hour an ambulance arrived and took us to the Station Sick Quarters at RAF Hemswell in Lincolnshire. After Mac, Tony, Dinty and Joe had their burns dressed, they were taken to Lincoln Military Hospital; Ralph and I returned to Snaith the following morning, were screened and granted eighteen days leave."

A report on this crash which appeared in the national press on 12 August 1943 stated that when an RAF plane crashed on a cottage at Cliff Farm, Snittersby, near Brigg, Peter Clarke the stepson of the farm worker who lived there, was standing in the road waiting for his stepfather to come home. He saw the Halifax with what appeared to be an engine fire head straight for the cottage and crash into it, setting it on fire, with bullets from the aircraft exploding. Peter found the door of the cottage jammed with debris but with difficulty managed to lever it open wide enough to drag his brother and sister out to safety. He then tried to reach his mother and baby sister but was driven back by the intense heat and when his father arrived there was nothing further he could do.

The crew of of this aircraft comprised W J Macpherson (Mac) Pilot, A T Ellis (Tony) Navigator, R V Payne (Rex) Air Bomber, C Silvester (Silvo) Wireless Operator, F S Moores (Dinty) Flight Engineer, J M Grudzein (Joe) M/U Air Gunner, and W R Clow (Ralph) Rear Air Gunner.

THE NIGHT ANDY LOST HIS NOSE

An unusual accident occurred to Halifax MZ465 MH-Y piloted by F/L Andy Wilson which took off on the 13 Jan 1945 for an operation against Saarbrucken. During the operation the Halifax was flying at a height of 7,000 feet and at 2010 hours had reached a position 40.15N, 14.08E. At this stage the Pilot was checking the reading on his DR compass repeater preparatory to changing course but on looking up he suddenly saw a Halifax crossing in front of his aircraft from starboard. He had no time to prevent the collision which occurred, the rear port fins of the aircraft which hit him taking away ten feet of the nose of his aircraft and two members of his crew with a tremendous vibration. (Photo 46). The other aircraft, which was LL590 from No 347 Free French Squadron at Elvington, crashed killing four of the crew. Andy Wilson's aircraft dived and lost about 4,500 feet before the Pilot managed to regain control. On levelling out it was found that the ASI, DRC, intercom, 'Gee' and H2S were unserviceable and the artificial horizon and climb and descent instruments on the BFP were fluctuating. The control system was still functioning but the aircraft was very heavy to handle with a continual tendency to turn to port. The pilot climbed the aircraft to 11,000 feet at which height it stalled and lost height finally levelling off at about a height of 7,500 feet on a north-westerly course. The Wireless Operator tried to operate the T1154/R1155 radios for a short period to send out a distress message but found there were numerous blue flashes due to shorting, so he switched off. The IFF was switched to the distress position at 2015 and 11 Group responded to it.

When the aircraft reached England there was 10/10 low cloud at 4,000 feet and the Pilot did not break cloud until he saw Sandra lights indicating the presence of an airfield. On breaking cloud he was given a green Very signal by the ACP to land at Ford aerodrome. A steep approach was made with the aircraft swinging badly as the speed was reduced, but a perfect landing was achieved. Andy did not receive any official recognition for this feat of airmanship. Later on when discussing the incident with W/Op Ron Holmes he told him that "The old man at Snaith was more concerned about his bloody aeroplane than he was about the two men killed in my collision. They don't like you bending their aeroplanes at Snaith". SEVERELY DAMAGED BUT RETURNED

An example of the severe damage which a Halifax could suffer and still get back to base is that sustained by MH-B HR868. This aircraft took part in a raid on Frankfurt on the night of 20 Dec 1943 piloted by P/O Mackenzie. On the way to the target the aircraft was attacked by an enemy night fighter firing cannon shells, some of which went the full length of the fuselage. The Bomb Aimer was fatally wounded and taken to the rest position where the crew rendered first aid, but he died before reaching base. Incendiaries in the bomb bay were set on fire, the wing bomb bay doors jammed partly open, the flaps dropped 15 degrees and the port elevator was considerably damaged (see photo No 45). The captain jettisoned the HE bombs but was not able to jettison an SBC containing 4 lb incendiaries, however he managed to bring the aircraft back and land safely. The Armourers reported that when they came to open the bomb doors to remove hang ups, they found the interior of the bomb bay covered with the dead crewman's blood.

"IT'S AWFULLY DRAUGHTY WITHOUT THE 'PERSPEX'"

The background to the Villers Bocage operation on 30.6.44 is reported in Chapter 7 and as already mentioned elsewhere, during this period of operations maximum effort was expected from the squadron when participating in an operation. F/Lt Jim Feaver, the captain of MH-S, was detailed for this raid but was kept waiting for the order to go ahead since the operation was postponed several times because of the weather over the target. Two of Jim's crew members were unfit so he had to borrow a Navigator and a Bomb Aimer from another crew which was not on the Order of Battle. These temporary crew members were Navigator John MacCoss and Bomb Aimer Ian Craib, but at the last minute Ian was replaced by S/Ldr Simmonds. S/Ldr Simmonds was acting Squadron Commander and at the main briefing one of his instructions was that if cloud obstructed the target the squadron should descend to 4,000 ft to bomb.

It was a fine summer's evening when MH-S took off at 1901 hrs and John gave Jim Feaver a course to fly crossing the South coast heading for France. Having reached the operational height of 14,000 ft on track for the Normandy battle area it was necessary to dog leg three times to maintain the ETA at the target. As 'S' Sugar was crossing the French coast a message was received from the Master Bomber stating "cloud base at 4,000 ft". As mentioned in Chapter 7 the Master Bomber was bringing the aircraft down to low altitude to ensure bombing accuracy, this order being cancelled when the cloud over the target cleared. Jim Feaver made a rapid descent and levelled out at 4,500 ft, five or six other aircraft had taken similar action, but as the cloud had cleared over the target the bombers were stacked from 4,500 to 14,500 ft.

On approaching the target area the Bomb Aimer excitedly identified the concentration of German armour which was their target and the bombing run was commenced. Over the target the Flight Engineer, F/O Wallie Stocker, was standing in his position under the astrodome watching the aircraft above, one of which was only a few yards away, opening their bomb doors and releasing their cargo of bombs, some of which Wallie heard whistle past. The bomb doors were open and the Bomb Aimer had just called "Bombs Gone" when the aircraft was hit by flak and lurched violently. A howling gale started to blow through the aircraft because all the Perspex in the nose cone, windscreen, and astrodome had shattered, together with part of the starboard side nose section. The starboard inner engine had to be feathered because of damage and petrol was pouring out of a main tank. This meant that the Flight Engineer had to adjust the fuel transfer system to ensure that the remaining petrol in the damaged tank could be used up as soon as possible. After the explosion Navigator John MacCoss was trying to adjust the 'Gee' set, which appeared to have become u/s, when he noticed that his hand was covered in blood. Jim Feaver then ordered the Bomb Aimer to take John back to the rest position in order to render first aid. They had barely reached that position when the aircraft was again hit in the nose. The W/Op, F/sgt Eric Millet, who had some protection in his station under the Pilot nevertheless received a nasty wound with a piece of shrapnel sticking out of his right arm. Nick Simmonds who had his back towards the front of the aircraft received a serious flak wound in a painful place, being known thereafter as 'Flak up your jacksey Nick Simmonds'. Whilst all this was happening the gangway had become very slippery after flying through a rain storm.

The Pilot took evasive action involving a violent diving turn to starboard which proved successful as no more hits were received. Some of the electrics had failed, reducing the amount of instrumentation available and this combined with the gale blowing through the aircraft producing a loss of stability, made the Halifax very difficult to fly. After leaving the target area the skipper carried on with the difficult task of controlling the aircraft keeping in constant touch with the Flight Engineer to assess the situation. When the French coast came into view a decision was made to carry on to try and reach Sussex and then shortly after crossing the coast the Rear Gunner, Jock Smith, reported fighters dead astern but to everyones relief they turned out to be Hurricanes providing an escort back to England. On approaching Ford airfield the Flying Control was contacted via the distress frequency and a direct approach authorised. A successful landing was completed and the end of the runway reached with the pilot turning off on to the peri track. At this point the two engines which had brought them back safely suddenly decided to cut out. The skipper had carried out an excellent piece of airmanship by bringing the badly damaged aircraft across the channel to land safely, having pre-dated Andy Wilson's landing at the same airfield by seven months.

The three injured crew members were taken to hospital, John MacCoss was like a human pin cushion with about fifty pieces of shrapnel embedded in his skin. Thankfully all the injured crew members were eventually back on operations after a spell in hospital and sick leave. On this sortie 11,000 tons of bombs were dropped, with the loss of two aircraft one of which was a Lancaster Flying a short distance from 'S' Sugar on its port side. The operation thwarted the German attack.

BIRD STRIKE

On the 29th January 1945 Pilot Dave Waddington along with W/Op Ron Holmes and a Navigator and Flight Engineer were flown by F/O Bamsey in MH-F to Skipton on Swale to pick up a Halifax. The resident unit, 424 Squadron of the RCAF was converting to Lancasters so their Halifax aircraft were being disposed of, three of which were transferred to 51 Squadron. Dave Waddington's crew picked up a Halifax, presumably LW194, and flew it back to Snaith. At Snaith they were asked to take it up for an air test to find out if there were any snags present. On taking off the aircraft had reached a height of about 250 ft at full throttle when it was hit by a very large flock of seagulls. The 'Perspex' of the windscreens was shattered, with chunks of dead seagull flesh scattered all over the cockpit and adorning the Pilot's face. The air intakes to the engines were blocked and propellors bent. Dave Waddington managed, with great difficulty, to keep control of the aircraft and by a feat of airmanship landed it safely. The 'bent'

aircraft was then towed into the hangar for the necessary repairs.

DAMAGE TO A SQUADRON AIRCRAFT MADE THE NATIONAL PRESS

There was a write up in the national press about the raid on the 7th September 1943 against the armament centre at Mannheim and Ludwigshaven, twin towns on the opposite banks of the Rhine. The report claimed that 1,500 tons of bombs were dropped and included details of the damage sustained by a Halifax flown by Michael Foster. This was one of 21 aircraft from 51 Squadron operating that night, although as would be expected for security reasons the squadron to which the aircraft belonged was not mentioned.

Half an hour after leaving the target aircraft MH-D (see photo 41), was hit by a fighter's cannon shells and a tank in the starboard wing went on fire with a jet of flame streaming out backwards like a gas burner. The petrol tank kept on burning for about one and a half hours until they reached the French coast at which point the petrol tank exploded. Much to the surprise of the crew this blew the fire out (rather like blowing out an oil well fire with explosives). This resulted in the starboard aileron becoming buckled with the aileron control almost useless.

The aircraft was flown home shuddering and shaking and as a consequence was given a priority landing at Snaith. Just before landing the Pilot had to cut the starboard inner engine and feather it because of lack of petrol. The Rear Gunner reported to the press that there was a hole 3 ft across under the wing with enough space to put a dining room table in.

"LOOK OUT SKIPPER THERE'S A TRAIN COMING!"

On the 4.4.43, fifteen aircraft were detailed for an operation against Kiel with a bomb load of 2 x 1.000 lb HEs, 540 x 4 lb incendiaries, and 56 x 30 lb incendiaries plus a fuel load of 1,882 gallons. One of these aircraft was MH-Z, DT580 piloted by Claude Wilson in place of his normal aircraft, MH-V, which was unserviceable. When taking off, Louis Wooldridge in the mid upper turret noticed wisps of white smoke emitting from the exhaust manifolds of the four Merlin engines, usually the sign of a glycol leak. About half way down the runway with the tail up and approaching the final bounce before getting airborne, Louis noticed that

POST-OPERATIONS AND LOSSES

Photo 73 Crew Of MH-Z

the emissions had changed to a dense white cloud. Over the intercom he heard the Pilot comment to the Flight Engineer that the engines wee loosing power, so he broke in to mention the smoke, at which juncture the Flight Engineer 'Ginger' Anger reported that the fire extinguishers on all four engines had been activated, the effect being to reduce the power of the engines. The Halifax was fitted with impact switches which automatically activated fire extinguishers in the event of a crash.

As a consequence of the foregoing information the Pilot made a decision to abort the take-off, slamming the tail back down on the runway and applying the brakes as fiercely as possible, without nose diving the aircraft. By this time all the emergency vehicles parked outside the control tower were on the move towards the aborting aircraft and the mid upper gunner saw the smoke of an express rain approaching from the Selby direction. At the end of the runway there was a stretch of grass which led to the wooden fence bordering the railway embankment. Since he did not want to finish up on the railway line in the path of the approaching train, the Pilot ordered the crew to brace themselves for a sharp turn to port. Because of the rotation of the propeller this was the natural direction of swing of the aircraft. The Pilot cut the engines and used the rudder and port brake to turn the aircraft. This was a 'Dicey' operation since the strain on the undercarriage could snap it of and cause it to penetrate the wing tanks with the possibility of a fire or an explosion.

The aircraft swung to port and came to rest with the starboard wing overhanging the railway fence as a packed express train flashed past with the passengers waving to the Halifax crew. The aircraft was towed over to the hangar for engine and undercarriage repairs and since this was the only spare aircraft the crew were stood down from this operation.

THE RUNNYMEDE MEMORIAL.

The bodies of aircrew shot down over Europe are buried in numerous cemeteries tended by the Commonwealth War Graves Commission, such as the Reichswald war cemetary near Kleve. However many bodies were never recovered so their sacrifice is recorded on the Runnymede Memorial in Surrey where 20,455 names were inscribed. These include the names of 236 aircrew from 51 Squadron.

One such crew is that captained by P/O W Locksmith, which were lost in an operation against Duisburg on 12.5.43, flying in Halifax II HR786, MH-J. Shortly before reaching the target they were picked up by a blue radar controlled searchlight and then coned by the ancilliary searchlights. This aircraft was about 800 yds ahead and to the starboard of aircraft HR838, whose crew observed their plight. The Pilot made varying manoeuvres to try and escape the from the cone of light, without success, so the flak batteries opened up on the 'sitting duck'. The aircraft appeared to receive a fatal hit because it went into a steep dive, disappeared from view and failed to return from the operation.

In 1990 Louis Wooldridge learnt from sources in the Amsterdam area of Holland that this aircraft crashed at Jisp in Holland and buried itself in marshy ground. The bodies of the two Air Gunners were found and are buried in the Harlingen and Amsterdam cemeteries. The other bodies were never recovered and their names are recorded on the Runnymede memorial, but there are plans afoot to recover the aircraft and the bodies.

In October 1992, which by coincidence happened to be the 50th anniversary of the arrival of 51 Squadron at Snaith, a programme called 'Splendid Hearts' was broadcast on BBC television. This featured the Runnymede Memorial and demonstrated the trauma involved when the loss of a loved one was compounded by having no grave at which to mourn. The family of a 51 Squadron airman whose name is inscribed at Runnymede featured in the programme. F/Sgt William Vernon Willson, who was the airman in question, lost his life as the Navigator in Halifax III MZ507, which failed to return from an operation against Berlin on the night of 24/25 March 1944.

Over Germany an explosion in the nose of the aircraft ejected the Navigator Bill Willson and the Bomb Aimer John Scott (RAAF) without having a chance to collect their parachutes. The Signaller Alan Sidebotham also went out of the aircraft but fortunately he had managed to collect his parachute so he landed safely and finished up in a POW camp. Three of the crew (Pilot, Flight Engineer and rear Air Gunner) died after the aircraft crashed and the mid upper Air Gunner managed to crawl out of the turret, but was seriously injured.

Bill Willson's brother recently decided to try and find the Navigator's grave so he contacted Jim Gill (the Sqdn. Association Secretary) for possible sources of information, which include the AHB of the MOD. With the re-unification of Germany and ready access to the Eastern sector, information on the location of the grave became available. Consequently several members of the family accompanied by the sole surviving crew member, Alan Sidebotham, then visited the grave with the help of the BBC. The grave, which contained the bodies of Bill Willson, John Scott and Alf Taylor the rear AG, was located at Parchim, near the site of the Luftwaffe airfield to which the bodies were first taken.

AN EXAMPLE OF PERSONAL DEDICTION

On 14th November 1944 a crew captained by F/Sgt C W R Millard took off from Snaith in Halifax MH-H, LK844, for a training flight. Sadly the aircraft broke up in a high speed dive and crashed in a field near Tingley Cross Roads on the main Bradford to Wakefield road, all the crew being killed. A witness to the crash was a local schoolboy, 13 year old Walter Townend, who was so moved by the incident that in later life he decided that there should be some recognition of the crew's sacrifice. Walter therefore set himself the task of providing a memorial to the crew at Tingley Cross Roads near where the crash occurred. A dedication ceremony was carried out on Remembrance Sunday 12th November 1989 which was attended by relatives of four of the crew whom Walter had managed to contact, plus past and present members of the squadron. The memorial was unveiled by Dicky Pearce and George Booth of the Squadron Association who had flown in LK844, which was a veteran of 49 operations when it crashed.

CRASHES AT SNAITH

Numerous aircraft crashed at Snaith for various reasons and the following reports on a number of these incidents have been compiled from information at the Air Historical Branch of the MOD. Thanks to serving RAF Sgt Neil Henshaw (whose father served with the squadron) for his help in obtaining this information.

On the night of 25/26 May 1943 HR747 was returning from a raid on Dusseldorf when the pilot P/O R J Cribb carrying out a landing on QDM 231 overshot the runway. Having found that he could not get the aircraft to climb, the Pilot attempted to land in a field on the south side of the Heck-Pollington road, at the end of the runway. The hydraulics in the aircraft had been damaged by flak meaning that the undercarriage would not retract for a belly landing, so that when the aircraft landed it skidded for a considerable distance hitting two trees in the process. It eventually finished up in a large ditch to the west of the quarry, where all the crew emerged uninjured.

On the 25 Oct 1944 Halifax LL612 returned from a raid on Essen. When coming in to land the Pilot did not close the throttles until after touch down with the result that he was coming in too fast to land safely, so he should have gone round again. However he attempted a landing but the speed of the aircraft was such that he overshot the runway with the undercarriage collapsing. The aircraft then crashed through two hedges before stopping. One member of the crew was seriously injured and the Pilot had his log book endorsed.

In very poor visibility due to a ground mist, Halifax LV865 MH-Y piloted by F/O Twilley took off for Boulogne at 0727 on the 17 Sept 1944 with a full bomb load. A problem was experienced with one of the starboard engines during take off, producing a swing which the pilot could not correct. The Pilot attempted to get airborne at 110 mph, a speed which was too low for take off as a result of which the starboard wing hit the ground and the aircraft crashed into a fusing hut in the Bomb Dump. In this crash one crew member was killed and two seriously injured. Examination of the offending starboard engine after the crash revealed that some of the plugs had oiled up.

Aircraft MZ870 was taken up for a cross country and bombing execise on 1 Oct 1944. During the flight a hydraulic failure occurred because of a fluid leak from a faulty union in the pressure line, which was a frequent defect in the hydraulic system. Because of this leak the bomb doors would not close after the bombing exercise. The Pilot was inexperienced and when coming in to land with the bomb doors open came in too fast, as a result of which he overshot the end of the runway. The crew were uninjured in the crash.

During a night exercise on 27 Oct 1944 aircraft NR128 MH-S encountered problems with the starboard inner engine as indicated by the engine temperature and oil pressure readings. As a consequence the Pilot had to shut the engine down. When coming in to land on three engines the Pilot came in too fast and overshot the runway with the result that the undercarriage sheared off. One member of the crew was seriously injured.

Halifax NP932 piloted by F/O Chopping, with P/O Klovell as Co-Pilot, took part in an operation on 14/15 March 1945 against Homberg. On returning to Snaith the Pilot when coming in to land on the main runway QDM 139 carried out two overshoots satisfactorily. Then on the third approach Flying Control gave the order "Pancake" and the Pilot replied "Overshooting". The aircraft appeared to be carrying out a normal overshoot at 200 ft above the runway in use but there was a sudden flash followed by an explosion near the lead out funnels. The aircraft had crashed to the North of No 1 WAAF site killing all 8 crew members. Examination of the aircraft after the crash showed that the throttles had not been locked by the Co-Pilot and had probably vibrated loose. It was believed that the Co-Pilot sitting in the Engineer's seat may not have understood the Pilot's order to lock the throttles.

After a period of maintenance work in the hangar JN922 was taken up for an air test on the afternoon of Sunday 5 Dec 1943, piloted by F/Lt McCreanor. On completion of the air test, when coming in to land, the Pilot found that only one undercarriage wheel would come down. He therefore circled the airfield whilst trying to get the offending undercarriage leg down and deciding on a course of action. News about this aircraft spread rapidly and a large number of maintenance personnel were stood around in front of the main hangar watching the aircraft in trouble. The author was standing near two Riggers and heard one remark to the other "Who signed the 700 for that kite?". The Pilot eventually decided to come in and made an excellent job of setting down on one wheel. After touch down he ran almost the full length of the runway until the speed dropped at which stage the unsupported wing dropped and the aircraft swung off the runway. The crew all walked out safely probably recalling the old motto that 'Its a good landing when the crew can walk away from it'.

PRISONERS OF WAR

In discussing losses, mention should be made of those members of the squadron who managed to escape death by parachuting or crash landing into enemy territory, a total of 9,000 airmen finished up in POW camps. These airmen, although saved from death had to suffer the privations of hunger, illness, poor living conditions, malnutrition and monotony which were the lot of a 'Kriegie' (From the German, Kriegesgefangene, ie POW). The information reproduced here is based on the experiences of some of the 51 Squadron POWs. Those airmen sent to Wermacht camps appeared to suffer most.

After capture prisoners could receive rough treatment at the hands of the civilian population, police, military, and Gestapo. They would be interrogated by the Luftwaffe at a place like Dulag Luft, the Luftwaffe Interrogation Centre for POWs. All sorts of treatment was meted out to try and obtain information from them other than Number, Rank and Name. This could vary from the 'Good guy' approach of an interview with a pseudo 'Red Cross' official to the 'Bad guy' approach with threats to execute them as spies if they had been captured in civilian clothes. Squadron members were shown a book entitled 51 (B) Squadron with lists of aircrew and crosses indicating the dead ones, in an effort to entice them to talk about the squadron and thus supply information about it. Fred Heathfield was asked how W/C Franks and G/C Jordan were getting on, the fact that the Luftwaffe had the latter name in their files showed how up-to-date they were with their information because Jordan had taken over from G/C Gray only after Fred had been shot down.

From Dulag Luft the airmen were sent to a Stalag after their sheepskin Irvine jackets and flying boots had been taken off them, the latter being replaced by German army boots. Prisoners who had been captured in civilian clothes were issued with a selection of military clothing such as ill fitting old French uniforms. The post war films of POW camps with airmen wearing smart uniforms, caps and silk scarves are looked on with derision by ex 'Kriegies' since they were very poorly clad.

In 1943 the amount of accommodation available to the Luftwaffe was limited, with the consequence that when the RAF started to suffer high losses commencing with the 'Battle of the Ruhr' there was insufficient accommodation in Stalag Lufts for aircrew prisoners. The Germans therefore provided accommodation for aircrew prisoners in army Stalags managed by the Wermacht. In Stalag IVb quite a number of 51 Squadron aircrew met up, including Fred Heathfield, Tom Nelson, Bill Barnet and 'Curly' Manning. At this Stalag there was a Navigator from 51 Squadron who had been trained as a 'Code Writer' so that he could send messages back to England using a code hidden in his letters. These letters were decoded by the authorities before being passed on to the relatives' addresses.

In army camps such as Stalags IVb and VIIIb, a small compound was set up in the middle specifically for RAF prisoners. These compounds contained up to half a dozen huts and were wired off from the rest of the camp. The occupants were treated differently from the rest of the camp since the Wermacht did not like the RAF, being concerned about them escaping. Consequently they were unnecessarily harsh. Initially in 1943, some RAF personnel in these camps were locked up for twenty three and a half hours a day. In some Stalag Lufts the food was communally mixed with the Red Cross supplies whereas in Army Stalags the food was issued out to individuals. The food was very poor, starting with mid morning 'ersatz' coffee, reputably made from acorns, which for the afternoon 'brew' could be replaced by 'mint' tea, both were foul brews but wet and warm, served in buckets. Lunch was soup made from cabbages or green turnip tops with 3 to 5 small, cold, boiled potatoes. There was a ration of black bread, the quantity issued was supposed to be a small loaf between four men. In Britain this size used to be called a small tin. On occasions this ration could be reduced to as low as one loaf between ten men. The normal procedure was to cut the loaf into the appropriate number of portions and draw cards for turns at selecting a portion.

Occasionally millet seed or pea soup was served up but this time without potatoes and there was never any meat present. Occasionally drums of Sauerkraut, shredded cabbage pickled in brine, were issued and the empty drums could become useful buckets. Sometimes either cheese or wurst was supplied. The cheese could be covered in slime and stank to high heaven. The wurst contained raw meat or offal with the possibility of tape worm germs being present. On some days a small pat of margarine or a teaspoonful of 'ersatz' jam was provided, this was made from beetroot or turnip and probably thickened with sawdust.

The food issued by the Germans was augmented by Red Cross parcels. At one period the guards were concerned in case the parcels were used as rations for escapees, so they used various techniques to discourage this. They would take the tops off the tins before issuing or pierce holes in them. On occasions they could be particularly vindictive by emptying all the contents of a parcel which could include tea, coffee, rice, chocolate, meat stew, corned beef, cheese and biscuits into a billy and giving them a stir with a bayonet for good measure. Parcels were supposed to be issued weekly but on many occasions the period between parcels was much longer and the number of persons allocated to a parcel could vary so combines were formed to share them. The POWs could not have survived without these parcels but even then the rations were so low that at the end of the war the majority of airmen were debilitated.

As mentioned above, in some Stalag Lufts communal feeding was carried out in the huts with one person being allocated the task of cooking the food. The cook had control of the rations provided by the Germans and the food received in Red Cross parcels. An unwritten rule in Block 66 of Stalag Luft 3 was that the occupants of the hut did not criticise the cooking ability of the chef. It was permissible to complain about the lack of variety in the menu or the quantity served but not how it was cooked. One evening after an indifferent meal Bobby Stark made the mistake of suggesting that the cooking could have been better. Within minutes he was appointed cook, a job that was his for the next fourteen months.

The normal lunch time issue for Bobby Starks's hut was 'Kohl-Rabi' (turnip soup) or 'Barleygoo', barley cooked in water plus two slices of bread. He tried to improve the 'Barleygoo' by the addition of 'Klim' (American dried milk powder) to provide what might euphemistically be called "Cream of Barley Soup". One of Bobby's monthly 'Cordon Bleu' achievments was a chocolate pudding served with 'cream'. The ends of each loaf of black bread were placed in a cardboard box over a period of weeks until there was sufficient to grate down to fine flower. Items from Red Cross parcels comprising raisins, currants and cut prunes were mixed with margarine, a little milk powder, some sugar and a bar of precious chocolate. The pudding was cooked in the oven for one hour in the afternoon and a further thirty minutes before serving. The cream was a thick, well beaten, mix of 'Klim' and water. This chocolate pudding was

POST-OPERATIONS AND LOSSES

rather 'heavy' but the prisoners did at least retire to their bunks with full stomachs once a month.

The Army Stalag huts were about 80 ft by 30 ft with no glass in the windows, which meant they were very cold in winter and snow could blow through the windows onto the beds. Sacking was used as curtains. These huts housed 180 airmen in three-tier bunks with a sack palliasse and a single threadbare blanket. POWs had to make their own cooking and eating utensils from the various metal containers obtained from the Red Cross parcels. The latrine and washing facilities were very rudimentary with 48 seater latrines in communal blocks of 12 over a huge cesspit. The water supply for washing was very limited and earth lats. were attached to the huts for use at night. Regular delousing sessions were carried out. The latrine cesspits were regularly emptied by Russian POWs and the contents spread out on the surrounding fields so that the odour emanating from the camp could be detected even when out of view. Punishment for POWs was up to 28 days solitary confinement in the 'Cooler' on bread and water.

Whilst food and health were major factors in the life of the residents of a Stalag, their morale was also important. The POWs looked forward eagerly to letters from home but since these were censored it was difficult to obtain news of the war by this source. Consequently a lot of effort was put in by prisoners to establish clandestine radios to receive BBC news broadcasts. I am indebted to Fred Heathfield for the following report on his experiences of radios in POW camps.

In Stalag IVb the first POW radio in the camp was built by a Navigator from 100 Squadron, Sgt Eric Gargini, a radio expert in 'Civvy Street'. It was a tremendous boost to the camp morale to be able to receive the BBC news every day including the report of the Normandy landings on the morning of 'D' Day. The Germans knew about this radio and searched for it without success. On one occasion, during a search, it was passed around the hut like a rugby ball and then out of the window to be hidden in another hut. A sergeant who could write shorthand at 180 words per minute copied the BBC 9 pm news every day and then read it back to the occupants of his hut. A transcript was sent around the rest of the huts. On Xmas day 1943 he recorded the King's broadcast and read it out immediately it had finished.

Later on an RAF Wireless Mechanic named Walter Briggs arrived at the camp and worked with Gargini in constructing sets for the various huts. He managed to get radio parts smuggled into the camp and Gargini obtained a copy of Vol 1 of The Admiralty Manual of Wireless Telegraphy, probably via the Red Cross book service. This provided very useful technical information. A radio was provided for Fred's hut, size about 8 x 6 X 6 inches. This was mains powered with 3 valves on a metal chassis. Since the valves were not designed for the function they were required to perform, a compromise circuit was necessary. The set was hidden in a cavity made in a brick pillar in the hut and covered by a board. Operating the set was a hazardous task since it could only be reached at arms length and the mains electricity which was fed into it from the lighting circuit was via hidden bare wires. A camouflaged wire aerial was connected to the set and a telephone earpiece was used as a headphone. The signals received were weak, the set needed constant retuning, and it was badly affected by the damp which occurred in the cavity. This meant that on occasions the set had to be removed from the cavity and dried out.

Gargini and Biggs became set manufacturers for the camp and had to produce various components from scratch. Examples were as follows: X ray film was purloined from the Germans and cut up to make the

Photo 57 via Val Hood
Drawing Of Layout Of POW Hut, From Val's Diary

dielectric for trimming condensers by interleaving it with metal plates. Fixed condensers could be made from aluminium foil using the wax scraped off from biscuit wrappers to impregnate paper dielectrics. A transformer was built into a one gallon size German jam tin. Types of radios about the camp included one built into a portable record player and one built into a broom head with the aerial running up the handle. A good hiding place for a simple set was in a footlight in the theatre, this was a dry location with a source of mains electricity.

To sum up, conditions and food in the camp were so wretched that after repatriation when the war ended many POWs needed a recuperation period to regain their health. Many POWs were unfortunate enough not to live to see repatriation. In some camps when the Russians advanced the occupants were force marched west and many died on the march.

The story of one 51 Squadron POW who landed amongst a friendly population has been recorded in detail in a Dutch book 'In der Schaduw van der Adelaar' (In the Shadow of the Eagle). The personal experiences of this airman, F/O Bobby Stark who is a member of the Squadron Association, are outlined below.

Bobby Stark's last operation with the squadron was on the night of the 13/14 May 1943, in HR790 piloted by P/O George Byres, for a raid against Bochum. The aircraft was shot down by a night fighter with the Flight Engineer and the two gunners being killed, the rest of the crew landing safely to finish up in a POW camp. Bobby Stark baled out through the escape hatch and as he descended everything seemed quiet in the bright moonlight and clear sky with its myriad of stars. Below him Holland stretched out and to the west he could see the Zuiderzee, descending into this could be disastrous. Then the streets and houses of a town came into view and he landed with a jolt on the flat roof of a building with the parachute draped over an adjacent house. Bobby was taken by neighbours into the house covered by the parachute. The occupier, a Mr Burger told him that he had landed at Almelo in Holland and the police had been notified of his arrival because they thought he was dead. The police arrived and as they took him away he gave Mrs Burger his air crew whistle as a souvenir.

The Bomb Aimer, Sargent Eames, landed in the countryside but was captured by German soldiers and taken to Amelo to be locked up with Bobby Stark. The next day they were taken to Hengelo where they met the German pilot who had shot them down along with three other bombers that night and given the inevitable meal of saerkraut. Subsequently they were transported to Dulag Luft for 'processing' like other 51 Squadron members, eventually finishing up in Stalag Luft III. After the war Bobby Stark received a letter from Mr Burger, written in English, an extract from which is reproduced below.

"Dear Mr Stark,
Almelo (Holland)
May 26 1947
I'll tell you about that night 13/14 May 1943 as good as I can. It was a very fine evening, warm and we went to bed at about 11 o'clock. I heard some planes come and one hour later there came many - very many. We heard they went to the Ruhr. We went out of our beds, because my wife was very fearful and we attended to the children (two boys: 10 years and 3 years old). German night-planes were in the air and that always was very dangerous. You were loaded with bombs and when you should be shot down, the bombs were for us - you understand.
We went to bed again at 2 o'clock in the night. Then the English planes went home and passed Almelo again. We laid in our beds, somewhat dozy, because we were tired. Each night, it was the same story. At one, we heard the voice of our neighbour (time 3:15) and a screaming noise in the air. My neighbour cried my name and we heard a heavy blow. The windows of our sleeping room were covered with a yellow haze. Because I was not quite awake, I thought a bomb was fallen into my garden. I cried to my wife: "Take quickly the children and go downstairs, I'll see what I can do". When I came into the kitchen, with eyes like dishes, my neighbour said: "He is as dead as a door nail". I asked: "What, who?" Then he told me, that a man with a parachute was fallen on the small flat next to our house and the parachute was hanging on our roof. That was the yellow haze, I had seen. What now? You must know, that in Holland a general strike began on the 10 May 1943. The Green Police - the best murders of the German murders - came into our town and we had to be indoors from 8 in the evening till 6 in the morning. When one came in the street in that time., they shot him down and it did not matter, if he was 8 or 80 years old.
We meant, you were dead, there was no doubt and we had to ask the help of the police to take away your corpse. I did not make me sure of the fact, that you were dead, because I can't see blood etc and thinking of the heavy blow - I supposed your limbs laid distributed on the flat. I went to the other side of the street to a telephone and asked help of the police with a stretcher. When I came home, I saw you sitting on a chair - you were very quiet and my wife was making tea. You had only a scratch on your nose. I began to ask several things and you answered. In no time 12 or 15 inhabitants of our street came in and we were very enthusiastic. For us, you were an oasis in the desert. You came from a free country. The Dutch police came to take you with them and you shook hands with all of us. I

POST-OPERATIONS AND LOSSES

asked you the address of your parents and I did what I could, to set your parents at ease. From you we got a flute, that was fixed on your uniform. That flute is now hanging on a nail in the wall as a pleasant rememberance of a moved night.
Perhaps you have wondered, that we could not help you, to come out of our country, but even if I had not warned the police, I could not have helped you, because too many men had seen you and a in town, there is always treason and moreover, the German Green Police had seen you from out of their headquarter in a school near of our house. This is the story of the night 13-14 May 1943. When you wish to know more then write."
Sincerely yours
Burger

Bobby Stark returned to Holland in 1982 to visit the graves of his dead colleagues and to his surprise was given a VIP reception and presented with a plaque which had a piece of Halifax HR790 mounted on it.

Some aircrew members who had to bale out managed to escape capture and suffer the privations of being a POW, often with the help of the resistance. Ealier on this chapter mention has been made of F/O Nock's escape, but other squadron members escaped capture, two of whom were Fred Kirkwood and Peter Hinchliffe.

Fred Kirkwood was shot down during the Tergnier operation on 11.4.44 and Jim Gill recalls how he suddenly reappeared in the Officer's mess some months later, to the surprise of everyone present. Peter Hinchliffe was a Navigator in MH-W, an aircraft with the famous 'Winsome Waaf' motif, see the nose art photos. Peter was shot down on 4/5th November 1944 during a raid on Bochum, he baled out and landed about 1,000 yards from the German positions in a forest and just within the American lines. On landing the parachute became attached to some telephone wires so had to press his release box to drop to the ground in the dark. After he joined the Americans their positions were shelled before he left to rejoin the squadron. When he arrived back at Snaith one of the persons most relieved to see his safe return was his future wife Irene, a WAAF Teleprinter Operator at Snaith. She had learnt very quickly about his failure to return from the operation since she had the sad task of sending out the telegrams to next of kin of missing aircrew.

Chapter 7

ANALYSIS OF OPERATIONS 1943-45

At the time of publication of this book there is a current degree of criticism regarding the bombing tactics employed by Bomber Command, linked with the unveiling of the memorial to Sir Arthur Harris outside St Clement Danes church in London. This analysis should demonstrate the significant part 51 Squadron (along with the rest of Bomber Command) played in the successful pursuit of WW2. Hopefully it will help in replying to the armchair critics (many of whom did not experience the traumas of WW2), sitting in their ivory towers and denegrating the actions of men and women of units like 51 Squadron, whose sacrifice and devotion provided them a safer world in which to live.

EARLY DAYS

The squadron arrived at Snaith from Chivenor in October 1942 and the Whitley aircrews had to convert to the Halifax aircraft the squadron was then being issued with. This was achieved by attending a Heavy Conversion Unit plus practice with the squadron. Their numbers were bolstered by the arrival of new members of the squadron from a Halifax HCU. The initial aircraft were early Mk II's, some of which came from 130 Squadron at Kirmington following its conversion to Lancasters. When up to complement the squadron had to go though a 'shakedown' period during which both air and ground crews had to become familiar with the new aircraft, and participate in a number of minelaying operations in order to become operational as a Halifax squadron. On the 14/15 Jan 1943 the squadron carried out its first main force Bomber Command operation from Snaith. Five aircraft took part in a raid code named 'Pickerel', the target being Lorient U-Boat base with, the aid of PFF marking. This being a major change from the Whitley operations where they had to bomb blind at night.

From then until March the squadron took part in various operations. German targets included Dusseldorf on 27/28 Jan 1943 which was the first operation when 'Oboe' Mosquitoes carried out ground marking. Bombing was well concentrated as a result of this accurate marking, without which the target would have been difficult to identify due to thin cloud along with the usual Ruhr ground mist. Other operations included a U-Boat base at St Nazaire, Turin in Italy and minelaying. The number of aircraft available for an operation varying from 3 to about 12 aircraft. Bomber Command losses were starting to mount up, the average Bomber Command losses over the next 12 months averaging as high as 6%, this could indicate the complete loss of a squadron in 17 operations without replacements, but a few crews did manage to complete a tour of 30 Operations. Since a number of crews were lost in the first few operations this meant a few crews could still complete an operational tour and keep the average at 6%. In 1943 Bomber Command was forecasting that their aircrews had a 1 in 3 chance of surviving the war. In his statement at the end of the war, ACM Harris expressed his sorrow at the grievous casualties suffered by Bomber Command aircrews. Commenting on how their losses mounted over the years with negligible chances of surviving one tour of operations and the chances of surviving two tours being mathematically nil. Yet survivors still volunteered for a third tour. During the war 55,000 Bomber Command aircrew were killed.

One of the few crews which survived a tour after taking part in the first operations carried out by the

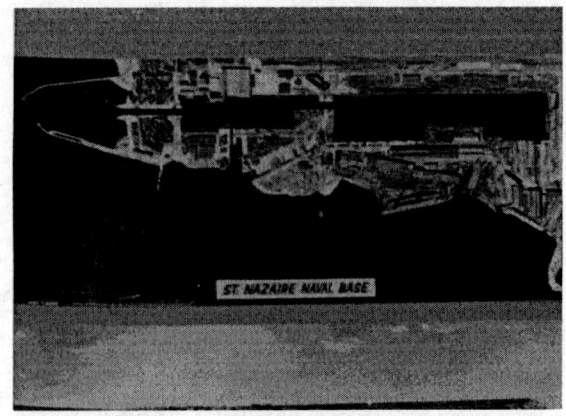

Photo 60 Jaric via 51 Squadron
Model Of St Nazaire Target

ANALYSIS OF OPERATIONS 1943-45

squadron at Snaith was the one captained by Sgt Claude Wilson. On their seventh operation they went to Hamburg on the 3/4 March 1943 in aircraft 'T' Tommy and as an example of the hazards of sorties in early 1943 a report by their Air Gunner, F/O Les Sharp DFC, is given here.

"We took off from Snaith at approximately 2200 hours, no problems flying out, except for small amounts of flak on reaching the German coast, no damage incurred. We arrived over the port of Hamburg between 0030 hours and 0100 hours, marker flares already dropping and commenced the bombing run at the height of 21,000 ft. Suddenly we were picked up by a master searchlight and within seconds were coned by many others. Then our world went mad. Claude Wilson, our Pilot, threw the aircraft into a series of evasive actions, at the same time jettisoning all our bombs. Flak was everywhere and our world turned upside down, we twisted and turned all over the sky, then suddenly the lights were gone and Sgt Wilson levelled out and was asking for a course home. It was then, as rear gunner, battered and bruised, I noticed, as I thought, smoke coming from the port outer engine. I conveyed this news to the Pilot and Flight Engineer, who on checking my warning, closed the engine down. This proved to be a glycol leak not a fire, but in any event the engine had to be closed down. We were still in the Hamburg area so the Navigator, Sgt Peter Finnett, reminded the Pilot that balloons over Hamburg were at 5,000 ft, the height we had arrived at through evasive action! We were now a target for light and some heavy flak but had managed to climb to 6-7,000 ft and fortunately had not encountered any balloons. We survived this, then suddenly we were over the coast and on course home. We now had roughly two or three hours flying ahead of us before reaching base so settled down, but still watching for night fighters. After a short time of peace the Flight Engineer came on the intercom with the news that the starboard outer was causing trouble, this turned out to be a serious problem and the Pilot ordered the engine to be feathered and closed down. At approximately 0200 hours we were operating on two engines with two hours flying ahead. The possibility of ditching in the North Sea in March was not a pleasant thought and morale wasn't very high at that moment. It soon became clear we were not holding our height and the conversation was on what to jettison. The Pilot agreed to carry on as we were and although still losing height 'T' for Tommy made it to Manston. At 900 ft we swept into Manston on two engines and Sgt Wilson made a great landing.
We were taken to the Station Sick Quarters where our bumps and bruises were treated. given a large Navy rum and after a quick de-briefing taken to our sleeping quarters, where the rum took its toll! Next day we were collected from Manston by a Halifax, sent from Snaith, and were back on 'Ops' on 5 March, this time a trip to Essen. The next day was my birthday, I was 22 years old. I was the oldest member of our crew!" The previous 'T' Tommy had a very spectacular end in Feb 1943 as described in Chapter 10.

BATTLE OF THE RUHR

On the 5/6 March 1943 what is now known as the 'Battle of the Ruhr' commenced. The Ruhr was the powerhouse of German industrial production and contained many important industrial targets. It covered an area of some 2,000 miles, had a population of over 5 million. It was the source of 90% of German steel production because of the ready source of Ruhr coking coal and the proximity of the Lorraine iron ore deposits. The largest towns in the Ruhr were Essen, Dortmund, Duisburg, Gelsenkirchen, and Bochum with populations over 3,000. In view of the foregoing the Ruhr was well defended being euphemistically nicknamed 'Happy Valley' by the aircrew. The target for the first raid in the battle was the Krupps works in the centre of Essen. It was a moonless night but Pathfinding was carried out by 'Oboe' Mosquitoes which dropped red TIs at 2100 hrs on the aiming point. The 12 aircraft detailed by 51 Squadron went in with the first of three waves for a concentrated raid which lasted 38 minutes, dropping their bombs on accurately placed green TIs. To assist the main force Pathfinders used a technique they had now developed which involved dropping yellow track marking flares at the start of the final leg. In this raid 42% of the aircraft which bombed the target dropped their bombs within three miles of the aiming point.

Mention has been made in Chapter 5 that one of the hazards of operating in the bomber stream was the possibility of being hit by bombs from aircraft operating at a higher level. The problem was particularly true in 1943 for the Mk II Halifaxes which had a lower operating ceiling than the Lancasters. Claud Wilson's crew in aircraft HR838 in an operation against Duisburg had a personal experience of this hazard. The mid upper gunner observed a Lancaster bomber with bomb doors open about 1,000 ft above them, crossing from the port quarter to the starboard bow so he immediately warned the captain. The Pilot therefore carried out an immediate evasive action to starboard so that the aircraft was practicaly standing on its wingtips. Large and small bombs whistled past on either side of the aircraft, fortunately missing it.

For background knowledge of the Ruhr operations it is worthwhile analysing the Krefeld raid on 21/22 June 1943 since this was a significant one which can be examined in detail. At the time of this raid the squadron was still operating the Series 1

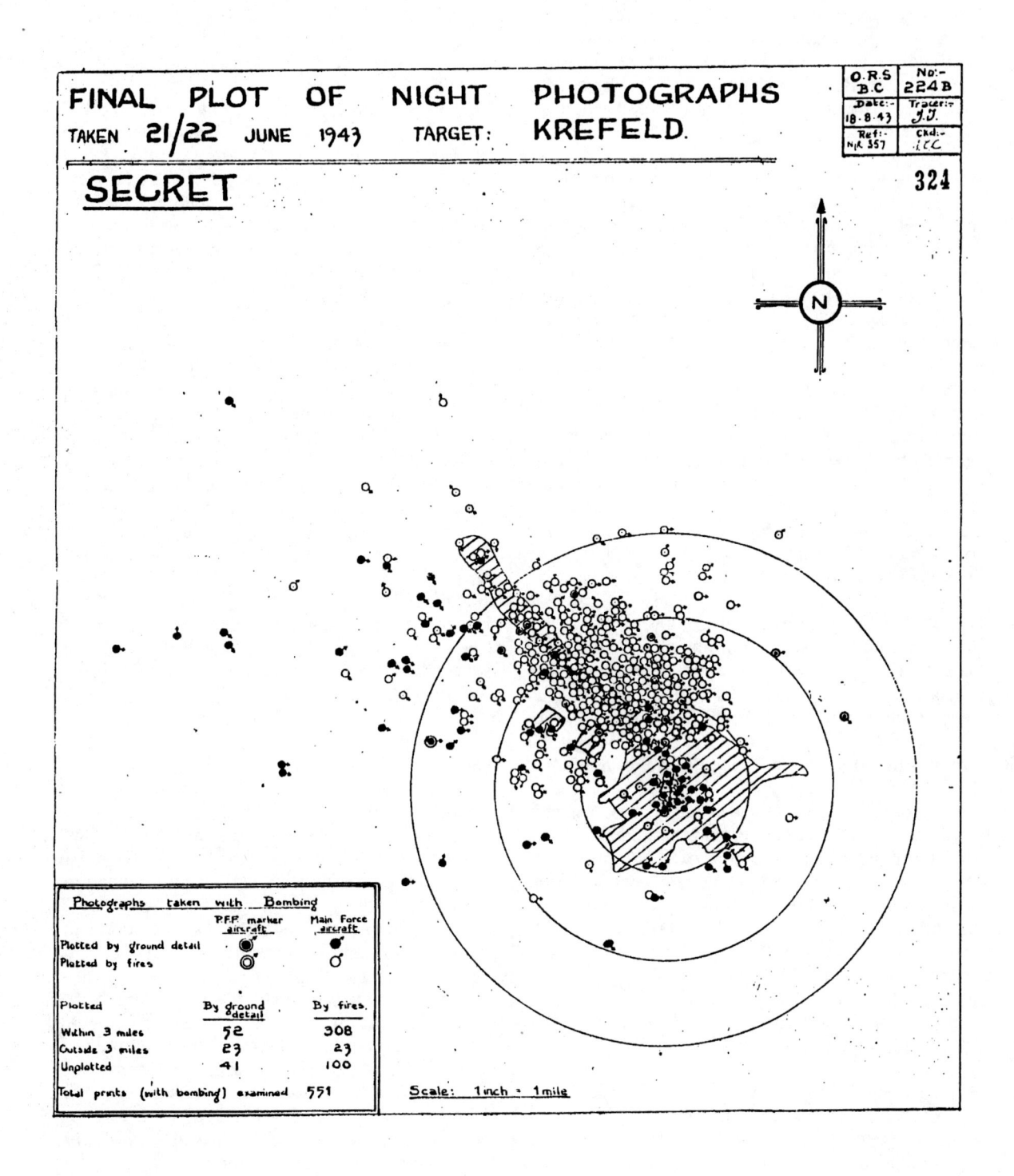

FIG 22 Pro Ref. Air 14/3410 - XC/A 016226
Bomb Plot For Krefeld Raid
Crown Copyright

ANALYSIS OF OPERATIONS 1943-45

(Special) and Series 1A versions of the Halifax Mk II fitted with Merlin engines, which had problems with the height they could attain with a full bomb and fuel load. In addition the aircraft at this period were still fitted with the original fin and rudder which gave overbalance problems. The Halifax was therefore considered by Bomber Command to be inferior to the Lancaster a situation which was rectified when the Mk III came into service.

At this time there were many secret facets of the aircrew's involvement in the battle of wits between the Bomber Command offensive and the German defences which were not general knowledge. When the squadron's aircraft, along with the rest of the Command were being prepared for a raid in June 1943, testing of the T1154, R1155 radios in the aircraft would be carried out early in the day before bombing up commenced. However, the Luftwaffe listening service was monitoring the transmissions so that the timing of the radio tests could give them a hint that a raid was imminent. The aircraft also carried two items of radar equipment which could be of value to the enemy, these were the IFF set and the 'Monica' tail warning radar. The latter was being fitted in 51 Squadron aircraft from June 1943 onwards so that many of the aicraft engaged in the Krefel raid were using this equipment.

During the early stages of the Battle of the Ruhr, 'Monica' had not been compromised by the enemy because it was fairly new. However, as the campaign proceeded the Luftwaffe identified the Monica transmissions and used them to home in on. With regard to the IFF, an idea had circulated amongst the aircrews that if switched on it could act as a jammer for the bluish coloured Wurzburg controlled searchlights, This idea gained so much credence with the aircrew that at one period a modification of the Mk II IFF involved the fitting of a 'J' (jamming) switch so that the set could be switched on permanently. Apparently Command believed that this item could boost the morale of aircrews during a period when casualties were high, but actually it was a lethal device for the aircrew. In 1944 RAF intelligence established that German tracking stations were able to trigger the transponders in IFF sets and use this information for tracking purposes.

By the time of the Krefel raid the majority of Luftwaffe twin engine night fighters had been fitted with Lichenstein C1 FuG 202 AI Radar developed by Telefunken and operating on a frequency of 490 Mhz, its performance being similar to that of the RAF AI Mk 4 system. Their AI radar system was given the code name 'Emil Emil' by the Luftwaffe ground control organisation. This meant that under the guidance of the GCI Controllers in the 'Himmelbet' Sectors using Wurzburg Radar, night fighters could be guided on to the bomber stream in such a position as to be able to use AI radar to home in on a target. The RAF were fully aware of the capabilities and frequencies of the Wurzburg and Lichenstein radars thanks to the efforts of both 51 and 192 Squadrons, the latter being a parent of the current squadron. The 'Whitley Boys' of 51 Squadron, had in 1942, participated in the Bruneval Raid which resulted in the capture of vital components of a Wurzburg radar for examination by TRE, and information on the Lichenstein radar was obtained by 192 Squadron. The Elint Flight which became 192 Squadron sent a Wellington 1C (DV 819) on a 'Ferret' Flight with the hazardous task of being intercepted by a night fighter. When the night fighter's radar locked on to the Wellington the Special Wireless Operator on board analysed the radar transmissions and recorded details of them. The aircraft was severly damaged by cannon shells and the Special Operator hit. The aircraft got back to Britain but could not land so the Wireless Operator was dropped by parachute with the vital information, whilst the Pilot ditched the aicraft in the channel. Fortunately, all the crew were rescued. As a result of the foregoing the RAF had an answer to these radars in the form of 'Window', but were reluctant to use it until the Hamburg raid in July 1943. During the Krefel and Ruhr raids the Squadron did not have the protection afforded by 'Window' so that the night fighters could make maximum use of their AI radar.

The only radio countermeasure available for use by the squadron was the use of 'Tinsel' which, as mentioned earlier, was a jamming signal sent out by a Wireless Operator who would monitor the lower GCI frequencies in the 3-6 Mhz band and then jam with audio noise from his carbon microphone via the T1154 transmitting on the same frequency as the GCI controller. The object was to upset the night fighter control system. The higher GCI frequency of 34-42 Mhz was jammed by high power transmitters in Britain. A development of this system was 'Special Tinsel', whereby the RAF listening station at Kingsdown monitored the GCI controller's transmissions and measured their frequencies. This information was then sent to the Wireless Operators in the aircraft and was a system which had its greatest success in August 1943, but the Germans eventually countered it by rapid changes in frequency.

The RAF also had to cope with jamming operations carried out against them by the Luftwaffe. By June 1943 the squadron's Navigators were fully familiar with the 'Gee' equipment which had been in use by Bomber Command's mainforce since Spring 1942. Over Britain the Navigators could get good fixes but when they approached the Dutch coast heading for Krefeld the effects of heavy jamming of the FM type by the Germans became evident and made it difficult to read the traces on the cathode ray tube. The maximum range attainable with 'Gee' was normally about 400 miles. The Eastern 'Gee' chain was in operation during the Krefeld raid, employing the 'Virginia' frequency throughout, plus the 'Zaneville' frequency between 0130 and 0230 to cover the period when the main force was on the target area. The hope was that the Navigators would find one of the frequencies usable. The frequencies could be altered by the Navigator via the RF unit in the 'Gee' receiver.

The squadron's objective was to bomb as near the given aiming point as possible, but the problem with the Ruhr was that being an industrial area, even on a clear night there could be a ground haze to obscure the target. The aircrews' nickname of 'Happy Valley' for the Ruhr was a deliberate misnomer because of the above problems and it's strong defences of searchlights and concentrations of 88, 105 and 128 mm anti aircraft guns. In view of this the aircrew did not want to hang around trying to identify the target, so accurate target marking was of prime importance, hence the value of the Pathfinder Force's target marking activity. When the squadron first started operating at Snaith the Pathfinder Force had commenced trials with Mosquitos navigating and target marking by means of the 'Oboe' radar system. After identifying the 'Oboe' transmissions the Germans set up a jamming system so the RAF's answer was to increase the frequency and modify the transmissions. For the Krefel raid the K-Oboe system was used for the first time and was therefore unaffected by German jamming. This contributed greatly to the success of the Krefel raid because the ground markers were very accurately placed by the 'Oboe' Mosquitos and being a clear night with little cloud over the target the PFF were able to place their TIs accurately. This meant that when 51 Squadron arrived at Krefeld in the region of 0200 hrs they had an excellent target to aim at and dropped about 100,000 lbs of HE bombs, the total tonnage dropped by the main force being about 2,306 tons.

When the German bombing raids on Britain early on in the war were analysed, it was shown that the incendiaries could be more destructive than an equal weight of HE bombs. The reason for this being that it was possible for incendiaries to have an almost unlimited effect. The incendiaries were particularly effective with combustible targets and could produce destruction out of proportion to the weight of the bomb as demonstrated in the Krefeld raid. The Hamburg fire storm raids in July are very well documented, but it may not be generally realised that the Krefeld raid was the first occurrence of a major fire storm, the bomb loads containing a high percentage of incendiaries. 51 Squadron was the exception because of an emergency bomb load due to the bomb dump explosion. Because of the accurate bombing a large concentration of incendiary fires occurred giving a high intensity conflagration with the result that an updraught of hot air was produced causing winds of up to hurricane velocity to flow into the fires to replace the updraught. This wind could carry burning debris and feed the fires to such an extent that the Krefeld fire services were unable to cope resulting in a high level of devastation.

The HE bombs dropped by 51 Squadron added to the destruction because in addition to damaging buildings and allowing access of air, HE bombs could break gas mains, thus adding to the fires, destroy the water mains needed to fight the fires and produce rubble and craters which could hamper the fire and rescue services. The fires raging over a large area of the city lasted for several hours and with the fire services unable to cope, 47% of the built up area of Krefeld was destroyed involving the destruction of 5,517 buildings. Post raid photo analysis reported that 75% of the aircraft bombed within 3 miles of the aiming point, the Bomber Command bombing plot being shown in Fig 22.

The weather over the target produced a cloud cover of 4 to 6 tenths comprising thin patches of strato-cumulus with tops at 8-10,000 ft. During the latter part of the attack the cloud cleared to 0 to 3 tenths and the visibility was moderate to good. There was a slight ground haze, typical of the Ruhr, but bombing conditions were good. Flak was moderately heavy backed up by searchlights operating in cones.

However it was not all on the side of the RAF that night and heavy casualties involving 6.2% of main force occurred, which compared with an average loss of 4.7% during the Battle of the Ruhr. As mentioned in previous chapters the twin engine night fighters were under GCI control, these were later on code named 'Zahme Sau'. However at the time of the Krefeld raid the 'Wilde Sau' free ranging single seater night fighters had started to operate. Post raid reports mentioned encounters with Bf 109 and FW 190 aircraft. Of the 42 bombers shot down that night at least 30 of these were due to night fighters. Over the target both controlled and 'Wilde Zau' fighters could operate since the flak had restricted its height to under about 18,000 ft to allow the night fighters to operate above it. Pilot Fred Heathfield reported seeing numerous encounters over the target as indicated by tracer fire. Fred had difficulty in gaining height so he was hit by flak and since his loss was a very interesting one it is described in detail in Chapter 6.

Whilst the twin engine fighters had the advantage of AI radar, over the target both they and the single engine fighters could take advantage of the illumination afforded them by the intense fires on the ground and the three quarters full moon. The target defences included bluish coloured marker searchlights controlled by Wurzburg radar which would lock onto a bomber so that the uncontrolled searchlights could follow it and cone the aircraft. When caught in a searchlight like this a bomber was a sitting duck for flak or night fighters and it had to be a very lucky or skillful pilot who was able to escape from the beams.

Having dropped their bombs the pilots left the target area as quickly as possible, setting a course for Noordwijk on the Dutch Coast. On the return journey their problems were not over since the night fighters were still active with the assistance of their AI radar, 50% of the night fighter interceptions taking place on the return journey. There were several areas of high flak concentrations, at Eindhoven, Amsterdam, Rotterdam, Utrecht, Lleyden and the Dutch Islands plus a flak ship operating off the coast near Noordwijk. After leaving the Dutch Coast heading for the landfall at Southwold the Navigator could now rely on being able to get a 'Gee' fix, and also for this raid they had the advantage of clear weather.

When they reached Snaith, Flying Control had some problems bringing the aircraft in because a localised early morning fog developed. Consequently the Flying Control Officer had to divert three aircraft to land away, the first of which arrived back about half an hour after the last one to land at Snaith. The diversion airfield was Pocklington which was fog free. Dave Storey the Navigator in Sgt Morris's crew remembers the incident very clearly because when he stepped out of the aircraft at Pocklington a voice said "Dave, what the Hell are you doing here!" One of the ground crew which greeted them on landing was an old school chum of Dave's. After debriefing and an operational breakfast the 51 Squadron aircraft flew back to Snaith where the visibility was now suitable for a landing. The squadron was fortunate in only losing one aircraft on this raid.

To sum up, the RAF achieved a very successful raid thanks to the accurate marking by the PFF and the assistance of the clear weather. However, against this the Luftwaffe were very successful in the number of aircraft shot down helped by the free use of Wurzburg ground radar and Lichenstein AI radar for detection, tracking or final contact with the bombers. The RAF aircraft were also being compromised by the ability of the Luftwaffe listening stations to analyse radio activity as a guide to Bomber Command's activities and Ground Stations ability to trigger the RAF IFF sets and hence track the bombers. The recent development of deploying 'Wilde Sau' night fighters was successful because of the clear weather, three-quarters moon and high illumination over the target due to ground fires. Six of the mainforce aircraft were damaged by bombs dropped by another aircraft, one of the hazards of the bomber stream.

A typical height flown during the Battle of the Ruhr was about 18,000 ft upwards, but there was a case when a low level approach was tried before climbing to about 19,000 ft before bombing. The reason for this low level approach could have been to assess its effect on the Kammhuber Line defences. Les Sharp, with additional information from Louis Wooldridge DFC his fellow Air gunner, has produced the following report on such an operation on 20 April 1943. This raid on Stettin which was 650 miles distant from Snaith is reported to be one of the most successful attacks beyond 'Oboe' range carried out during the 'Battle of the Ruhr'. The loss rate for the Main Force was 6.2%.

"The take off time was 2115 hours with operational orders to fly at 16,000 to 18,000 ft initially, then over the North Seat to come down to a low level height and maintain this until nearing the city of Stettin. On reaching the target we were ordered to bomb at a height of 19,000 to 21,000 ft. On the night chosen for this operation there was a full moon, and on the flight to Stettin we flew 'on the deck' with orders to the Gunners to fire at anything on the ground that was moving. On approaching the Danish coastline, near the Kiel Canal outlet, the Mid Upper Gunner observed a U Boat on the surface which carried out a crash drive at the approach of the low level Halifax. Crossing Denmark we were greeted by a Danish family waving large white towels, readily visible in the bright moonlight and over the Baltic sea near Lubeck and Rostock the crew observed two Lancasters shot down into the sea. We fired at the

ground several times when we flew over airfields and military installations. The low level flying continued until the time came for us to climb to our bombing height. We did our bombing run in spite of heavy flak and dropped our bombs on the red and green marker flares with good results. After "bombs away" we turned for home to resume our low level return.

Over a German town the Mid Upper Gunner spotted a Town Hall clock which indicated 0130 so he fired at it and saw the clock faces disintegrate, hoping it would make the German war workers late for work. The enemy was now aware of our tactics and the light and heavy flak guns became more of a problem, the radio aerial above the fuselage was shot away but no major damage occurred. To our port and starboard we could see aircraft going down, either hit by flak or hitting pylons or hills. We continued on our way with the gunners firing at airfields and military bases and then, after a course alteration, things became quieter. The Navigator now gave the Pilot a course, ten miles south of Esbjerg, to cross the Danish coast, with orders to then climb to a sensible height (16,000 to 20,000 ft).

We continued for a few minutes then all hell broke loose with two searchlights hitting us at 300 ft with flak pouring into the air in red, green and white tracers. The next thing we were conscious of was going skywards still in a fairyland of lights. By now the Pilot, Sgt Wilson, amid some rude words, had control of the aircraft and we were fortunate that when dazzled by these searchlights he had pulled back on the joystick causing the aircraft to go upwards instead of the reverse, in which case we would have made a mess of the town of Esbjerg and ourselves. Still uncomfortably low we were crossing the Danish coast at about 1,000 ft and a lone gunner on the beach had a pot shot at us, causing no harm. The trip over the North Sea was uneventful and we landed at Snaith at 0545 hours, making our total flying time 8 hours 30 minutes, a trip we shall never forget. During the debriefing the Esbjerg incident was reported to the I/O Officer, solving the mystery of the lone Halifax reported by the other crews as having had a fierce encounter with the ground defences."

During the Battle of the Ruhr the squadron had lost many aircraft and a lot of good men. The official closing date for the battle was 14 July by which time the squadron losses were 56 aircraft and 288 aircrew killed or POW with 13 ground crew killed. These figures were for the period since the start of operations in January. A suitable postscript to this campaign survey is a contribution by Air Bomber Geoff Tavener DFC, who carried a copy of the New Testament & Psalms in his battledress pocket throughout 41 bombing operations.

Geoff's comments are as follows:- "As well as having the title 'Happy Valley' the Ruhr was also called the 'Valley of the Shadow' which could relate to Psalm 23, Verse 4 'Yea, though I walk through the valley of the shadow of death, I will fear no evil: for Thou art with me; Thy rod and Thy staff comfort me'. Once the target was reached and the bomb load dropped, the chief aim in life was to pass through the Valley and out of it at all possible speed. The fact of David, the writer of the Psalm, walking can only be a measure of his faith and courage! Many of us who survived the war-time flying experience must wonder why we were spared and whether we have justified our survival by having been an influence for good in the lives of other people. Maybe it is not too late to do something about it now, even at this eleventh hour."

DEEPER INTO GERMANY

After the hazardous 'Happy Valley' campaign had finished the squadron became involved in the lead up to the possibly more disastrous campaign called the 'Battle of Berlin' which started in August 1943 and during this period the squadron took part in two memorable operations. Firstly there were the Hamburg operations of 27 July to 2 August, which have been well documented, but it is worthwhile commenting on them from the squadron's point of view. Successes achieved by the German defence system have already been discussed, and the Hamburg raid was one of the watersheds in the RAF's countermeasures war against them because it was the first use of 'Window' to neutralise the enemy's radar system.

'Operation Gomorrah'

During the 3rd week in July 1943 a large consignment of brown paper parcels size 12 x 2.5 x 2.5 inches was under secure storage at Snaith. These bundles each contained 2,000 'Window' strips size 30cm x 1.5cm made of very thin aluminium foil bonded to black paper. Later production of 'Window' was 27 cm long with a brown paper backing. Aluminium foil used for these strips was already available for the production of paper capacitors used in radios etc. The length of these strips was such that they acted as half wave dipoles resonating and re-radiating a signal at the frequency of 450 to 500 MHz, as employed by 'Wurzburg' ground and 'Lichenstein' airborne radar. One bundle when dropped by a squadron aircraft would produce the same radar response as a Halifax aircraft.

Around tea time on the 24 July the aircrew went in for briefing for the Hamburg raid and when the curtain went back to reveal the target map, the aircrews noted with satisfaction that the raid did not require a deep penetration into Germany. At this session after the normal type of briefing there was some new information never before communicated.

ANALYSIS OF OPERATIONS 1943-45

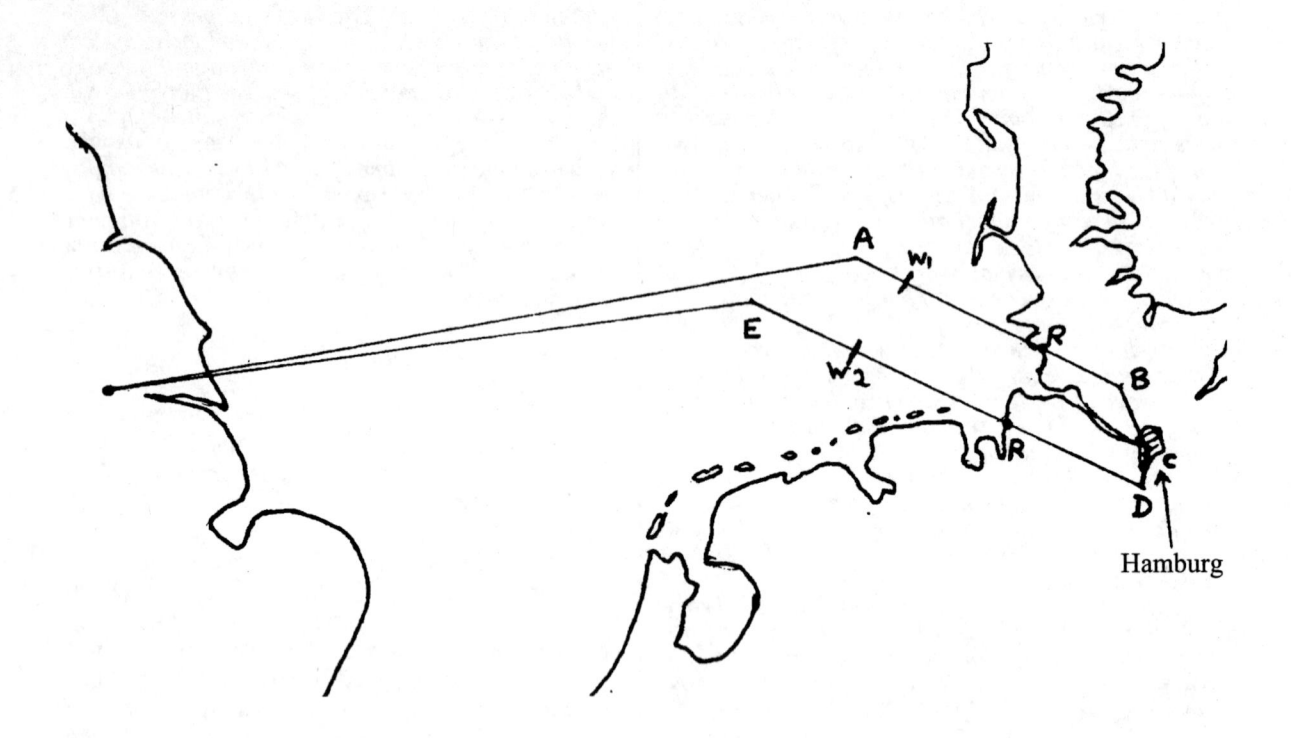

Map 11

Route Map For Hamburg Operation

A,B,C,D,E=Turning points
W1=Window dropping commences
W2=Window dropping ceases
R=PFF Track marking flares

The crews were told that bundles of a new radio countermeasures weapon in the RAF's armoury would be dropped in the region of the target. At the briefing the squadron CO, W/C Franks, read out an announcement from Bomber Command to all crews. This stated that they were using the new RDF countermeasure called 'Window' which involved dropping packets of metal strips which gave the same reaction to RDF as a Halifax This would confuse the German defences so that attention would be wasted on the 'Window' strips. It was emphasised that 'Window' was a communal exercise and protection was gained not from a single bundle an aircraft dropped, but by all bundles dropped by the bomber stream, which should be kept as concentrated as possible. It was realised that the task of dropping these bundles would be difficult for airmen hampered by oxygen, intercom leads, and darkness plus the problem of activity at altitude. It was essential to release bundles at correct intervals and adhere to the specified route. The CO concluded by saying that 'Window' was so devastating to the RDF system that the RAF withheld from using it until they could devise a defence against it. The raid was considered so important that S/Ldr Charlie Porter, the 'C' Flight Commander flew in Sergeant Cates' aircraft as a Bomb Aimer.

At their briefing the Navigators were given two points on their tracks at which window dropping had to start and stop. This was at Long. 8 degrees East on the way in and 8.5 degrees East on the way out (see Map 11). The Wireless Operators had the responsibility of timing the operations because the bundles had to be dropped down the flare chute at the rate of one per minute. Each aircraft dropped over 100,000 strips of 'Window' during the operation falling at a rate of about 300 ft per minute. This was not a very popular activity, sometimes 'Window' strips would fly back into the aircraft to be collected up in the dark and there was another problem in that on ejection from the flare chute the bundles could hit the IFF stub aerial and damage it. When the bundles of 'Window' were delivered to the aircraft by the groundcrew they were given the cover story that they were a new type of 'Nickel' (Propaganda leaflets) and on no account must the packets be opened till the aircraft was airborne. As an additional item of security all aircrew were confined to camp after the briefing and public phone boxes locked up.

This was a maximum effort raid so the squadron provided 24 aircraft and the route given to Navigators is shown in Map 11. The convergence for the bomber stream was at Point A and the 'Window' dropping points are indicated. No 4 Group provided 175 aircraft, including 17 Wellingtons, which were still operating with the Group at this stage. The 4 Group contingent in the approx. 200 mile long bomber stream was the largest contribution by any Group. The 4 Group aircraft attacked the target in two of the six waves, ie the fourth wave from 0126 to 0134 and the fifth wave from 0134 to 0142. The PFF laid track markers which were actuated by a barometric fuse and scattered yellow pyrotechnics, the target itself being marked by red TIs followed by green 'backers-up' TIs. As well as visual marking aircraft PFF were using 'Y' aircraft employing H2S for target identification. Hamburg being a coastal target, its returns from the built-up areas and the water provided identifiable differences so making it an ideal H2S target. This advantage of an identifiable target was however marred by the fact that H2S was a very new piece of equipment and still under development with the result that only 40% of the sets were serviceable.

The effect of the 'Window' strips became very obvious to the air crews as the searchlights seemed to be aimlessly probing the sky looking for targets, different from the normal situation, when 'Wurzburg' controlled searchlights could help the uncontrolled searchlights to find the target. The flak batteries not able to rely upon the gun laying radar also became very inaccurate in their shooting. The effect on the German radar system was to produce a display on the radar screen which could not be interpreted successfully by the operators. In order to assess the effect of 'Window' the Wireless Operators at the briefings were told not to carry out 'Tinsel' jamming operations so that the 'Y' listening service in the UK could monitor the reactions of the Germans. Their reports indicated a state of panic and confusion amongst the German GCI controllers. 'Window' did not affect 'Freya' E W Radar but it jammed 'Wurzburg' which was used for close range detection and fighter control along with the Leichenstein AI radar in the night fighters.

On the first of the Hamburg raids a 51 Squadron aircraft captained by Sergeant W J Murray was lost. This was a novice crew on its first operation which was 60 miles outside the bomber stream on the run-in to target and since it was not camouflaged by the 'Window' emissions of the mainstream it would be detected by a night fighter's AI radar. It was shot down near Sonderborg by a Ju 88 of NJG3 and crashed on the north bank of the Flensburg Fjord, all the crew being killed. Another inexperienced crew captained by Sgt A Fletcher on their first operation were luckier on the run-in, since their Rear Gunner managed to shoot down their attacker, a Dornier 217. The rest of the squadron carried out the mission successfully and returned to base.

The raid was followed by three further raids on the 27/28 July, 29/30 July and 2/3 August. On the second raid some fires were still burning from the first raid, The aircraft had increased the incendiary content of their bomb loads and the conditions were very warm and dry. The result was the famous Hamburg fire storm which was similar to the one described earlier for the Krefeld raid but much more severe having been described by air crew as a 'Sea of Fire'. On the way back the fire storm was so severe that the rear Air Gunner could see the fires during a considerable period of the flight back to England. Severe flak was encountered over Cuxhaven on the way back. The following night Hamburg was given a respite because Bomber Command knew that smoke from the fires would make target identification very difficult so that the third raid was delayed until 29/30 July, when although no fire storm developed the damage was nevertheless severe. The squadron was not given a night off on the 28/29 since they had to take part in a raid on Essen.

A fourth raid was carried out on the 2/3 August but this time fate took a hand on behalf of the enemy and severe weather conditions of 10/10 cumulonimbus cloud, heavy icing and thunderstorms were a disaster for the bomber stream, this was known by the RAF as the 'Night of the Storm'. Due to the weather conditions only a small proportion of bombs were dropped on the target. Dave Storey has given a graphic description of this operation.

Dave reported, "We found the weather more terrifying than enemy action and were literally hurtled 30 or 40 feet into the air at frequent intervals by the vast currents of air in the towering cumulo-nimbus thunder clouds. Lightning continually flashed all around us and static electricity called St Elmo's fire covered the whole of the plane making it appear that we were actually on fire. This static leapt from the propeller blades, covering the wings in blue flame and dancing all around the cockpit and the fuselage. Just as terrifying as the vast upcurrents and the static fire was the bombardment of the fuselage by huge chunks of ice being hurled from the propeller blades. Blocks of the size of legs of mutton. We could not get out of this vast cloud because the increasing weight of ice on the aircraft prevented us from climbing. We also tried to get underneath it but the cloud base was too low. In desperation we flew in all directions to get free of the cloud and the ice. We dropped our bombs on ETA, which was all we could do, not having the slightest clue of our true position. The magnetic compass was totally useless owing to the huge amounts of electrical energy in the clouds.

The foregoing problems constituted a total disaster for all the Navigators as we had to make wild guesses about our positions. I presumed a position somewhere to the North/East of the target and when we finally got into slightly improved conditions we set course for home from this assumed position. The whole force was requesting QDMs (Position lines from DF Stations) two or three of which could be used to fix a position. However, the demand was so great that priority was given to those in dire trouble, 'Darky' cases etc, of which there were many. All others had to wait their turn. We eventually got a fix and were able to find our way more or less in the right direction. Once we got within 'Gee' range all our troubles were over. Without doubt this was our most frightening trip since the forces of nature can out do anything that man might attempt. Back at Snaith the squadron found clear conditions for landing."

During these operations the squadron lost two more aircraft to night fighters. JD309 captained by Sgt A Fletcher, a crew on their fourth operation which shot down a night fighter on the first Hamburg raid was itself shot down on the 30 July having crashed into the sea with no survivers and HR 859 captained by W/O E R Sklarchuck on their fifth operation was shot down on the 3 August. As a result of this series of raids, in addition to the damage Hamburg suffered due to high explosive bombs and fires, 180,000 tons of shipping was sunk.

The use of 'Window' was to produce a considerable reduction in casualties from about 6% average for the Command before the use of 'Window' to about 2.5% for the Hamburg raids. The Germans attempted to limit the effects of 'Window' by getting the GCI controllers to give out running commentaries to night fighters and committing some 'Thame Sau' aircraft to take part in freelance operations alongside the existing 'Wilde Sau' aircraft. These raids forced the Luftwaffe to alter their defence tactics with increased flexibility in the use of their resources in order to try and overcome the effects of 'Window'. In the long run these changes would be to the detriment of the RAF.

Peenemunde

The second memorable operation was 'Operation Hydra', the target being Peenemunde a research and production site for Hitler's 'V' weapons on the Baltic coast. When the site had been identified by photo reconnaisance and intelligence work, Duncan Sandys the Deputy Minister of Supply, put in a recommendation to the War Cabinet that it should be bombed and this was agreed upon at a meeting on the 29 June 43. It was important that this target should be bombed efficiently first time so a long, moonlit night was needed, which was contrary to normal policy, and the night of 16/17 August was chosen. This was a 'Goodwood' maximum effort raid so 51 Squadron provided 24 aircraft, all of which bombed the target. At the briefing the air crew were given a cover story about the nature of the target, being told as an incentive that the target was involved in radar research which could be used against Bomber Command aircraft and they were also warned that the target was so important that if they did not achieve their objective in this raid they would be sent in again. The bomb load was mainly the maximum number of HEs but some aircraft carried a 100% incendiary bomb load.

The Squadron would go in with the first wave at a low height of 7,000 ft, their objectives being the Scientists' and Engineers' living quarters. This was the first use of a Master Bomber to control the operation. Squadron aircrew reported the arrival of night fighters on the return journey with long running fights in the bright moonlight, with bombers being attacked all around and the sky full of tracers. There was a report that during the operation, Air Gunners from 51 and another 4 Group aircraft opened fire on each other by mistake.

P/O Nick Richards' aircraft, HR732 MH-Y, sustained an engine failure and the crew jettisoned all unessential equipment so that they could bomb the target. Because of the loss of the starboard inner engine they were denied the use of the Pesco vacuum pump which operated the Mk XIV bombsight sighting head gyro and components in the computer. The Bomb Aimer 'Dixie' Dean therefore had to estimate the sighting angle and the point at which to release the bombs. The crew returned safely having come back at a very low level to avoid night fighters. The Pilot was awarded the DFC for this sortie, after which the crew was screened from ops.

The squadron's route for the operation was Snaith; out over Flamborough Head; 55.20N 80.29E; 54.24N 13.40E; Island of Rugen; Peenemunde; Mando; Snaith. Bomber Command had carried out a successful diversionary operation by sending eight Mosquitos to Berlin with 'Window', capitalising on its successful use in the Hamburg raid. This 'Spoof' raid attracted the attention of some 200 night fighters, consequently only a few night fighters arrived at Peenemunde to catch the last wave of bombers. Nevertheless 29 aircraft in the last wave were shot down, out of a total loss of 40 aircraft, which was a loss of 6.7% of the total force. Since 51 Squadron was fortunate enough to be in the first wave it suffered no losses. The attack was successful since the 'V' weapon programme was put back at least two months.

BATTLE OF BERLIN

On 23/24 August the squadron participated in the start of the Battle of Berlin with a maximum effort of 27 aircraft from all three flights of the squadron, which were operating with the Code letters MH and LK. Berlin, in addition to being the capital of Germany, was an important industrial target. A large number of the factories producing important war materials were integrated with the domestic areas. This meant that it was not possible to destroy these factories without an area bombing campaign.

Between 23/24 August 1943 and 24/25 March 1944, which was the final raid on Berlin in this campaign, the squadron took part in 9 raids. During this period the German defences were starting to recover. However, Berlin was not the only target and the squadron participated in 48 operations with about 800 sorties involving a loss of 43 aircraft (loss rate of 5%) and about 240 aircrew. These losses meant that it was difficult for an aircrew member of the squadron to attain the 30 operations required for a tour.

One of these operations was a raid on Leipzig on 19/20 February 1944 and the squadron was very fortunate not to lose any aircraft on that operation because the losses amongst the Halifax squadrons were approx 14%, the majority of these being Mk II aircraft. As a result of this the Mk II Halifax was withdrawn from operations over Germany. But since 51 Squadron had converted to the Mk III aircraft it continued to operate in the Berlin campaign. Number 158 Squadron at Lisset converted to the Mk IIIs before 51 as a result of which on 23rd of December aircrews from the squadron had to travel to Lisset by road and ferry several Mk II aircraft to 51 Squadron the following day. A problem arose when the aircraft arrived at Snaith, because due to fog landing was quite hazardous and one aircraft hit the runway with such force that it bounced the height of a house and caused several men who were working on the runway to scatter.

The experiences of P/O John Morris's crew as described by Dave Storey exemplify some of the problems encountered in this Leipzig raid:

"Shortly after we became airborne it was discovered that the aircraft heating system had failed, which was the start of our troubles. Once we reached our operational height of of around 18,000 to 20,000 feet the cold was beyond description. The thermometers read -25 below and although we were warmly clothed this cold penetrated everything. Unfortunately it was impossible to navigate with thick gloves on, all I was able to wear was my thin silk gloves with fingerless wool mittens on top. The metal Dalton computer and dividers were so cold it was like handling hot metal. After the trip I discovered all my finger tips were slilghtly frost bitten, also my heels. Strangely enough one would have expected the toes to be more affected than the heels. But the skin of the latter was hard and shiny, just like a mild burn. We had to keep removing the oxygen masks to break the ice caused by the condensation of our breaths. We all carried Thermos flasks of hot coffee which was more than welcome on this occasion. However the cold was so intense that coffee which I spilt on my navigation chart froze instantly on contact and had to be hacked off with a penknife before I was able to continue with my plotting.
Nick Simmonds (Our Flight Commander who was flying with us) tapped me on the shoulder and shouted "Bloody cold up here Storey, I've got one heating pipe shoved down my front and another up my backside and I'm still frozen", which was quite natural as there was no heat coming through at all. (This was nothing compared with that which the rear portion of Nick's anatomy would suffer on the Villers Bocage raid). Shortly after this I nearly jumped out of my skin due to the noise caused by Nick Simmonds firing off the Vickers K gun in the nose. The object of this exercise was to warm his hands on the barrel. The intense cold was not our only worry since the the met forecast winds were exactly 180 degrees out. Instead of flying into a head wind we had a very strong tail wind in the region of 80 to 100 mph. This meant we were very much ahead of time all the way along the route and had to constantly fly triangular dog leg courses to lose time. We flew 3 minute and 6 minute dog legs at frequent intervals in a desperate attempt to loose time but we could not loose enough with such a strong tail wind, which was the complete opposite of the forecast on which the operation had been planned.
The Pathfinder Force with its more sophisticated equipment was sending back estimated winds to Bomber Command which were averaged out and

retransmitted to the main force. On this occasion these broadcast winds appeared to cause more confusion to an already confused main force and many rejected them because they were 180 degrees different from the original forecast winds. I decided quite early on to use the broadcast winds on the assumption that the PFF with their superior equipment knew what they were doing.

We were flying on a northerly route with the purpose of misleading the Germans into believing that we were making for Berlin. The final approach to the target was to be made from a turning point well north of Leipzig, marked by a PFF route marker flare. When we spotted this flare we found ourselves south west of track and accordingly altered course visually for this marker flare and replotted our course for the target using the broadcast wind. We duly arrived over Leipzig 20 minutes before zero hour in spite of all our efforts to lose time, due entirely to those contrary winds. I therefore decided that the only sensible thing to do was to fly a Radius of Action in the direction of the lightest flak area. This manoeuvre would take us away from the target area and bring us back exactly on zero hour, a far better alternative to flying around the target area whilst being coned by searchlights and pumped full of flak for 20 minutes. We arrived back over Leipzig exactly on zero hour, just as the first flares went down. We dropped our bombs on the sky marker flares, since the target was covered by cloud, and immediately started on the long journey home against those appalling head winds and still frozen to the marrow. It was reported that the majority of the force dropped their bombs in the wrong area that night as a result of rejecting the broadcast winds. The raid was therefore a flop. Although we did not suffer from enemy action ourselves that night we did endure the indescribable cold."

The Leipzig disaster, as far as the squadron was concerned, was eclipsed six weeks later by their last operation in the Battle of Berlin. The German defences were now recovering from the setbacks they had encountered following the Hamburg raids. This recovery is best described by examining in detail the Nuremburg raid, at the end of the Battle of Berlin, which was a very traumatic experience for 51 Squadron and can be contrasted with the Krefeld raid. As discussed the Krefeld raid showed the efficiency of the German defences before the major radio countermeasures were in force by the RAF. The Nuremburg raid took place after the RAF had put numerous countermeasures into force, including 'Window' and 100 Group support, so that various Luftwaffe systems such as Wurzburg and AI radar FuG 202 could be neutralised. However, the Germans had another card up their sleeve because they had produced the Lichenstein SN-2, FuG 220 AI radar with various variants, developed from their ASV radar and operating in the frequency range 37.5 to 118 Mhz. This system had a cumbersome aerial array and could be considered primitive by comparison with the 490 Mhz FuG 202, with the disadvantage of a longer minimum range. However, the longer wavelength of the system (3 metres) meant that it was unaffected by the 'Window' strips currently in use. The disadvantage of longer minimum range was overcome by including a modified version of FuG 202, Lichenstein C1-Weitwinkel with a single quad dipole, for final closure to visual contact at around 300 feet. (See Figure at the start of this chapter).

To complement the foregoing, night fighters, including single seater 'Wilde Sau' aircraft, were fitted with a 'Naxos' receiver for homing in on H2S transmissions and a FuG 227 'Flensburg' to home in on 'Monica' transmissions. In addition the Luftwaffe having replaced their original 'Wurzburg' radar by the more efficient 'Giant Wurzburg', had added the 'Naxos' receivers to the older 'Wurzburg' to produce 'Naxburg' receivers, and developed another system called 'Korfu'. Both were ground based installations for monitoring H2S transmissions and were effective enough to be able to detect them whilst the aircraft were still over England. The normal 'Naxburg' range was 100 to 160 miles but two sets on a 2,000 ft mountain achieved a range of 250 to 300 miles.

At Snaith, on the 30th March, the ground crews were busy preparing the aircraft for an operation. Looking at the fuel and bomb loads they knew that the aircrews were in for another long haul but obviously did not realise what a harrowing event the squadron was due to experience. Snow had fallen in Yorkshire so the Riggers were given the job of applying de-icing paste to the leading edges of the wings etc. A number of machines had to be withdrawn from the list of available aircraft because of serviceability problems. On 'C' Flight 'U' Uncle was found to be u/s so the crew captained by Sgt Keith Alderson were stood down. In the afternoon however a new crew list was drawn up so they were allocated MH-S a new arrival on the squadron from 48 MU the Handley Page Halifax repair depot at Clifton (Rawcliffe), York. At 1840 hrs the crew took off in this aircraft for an air test whilst the armourers stood by ready to bomb up. This new aircraft was found to be less serviceable than MH-U, since it could not be trimmed to fly hands off and the maximum speed was 170 mph. The Pilot therefore landed and reported the problem to the Flight Commander, Nick Simmonds. He had to make a difficult decision about the aircraft since Bomber Command had called for a maximum effort and there were no spare aircraft available.

ANALYSIS OF OPERATIONS 1943-45

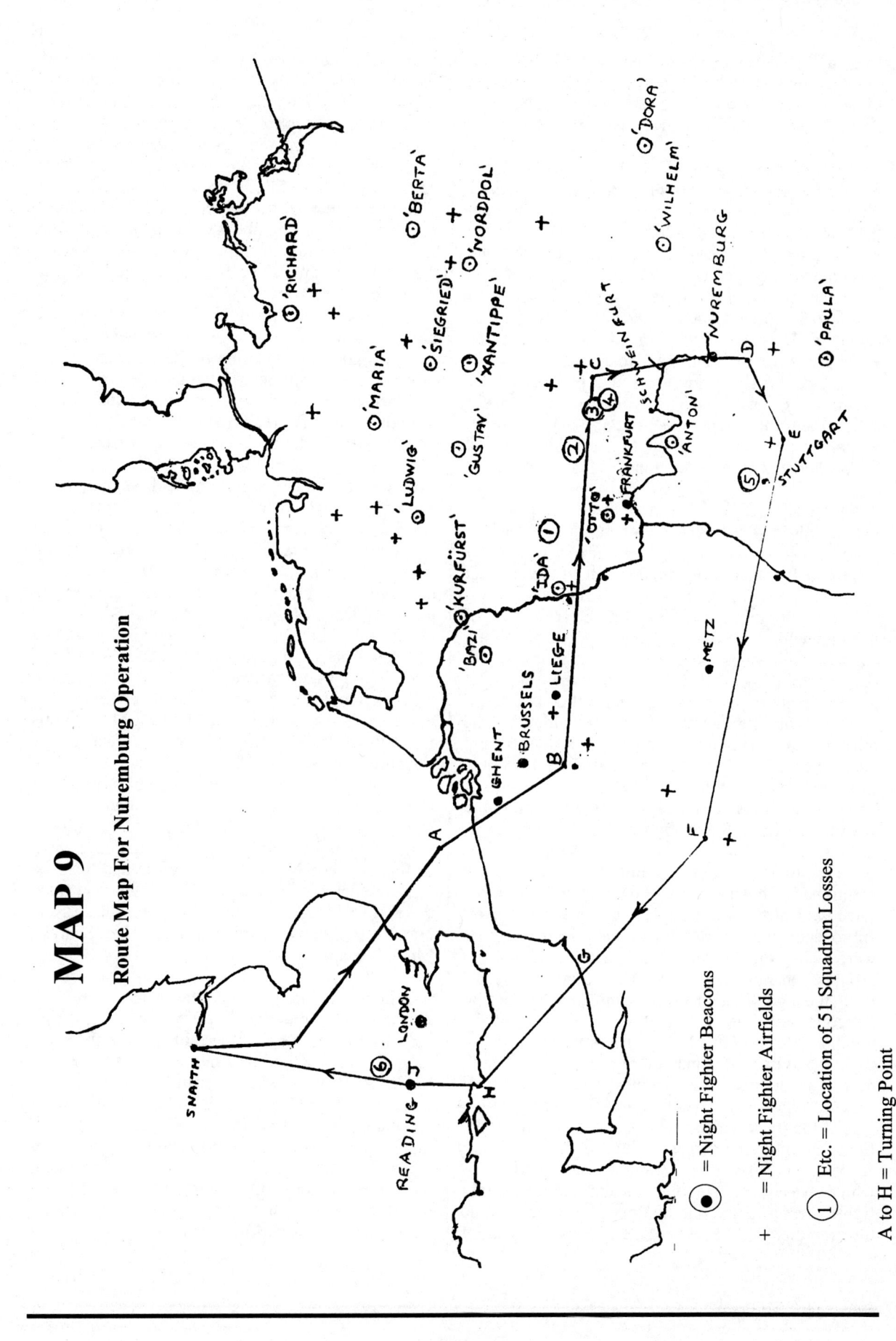

MAP 9
Route Map For Nuremburg Operation

◉ = Night Fighter Beacons

+ = Night Fighter Airfields

① Etc. = Location of 51 Squadron Losses

A to H = Turning Point

Eventually a decision was made to scrub MH-S from the operation, so that the crew were stood down. In view of the squadron's experiences in this operation the crew were glad they had to give it a miss.

The squadron commander W/C Ayling was on leave and Larry Ling was not taking over as CO until the 1 April so Flight Commander, Peter Hill, carried out the briefing at about 1830 hrs. He lead the squadron by getting together a 'scratch crew' and commandeering aircraft MH-F. The Station Commander G/C Fresson had welcomed a party of newspaper correspondents and photographers to Snaith. They were visiting the station on the authority of Bomber Command to cover the activities of a typical bomber station and took photographs of the briefing, the Station Navigation Officer (S/Ldr Jousse) and the Navigation Leader (Doug. Rubery) preparing the flight plan for the raid, the Control Tower and a debriefing session.

After the take-off from Snaith for the Nuremburg raid the Squadron Navigators quite happily switched on their H2S sets, thankful for the assistance of another electronic navigation aid, but unaware of the fact that they were providing a weapon for the enemy. Consequently the Luftwaffe could detect the start of the raid whilst the bomber stream was assembling over England and prepare to monitor it all the way to the target. The enemy did not know that the target was Nuremburg and in fact initially they thought it was Frankfurt but they could track the aircraft. The RAF set up a diversionary raid with Mosquitos, but since these aicraft were not fitted with H2S, the Luftwaffe was not fooled. They could distinguish between the diversionary raid and the main bomber stream with its H2S transmissions.

At the time of this operation, as previously mentioned, the squadron had converted to the more effective Halifax Mk III and as the squadron aircraft approached the 'Kammhuber line' the battle lines were being drawn up. Aware that a raid was in progress, thanks to the lack of radio silence by the RAF, the night fighters were assembled at their Radio Beacons including some alongside the track of the bomber stream, see Map 9. The Luftwaffe Third Fighter Division was massed at radio beacon 'Ida', near Aachen and other fighters were waiting at beacon 'Otto' near Frankfurt, not far from position 'C' on the track which was the turning point for the final run into the target. With the help of their 'Naxos' and 'Flensburg' monitors and the AI radar, which wasn't being jammed, the German night fighters could detect the bomber stream as it came towards them. AI radar contacts, assisted by night fighter flares dropped by German bomber aircraft above the track of the bomber stream to illuminate it, plus a moonlight night and contrails produced by the aircraft, all contributed to the chance of a final visual contact being made. Under these conditions, even the 'Wilde Sau' aircraft, which were considered to have filled gaps in the Radar defences produced by the use of 'Window', were also able to achieve successes and the RAF bomber stream was virtually flying into a trap. In order to compound the RAF aircrews' difficulties, the German 'Heinrich' jammers were subjecting the 'Gee' transmissions to heavy jamming so that the navigators had to rely on broadcast winds for an accurate DR plot. On this operation very strong winds were encountered and the meteorological forecast winds were so inaccurate that many aircraft were off track with the result that the bomber stream started to become dispersed.

The twin engine night fighters had, as mentioned earlier, another very effective and fairly new weapon in their armoury, namely an upward firing cannon at the rear of the cockpit, code named 'Schrage Musik'. The technique with this weapon, after visual contact was established, was to fly underneath their target and aim upwards to hit the petrol tanks in the wings. The bomb bay had to be avoided because an explosion there could wreck the night fighter as well as the bomber. At this stage the RAF were not fully aware of the danger of this type of weapon, despite the fact that upward firing guns for anti Zeppelin defence were known to 51 Squadron in World War 1. As the squadron, intermingled with the bomber stream, moved into Germany and closer to the night fighter concentrations, the aircrew started to see on both sides of them the tragic sight of aircraft going down in flames. The Navigators therefore had to make regular entries in their log of 'Kite down' and since the night fighters were not using incendiaries the crews were not aware this was due to the 'Schrage Musik' weapon.

An important target was the Maschinenfabrik Augsburg Nuremberg (MAN) works, a significant industrial objective, but the raid was a failure, the target being obscured by cloud with part of the PFF marking Schweinfurt by mistake. Some of the aircraft with no H2S and hence dependent on very inaccurate forecast winds, were so much off track that they bombed Schweinfurt which is 55 miles NW of Nuremburg. The Pathfinders were late with the result that some of the aircraft had to circle the target, with bombers milling around risking collisions and the marking was poor. The result was an excessive creep-back of the bombing, and very little damage achieved. All this was in direct contrast to the Krefeld raid. After leaving the target the bomber stream became more widely dispersed and interception more difficult for the night fighters. Nevertheless, 51 Squadron lost two aircraft on the return journey giving a total loss of 6 aircraft on this raid, 35% of aircraft despatched, a tragedy for the squadron.

The squadron aircraft lost on the raid were firstly, LV822 piloted by F/Sgt Wilkins which was shot down by night fighters and crashed at Guntersdorf near Helborn, with 7 aircrew killed. The second aircraft, LW544 piloted by Sgt Brougham, was also shot down by night fighters and crashed at Wahlen, north west of Alsfeld. Five men were killed and two taken prisoner. Sgt Binder was piloting LV857 the third squadron aircraft to be shot down by a night fighter and it crashed at Schwarzbach, north east of Fulda, with the loss of all the crew. A fourth aircraft piloted by F/Sgt Stembridge was shot down by a night fighter and crashed at Fladungen, east of Fulda, with 2 crew killed and 5 taken prisoner. Squadron Leader Hill on his 13th operation of a tour was believed to have been downed by flak over Stuttgart and crashed at Bietigheim, north of Stuttgart, with everyone killed. The last squadron aircraft to be lost was piloted by P/O Brooks on his 19th operation. The aircraft made it back to the UK but crashed at Stokenchurch, north of Reading. It is believed that it was trying to land at one of the airfields in the vicinity. When a recue party from Benson arrived at the crash site the pilot was still alive but died shortly afterwards.

A member of P/O Brooks' crew, the Mid Upper Air Gunner D.Churchill, was married to Anne Duffy a WAAF MT driver at Snaith who was expecting his child. Like many other WAAF drivers she would have the task of transporting the crews to their aircraft in an aircrew coach, many of whom including her husband she would not see return. Her son Dennis Churchill, named after his father, rather poignantly recently attended a squadron memorial service at Selby Abbey to commemorate a father he sadly never knew.

To recap, everything was against the Squadron that night. Their aircraft appeared naked in the moonlit night with icing conditions producing tell tale contrails as a give-away to the enemy, cloud over target and strong winds with inaccurate wind vectors transmitted to the bomber stream. The target was out of range of 'Gee' but even in the earlier stages it was being jammed by the enemy. The night fighters were lying in wait for the squadron and the H2S and 'Monica' radar aids were being compromised by the enemy and used as a homing device. The fighters also had the advantage of an AI radar system that was not being jammed, so that they could make maximum use of their 'Schrage Musik' weapon.

OPERATING FOR SHAEF

With 'Operation Overlord' in the offing the Air Staff required Bomber Command to participate in a strategic bombing campaign in support of the forthcoming operation. ACM Harris was not very pleased at this and a report on the bomber offensive states that he detested the objectives laid down because it took him away from his major objective of destroying German industry. However from April onwards it was a very fortunate respite for Bomber Command which had lost a lot of aircraft and aircrew in the past few months.

Based on what was known as the Zuckermann plan, ACM Portal, (Chief of the Air Staff), laid down a list of strategic targets in the French railway system to be attacked starting on the 6 March. As mentioned Harris was not very pleased at this because he considered that his bomber force would not be very effective against the strategic targets stated, but he had to obey the directive. As a consequence he committed 4 and 6 Groups to the task so that he could continue to use his Lancasters, which he considered superior to the Halifax, for his area bombing campaign. However many 4 and 6 Group squadrons had now been converted to the successful Halifax Mk III and starting on the 6 March the squadron participated in attacks against railway targets at Trappes, Le Mans, Aulnoy, and Coutrai. To Harris's surprise the 'Halifax Boys' turned the tables on him by carrying out some very effective attacks on these targets. On the night of 6/7 March the squadron joined other 4 Group squadrons for the raid against Trappes. This was a very important rail depot and set of marshalling yards near Paris. The target was marked by 'Oboe' Mosquitoes and 15 aircraft from the squadron along with 246 other Halifax aircraft dropped a total of 1,258 tons of bombs with great accuracy.

The last raid of the month on Vaires, near Paris was particularly effective with two ammunition trains being blown up and a lot of troops killed. In the words of an aviation historian, Harris was 'Hoist with his own petard'! The Air Staff were then convinced that Bomber Command was not as blunt a weapon for strategic bombing as Harris had

ANALYSIS OF OPERATIONS 1943-45

claimed and could operate outside the pattern it had normally employed up to then. Sadly after fulfilling Portal's requirements concerning the March railway targets the squadron had to participate in the abortive Nuremberg raid at the end of March as reported earlier in this chapter. After Nuremberg the commitment to the 'Overlord' programme was a very fortunate respite since it gave 51 Squadron a chance to recoup from the deep penetrations into Germany which had taken such a toll of the squadron and yet still carry out important operations which would help to win the war. The Berlin raids were very costly to both 4 and 8 Groups and in fact AVM Bennett considered that several more operations against that target would have broken the back of his PFF. The official date of transfer of major Bomber Command effort to the pre-invasion targets was the 14 April and this campaign involved the squadron in strategic operations, up to, during and after the 'D' Day invasions. They participated in the pre-invasion 'spoof' ops. whereby for every strategic target in the invasion area, two in the Pas de Calais area would be attacked. The purpose of this ploy was to convince the German High Command that the main invasion would take place in the latter area and that the landing on the Normandy beaches was a diversionary operation.

Operations were continued against the French railways because of their strategic value. They provided an important communication facility for the German Army as they could be used for the rapid transit of troops and Panzer divisions to any part of the invasion area. The Zuckermann Transportation Plan therefore envisaged the neutralisation of the French railway system by bombing the main French railway centres. The effective working of a railway system was dependent upon its traffic control centres, marshalling yards and locomotive running and repair sheds, which were often grouped together in one large complex. The squadron's contribution to this operation is shown in Map 12. In the Zuckermann Plan, 80 railway centres in NE France were to be attacked by the various air forces, 25 of which were allocated to Bomber Command. General Montgomery wanted the rail system out of action within a wide radius from the beach head and the plans had to make provision for ensuring that the lives of French citizens were not needlessly put at risk. These ops. were of prime importance to the Allied cause for the run-up to the D-Day landings on the Normandy beaches and the support operations after the landings. In addition to the Transportation Plan objectives, targets included heavy batteries in the German coastal defence system, and radio listening stations. On the day before D-Day the squadron sent 10 aircraft to bomb a coastal battery at Herquelingue in the Pas de Calais which was one of the D-Day deception targets.

For Operation 'Neptune' on the 6 June, the seaborne landing phase of 'Overlord', the target for the squadron was one of the ten 'Neptune' batteries to be attacked by Bomber Command. The squadron's objective was target number 10/J/178, a heavy battery at Mont Fleury overlooking the 'Gold' beach, where the 50th T.T. Division ('The Geordies'), 7th Armoured Division and 42nd R.M.

Photo 76 via D. Churchill (Junior)

Four members of P/O Brooks' crew lost on Nuremburg raid (D. Churchill on right)

Photo 77

Via

D. Churchill (Junior)

M/T Driver A. Duffy wife of D. Churchill

Commando landed. When the aircraft were being prepared on the 5 June for this operation, both ground and air crew realised that something important was in the wind since certain special preparations had to take place. One example is the fact that the Radar Mechanics had to immobilise the IFF sets by using locking wire on the switches in the control unit (Fig 39) and Type 27 'Gee' RF Units were made available for all Navigators.

At the briefing the aircrew were told that the type of target they were attacking but not the reason for the operation, although they guessed something special was going on, particularly as both ground and aircrew were confined to camp. Bomber Command had now realised the importance of radio silence, so a restriction was put on the use of H2S and IFF was banned, hence the action by the Radar Section. The Navigators were briefed that H2S was not needed because special frequencies would be in use for the 'Gee' chains and all aircraft were fitted with the tunable Type 27 RF unit to receive them. If the Channel chain was used on D-Day then the RF unit setting was 27/110/1 with an ALU setting of 7.

Twenty-four aircraft were detailed for the operation with a bomb load of 9 x 1000 lb and 4 x 500 lb HEs, but one had to cancel due to technical failure. Take off was between 0228 and 0258 and the target was bombed between 0437 and 0442. The Pathfinder Force had marked the target but there was 10/10 cloud at 10,000 ft, some crews bombed at 10,500 ft and others came below the cloud to bomb. Most of the crews could see the markers through the cloud. There were no aerial combats and negligible opposition was encountered. After the operation the aircraft flew west returning over the Cotentin Peninsular and back across the Channel. Through breaks in the cloud they could see the Invasion Armada. Twenty-two aircraft landed at Base between 0648 and 0728 and one landed away short of fuel. The following morning when personnel were entering their various messes they heard the BBC news over the Tannoy reporting the landings and cheers went up.

Back on the beaches in the chilly first light of dawn the assault craft headed towards 'Gold' beach and thankfully the bombardment of the German positions had been effective. The assault components of the 69th and 231st Brigade moved as fast as possible across the bullet swept beaches. The Royal Engineers landed their armoured support vehicles with flail tanks clearing mines and other vehicles opening exits from the beach and neutralising strong points. Examination of the Mont Fleury Casemates

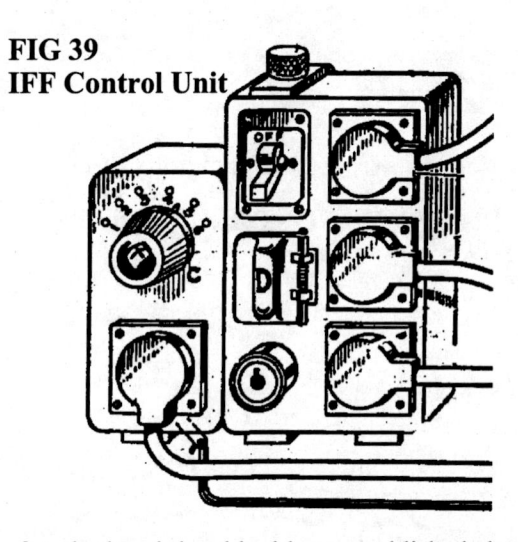

FIG 39 IFF Control Unit

after the beach head had been established showed that they were very strongly constructed and therefore difficult to destroy but the bombing had been successful in that it had destroyed the ammunition store and all the supporting buildings. The result of this was that when the Infantry captured the bunkers they found that the gun crews had to cease firing because they had run out of ammunition due to the destruction of their ammunition supply by the bombing, also the gun crews were dazed and demoralised by the bombing.

When the Allied Forces were fighting to establish their beach head after the Normandy landings, support operations by Bomber Command were quite important. Heavy attacks were carried out against certain railway centres, the objective being to cut off rail traffic to the invasion area from Southern France, North East and Eastern France and the Brest Peninsular. Then on the 30 June 1944 an army support operation took place. The 2nd and 9th Panzer Divisions were moving up to carry out an attack on the junction of the British and American armies. Consequently a heavy attack on the road junction at Villers Bocage, through which they would be passing, was planned. 51 Squadron supplied 23 aircraft for the raid which was controlled with great care by a Master Bomber in the last light of evening. Because of the problems of dust and smoke from the bombs obscuring the target the Master Bomber ordered the bombers down to 4,000 ft to ensure that they bombed on the markers and a total of 1,000 tons of bombs was dropped.

One of the most useful operations carried out by the squadron in direct support of the Allied Armies was in the break out from Caen code named 'Operation Goodwood'. About a fortnight after D-Day the

ANALYSIS OF OPERATIONS 1943-45

MAP 12

51 Squadron Strategic Operations in 1944

'OVERLORD', 'NO BALL' and ZUCKERMANN Strategic Targets

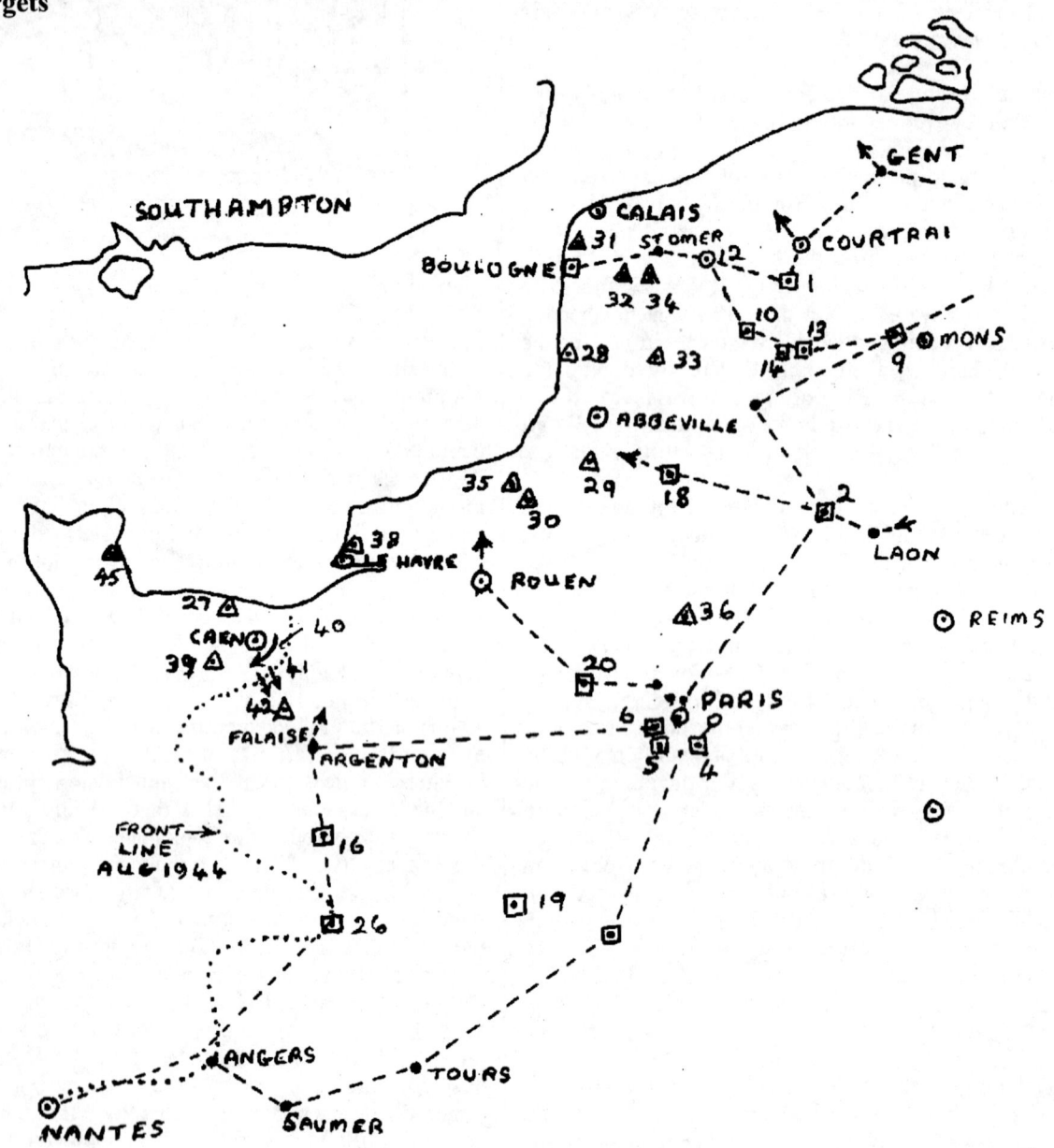

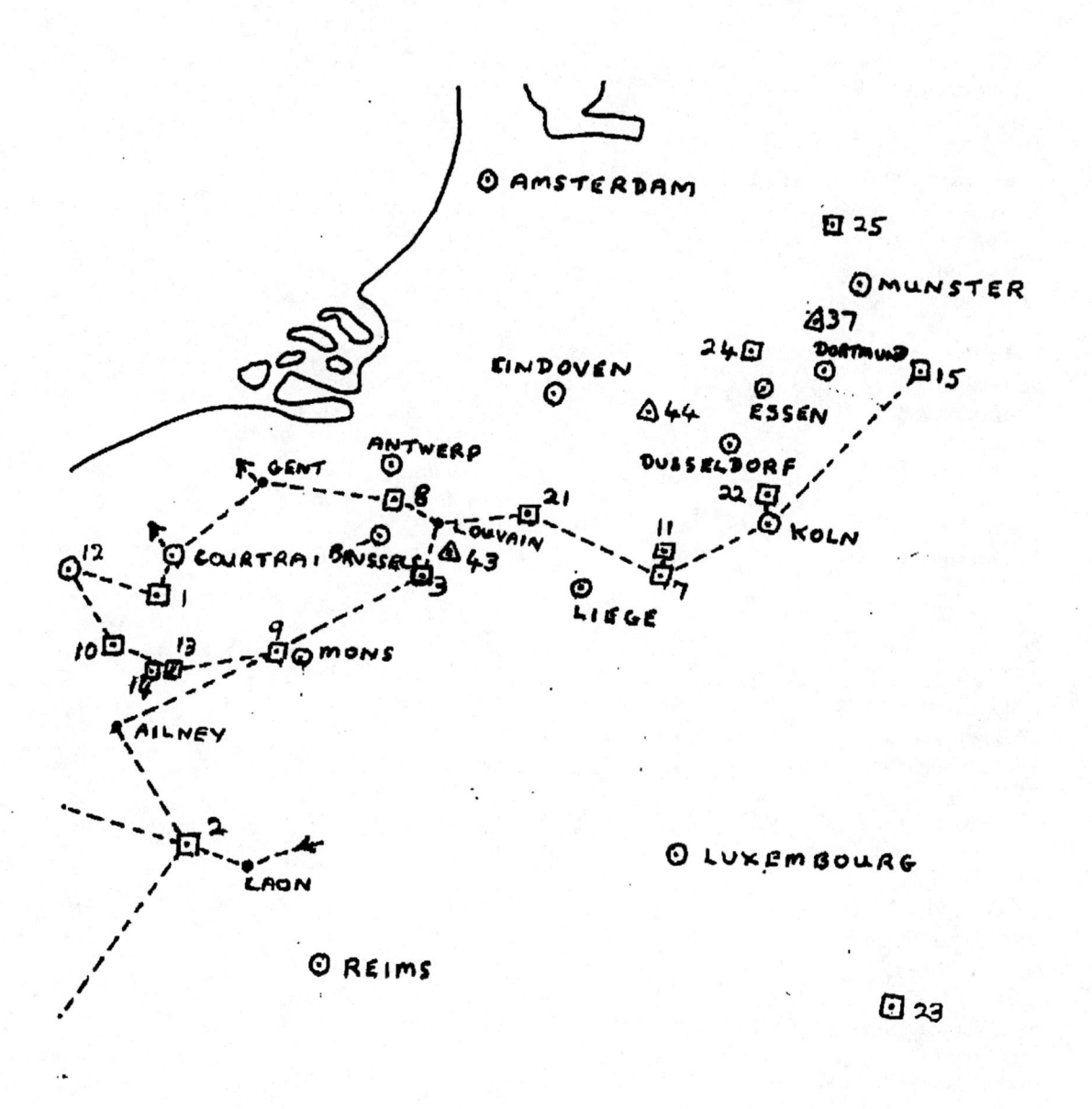

ANALYSIS OF OPERATIONS 1943-45

⊙   Towns and citys

— — —   Railway System

▫ 2   Railway targets attacked by 51 Squadron

•   Railway targets for other squadrons

△ 30   Other strategic targets

• • • • • •   Allied front line August 1944

Key To Strategic Targets In Map 12

Railway (Zuckermann) Targets
1 Lille
2 Tergnier
3 Ottignies
4 Villeneuve St George (Paris)
5 Massey Palaiseau (Paris)
6 Trappes (Paris)
7 Montzen
8 Malines
9 St Ghislain
10 Lems
11 Aachen
12 Hazebrouck
13 Somain
14 Douai
15 Soest
16 Alencon
17 Orleans
18 Amiens
19 Chateadun
20 Mantes La Jolie
21 Hasselt
22 Opladen
23 Saarbrucken
24 Recklinghausen
25 Rhein
26 La Mans

Gun Batteries
27 Mont Fleury
28 Colline Beaumont
45 Morsalines

'V' Weapons Sites
29 Oisemont
30 St Martin L'Hortier
31 Marquis/Mimoyecques
32 Lumbres
33 Siracourt
34 Wizernes
35 Croixdalle
36 Thiverney

Military Establishments
37 Dulmen
38 Le Havre

Army Support Operations
39 Villers Bocage

40 "Operation Goodwood"
41 "Operation Totalise"
42 "Operation Tractable"

Airfields
43 Tirlemont
44 Venlo

The following strategic targets are not recorded on map 12:
Vaires
Bingen
Opladen
Herquelingue
Pont Asbagnol
Le Grand Rossignol
Les Cateliere
Nucourt
Bois De La Haie
Anderbek
Bois De Cassan
Bourg Leopold
Alyis Le Havre
Fouillard
Foret De Nieppe
Ferme D'Urville

ANALYSIS OF OPERATIONS 1943-45

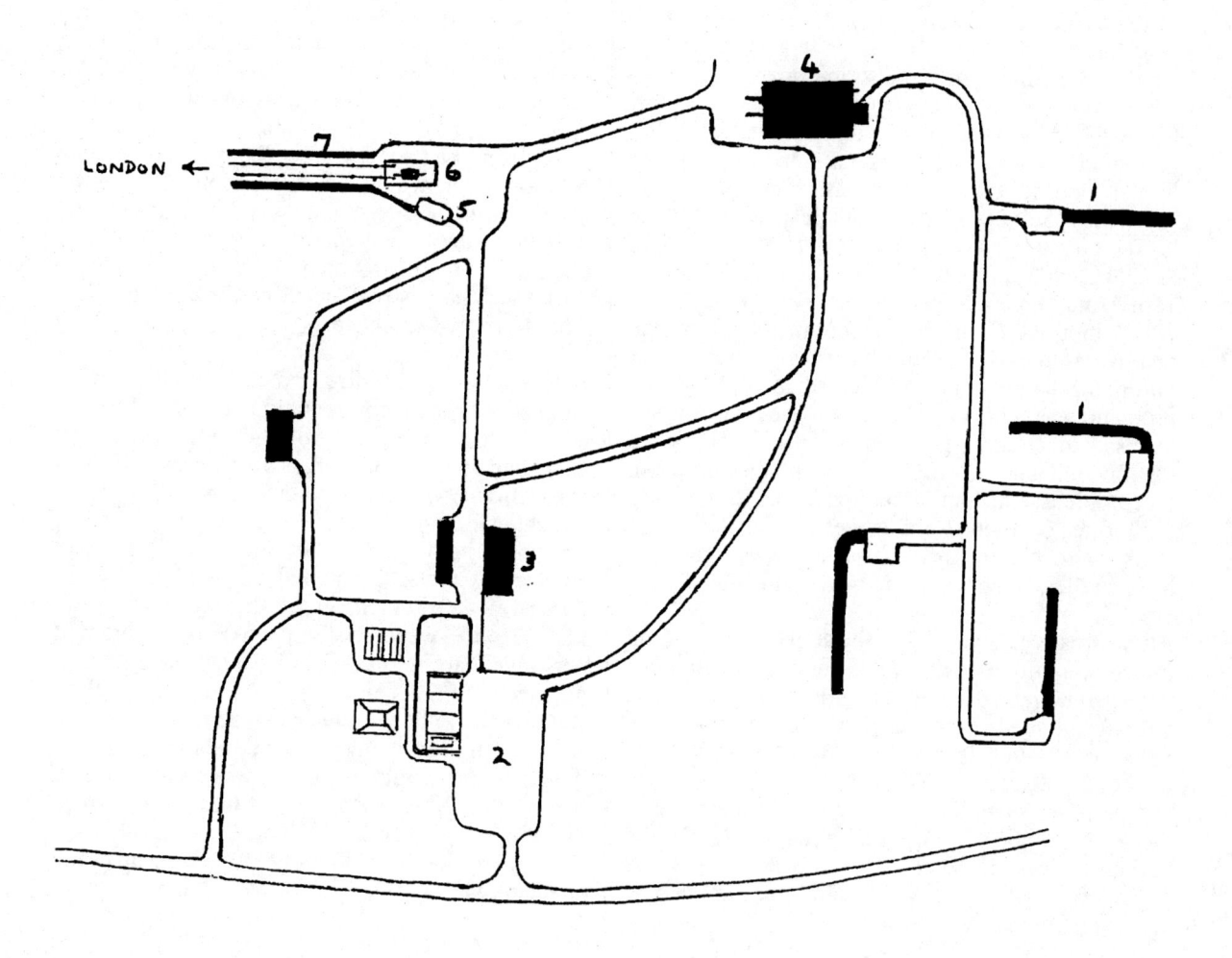

Map 13

Sketch Map Of Layout Of A Typical Establised 'V1' Site
Key
1=Shelters ('Ski' Shaped)
2=Assembly Area For V1's
3=Technical Offices
4=Gyro Compass Deviation Correction Building
5=Firing Shelter
6=Firing Mechanism

Allies had only gained about one fifth of the territory they had planned to occupy by mid July. They were therefore pinned down in a narrow bridgehead about 10-20 miles deep. It was a critical situation since the Germans were not yielding ground so a break out was essential before they achieved a large build up in front of the Allies. It was also important to prevent the movement of armour to the American sector. Since the Allies had plenty of tanks available an armoured attack was planned and the name 'Goodwood' for the operation was an apt one since at the word 'Go' the tanks would leap forward like horses out of a starting gate. A strong 'left hook' around Caen from the North East was planned, led by 11th Armoured Division followed by the Guards and 7th Armoured Divisions. Some members of the guards armoured division had been stationed at Pollington barracks on the East of the airfield. The problem was that the attackers' flanks would be exposed to German fire. On their left flank were fortified villages east of Caen. The villages had been turned into a system of linked strong points covering each other by mutual defensive fire On their right flank were the factory areas of Caen, such as Mondeville, which were also heavily fortified.

At the break of dawn, before the attack, 51 Squadron joined one of the strongest air armadas in history to tear apart targets successfully marked by 'Oboe'. The aircraft bombed from medium heights, between 5,000 and 10,000 ft. Bomber Command dropped a total of 5,000 tons of 500 and 1,000 lb HE bombs, in two narrow rectangles on either side of the route of the Allied armour. TIs were dropped by PFF for the various waves of bombers to prevent the Bomb Aimers from taking the clouds of dust as their targets or from bombing short. When the Germans saw dark objects detach themselves from the leading aircraft in the bomber stream and realised they were bombs they either climbed into the tanks and closed the flaps or got underneath them. These Panzer troops went through the most terrifying hours of their lives with colleagues knocked unconscious by blast, tanks blown over, set on fire or buried in earth. No German fighters were encountered because of air superority and there was no serious flak because the 88 mm guns were operating in an anti-tank role. The 16th Luftwaffe Field Division and the 21st Panzer Division were badly affected, even German troops which were not casualties were dazed by the raid which reduced their operational effectiveness.

By mid August 1944 an Allied breakout was planned with the objective of trapping the Germans in what became known as the Falais Gap, so on the night of the 7/8 August, 22 aircraft from the squadron took part in 'Operation Totalise'. The plan was for two columns of armour accompanied by armoured infantry carriers to advance rapidly through the middle of the enemy defences, the flanks of the advancing columns being covered by a 1,000 bomber raid. When a gap had been produced the 4th Canadian and 1st Polish Divisions would follow through it. The squadron aircraft joined about 1,000 bombers from Bomber Command when a total of 3,500 tons of bombs was dropped on enemy positions on both side of the Falaise Road. After the bombing the Allied columns pushed ahead and achieved their objective with a very low loss of tanks and very little resistance. This was considered to be a very easy action thanks partly due to the help from Bomber Command.

A follow up to 'Totalise' which took place on 14 August was called 'Operation Tractable'. Nine aircraft from the squadron helped support the Canadian 3rd Division offensive towards Falaise in conjunction with US troops advancing from Argentan South of Falaise, by bombing German positions holding up the advance. The rapid advance by the Allies started at 1200 hours on 14 August with 160 tanks in the first wave and 90 in the second wave accompanied by armoured personnel carriers in order to swamp the anti-tank defences. Nine aircraft from 51 Squadron acompanying the Bomber Command force swept low over the advancing armour bombing the enemy defences. A terrific dust cloud was created by the bombing and the tanks crashed through it at zero visibility. The Master Bomber concentrated on keeping the bomb line moving forward ahead of the advancing armour.

However a very unfortunate 'Friendly Fire' incident occurred because the Canadian Regt. de la Chaudiere was using yellow recognition flares, the standard recognition colour for friendly troops. This information did not seem to have got through to Bomber Command, because PFF were using yellow and red TIs. The problem was compounded when an Auster Spotting aircraft flown by the army started to fire red Very cartridges over the ground markers to warn the bombers, but this only exacerbated the situation because of the red TIs. Nearly 400 Canadians were killed or wounded. The ground operation was successful since by the 15 August the Canadians were pressing on towards Falais, along with the Americans moving up from Argentan in the South, to close the Falaise gap and trap a large number of German troops, see Map 12.

The 'V' Weapon Campaign

The squadron had participated in the Peenemunde raid to retard the production of the V1 Flying Bomb, which employed a ram jet engine using a propellant mixture of hydrogen peroxide and potassium permanganate and was launched on a compass heading. The compass in the V1 was linked to a gyroscopic controlled Askania automatic pilot. A propeller operated journey counter activated a device to dive the rocket onto a target, when the appropriate distance had been traversed. By mid 1944 this weapon was in full production and operating from sites in France and the Low Countries. Because of the shape of some of the buildings they were known as 'ski sites' and the layout of a V1 site is shown in Map 13. In the compass building a process to correct the compass deviation was carried out. This was necessary because of the large amount of steel present.

The campaign against V weapons in general was given the name 'Operation Crossbow' with the V1 sites code named 'No Ball' sites and given identity numbers. Some were well defended by flak batteries, such as the Oisemont site backed up by the Abbeville battery of 30 guns (88mm, 27mm & 20mm) which was attacked by the squadron on 1 July 44. There were also V2 rocket sites, e.g. Wizernes and a V3 site at Mimoyecques-Marquise to be attacked. The V3 weapon was a 'Supergun' and at Mimoyecques multi-barrel guns with each barrel 400 ft in length were set in the hillside and targeted on London, the objective being to rain 6" shells on London at the rate of one per minute. The design of the Iraqi Supergun, which came to light in 1991 as a result of the Gulf Campaign, was based on research information available from the V3 programme.

These V weapon sites existed until the Allied Forces captured the sites, the last ground launched V2 being despatched on 3 September 1944.

DEVELOPMENTS IN THE RADIO COUNTERMEASURES WAR

During 1944 there were various developments in the Radio Countermeasures war which were of assistance in the planning of the bomber offensive. In January 1944 it was discovered that Luftwaffe Air Signals Regiments were sending out to the ground controllers ranges and bearings of RAF bombers up to 350 kilometers away, obtained by interrogating the bomber's IFF with DF equipment. Information obtained from the decoding of Enigma transmissions showed that for a number of raids during the Battle of Berlin, about 20% of the aircraft losses were the result of detections by the monitoring of IFF sets.

The RAF achieved a major success on 13th July 1944 when a Ju 88, fitted with AI FuG 212, 'Naxos' and 'Flensburg', landed in error at Woodbridge in Suffolk. The RAE used this aircraft to carry out evaluation trials on the detection of H2S and 'Monica' transmissions. As a result of these findings the RAF realised the importance of radio silence since RAF radar could be compromised and they became fully informed of the new developments the Luftwaffe had carried out with their AI radar to counter the effects of 'Window'. When the squadron was again involved in the bombing of industrial targets in Germany, in view of the lessons the RAF had learned, the control of radio emissions came into force. In July 1944 'Monica' was removed from all aircraft, IFF transmissions controlled and the use of H2S restricted. In fact 192 Squadron was given the task of monitoring the bomber stream for H2S transmissions. Also a new size of 'Window', MC2, a concertina type, was employed for jamming Fug 212 AI radar. As a result of the foregoing developments when the raids into Germany did recommence the Luftwaffe were taken completely by surprise because of the radio silence, so much so that they tried to intercept Mosquito spoof raids. Interceptions by the Luftwaffe became much more difficult because to be effective they needed 200 kilometers of warning, before the bomber squadrons entered German territory.

BACK TO GERMANY

Night attacks on German cities were carried out during the non moon period in July and day raids with fighter escort were carried out alongside the strategic bombing offensive during the summer period. The aircrew and ground staff had never worked so hard. Sometimes squadrons flew two sorties in 24 hours and during a large period of 1944 no leave or 48 hour passes were available for ground crew who had to work long hours. Aircrews had the number of operations required to complete a tour increased to about 35 ops because a high proportion of these were now carried out over France. The first major raid on a German city since the Battle of Berlin was on 23/24th July to Kiel which was a major U-boat base with important naval facilities. The bomber force appeared from behind a 'Mandrel' screen, provided by ground 'Mandrel' transmitters on the south coast of England plus No 199 Squadron Halifax aircraft each containing 8 'Mandrel' jammers for different EW radar frequencies along with 'Shiver' jammers for use against 'Wurzburg' (Map 14). Aircraft from 101 Squadron could provide 'ABC' transmitters for

ANALYSIS OF OPERATIONS 1943-45

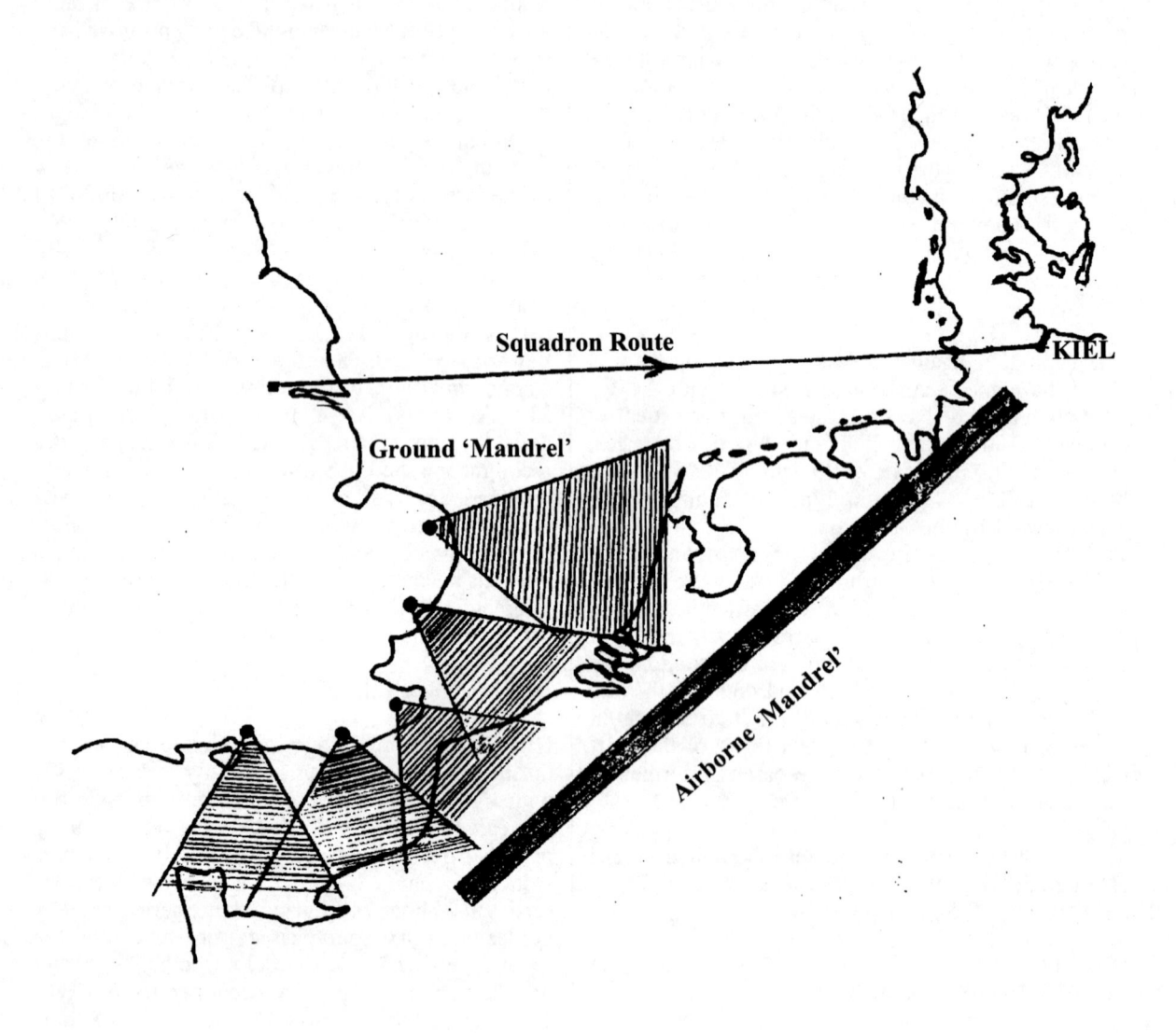

Map 14

Pictorial Representation Of Radio Counter Measures 'Mandrel' Screen For 1944 Kiel Raid

jamming the German night fighter ground controllers R/T. Radio security measures were imposed on the main force, radio emissions being controlled by putting restrictions on the use of equipment such as H2S and IFF. When spoof raids were carried out by the Special Window Force, the Germans could not distinguish between these and the main stream aircraft because of the lack of radio emissions to betray them. At Kiel, 621 aircraft bombed the port facilities and shipping very heavily, causing major damage. The foregoing measures fooled the defences and caused confusion amongst the night fighters. As a result of this Bomber Command losses were only 0.6%, and all 51 Squadron aircraft returned safely. In the return to Germany there were 12 night operations in both August and September.

Oil Targets

Synthetic ('Erzatz') oil production was of prime importance to the German war effort, in particular to fuel their aircraft and Panzer Divisions. The story of German synthetic oil production started in 1925 when two scientists, Franz Fischer and Hans Tropsch, made a discovery which the Germans rapidly developed during the 1930s for the production of synthetic petrol. This meant that when war broke out in 1939 they had an indigenous source of petroleum. The Fischer-Tropsch process, as it was called, used coal as a feedstock, a raw material of which Germany had a ready supply. In order to increase coal production during the war Germany employed both slave labour and prisoners of war in the coal mines. Coal production reached over 500 million tons a year, double that in Britain.

In the Fischer-Tropsch process powdered coal was heated with a catalyst to produce a mixture of hydrogen and carbon monoxide. These gases known as Synthesis Gases were reacted together under high temperature and pressure in the presence of special catalysts with a high surface area. The result of this reaction was that the carbon monoxide and hydrogen produced a mixture of hydrocarbons. The mixture generally included 25% of propane and butane gases (useful for heating purposes), 30% petrol, 14% diesel fuel and some other products which could be used to make synthetic soaps and fats. The main oil production plants were located at Sterkrade, Gelsenkirchen, Harborg, Bottropp, Hemmingstedt, Kamen and the Rhenania Ossag refinery at Dusseldorf. An increased concentration of attacks on these installations was started in 1944 and 51 Squadron played its part in the raids on these important targets. The Order of Battle for a Sterkrade operation is shown in Fig 17.

There is an interesting observation which was possibly due to the differences between the German synthetic fuels and the British 100 octane petrol which came from natural sources. Louis Wooldridge DFC in his two tours as an Air Gunner saw numerous aircraft shot down. His observations were that you could distinguish between exploding German and British aircraft by the colour emitted by the burning aircraft. British bombers produced a bright reddish glow by contrast with the German night fighters which exhibited a white glow.

The effectiveness of the bombing campaign in reducing the synthetic petroleum production facilities is shown by the fact that in March 1944 it was 927,000 tons but by June 1944 had been reduced to 472,000 tons. With the Ploesti oil resources cut off and the effect of the bombing campaign the German fuel situation became catastrophic by September 1944, so much so that the Luftwaffe had to reduce its training periods because aviation petrol could not be spared. The shortage of aviation fuel was also a factor in slowing down the development of the jet fighters.

In addition to oil installations, chemical factories were important targets since these were producing materials for the munitions of war. Rocket propellants were being developed by the I G Farben factories, one of these being the chemical works at Ludwigshaven which was accordingly bombed by 51 Squadron on 2/3 December 1944.

After the major break out from Normandy the German armies were broken and there was a swift advance to the German frontier but the front line was so widespread that the advance slowed down. Bomber Command had been under directives from SHAEF during the summer of 1944 in order to support the ground campaign and although it was released from this control in mid September strategic ops. were still on the cards. The Channel ports had to be captured with aerial support, petroleum and ammunition storage facilities needed to be destroyed to limit the use of German vehicles and aircraft and communications targets were still important. During 1944 the number of aircraft available to the squadron had increased markedly which contributed to the ability of the main force to easily provide 1,000 aircraft for a maximum effort. Four Group had now become accustomed to bombing relatively precise targets on markers laid blindly by 'Oboe' Mosquitoes. Also high standards of accuracy could be achieved in daylight operations. Regular raids on German cities could now be carried out.

A second Battle of the Ruhr commenced in the Autumn, daylight raids were now possible. Fortunately the German air force was deteriorating, which meant fewer losses. The last Battle of the Ruhr took place between October and December 1944 and was very devastating to the enemy with 60,830 tons of bombs being dropped for a low loss rate. Mention has been made earlier of the difficulty aircrew had in completing a tour of ops. particularly during 1943. A similar consideration could be applied to the aircraft with regard to the number of ops. they participated in before being shot down or crashed so that many aircraft did not even achieve the number of flying hours which necessitated a Major inspection. But one particular aircraft had a charmed life, this was MH-E with nose art 'Expensive Babe' (Photo 32). It completed 100 ops. with the raid against Osnabruck on 6/7 December 1944 and survived the war.

THE FINAL CAMPAIGN

1945 was the beginning of the end and the squadron continued operating against a variety of targets. By the end of January operations against oil installations had reduced oil production to 29% of its peak output and the continuous bombing reduced it even further to only 5% by the end of April. Attacks on transportation targets had devastated the German railway system which severely restricted the movement of strategic materials. Other targets were U-boat bases and construction yards, facilities for manufacture of war materials and fuel or ammunition dumps.

With regard to the latter targets there is one operation which is worth examining in detail and which can be entitled 'The night 51 Squadron (and the rest of 4 Group) missed the target'. On Sunday 14 January 1945, 4 Group was given an important strategic operation, namely a Luftwaffe fuel dump. The squadron operational report after the raid was that 21 aircraft were detailed for a night attack on an oil dump at Dulmen but the take off had to be delayed for four and three quarter hours. One aircraft cancelled with engine trouble so twenty aircraft took off between 1855 and 1917 hours. The aircraft which reached the target reported that there was only a slight haze over it so that it could be easily identified. The PFF marking was well concentrated and between 2319 and 2322 the squadron dropped 195 x 100 lb and 114 x 250 lb bombs on the markers. Only one small ground explosion was observed at 2223 and none of the fires which should occur with a fuel dump were observed. All the squadron aircraft returned to base between 0122 & 0202.

Bomber Command analysis of the operation which was based on photo reconnaissance reported that 100 Halifax Aircraft from 4 Group, supported by 15 PFF aircraft attacked a Luftwaffe fuel storage depot at Dulmen, near Munster. Most of the bombs missed the target and fell in fields to the south of it, only slight damage being inflicted on the the fuel store. One 4 Group aircraft, belonging to 578 Squadron, was lost.

On Monday 15 Jan 1945 as a result of the foregoing analysis the Instrument Section bombsight specialists were detailed for a special task. This followed a request from the Bombing Leader (F/Lt Ken Dean), acting on instructions received from a higher authority. All the Mk XIV bombsights computers had to be removed from the aircraft and checked in the calibration room in the Instrument Section. Four Instrument personnel with bombsight expertise, including the author, worked continuously overnight for up to 18 hours to check all bombsights, return them to the aircraft and carry out re-installation procedures.

All the bombsight computers were found to be within the tolerances laid down in the AP and satisfactory installations were carried out, the task being completed in time for the aircraft to be available for the forthcoming Magdeburg raid on the 16/17 January. Subsequent to the above, information was fed back to the Instrument Section that for the operation in question the forecast winds provided by the Meteorological Service were incorrect. If wind vectors, which had to be fed into the bombsight computer manually, were incorrect, then bombing errors would occur.

As 1945 unfolded, due to the gradual destruction of the Luftwaffe and the advance of the Allied Forces, the RAF could operate more freely than previously, also there were sufficient aircraft to sustain two large raids on the same night. Because of the fluidity of the Allied front line a problem for the squadron when bombing German targets near the front line, was to ensure that no bombs were dropped on the Allied side of the bomb line, an example of which is shown in Map 7. The amphibious Rhine crossing by the US 9th Army and British 2nd Army took place on the 24 March and this was supported by bombing operations against the Ruhr which was still supplying fuel and munitions to the German front line on the Rhine. Then as the war drew to an end the effort required diminishd so that on the 15 April 1945 the squadron was reduced to two Flights to carry out the last operation at Snaith, the target being the Naval Base

ANALYSIS OF OPERATIONS 1943-45

S E C R E T

51 SQUADRON, R.A.F. STATION SNAITH
Battle Order - Serial Number 641. 18/8/1944
Officer I/C Flying S/Ldr Varey

AIRCRAFT	CAPTAIN	NAVIGATOR	BOMB AIMER	WIRELESS OPERATOR	FLIGHT ENGINEER	M.U. GUNNER	REAR GUNNER
A	F/O Coldrick	P/O Markham	Sgt Rounce	Sgt Butterfield	F/Sgt Dobson	Sgt Lea	Sgt Bowan
B	F/O McKnight	F/Sgt Cider	F/Sgt McKay	F/Sgt Flees	F/Sgt Toobay	F/O Paradise	Sgt Smith
E	F/O Boyers	Sgt Russell	F/Sgt Murphy	F/Sgt Ramsey	Sgt Jenkins	Sgt Blamire	Sgt Fry
H	F/Sgt Abell	Sgt Marsh	Sgt Howat	F/Sgt White	Sgt Merrill	Sgt Rouse	Sgt Jones
J	F/O Willies	Sgt Vaight	F/Lt Scott	Sgt Polden	Sgt Howard	Sgt Burgess	Sgt Davies
L	F/Lt Richardson	F/O Grose	F/O Preston	Sgt Crisp	Sgt O'Conner	P/O Butson	Sgt Barrington
N	P/O Quan	Sgt Franklin	F/Sgt Anderson	F/O Kempson	Sgt McLaren	Sgt Cartwright	Sgt Adams
O	F/O Harwood	Sgt Henson	F/O Sweeney	Sgt Trembling	Sgt Smith	Sgt Morris	Sgt Bennett
R	F/Lt Gilchrist	Sgt Rolph	F/Sgt Wise	Sgt Babadursingh	Sgt Meyers	Sgt Wilversten	Sgt Kimey
S	F/Lt Feaver	F/O Howson	F/O Bachelder	F/Sgt Millet	P/O Stocker	F/Sgt Grainger	F/Sgt Smith
T	F/Lt Pettifer	F/Sgt Hayward	F/O Davey	F/O Wilson	F/Sgt Royles	Sgt Hatton	Sgt Westhead
U	F/O Ripper	Sgt Staple	P/O Phillips	Sgt Cooke	Sgt Geddes	Sgt Dubber	Sgt Sherwin
V	Sgt Bielby	Sgt Brown	Sgt Budgen	Sgt Williams	Sgt Warren	Sgt Whittaker	Sgt Timms
W	W/O Potts	F/Sgt Frew	F/Sgt Hobbs	F/Sgt Batey	Sgt McGowan	Sgt Howard	Sgt Hale
Y	F/O Black	F/Sgt Stephenson	F/Sgt O'Donohue	F/Sgt Morell	F/Sgt Carruthers	F/Sgt Scott	F/Sgt Dent
Z	F/O Moore	F/Sgt Tinning	P/O Tavener	F/O Geddes	Sgt Micklethwaite	F/Sgt McVey	F/Sgt Connors

PRE-BRIEFING :	1900 hrs	DISTRIBUTION :	O.C. 51 Squadron	Base Messing Officer
MEALS :	2100 hrs		O.C. 'A' Flight	Station Operation
MAIN BRIEFING :	2150 hrs		O.C. 'B' Flight	Sqdn. Photo. Section
TRANSPORT :	2225 hrs		O.C. 'C' Flight	Nav.Officer
			Officers' Mess	Intelligence
			Sergeants' Mess	Sqdn. Armoury
				Transport Officer
				N.C.O. I/C Cloakroom
				Medical Officer
				Radar Officer

Signed : F/Lt T Creasey, Adjutant - For : Wing Commander G W M Ling, C/O 51 Sqdn.

FIG 17 via J. Feaver. Order Of Battle For Sterkrade Operation

ANALYSIS OF OPERATIONS 1943-45

and airfield at Heligoland. The squadron moved to Leconfield on the 20 April and carried out their last Halifax operation on the 25 April, the target being the Coastal Batteries at Wangerwooge.

The squadron had played its part in the contribution made by Bomber Command to the war effort over the preceeding years. This contribution can be summed up by quoting from a published military assessment of the war in Europe. This stated that there were six noteworthy reasons for the success of this campaign, one being the destruction of German war industries and communications by the Allied Air Forces.

At Leconfield after hostilities had ceased in Europe 51 Squadron was tranferred from 4 Group to 48 Group in Transport Command. The squadron had the sad task of delivering its Halifax aircraft to storage airfields such as 45 MU at Kinloss. When the crew returned from a delivery trip the only item they brought back with them was the 'Gee' set. The squadron was then very busy converting to the Stirling Mk V aircraft which it had taken delivery of for transport duties. During the training period with the Stirlings the squadron took part in the 'Cooks Tours' sorties, whereby ground crew were taken for flights over Germany to view the damage inflicted on German cities by Bomber Command. Unfortunately the majority of ground crews who had supported the squadron at Snaith missed out on this opportunity since some had stayed at Snaith, and a high proportion had been posted away.

Snaith remained in No 4 Group which was tranferred to Transport Command as a training group and 1516 BAT Flight was posted to Snaith to train aircrews in beam approach and the use of radio navigation aids. One interesting piece of information is that Jimmy Edwards the famous comedian with an RAF handlebar moustache, who gained a DFC as a Dakota Pilot at Arnhem, came to Snaith for a Radio Ranging Course in 1945.

Chapter 8

TECHNICAL SUPPORT

At Snaith, as at other units, the technical support by Engineering Personnel required to keep the maximum number of aircraft armed and operational was of prime importance to the Bomber Command offensive. The squadron reformed in 1937 with antiquated biplane bombers which were based on WW1 aircraft design. However due to the rapid developments which take place in wartime, in five short years the squadron was operating with the Halifax four engined heavy bomber, an efficient fighting machine containing much new and complicated equipment.

Since the major components of a Halifax were its airframe and method of propulsion, the largest groups of airmen servicing the aircraft comprised tradesmen of the Engine and Airframe discipline, either Fitters or Flight Mechanics. But in addition to the foregoing, in order to cope with the myriad of technical auxiliary equipment installed in a Halifax, some of which was quite advanced for the period, there were the Ancilliary Trades with whom the Engine and Airframe trades had a friendly rivalry, jokingly referring to them as the 'Gash Trades'. The Ancilliary Trades comprised Electricians, Instrument Repairers, Wireless Mechanics, Radar Mechanics, Photographers, Safety Equipment, and not to forget the important trade of Armourers (Bombs & Guns), answering to the nickname of 'Plumbers'. All RAF trades were listed in five Trade Groups, classified according to responsibility and pay, with Group 1 being the highest paid trade group. For trades having personnel in the top two groups such as Fitters (Group 1) and Flight Mechanics (Group 2) promotion to NCO status was generally restricted to Group 1 tradesmen.

When 51 Squadron moved to Snaith, all tradesmen involved in aircraft maintenance were members of the squadron and hence directly responsible to the squadron CO, through the squadron Engineering Officer. With the advent of the Halifax the squadron operations became more complex and the pressure on the engineering services increased markedly. A decision was made by Bomber Command to relieve the squadron COs of some of their responsibilities and form a new servicing organisation. Consequently when 578 Squadron was formed at Snaith in Jan 1944 from 'C' Flight of 51 Squadron the new Engineering system was set up. This meant that the Engineering support system was split into 3 Groups (A forerunner of the post war First, Second & Third line servicing) under the appropriate Engineering Officers. The groups were Flight Servicing for carrying out daily inspections and any maintenance carried out on the flights, a Squadron Servicing Echelon (No 9051) for Minor Inspections and repairs of a category normally carried out in the hangar and a Major Servicing Unit to carry out Major Inspections, major repairs, and acceptance checks and modifications on aircraft delivered to the squadron. Even new aircraft delivered from the manufacturers required an appreciable number of modifications to be carried out, also an important task was the de-bugging of new aircraft. Because Burn was a satellite of Snaith it did not have a Major Servicing Section so all Major Inspections were carried out at Snaith.

Technical support was also provided by the station itself in the form of the Station Armourers. They were responsible for the supply of ammunition belts filled with .303 ammunition by means of a belt filling machine in the Station Armoury and the maintenance of guns. The Armoury staff included WAAF Assistant Armourers. The preparation of bombs in the Bomb Dump was also the reponsibility of the Station Armoury but in view of the heavy nature of the work involved this was normally restricted to male personnel. The Station Workshops employed Fitters (General), Turners and Carpenters. There were also parachute packing, and Mechanical Transport Sections, the latter providing the numerous MT. vehicles necessary.

The operational pressures which necessitated the formation of the aforementioned engineering organisation affected the ground crews themselves. They worked 7 days a week for long hours with very occasional days off. Then, from early 1944

TECHNICAL SUPPORT

onwards, there were no leave or 48 hour passes for groundcrew, the aircrew still being given their well earned operational leave after a number of operations. In his Special Order of the Day at the end of the European war, ACM Harris commented on the devoted service of the ground crews. He referred to how they tended aircraft in bitter weather with the prolonged misery of wet and cold and achieved extraordinary records of aircraft serviceability.

There was a tremendous rapport between aircrew and groundstaff, the aircrew realising how much they relied on their ground crews who took a tremendous personal interest in both the aircraft and the crews who flew them. Ground crews working on the flights in all types of weather were characterised by their leather sleeveless jerkins known as 'Goonskins' and Wellington boots, with white sea boot socks turned over the tops. These were essential for tramping through the winter mud and the white socks were necessary to prevent the tops of the Wellingtons from chafing the legs. What generally happened however was that the feet of the socks wore out without replacements being available so it was interesting to see some of the groundcrew putting on the white socks with little or no feet in them over their normal short blue socks. The Engine Trades and the Riggers were often characterised by oil stained small packs slung over their shoulders and greasy hats.

Out on the flights under the umbrella of the Flight Servicing Organisation the ground crew allocated to each aircraft normally comprised a Sergeant Fitter in charge supported by Corporal Fitters (Airframe and Engines), four Flight Mechanics (Engines), one for each engine and Flight Mechanics (Airframes), generally referred to as Riggers. The servicing personnel working out on the open dispersals on the flights had to operate in all types of weather often waiting overnight for their allocated aircraft to return. The conditions in winter could be quite harsh. Also when an aircraft became unserviceable the ground crew had to continue working on it until it became serviceable.

There were only a few buildings around the dispersals, mainly Flight Offices, so many of the ground crew built their own dugouts covered over with corrugated sheets or whatever materials were available and banked up with earth. A rudimentary heating system which was installed in these dugouts, was given the name 'Foo Foo' stoves, based on a design brought to Snaith by Fitters such as Steve Brown who had served in the oil producing areas of the Persian Gulf. These stoves consisted of three old ten gallon oil drums, one of which had its lid cut off and the other two which containing oil or water with taps fitted to allow the oil or water to drip into the open drum. The oil which dripped into the drum was set on fire and the water allowed to drip on to it causing a flare up like water onto a hot chip pan fire. These stoves which operated on waste sump oil could glow red hot when operating and could be used to make toast on. They were very popular with the ground crew despite the stench they produced. An even more foul atmosphere resulted on an occasion when an armourer dropped a Very cartridge down the dug out chimney producing immediate evacuation. The Station Medical Officer recognised the problems of working in inclement weather by recommending that hot showers or baths should be available for the ground crews when the came off duty on the flights.

Photo 61 Trolly ACC. And Chore Horse

On the dispersals, familiar sights were the maintenance platforms for working on the engines or gaining access to parts of the fuselage. A regular sound was the hum of a 'Chore Horse' petrol engine driving a generator to charge the heavy duty accumulators used for starting the aircraft's engines. These accumulators housed in a portable two wheeled 'Trolley Acc.' were a very important item of equipment since starting an aircraft's engines produced a heavy drain on batteries and if the internal accumulators were used they could soon be discharged. It could therefore be a chargeable offence to start up on the internal accs, when 'Trolley Accs.' were available. However there were occasions, due to an operational contingency, when this rule had to be ignored without informing the authorities. One case was during the Ardennes offensive, known as the 'Battle of the Bulge', when the kites were all bombed up and ready to go in the atrocious weather, which had assisted the German offensive by restricting Allied air support. The 'Trolley Acc.' for for S-Sugar was flat so the Cpl Fitter started up the port inner on the internals and then ran this

124

engine so that the generator in it was charging up the accs. and producing enough current to start the other engines. Some other aircraft then followed suit.

There was a shortage of tools for issue at Snaith and when tradesmen newly arrived on the squadron reported to the stores to draw a tool kit it was rare for them to be issued with all the items on the list of tools they were entitled to. The dedication of the ground crew is demonstrated by the fact that a number of them purchased tools out of their own money. The ubiquitous adjustable spanner was an essential item of equipment and for difficult to access nuts special tools had to be obtained or devised. When civilian engineers working for aircraft or engine manufacturers arrived at the station to carry out special work on the aircraft the RAF tradesmen looked on with envy at the comprehensive tool kits containing many special tools which they brought with them. Therefore on occasions some of these tools went missing and finished on the flights. By comparison the American Airforce was very well supplied with tools and every new American aircraft was delivered with a full set of tools. A ground crew team had an eye opener when they went to an American airfield to carry out some work on a Halifax aircraft which had force landed there. Reporting to a Master Sergeant in the Engineering section they were told the aircraft was on the other side of the airfield. "Any bikes available" they asked, "Sorry Bud, no bikes available, but if you'd like to go over to the Motor Pool you can draw out a Jeep". An astonished silence from the RAF boys, overawed at the facilities available, was followed by a further comment from the Yank, "If you need a mobile crane I should be able to fix you up with one and if you want any tools, just holler". Another maintenance problem was a shortage of spares and it was sometimes necessary to 'cannibalise' an unserviceable aircraft for an essential spare for another aircraft. On occasions a damaged aircraft may be set aside for such a purpose, this kite being commonly referred to as the 'Christmas Tree'.

The Flight Sergeant in charge of maintenance on a Flight was responsible for checking on the serviceability of the aircraft with the Form 700s being lodged in his office. When aircraft were needed he was a familiar sight wandering around the various dispersals on the flight calling out "Sign up", so that the various trades would sign the 700 to confirm that the aircraft were serviceable. There was also a Form 700A kept in the aircraft for use if it had to land away from base and hence inspected or serviced on another airfield. Having considered ground crew support in general the activities of the various trades can be considered in detail.

ENGINE TRADESMEN

Over the period of operation with the Halifax the engine trades had two makes of engine to deal with. The majority of Mk II Halifaxes were fitted with Rolls Royce Merlin Mk XX or 22 inline engines and the Mk III with Bristol Hercules Mk XVI radial engines, the latter providing a better performance so the squadron happily converted to the Mk III aircraft in January 1944, when the engine trades had to become proficient in servicing the new engines. The Hercules engine was a 14 cylinder sleeve valve engine, sleeves inside the cylinder bore with cut-outs acted as valves to control exhaust and inlet ports in the cylinder wall in place of the normal poppet valve arrangement. The engine had two rows of cylinders with compression ratios of 7 to 1 and a two speed supercharger of the centrifugal type with two gear ratios of 6.68 to 1 for 'M' gear and 8.35 for 'S' gear. The low gear was used for take off at low altitudes and the high gear for maximum power at higher altitudes. A Pesco fuel pump fed 100 Octane fuel to Claudel Hobson inverted twin carburettors, along with an automatic boost control. Under icing conditions as indicated by a drop in boost pressure, warm air could be fed to the air intakes to the carburettors. The pitch of the propellors on the Hercules engine could be altered by means of a De Havilland Hydromatic feathering unit, operated by oil pressure with a normal pitch range of 35 degrees. This equipment was important when an engine cut out since the unit could provide a further 45 degrees for feathering to prevent the propellor from windmilling. Each engine had a Methyl Bromide fire extinguisher which in addition to the Pilot's switch could be operated by a Graviner impact switch in the case of a crash.

The jobs routinely carried out by the engine tradesmen on the flights were the changing of oil coolers, starter motors, spark plugs, magnetos etc. There were occasions when a major job such as an engine change had to be carried out on the flights. Engines could be tested by running them up, normally by a Sgt or Cpl Engine Fitter and since each engine had two sets of plugs and two magnetos, one check was to switch off a magneto and by keeping an eye on the rev. counter look for a reduction in engine speed, known as a 'mag drop'. 'Mag drop' readings could indicate if there was a fault on the engine. When the Engine trades saw a 'Merlin' engined aircraft coming back with white vapours streaming out of the exhausts they knew that they had a glycol coolant leak to deal with. One messy job which had to be carried out was to coat the exhaust with a red compound to reduce the glow in the dark.

There was an Engine Bay in the main hangar where engine power units were prepared. In an engine change the the complete power unit was replaced and the u/s unit returned to the Bay for the fitting of a new or overhauled engine. The power unit in addition to an engine contained all the necessary ancillary items linked to the engine.

AIRFRAME TRADESMEN

The Airframe tradesmen, along with their engine colleagues, were regularly involved in removing panels and cowling covers using the ubiquitious, long, pump action, spiral rachet screwdrivers, so these tools almost became a tool of office. The Riggers in the Maintenance section had a workshop with their motto, 'Ubendum, Wemendum', over the entrance.

In addition to the main structure of the aircraft there was a wide variety of equipment in the aircraft which was the responsibility of the Airframe tradesmen comprising:-

Hydraulics - Pressure for hydraulics accumulator was provided by a Lockheed EDP pump and the items operated by hydraulic pressure were the undercarriage, flaps, bomb doors, and air intake. There was a special hydraulics section with an NCO in charge who had attended a course at Messier's in Warrington.

De-icing Facilities - These were provided by a Rotax hand pump to spray the windscreen through small jets, in addition in severe icing conditions the Riggers would apply 'Kilfrost' de-icing paste to the leading edges of wings, rudders etc. A hazard for Riggers when applying this paste to earlier marks of Halifax was the presence of the Martin Cartridge Cable Cutters located in the leading edges of the wings. The principle behind these was that if the aircraft hit a barrage balloon the cable would slide along the leading edge of the wing into the jaws of the cable cutter at which point a chisel would be fired by an Eley-Kynoch cartridge to cut the cable. In winter liberal applications of anti-freeze grease were necessary to ensure operation of the device. It would be very easy for a Rigger to lose a finger if it inadvertantly entered the cable cutter slot when working on the leading edges of the wings.

Pneumatics - Air pressure at 300 PSI was stored in an air bottle behind the Engineer's bulkhead, pressure was provided by a Heywood compressor on the port inner engine and the pressure controlled by a Heywood pressure regulator. The Dunlop air brakes were operated by pneumatic pressure, controlled by levers on the control column and Dunlop differential relay units attached to the rudder bars.

Heating - The crew stations were heated by hot air from the flame dampers, fed into the fuselage by pipes.

Flying Controls - These were controlled by the sliding movement of push-pull tubing running in 'Tufnol' bearings with locking devices to secure controls when the aircraft was parked.

As exemplified in Chapters 5 & 6 the early fin and rudder systems on the Mk II Halifax caused handling problems, so from Sept 1943 onwards Bomber Command required modifications to be carried out on the tail unit. Consequently a working party from 13 MU at Henlow visited Snaith to work alongside the squadron Riggers to replace the existing fin and rudder.

ELECTRICIANS

Since so much of the equipment in the aircraft was controlled by electricity the Electricians had to interface with the majority of the other trades. The main source of power was four 12 volt lead acid accumulators located forward of the rear spar in a series parallel layout to provide a 24 volt, 80 AH source. This DC main supply was controlled by a Ground/Flight switch so that the internal equipment could be fed from either the internal accumulators or an external trolley acc. plugged into a socket either under the starboard mainplane or on the fuselage side near the rear turret, the latter used for turret testing. In flight the accumulators were kept charged by means of 3 x 60 amp, 1500 watt generators on the P/O, P/I, & S/I engines, the charging system being controlled by a voltage regulator and accumulator cut out. The main electrical panel was situated near the Wireless Operators' position with a voltmeter installed on it so that the power supply could be monitored.

A fault in the charging circuit of one Halifax caused a problem for the Wireless Operator during an operation. He observed that due to a fault, overcharging was taking place, with the result that excess gassing was taking place in the accumulators. The W/Op. decided that the best course of action was to disconnect the accumulators, so he removed one of the connecting leads. Unfortunately an explosive mixture of air and hydrogen had developed and a spark produced by the disconnection ignited this mixture. The result was that the accumulators exploded and sprayed the W/Op. and the fuselage with dilute sulphuric acid. Fortunately the airman's face was turned away when the explosion occurred so that it was not sprayed with acid but his clothing was damaged.

In order to provide a supply of fully charged accumulators there was a battery charging room in the South West corner of Hangar No 1. Some of the Electrical Section WAAFs worked in this room and one voluntary task was 'brewing-up'. For this job they had a makeshift immersion heater which had been rigged up by the Electricians comprising two carbon electrodes from a beacon connected to the mains. One day a WAAF was busy in the room when she heard a voice behind her, "I believe you make the best coffee on the station here". "You'll have to wait!", she remarked sharply. When she did turn round she saw to her surprise it was the Commanding Officer standing there.

There were many items of electrically operated equipment which were the responsibility of the electricians. For a Daily Inspection the Electricians would check that all the lights were working, note that the micro-switches for the various indicator lamps such as undercarriage warning and bomb doors were functioning, check the rotary converters (DC to AC) and the electrical controls for the bombing equipment. They would look out for 'earths' on the various auxiliary circuits, such as the Radar equipment, by isolating each circuit in turn and connecting the battery +ve or -ve to earth whilst checking for current flow with a meter. Possible causes of leaks could be AC grounding capacitors as used in rotary converters breaking down and allowing DC to flow to earth. The approriate tradesman would be informed that they had got an 'earth' on their equipment. At the end of the DI the main accumulator voltage would be checked by the meter on the electrical supply panel.

As mentioned earlier tradesmen had to carry out modifications on new aircraft to bring them up to operational standard and some important modifications were carried out by the Electricians on the equipment on the Air Bombers panel. The importance of checking the Air Bombers electrical circuitry is demonstrated by the report in Chapter 10 on the destruction of aircraft DT722 and DT7224. In order to facilitate this operation the Electricians at Snaith recovered a complete panel from a crashed Halifax, so that when a new aircraft arrived on the squadron they could speed up the modification programme by replacing the existing panel with a panel containing the requisite modifications.

There was another modification carried out by the Electricians which earned one of them the nickname of 'Dinghy' Evans, since he twice accidentally inflated the emergency dinghy. On the second occasion, a modification was being carried out on the electrical circuitry for the dinghy inflation equipment. The squadron had run into a problem with the dinghy immersion switch in the side of the fuselage inadvertently operating in very wet conditions. A modification was therefore devised, whereby a second immersion switch was installed in series with the first one, in order in order to reduce the chance of accidental operation. The second switch was installed in the fuselage on the opposite side to the original switch behind a hole prepared by the Riggers and covered with a grill.

On the occasion in question, the Electrician carrying out the modification had fitted a test lamp with an extension lead to the dinghy compartment to isolate the gas bottle activating unit. This lamp allowed the Electrician to check that the circuit was working. One of the Safety Equipment Assistants wanting to complete the installation of the dinghy popped his head inside the fuselage and shouted "have you finished with the lamp yet". Another tradesman, working with an inspection lamp which he had finished with, thought the comment referred to him and shouted "yes". The Safety Equipment Assistants then completed the installation of the dinghy and disconnected the Electrician's test lamp, removing the isolation from the activating circuit. The hatch cover on the dinghy compartment was replaced, and the 'erks' started to apply the sealing fabric around the edges of the hatch. Inside the Halifax 'Dinghy' Evans had completed his task and decided to test the circuitry by shorting out the two immersion switches with screwdrivers. This caused the dinghy to inflate with the result that two S.E. Assistants who were sitting on the dinghy hatch were catapulted off the wing. One was badly shaken and the other damaged his ankle.

When refuelling, bowsers had to make an earth connection to the aircraft and ground the bowser with an earthing stake before connecting the refuelling hose to the aircraft. One task of the

TECHNICAL SUPPORT

Bomb	T.V. Setting		
	long tail	short tail	
500 G.P.	1 840	1 600	
1 000 "	1 860	1 500	
250 S.A.P.	2 100	—	
500 "		1 420	
500 A.P.	1 850	1 720	
250 M.C.	2 730	—	
500 " Mk I-III, V	1 330	—	
" Mk IV			
1 000 M.C.	1 460	1 380	
250 A.N.M. 57	1 520	1 670	
500 " 64	—	1 660	
2 000 H.C. 65	2 100	—	
4 000 "	1 000		
8 000 "	1 000		
600 A.S.	1 150		
10 "	1 000		
11½ "	1 000		
Mine A Mk I-IV	1 000		
" Mk VI			
" 30 Mk VII Inc	1 000		

B.S. Mk XIV, Computor Ref: no: 9/2637
or B.S. Mk XIVA, Corrector Cam or 9/3472 type X
  Ref: no: 9/3417 type X
in HALIFAX No: MZ 851
Serial No: of Computor 5/10/42
  "   "   " Sighting Head 27340/42
Date of Installation 18/8/44
  "   " Ground Levelling 18/8/44

All-up Weight	Comp: scale	S/Head scale	All-up weight	Comp: scale	S/Head scale
47 000	6.4	7.6	57 000	7.8	9.0
48 000	6.5	7.7	58 000	7.9	9.1
49 000	6.6	7.8	59 000	8.0	9.2
50 000	6.8	8.0	60 000	8.2	9.4
51 000	6.9	8.1	61 000	8.3	9.5
52 000	7.1	8.3	62 000	8.5	9.7
53 000	7.2	8.4	63 000	8.6	9.8
54 000	7.3	8.5	64 000	8.7	9.9
55 000	7.5	8.7	65 000	8.9	10.1
56 000	7.6	8.8			

B.S. Mk XIV & T-1 Levelling Card ref: no: 9/3481

page 1

INSTRUCTIONS for FILLING IN TABLE on page 1
1. Obtain levelling scale settings for Computor & Sighting Head for a known All-up Weight, by ground levelling from pp. 2 & 3 (or in the case of an aircraft type in its introductory stage, by flight levelling).
2. Dealing with the Computor first, enter in line C of Form III the levelling scale setting under the all-up weight to which it applies. Subtract the quantity in line B from that in C & enter the result in line A.

Copy this into all the spaces in line A. Add successively A to B, & so obtain the scale settings for the whole range of possible weights.
Repeat the process for S/Head, in Form IV.
3. Copy each scale setting into its proper place on p. 1.
4. A valuable final check is made by making sure that each pair of settings in the Table on p. 1, subtracted one from the other, gives the same answer.

FORM III Computor

	47 000	48 000	49 000	50 000	51 000	52 000	53 000	54 000	55 000	56 000
A	6.4	6.4	6.4	6.4	6.4	6.4	6.4	6.4	6.4	6.4
B	0.0	0.1	0.2	0.4	0.5	0.7	0.8	0.9	1.1	1.2
C	6.4	6.5	6.6	6.8	6.9	7.1	7.2	7.3	7.5	7.6

	57 000	58 000	59 000	60 000	61 000	62 000	63 000	64 000	65 000	
A	6.4	6.4	6.4	6.4	6.4	6.4	6.4	6.4	6.4	
B	1.4	1.5	1.6	1.8	1.9	2.1	2.2	2.3	2.5	
C	7.8	7.9	8.0	8.2	8.3	8.5	8.6	8.7	8.9	

FORM IV Sighting Head

	47 000	48 000	49 000	50 000	51 000	52 000	53 000	54 000	55 000	56 000
A	7.6	7.6	7.6	7.6	7.6	7.6	7.6	7.6	7.6	7.6
B	0.0	0.1	0.2	0.4	0.5	0.7	0.8	0.9	1.1	1.2
C	7.6	7.7	7.8	8.0	8.1	8.3	8.4	8.5	8.7	8.8

	57 000	58 000	59 000	60 000	61 000	62 000	63 000	64 000	65 000	
A	7.6	7.6	7.6	7.6	7.6	7.6	7.6	7.6	7.6	
B	1.4	1.5	1.6	1.8	1.9	2.1	2.2	2.3	2.5	
C	9.0	9.1	9.2	9.4	9.5	9.7	9.8	9.9	10.1	

page 4

FIG 24 Bomb Sight Calibration For Halifax MZ851

TECHNICAL SUPPORT

CONDENSED INSTRUCTIONS for GROUND LEVELLING using B.S. Mk XIV & T-1 Clinometer ref. no: 9/3384
(For a fuller explanation see A.P. 1730A, vol. I, ch: 9)

1. Make absolutely sure that the computor gyro, bubble, & glide datum are accurately adjusted.

2. Enter the 4 readings each (taken to nearest 0·1°) required for Computor & Sighting Head, in Forms I & II respectively; each reading must go into whichever of the two spaces opposite its description is left blank. Take care that the end of the Clinometer marked 'Forward' is always placed on the part which is forward in the aircraft.

Note (i):—The readings on the Clinometer are false, deliberately. They are automatically corrected when working out the results on the Forms on this card.

3. Add up the 2 columns of numbers (including the printed ones) in each Form, & subtract the total of the 2nd column from that of the 1st. The results are the levelling scale settings for Computor & Sighting Head at Datum All-up Weight.

Note (ii):—On certain aircraft (e.g. Wellington & Halifax) a reading on the S H levelling scale may be got even when the bubble is level & the aircraft tail down on the ground. The shorter method of Form I* should then be used instead of Form I. Similarly, on aircraft with tricycle undercarriages, levelling scale readings on Sighting Head and Computor may be got when the bubble is level, & for these aircraft Forms I* & II* should be used.

Note (iii):—Clinometer readings on Computors Mk XIV & XIVA must be taken on the base-plate edge, on the T-1 on the machined flat on the top of the Computor box; on Sighting Heads, on the flat alongside the bubble.

FORM I Readings of :—

	+	−
Clinometer, on Computor on bench, bubble level	20·0	
Levelling scale of ,, ,, ,, ,, ,,	6·0	
Clinometer, ,, ,, mounted in aircraft		13·0
Clinometer, on Rigger's Datum	9·8	15·9
	35·8	28·9
	28·9	subtract
	7·9	

Levelling scale setting for Computor, at 58 000 lb

FORM II Readings of :—

	+	−
Clinometer, on Sighting Head out of a/c, bubble level	20·0	
,, ,, ,, ,, ,, mounted in aircraft		14·8
Levelling scale of ,, ,, ,, ,,	10·0	
Clinometer, on Rigger's Datum	9·8	15·9
	39·8	30·7
	30·7	subtract
	09·1	

Levelling scale setting for S/Head, at 58 000 lb

FORM I* (to be used instead of Form I, for aircraft on which a reading on levelling scale of Computor, mounted in aircraft & bubble level, may be obtained).

Readings of :—

	+	−
Levelling scale of Computor mounted in a/c, bubble level		15·9
Clinometer, on Rigger's Datum		15·9
		subtract

Levelling scale setting for Computor, at 58 000 lb

FORM II* (as for Form I*, but for Sighting Head)

	+	−
Levelling scale of S/Head mounted in a/c, bubble level		15·9
Clinometer, on Rigger's Datum	15·9	
	15·9	subtract

Levelling scale setting for S/Head, at 58 000 lb

TECHNICAL SUPPORT

Electricians was to check the resistance of the earth connection was not greater than half an ohm.

INSTRUMENT REPAIRERS AND COMPASS ADJUSTERS.

The Instrument Section was allied to the Electrical Section, both of which came under the control of the Electrical Engineering Officer. Originally the Squadron Instruments Section at Snaith was located in a building near the main hangar, but on 27 October 1943 it moved into one of the workshops in the main hangar facing the Control Tower. There was a wide range of anciliary equipment which was the responsibility of the Instruments Section. This included the Instrument Flying Panel, Magnetic Compasses and general instruments such as Engine Rev. counters, Boost, Fuel, Temperature, Air Pressure and Hydraulic Pressure Gauges. Specialised equipment included Gunsights, Auto Pilots, DRC, API and Mark X1V Bombsight. Some instrument personnel were sent on camera maintenance courses. The oxygen system was also the responsibility of the Instrument tradesmen, the gas being stored in 21 bottles at a pressure of 18,000 psi, 15 of which were under the Flight Engineer's platform and 6 behind the Flight Engineer's bulkhead with the main supply cock on his instrument panel. From this cock the oxygen was fed to the Mark Xa Master Regulator on the Pilot's panel which had a contents and delivery gauge and two control valves. Oxygen was always used at heights above 10,000 ft so this Regulator was employed to adjust the oxygen flow, according to the aircraft's height. The oxygen was fed to 13 Economisers whose function was to regulate the oxygen supply to the aircrew members in an economical manner. These only operated when the connecting tube was removed from the cut-out valve, the Air Gunners' positions employed bobbins as cut-outs. There was provision for portable oxygen sets providing 10 minutes supply to be located at each crew station and for use with 'G' Type masks, a short length of adaptor tube had to be provided.

When nitrogen purging of fuel tanks was introduced to provide an inert atmosphere in the tanks, this became the responsibility of the Instruments Section. One of the regular tasks carried out by the Instruments Section was modifications to the control equipment for the nitrogen bleed system necessary because of problems with operation of the system in service. These problems came about because the system had been brought into operation urgently which meant that some 'bugs' occurred in the system. This system became quite important when the Germans started using their 'Schrage Musik'

cannons which were aimed at the fuel tanks in the wings, since it was hoped that the risk of petrol fires could be reduced. The nitrogen was stored in 6 bottles in each bouyancy chamber in the root of the mainplane at a pressure of 1800 psi. The nitrogen flowed from these bottles through Palmer and Amal valves to all tanks. The Palmer valve reduced the pressure to between 10 and 30 psi and the Amal valve to about one quarter psi. The tanks vented to atmosphere through a Manley Regulus valve if the pressure in the tank rose to half a psi above atmospheric pressure.

The DRC (Distance Reading Gyro Magnetic Compass) was a valuable navigation aid as an adjunct to the Pilot's P4 Magnetic Compass. The advantage of this equipment was that the Master Unit could be installed in a position where the deviation was at a minimum and in the Halifax this was next to the Elsan toilet at the rear of the fuselage. The principle of the DRC was the 'North Seeking Mechanism' which was a rotatable frame containing a pivoted magnet and a gyroscope. By means of contacts and electromagnets the axis of a gyroscope was kept in alignment with the mean direction of the magnet. With aid of more contacts and an electric motor the rotatable frame was kept in alignment with the gyro. If the mean direction of the magnet was north the gyro and frame would also point north. The movement of the frame relative to the aircraft caused the transmitter to send impulses to repeaters containing a motor which was driven round by these impulses. The motor in turn drove a compass dial. The gyro rotated through the same amount as the aircraft rotated, relative to the 'North Seeking Cage' and indicated how the course had changed but the repeaters and the 'Cage' had to be synchronised. There was a variation setting corrector in between the 'Cage' and the repeaters so that the Navigator could obtain headings corrected for variation. There was a 'setting' switch to speed up control of the magnets over the gyro for use when starting up the DRC or the gyro had toppled as could occur with a 75 degree bank of the aircraft.

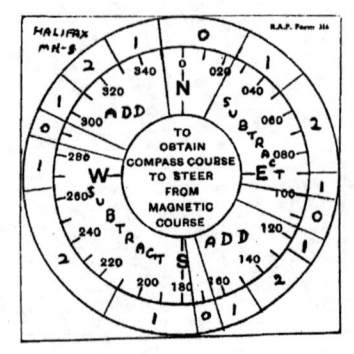

FIG 23

Compass Corrector Card For Halifax MH-S

The Instruments Section was responsible for the installation and repair of compasses and when operating with Whitleys was also required to carry out compass adjusting. However, when Bomber Command began operating with four engined heavy bombers a new trade of Compass Adjuster was initiated, whose members were all given the rank of Sergeant. The purpose of this was to give a level of authority which enabled them to render an aircraft unserviceable because of compass problems. Compass accuracy was considered of prime importance for accurate navigation. The importance of an accurate compass can be exemplified by an incident in early 1943 when a 4 Group Halifax returning from a raid on Berlin was so much off course that it landed at an airfield near Wick in the far north of Scotland. This extreme error in navigation was due to a faulty compass.

A regular task for the Compass Adjuster was to carry out a compass swing of the aircraft. The procedure was to attach a special towing hitch to the tail wheel of of the aircraft and connect it up to a tractor. The aircraft would be towed around in a circle by the tractor so that it could be lined up with the various points of the compass. The Compass Adjuster took the bearings of the aircraft with a hand bearing compass and shouted the readings up to a colleague in the cockpit who was reading the aircraft's compasses. The hand bearing compass readings were compared with the aircraft compass readings to estimate the Deviation and hence compile a compass corrector card (Fig 23).

Instrument Repairers with specialist training were responsible for servicing the Mk XIV (or American version T1) bomb-sight. This instrument was quite a specialised piece of equipment consisting of two units, the sighting head and the computer. Airspeed, height, and course were fed into the the computer unit automatically but a number of settings were applied manually. The manually set parameters were sea level pressure at the target, target height above sea level, the terminal velocity of the bombs, all up weight, wind speed and direction over the target. In the analogue computer, sighting angles and drift angles were calculated by an analogue mechanism incorporating small servo motors and pick-up bellows, the information being fed to the sighting head by flexible drives. The sighting head was in effect the bomb sight and comprised a collimator, glass reflector plate, drift scale and gyroscope. The collimator projected a graticule image onto the reflector plate for the Bomb Aimer to use as an aiming mark. The reflector plate was connected to the gyro and so geared that if for example the aircraft banked 20 degrees the reflector moved through half this, eg 10 degrees. Since the angle of incidence of the illumination was equal to the angle of reflection the sighting plane remained vertical whilst an aircraft banked. The reflector was adjustable in the fore and aft plane to allow for variations in Terminal Velocity of the bombs, and all up weight of the aircraft. There was special procedure for the installation of these bomb-sights and a calibration card with correction factors for use by the Air Bomber was produced. The card produced in an installation carried out by the Author is shown in Fig 24.

The Halifax was fitted with an autopilot nicknamed 'George' by the aircrew, its function being to take the strain off the Pilot by taking over flying the aircraft for a period. Originally the Mk IV Autopilot with two control plates was fitted to the squadron aircraft but in later Mk III aircraft this was replaced by the Mk VIII with a single control plate. The heart of the 'George' system was the gyroscope which maintained a constant attitude relative to the movements of the aircraft. Pick-off valves were activated by the gyroscope when an aircraft altered its course or attitude and these valves activated servo motors which applied the necessary movement to the control surfaces.

For a DI the Instruments personnel would need to check the various panel instruments, the bomb-sight, gun-sights, autopilot, astrograph API and the DRC were working satisfactorily. The oxygen system needed to be checked and charged up and the oxygen economisers tested to ensure that they were operating at 5 to 9 puffs per minute. The ASI and altimeter were operated by air flow from the pitot head supplemented by static vents in the side of the fuselage. The pitot head contained a heating element which had to be checked, its function being to prevent the orifices in the pitot head from freezing up. There were occasions under very severe icing conditions when the pitot head blocked up with ice, the result being no air speed indicator readings in the aircraft.

RADAR MECHANICS

Radar equipment which in 1943 was still referred to as RDF equipment for cover purposes was a top secret wartime development. The squadron had IFF sets in their Whitleys but did not use the 'Gee' navigation aid until they converted to Halifax aircraft. To service this new equipment the trade of RDF Mechanic, subsequently changed to Radar Mechanic, was formed and because of a shortage of

TECHNICAL SUPPORT

FIG 25 (Right)
'Fish Pond' Indicator Unit

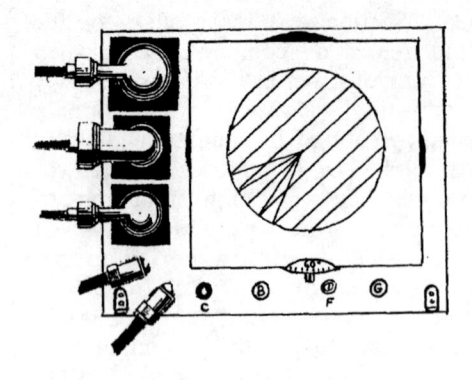

FIG 26 (Below)
'Fish Pond' Displays

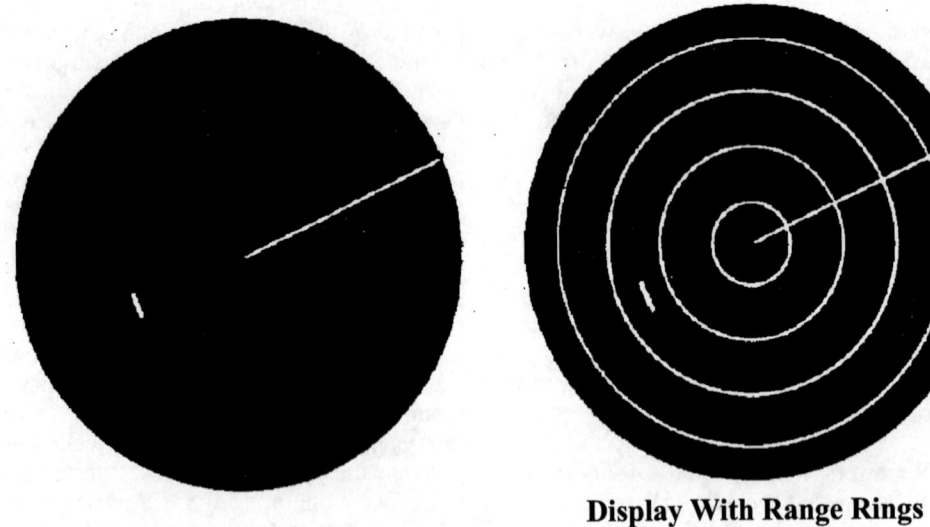

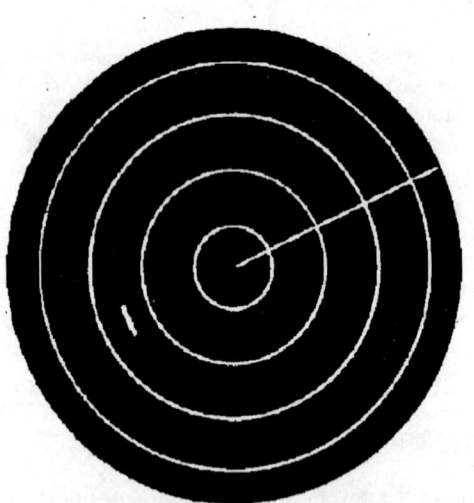

Display With Range Rings

FIG 27
H2S Scanner Unit

skilled recruits, personnel were recruited in Canada. A large Radar school was built at Clinton, Ontario, where Canadians were trained before coming to the UK. P/O Adams, the officer I/C the Radar Servicing Section at Snaith, was a Canadian and there were also some Canadian ORs in the section. The British Radar Mechanics included a number of WAAFs, the first WAAF Radar Mechanic to join the squadron, Myfanwy Griffiths, married the Radar Officer.

A special hut was built for the Radar Section to the west of T2 hangar No 2 and in view of the secrecy of the equipment access was restricted to authorised persons. The manuals for the Radar equipment were not included in the normal AP series being designated SDs (Secret Documents) and when not in use had to be locked in the section's safe. In addition two duty Radar Mechanics slept in the section with loaded rifles as a guard, which meant that members of the Radar Section were exempt from carrying out the normal guard duties.

The Halifax aircraft which the squadron started operating with in 1942 were fitted with the Mk II IFF and Mk I 'Gee' equipment and in November 1942 four aircraft went to Riccall to be fitted with 'Boozer' (AR5538). 'Boozer' as distinct from 'Monica' was a passive device which employed a receiver tuned to receive radar signals from 'Wurzburg' on 500-600 MHz and 'Lichenstein' radar signals on 490 MHz. When the aircraft was exposed to the transmissions from gun laying or master searchlight radar an orange light lit up on the pilots instrument panel and if a night fighter's radar was focused onto the aircraft then a red light came on. The intensity of the warning light varied with the location and range of the stalking aircraft. If off to the side and well behind the bulb would only flicker faintly whereas when dead astern and close up a clear unvarying light was produced. This device did not become a general fitting for the squadron aircraft.

A task for the section during 1943 was to replace the Mk II IFF by the Mk III version, and the Mk I 'Gee' by the improved Mk II version. The Mk I 'Gee' was a limited frequency system and its replacement by the Mk II with plug-in RF units for change of frequency to try and conquer jamming was important. A regular problem with Mk I 'Gee' equipment was spurious oscillations which showed up as a 'strobe jitter' and was caused by microphonic valves. The fault being due to variations in the mechanical construction of the VR91 (Civilian No EF50) valves. Mullard had problems with the manufacture of the EF50s from the initial development of 'Gee' sets. Valves which could be satisfactory in normal radio equipment were often unsatisfactory for use in 'Gee' equipment, so the section had a box full of valves which had been rejected. This problem did not occur when the EF50s were replaced by another type of valve.

Because of the secret nature of the Radar equipment it was fitted with detonators to destroy it, if it was likely to fall into enemy hands. Operation of the detonators was carried out by means of double switches under a hinged cover (two fingers had to be used to prevent accidental operation). Located in the Pilot's and Navigator's stations were Graviner impact switches which automatically detonated the equipment in the event of a crash. However there were occasions when a bumpy landing activated the switches and destroyed the equipment much to the chagrin of the Navigator. Later on in the war the use of detonators in some radar equipment was dispensed with, presumably because it was known that the enemy was aware of the equipment from captured sets. In June 1943 'Audible Monica' equipment was fitted to aircraft on the squadron and later on a few aircraft were fitted with 'Visual Monica', with an indicator unit based on the ASV Mk I Radar, installed in the Wireless Operators position.

Later on in 1943 H2S Radar equipment became available for use by the Main Force, so it was installed in some of the squadron's aircraft by the Radar Section. Later versions of H2S used wave guides to convey the signal from the scanner to the receiver but the early equipment used very thick coaxial cable and one Radar Mechanic reported that this cable was so thick that installing it was "like Wrestling with a Boa Constrictor". When the squadron converted to Mk III aircraft many of these were delivered already fitted with H2S and in these aircraft the tail-warning Radar was replaced by the 'Fishpond' unit which blanked out the ground return of the H2S signal in order to detect enemy aircraft underneath the Halifax. The Indicator Unit (Fig 25) was installed in the Wireless Operator's compartment on the left hand side of his desk, blips indicating aircraft between the kite and the ground, as shown in Fig 26. The direction in which they were moving was an indication of whether or not they were likely to be enemy aircraft.

In order to calibrate H2S equipment a 'Perspex' panel, which did not affect transmission of radar signals, was fitted in the airfield side of the Radar hut. A test H2S scanner (Fig 27) was lined up to transmit through the 'Perspex', Selby Abbey being used as a target. Some stations used corner reflectors for calibration. A rumour went round that radar microwaves could cause sterility, the consequence being that WAAFs would not work near the scanner when it was operating. As a result the WAAFs tended to work on 'Gee' and IFF which operated on lower frequencies. When aircraft first started operating with H2S the serviceability could be as low as 40%. However due to improvements in the equipment, by Jan 1945 the serviceability rate for H2S was 89% and for 'Gee' 97%.

WIRELESS MECHANICS

The Wireless Mechanics were responsible for servicing of the radio equipment in the Halifax. The T1154 transmitter and R1155 receiver (designed by Marconi) were used for long distance communications along with the associated DF equipment. There was also short range R/T equipment which could be operated by the Pilot and in the early Mks of Halifax this was the TR9 transceiver single channel unit remotely operated by a Bowden cable, but in later Mks it was replaced by the more efficient TR1196 transceiver with 4 stud push button selector boxes in the Pilot's cockpit and Navigator's compartment. The R/T equipment operated in the 50 metre band and had a range of about 10 miles. There was also an A1134 intercom system which could be linked into the wireless system. Small 2 volt accumulators were used to power the valve heaters and these had to be charged regularly by the Electricians and installed by the Wireless Mechanic. In the early days at Snaith when carrying out a DI the Wireless Mechanic could make a test transmission on the T1154. However, it was established that the Luftwaffe listening service was monitoring test transmissions which ceased when bombing up commenced, so that they could guess a raid was planned. As a consequence test transmissions with the radio equipment was restricted so that the Wireless Mechanic had to rely on meter reading for serviceability checks. Tests could be carried out with the short range TR1196 R/T equipment using a test transmission with a call sign issued by the Control Tower.

Problems in the intercom could reveal themselves as a howl in the microphone, one cause of this being faulty connections in the slip rings connections to the rear turret. In the words of a Wireless Mechanic, Norman Davidson, the Rear Gunners could cause a 'Wee' problem with the intercom connections if they were taken short in the turret and it leaked onto the slip rings producing a howl. Since Burn was a satellite station, newly delivered 578 Squadron aircraft used to come to Snaith for modifications and post delivery checks and older aircraft came for Major inspections. Consequently 578 Squadron tradesmen came over to work at Snaith on occasions and were involved in the solution of the 'howl' problem. If the Rear Gunner removed his intercom jack plug the howl would disappear but he could not be isolated from the intercom system so a remedy was necessary. The standard action was to gain access to the slip rings and clean them. However this was a rather tedious task involving removal of the 'Monica' dipole, part of the fuselage and the armour plating. As a consequence a modification was carried out whereby an alternative connection was provided for the intercom, with a second socket in the rear turret connected to the wiring in the rear fuselage by threading a connector through the top of the turret.

The numerous aerials fitted to the Halifax are shown in Fig 48. There was a problem with airmen standing on the 'Monica' dipole at the rear of the turret to clean the turret perspex, hence damaging it, so one solution tried was to put a notice above the aerial which stated, 'Danger high voltage, keep off'.

Ground crews could get involved in solving a lot of strange snags. Norman Davidson tells a story which although a slight digression from Snaith will be of interest to ex W/Ops. After he left Burn and Snaith he was posted to a Middle East airfield and like the author was one of the technical personnel that the RAF was short of so that their release was delayed till 1947. Post war squadrons like 51 when route flying or in transit called in at Middle East airfields with snags. One day an aircraft flew in with a report that the T1154 transmitter was smoking when operated. W/Ops were told to tune for 'maximum smoke' but this was ridiculous. The set had been changed at Luca but the fault remained. After a lot of heartache and sweat Norman found the problem, somewhere along the route a 'sprog' wireless mechanic had switched the power supplies under the bench (as in Fig 12) so that the HT supply was connected to the LT circuitry and the LT to the HT. Problem solved.

In later aircraft, in order to replace the pigeons carried in 1943, dinghy transmitters were stored on the port side of the fuselage aft of the rest position and any faults in these had to be rectified by the Wireless Mechanic. The design of these emergency transmitters was based on that of a captured German NS2 (Not Sender Gerate 21) emergency transmitter. There were two types of transmitter used by the RAF, the British Type 33 and the more widely available USA SCR 578 known as the

TECHNICAL SUPPORT

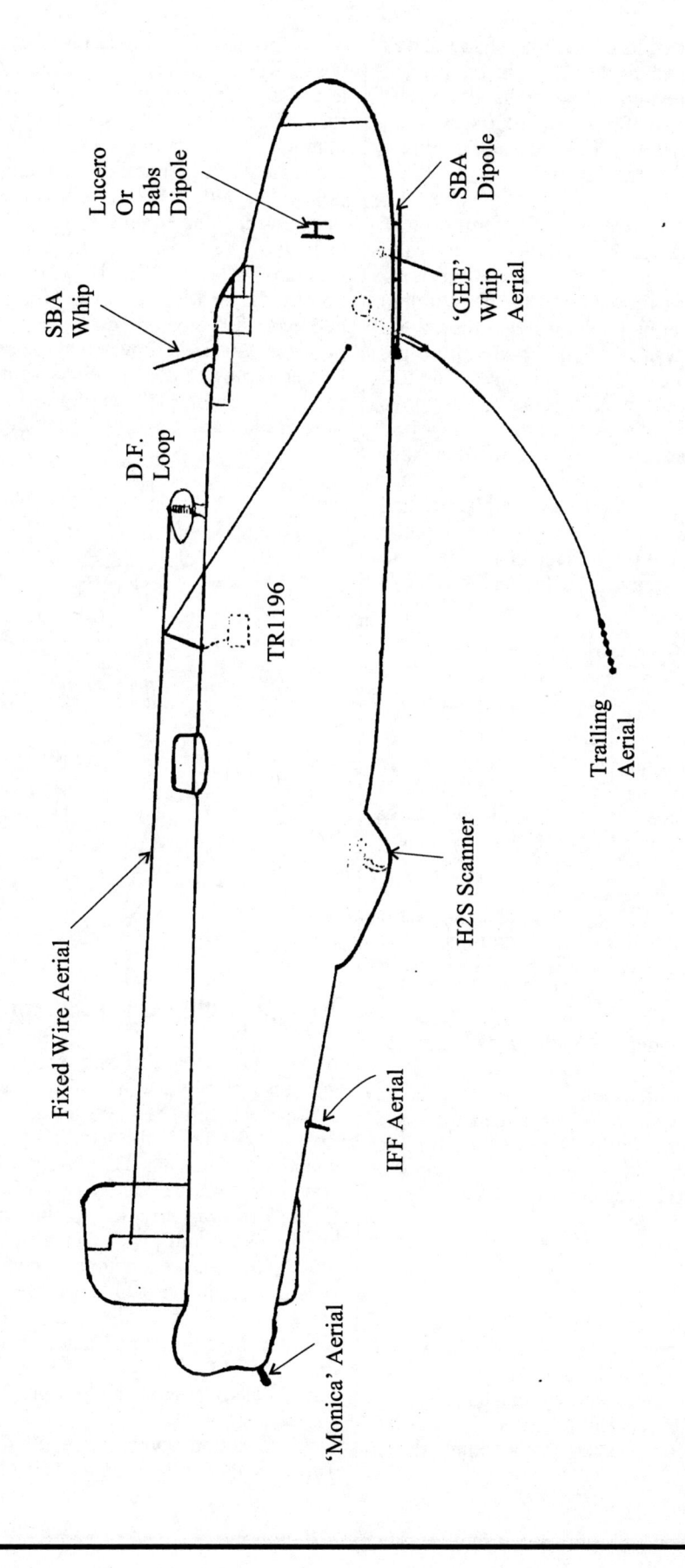

FIG 48 Aerial Systems On A Halifax

'Gibson Girl' because of its curvaceous shape. It was ergonomically designed so that it could be gripped between the knees when operating the handle for the generator. The radio had 300 ft of flexible wire as an aerial which could be elevated by means of a folding kite. The power output was 5 watts.

Then in 1944 when the amount of airborne radar equipment in use had increased, in order to reduce the load on the Radar Mechanics, the responsibility for the IFF equipment was transferred to the Wireless Mechanic. The IFF set had a detonator fitted till the end of the war and it was said that because of this the Germans did not capture an intact IFF set. The test procedure was for the Wireless Mechanics to remove a plug from the IFF set at the rear of the fuselage and put it into a test socket so that the two detonator buttons could be pressed to confirm that the detonator circuits were working. The Wireless Mechanics had an oscilloscope in their signals van so that a probe could be placed near the IFF aerial and a signal from it monitored by observing the display on the cathode ray tube.

SAFETY EQUIPMENT ASSISTANTS

The safety equipment used in the squadron included parachutes and inflatable dinghies. There was a special parachute building near No 1 Hangar where trained WAAFs carried out the important task of parachute packing. WAAFs were ideally suited for this task, since an airman's life could depend on their deft folding of a parachute.

In the event of having to ditch in the sea an inflatable dinghy was incorporated in the aircraft and was stored in the port wing covered by a panel sealed with aircraft fabric so that the panel could be readily ejected when the dinghy was inflated by a compressed gas cylinder. The Safety Equipment Assistant's job was to ensure that the safety equipment was installed and working correctly, bouyancy equipment not perished or damaged, gas cylinders satisfactory, and the GEC floating torches working. The dinghy was checked regularly for cracks and leaks and emergency equipment such as emergency rations installed.

ARMOURERS

51 Squadron being a bombing unit, the Armourers were very important members of the ground crew and theirs was a very physically demanding and hazardous task as exemplified by the bomb dump explosion. When an operation was planned the bombing up procedure started in the bomb dump when the list of bombs required for the operation was delivered to the NCO in Charge, his task being to ensure that the correct bombs were selected and fused as per instructions. The bomb dump was manned by the Station Armourers who carried out the fusing and preparation including insulation of tail units, aided by Armourers Assistants, for manhandling the bombs and loading them on to trolleys. The bomb sizes normally carried by 51 Squadron were 500 lb, 1000 lb and 2000 lb HE bombs, GP or MC. GP stood for general purpose and MC for medium capacity. The difference between MC and GP was that the MC contained a higher explosive content (50%) and a thinner wall than a GP bomb (34% explosive), so that it had a greater blast and fragmentation effect.

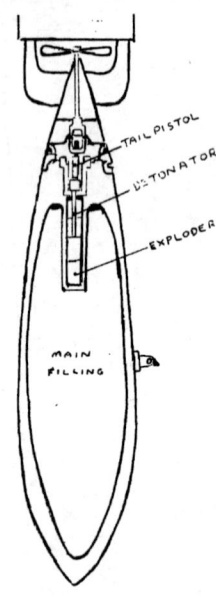

FIG 28 Tail Fused H.E. Bomb

A common bomb filling was Amatol/TNT in various ratios and other fillings were RDX and Tritonal which were more sensitive to impact than the Amatol/TNT fillings. Fig 28 shows the construction of an HE bomb. The exploder contained a more sensitive explosive than the main filling and was installed in the nose or tail of a bomb. The bomb pistol was a mechanical device which could strike a detonator containing a highly sensitive explosive such as Mercury Fulminate and these were fitted to the bombs when they were fused in the bomb dump before being delivered to the aircraft. The striker of the bomb pistol impacted with the detonator when the bomb struck the target.

Delayed action bombs were fitted with a special Type 37 pistol which could delay the striker from impacting the detonator for periods up to 144 hours. These Type 37 fuses contained a small phial of acetone dyed pink which rested on a cotton wool pad in contact with a celluloid disc. When the bomb dropped the impact broke the glass phial and allowed the acetone to come into contact with the celluloid disc. Since the acetone had some solvency power for nitrocellulose it would start to soften the celluloid. The celluloid disk held the firing pin against the action of a spring and when softened sufficiently it would release the pin and allow it to strike a detonator. The period of delay was governed by the thickness of the celluloid disc. Detonators were supplied in tin cans, each containing a dozen, and had to be handled carefully since Armourers were known to lose fingers and even hands during fusing operations. If bombs were handled roughly it was possible for the acetone phial to be broken as sometimes indicated by a pink stain on the outside of the bomb when the acetone leaked out.

Some delayed action bombs contained anti-handling device which meant that once the pistol was in place it could not be unscrewed without exploding the bomb, and this could cause problems if the pistol became cross-threaded and needed to be withdrawn. With the Type 39 anti-handling fuse a quarter of a turn anticlockwise to unscrew it would mean that the armourer could blow himself up. In such a case the bomb would need to be disposed of with the pistol still in place. It seems quite possible that problems with the anti-handling fuses could have been the cause of the bomb dump explosion. The various types of fuses were designated by code letters as follows : N = nose fusing; T = tail fusing; Inst = fused instantaneous; Inst R = fused instantaneous with rod, to explode just above the ground to produce cratering. The rod device was superceded by a barometric pistol in which air waves produced when the bomb was approaching the ground activated a diaphragm in the pistol which could explode the bomb before it struck the ground. LD 26 = long delay for 26 hours; D2 = time delay for 2 secs. Bombs were fitted with a propeller which rotated when the bomb was dropped, in order to arm the bomb.

The types of incendiary bombs employed were 4 lb, 4 lb Type 'X' and 30 lb, the Type 'X' incendiaries containing an explosive charge. The 4 lb incendiary bombs worked on the 'Thermite' principle whereby an aluminium and iron oxide filling was used to ignite a magnesium alloy casing which burnt for 7 to 10 minutes. The 30 lb incediaries contained phosphorous and rubberised Benzol, less efficient as fire raisers than the 4 lb bombs but the brilliant phosphorous cascade when they exploded affected the morale of the fire fighters. These incendiaries were packed in SBCs (Small Bomb Containers) in the bomb dump and held in place by retaining bars.

For 'gardening' operations mines had to be prepared and the various types were Type A and B Magnetic, Type D Acoustic, Type F Special Types for use against U Boats and Minesweepers, and Type G Acoustic/ Magnetic. There were dangers associated with the preparation and testing of sea mines especially the acoustic type. The Armourers had to test these for a positive circuit and during the 5 second test period the change in tempo of certain acoustic sources could detonate the mine. These sources included variations in the revolutions of M.T. or aircraft engines.

When the bombs had been prepared and loaded onto trolleys they would be hauled around the peri track by tractors driven by M.T. personnel, including WAAFS, to the Squadron Armourers waiting at the dispersal. At the Flights, Armourers would have been preparing the aircraft for the arrival of the bombs by carrying out their DIs. Each Armourer was allocated two aircraft and they would work in pairs to inspect four aircraft between them using a brush stale as one of their tools. The Armourer responsible for signing the Form 700 would go inside the aircraft and open the bomb doors. Then his colleague below would reach up inside the bomb bay with the stale and cock all the EMR units so that the bomb distributor unit could be operated to check they were working.

When the bomb trolleys arrived at dispersal the Armourers in the Flight would join up to form a team, usually four airmen plus a Corporal or LAC in charge. Each team had at least four aircraft to bomb up. There was a shortage of bomb trolleys at Snaith so bombs had to be rolled off the trolleys to release them for further bomb loads. This procedure worked satisfactorily with the British bombs with a safe filling but the American bombs were less stable so that when they were rolled off onto the hard dispersal accidents could occur. To overcome this the Armourers rolled the bombs off on to bundles of 'Window' strips to cushion the fall. This procedure was restricted to single men.

For the bombing up procedure Handley Page bombing winches were positioned either in the fuselage or on top of the wings and small access plates unscrewed so the winch cables could be dropped down. The bomb carriers which had been removed from the bomb bays were attached to the bombs by putting a carrier hoop through the lug on

TECHNICAL SUPPORT

the bomb case and clicking it shut. The bomb was then located firmly inside the carrier by screwing down the four carrier feet. The ball on the end of the winch carrier was fitted into a socket on the top of the carrier and the Armourer inside the aircraft told to "Wind away". Winching up the bombs meant slow hard work for the Armourers, so in 1944 in order to speed up the operation hydraulically operated winches were issued. The hydraulic power was provided by a Ford engine on a four wheel trolley driving a hydraulic unit and connected to the winches by pipes. Bomb loads were positioned so as to balance the aircraft when loaded and the bomb selector positions were chosen for balance during release. Because of the differences in terminal velocities the 4 lb incendiaries were dropped first, then the 30lb ones and the HEs last,

When all the bombs had been loaded into the bomb racks, plugs were put into their sockets and the Corporal in charge entered the aircraft, having ordered the rest of the crew to stand clear. He then connected up the accumulators and tested the bomb circuits. On the end of the carrier there was a fusing box with a release solenoid and a hook from the bomb would be connected to the fusing wire in the box. When the bombs were released over the target, fusing links would arm them. As the bombs fell the wire would pull the safety stop from the tail of the bomb allowing the rotor on the tail fin to rotate and unscrew the safety fork. However if the jettison bar in the bomb selector panel was operated then bombs would be released unarmed. When the Corporal was satisfied that everything was OK the bomb doors would be pumped shut, which would isolate the main bomb switch and the photo flash would be placed in the flare chute on the port side of the fuselage.

The bombing up procedure could take at least an hour for each aircraft so that with a 1300 hour start if everything went smoothly, bombing up should be finished by 1700 to 1800 hours and the tired Armourers would wearily wait for a vehicle to pick them up with their equipment. There were cases when a change of bomb load was required so it was a case of "De-bomb and bomb up again" which meant that the Armourers were then committed to stay on the flight and await the arrival of the NAAFI van for a mug of tea and a 'wad', helped by a 'Tenner' cigarette before bombing up again. Later on in the evening the replacement load, as for example two 1,500 lb mines, could arrive, the operation having been changed to 'gardening'. The second bomb up could be completed by about 2200 hours, by which time the aircrew would have arrived at the aircraft and could be standing by waiting for the go ahead.

The Armourers would keep their fingers crossed that they would not see a red flare fired from the Control Tower, meaning the operation was off. If this did occur it would mean a night off for the aircrew who would commiserate with their ground crew colleagues and hand them their coffee flasks to give the poor 'Plumbers' a drink before they got on with the thankless task of debombing again. Armourers never had a settled life, even with a stand down one third were on duty and the rest had to leave information as to where they could be found. A common occurrence was for Armourers to be called out by a Tannoy message or a notice flashed on the screen of the camp cinema, "All Armourers to report to their section immediately".

Even if the take off for an operation went off without a hitch the Armourers' tasks were not finished since the duty Armourers had to wait until the aircraft arrived back. The post operation task involved entering each aircraft with an inspection lamp on the forehead and a screwdriver to unscrew the bomb bay inspection plates to check inside for hang ups. Normal hang ups could be a problem for the Armourers but an ever dicier situation occurred during one operation. The squadron was operating in severe icing conditions and the result was that it affected the bomb release mechanism on one of the aircraft. In the EMR unit ice jammed the release hook in the closed position even though the solenoid was operating. Over the target all the bombs were released except the one with the jammed mechanism which meant that the crew flew back from the target with one bomb still hung up. When the aircraft reached warmer air the ice in the bomb mechanisms thawed out so that the aircraft returned with a bomb sitting on the bomb doors. The duty Armourers on their post op. check noticed this bomb which meant that the Warrant Officer Armourer was alerted and a special procedure had to be devised to remove the bomb. Bales of straw were obtained from a local farm and placed on a low loader, which was driven under the bomb bay. The bomb doors were then pumped open slowly and the bomb eased down on to the straw bales with some of the Armourers holding the tail to keep it horizontal. When safely located on the straw bales and lashed down it was driven away to be disposed of.

In addition to the bombing up procedure, another group of Armourers had to check the guns in the aircraft and install a fresh supply of .303 ammunition in belts. The ammunition mixture supplied in belts filled by the Station Armoury normally included tracer bullets (Identification red

TECHNICAL SUPPORT

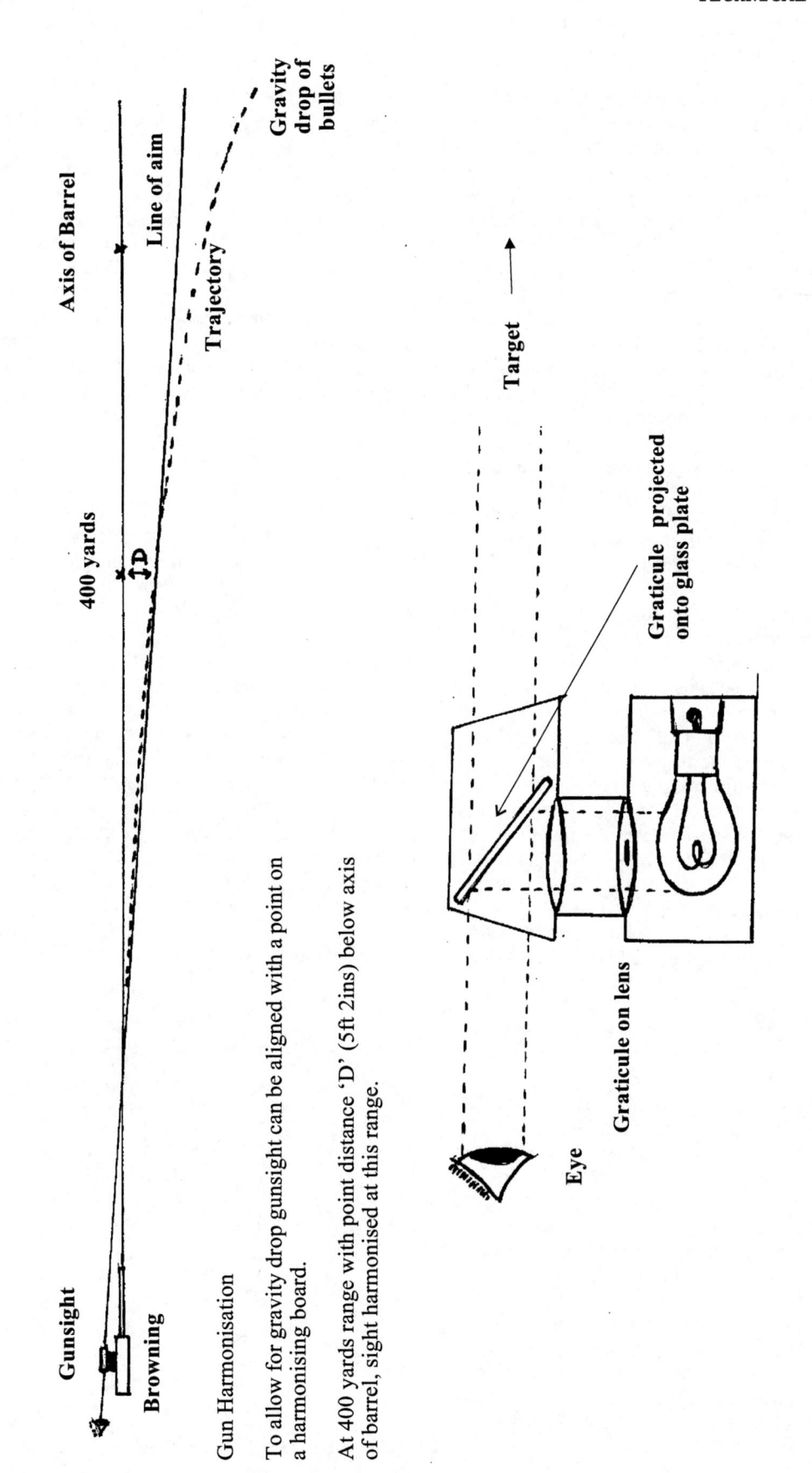

Gunsight

Browning

Axis of Barrel

Line of aim

Trajectory

Gravity drop of bullets

400 yards

D

Gun Harmonisation

To allow for gravity drop gunsight can be aligned with a point on a harmonising board.

At 400 yards range with point distance 'D' (5ft 2ins) below axis of barrel, sight harmonised at this range.

Target

Graticule projected onto glass plate

Eye

Graticule on lens

FIG 46 Gunsight And Harmonisation

139

annular ring on the base), armour piercing (Green annular ring on the base), incendiaries (Blue annular ring on base), and ball ammunition (Purple annular ring on the base). A Typical ammunition mix was 3 of ball, 1 of armour piercing, 1 of incendiary and 1 of tracer. Sometimes only two guns in a turret contained tracer bullets in their feed. The ammunition for the rear turret was gravity fed in tracks leading from elevated boxes on the rear port side of the fuselage. There was a mechanically operated feed assister and automatic reloading operated by the firing of the guns. Guns could be adjusted for left hand or right hand feed by means of the transport plate in the breech. To change the direction of feed it was necessary to lift up the plate turn through 180 degrees and replace it. The manufacturers specification for the maximum amount of ammunition which would be normally used in a Halifax was, 1,160 rounds per gun for the mid upper turret and 1,700 r.p.g. with a 4,800 reserve for the rear turret.

One job for the Armourers responsible for the guns, sometimes carried out in co-operation with the Air Gunners, was the harmonisation of the guns. This meant adjusting the guns to give the required cone of fire and lining them up with the reflector gun sight. Fig46 shows how the fall off due to gravity of the bullet stream, called the trajectory, is not a straight line unlike the view from a gun sight. Harmonisation meant that the guns were adjusted so that the point of impact at a given range was positioned on the line of sight at that range, in other words at the harmonisation point. To harmonise at 400 yds the 4 guns in turret could be aligned at a point at that distance and 5 ft 2 inches below the axis of the barrel. However to increase the possibility of hitting a target, even when the line of sight was not completely accurate the guns were harmonised so that the cones of fire overlapped with the increased possibility of a hit at the expense of bullet density.

For harmonisation a large board was used and this had red, yellow, blue, and green circles at the corners of a square with a sighting cross located between them. With a 400 yd harmonisation the circles were set at the corners of a 10 ft square and because of the bullet drop the sighting mark was 5 ft 2 inches below the intersection of the diagonals. On the north side of the airfield there were gun butts for for firing rifles and automatic weapons and a harmonisation range with datum marks for 100 and 400 yards. At Snaith, 400 yds was a rather restrictive distance at which to place the board if carrying out harmonisation on some of the dispersals since other aircraft, vehicles etc could get in the line of site. As a consequence a smaller board was employed, this could be used at 25 yards distance and still give the required result.

The harmonisation procedure was to place the board at the approriate distance from the turret, which had been set to zero in azimuth, open the breech of the master gun and place a gun aligning periscope in the barrel. The periscope cross wires were lined up on the appropriate circle on the harmonising board, which may have to be moved by an assistant. The periscope was placed in each gun in turn which was then lined up on the appropriate circle and finally the reflector gun sight was aligned on the aiming mark and locked in position.

PHOTOGRAPHERS

The use of bombing photography became so important for assessing the efficiency of bombing operations that all bomber aircraft were fitted with an F24 aerial camera. When the squadron aircraft were being prepared for an operation the photographers would load the camera with a magazine containing a fresh batch of film and ensure that the correct fuse capsule was set on the photoflash and the camera control was set to the bombing height. In the F24s used for night photography the focal plane shutter was modified so that the shutter was open and the film continously exposed when the camera was set. The shutter was closed when the new frame was wound over and capping blind operated. The exposure restarted when the capping blind operated. The camera was capable of taking 125 exposures but normally only 6 frames were used for the bombing

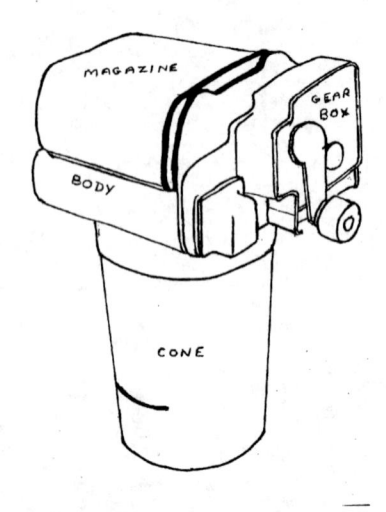

FIG 44 F24 Aircraft Camera

photos. The actual target exposure illuminated by a high candle power flash was called the Bombing Frame The other photos taken over the target zone were useful in that they recorded information which could be useful for assessment by the Operations staff. The information obtained could include searchlights, gun flashes, incendiary fires, and decoy targets.

When the Bomb Aimer pressed the bomb release switch it released the photoflash along with the bombs and also started the operation of the Camera Controller which operated the camera. Two frames were wound over before the photoflash ignited in order to ensure clearance of fogged film. The bombing frame exposure was made when the high candle power flash exploded. The photoflash was designed to make it fall slower than the bombs and explode behind the aircraft so that it illuminated the ground for about 1/30 of a sec without impinging on the photo frame in the camera. Approximately 4 secs after the exposure was made the Controller wound on two more frames. There was a possible exposure by frame 6 of the bomb bursts. In order to conserve this frame without fogging it the Bomb Aimer needed to press the `Bomb Tit' again to repeat the film cycle which meant that frame 6 would be wound on. When daylight operations started a modification was carried out on the camera cycle to enable it to take an extra picture coincident with the bomb release. The reason for this was that the normal single bombing frame in daylight was not reliable enough to give an indication of where the bombs were likely to hit..

After an operation the photographic section had to work fast to have the raid photographs ready for assessment by the I/O Section.

Photos 74 & 75 show 51 Squadron daylight bombing frame photos printed by the photographic section. Photo 75 was from a film exposed during an operation against Vaires Marshalling Yards near Paris. The information printed on the photo is as follows

PRINT NO: 2808
STATION: Snaith
DATE: 18.7.44
LENS SETTING: F8
HEIGHT: 13,000ft
Bg. & DIST FROM DATUM POINT: 155 17.57
TARGET: Vaires
BOMB LOAD: 16 x 500lbs
PILOT: F/Lt Richardson
SQUADRON: 51

Photographs of accurate bombing sorties were selected by Bombing Command and included in their Night Photography Reports. An extract showing the 4 Group entries in one of these reports is shown in Fig 54. This includes a 51 Squadron aircraft,`U' piloted by F/Sgt Alderson, with Sgt Holden as Bomb Aimer. This 51 Squadron aircraft's photo was chosen because of the accuracy of its bombing on this operation. During this

FIG 54   Bomber Command Night Photography Report

Report On Night Photographs No P.7   **Secret**
Photographs taken 11/12 June 1944
Target:- MASSEY PALAISEAU (France) Railway Junctions
4 Group Plotted Aircraft

Item No	Captain Taken	A/C	Print	Time	Plotting	A/C Heading
1	Sgt. Edwards	102E	4607	00:09	800yds	360 N.E.
2	W/O Bowden	578Q	188	00:12	750yds	286 S.S.W
3	P/O Page	102Y	4610	00:12	1050yds	308 S.E.
4	F/L Moore	102F	4608	00:15	1000yds	070 E.S.E
5	F/S Alderson	51U	2363	00:02	300yds	236 N.N.W

Air Staff Intelligence P.I.
Headquarters, Bomber Command.
13th June 1944

TECHNICAL SUPPORT

operation the flight commander, S/Ldr Nick Simmonds, whose exploits have been mentioned earlier in this book was leading `C' Flight. As a Bomb Aimer he took his aircraft down to low level and called out over the radio "Come on down its warmer here", to encourage `C' Flight. However other members of the flight declined his invitation and stayed at 15,000ft. Nick's aircraft collected a flak delivery for his pains.

MECHANICAL TRANSPORT

The support received from the M.T. section was essential for the efficient operation of the squadron and a wide variety of vehicles was provided. At Snaith the M.T. buildings are still in existence, if somewhat modified and in the old M.T. office the original vehicle state board can be seen painted on the wall. The efficiency of the M.T. section at Snaith is demonstrated by the fact that it was voted the best M.T. Section in 4 Group.

Bad weather, and in particular snow, was a hazard which the squadron had to cope with when operating in winter. The M.T. section had to provide equipment to help clear snow from the runways. In Feb 1944 because of heavy falls the snow ploughs were very active in clearing runways and the peri track. Depending on the wind direction, salt and sand gritting would be effective on some runways. With dry snow the snow blowers worked very well and could remove ridges of frozen snow but when the thaw started the snow melted and became slush with the result that it clogged the fans. In winter starting difficulties could be encountered and it was quite a common practice to get a heavy vehicle started and then use it to give tow starts to those vehicles experiencing starting problems. The variety of vehicles employed at Snaith is shown in the following table:

M.T. SECTION VEHICLES AT SNAITH

Prime Movers
Heavy Ambulances; Light Ambulances; Heavy Passenger Cars
Light Passenger Cars; Aircrew Coaches; Cranes; Motor Cycles;
Motorcycle Combinations; Freighters; Tenders 3 ton; Tenders 30 ton; Fire Crash Tenders; Light Tractors; Articulated Tractors; Vans 15 cwt; Vans 5/10 cwt; Bomb Carrying Tenders; Tankers 2500 gallons;
Preheater Vans; Snow Clearance Tenders; Signal Vans Type 316;
Light Tractors with winch;

Trailers
Floodlights; Landmark Beacon ('Pundit'); Petrol Trailer 900 gall;
Oil Trailer 450 gall; Preheater Trailer; Bomb Carrying Trailers
Airfield Caravan; Water Carrier Trailer;
Flat Trailers (eg for transporting oxygen gas cylinders);

Photo 64 (IWM CH6622)
Wireless Mechanic Servicing T1154 Transmitter

Photo 62 (IWM CH12630)
51 Squadron Ground Crew At Work Outdoors On Halifax MH-R

TECHNICAL SUPPORT

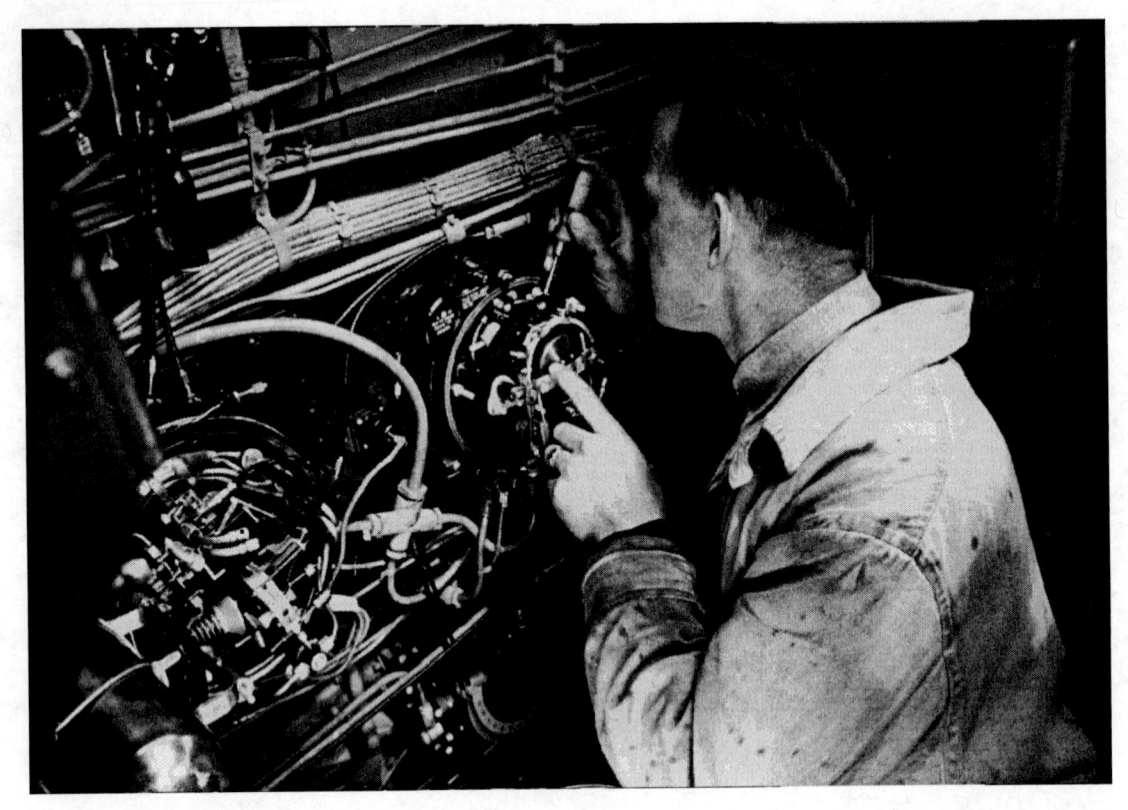

Photo 65 (IWM CH6607)

Photo 63 (IWM CH6600)

TECHNICAL SUPPORT

Photo 67 (IWM 6628)
Instrument Repairers Recharging Oxygen System

Photo 66 (IWM 6626)
Armourers Bombing Up With HE's And Incendiaries

TECHNICAL SUPPORT

**Photo 75
51 Squadron Bombing
Photo Of Tirlemont
Airfield**

**Photo 74
51 Squadron
Bombing Photo
Of Vaires
Marshalling
Yards**

Chapter 9

TRAINING AND PRACTICE

It was important to keep 51 Squadron up to maximum operational efficiency and in order to achieve this aircrew were required to participate in both ground and airborne training to keep an edge on their skills. Also in view of the technical advances during the war it was necessary for Ground personnel, both Officers and ORs, apart from training on the unit, to attend specialist courses at RAF Schools of Technical Training or courses organised by Manufacturers and Research Organisations. The latter included courses on Merlin engines at Rolls Royce, Hercules engines at Bristol Aircraft, Halifax airframes at Handley Page, Hydraulics course at Messier, D.R. Compasses at Ferranti and Radar equipment courses at RAE Farnborough and TRE Malvern.

For obvious reasons the RAF set great store by training as demonstrated by the regular publication of a training magazine called 'TEE EMM' and a variety of publications and wall charts all of which were displayed by the various crew leaders in their sections. Wartime members will recall a famous character, PO Prune who featured in these publications by regularly 'setting up a black', ie carrying out the sort of action which produced crashes and dangerous incidents, referred to as 'Pruneries. Anyone achieving one of these was awarded the H.D.O.O.T.I.F. (The Highly Derogatory Order of the Irremoveable Finger), which is reproduced in Fig 29. Consequently, a widely used term in the Squadron was 'Finger trouble' and a regular call to anyone who was not performing satifactorily was "Get your finger out".

**FIG 29
H.D.O.O.T.I.F.
Medal**

For ground training of aircrew there were various items of equipment on the station. The concept of simulator trainers for the RAF had been around since WW1, since they could be cost effective and time saving. It has been reported that in World War 2 there were 2,000 ground trainers in use and that these relieved the RAF from having to use 4,000 aircraft flying two million hours for training purposes, with a petrol consumption of 250 million gallons. Some of the WW2 trainers although predominantly mechanical ones were the starting point for modern simulators, which can be very complex. This sophistication is only made possible by modern integrated circuits and electronics, these simulators being so realistic that they can be used to assess a pilot's competence.

PILOTS

Pilots had access to a Link Trainer at Snaith particularly useful for practising instrument flying. This comprised a miniature aircraft shaped body, mainly occupied by a simulated cockpit, containing instruments and controls. The pupil climbed into the cockpit and a hood was lowered leaving him in complete darkness. A 'Blind Flying Panel', which was standard in all service aircraft during WW2, was just visible by virtue of the luminous markings on the instrument dials and a dim red light. The other cockpit aid was a stopwatch fitted into a special holder. The Instructor sat at a desk in the corner of the room, with headphones and a microphone to enable him to communicate with the pupil, as shown in photo No 30.

The Link Trainer first came into use in 1929 and was operated pneumatically, the turning motion being obtained by means of a bank of bellows operating cranks to rotate the shaft on which the trainer was pivoted and the pitch and roll was also effected by means of bellows. Movement signals from the trainer were transmitted to a three wheeled tracking device called a 'crab' which was located on the Instructor's desk. The 'crab', which was powered by electric motors, moved across a glass plate on the desk drawing lines with a stylus as it did so, which enabled the Instructor to follow the pupil's progress during a simulated flight.

The 'crab' turned as the pupil in the trainer operated his rudder and control column and moved at a speed relative to the speed set by the pupil. The Link Trainer could be made to simulate a take-off, climb, turn, dive, stall, spin, and even crash. Everything was copied by the stylus onto the glass. The Instructor could apply a wind speed and direction to the aircraft and also affect it with rough air and turbulance. Underneath the glass plate on his desk the Instructor could place a chart of say a cross country flight or Snaith airfield approaches and runways The airfield plan was particularly useful for landing or SBA exercises.

For the latter, signals to represent Standard Beam Approach could be sent to the pupil to enable him to carry out various exercises, which could include identifying a beam, flying through it, finding front or back beam, determining drift, and finally carrying out a complete beam approach and landing. Since there was no SBA equipment installed at Snaith and a pilot had to attend a course at a BAT Flight for flying training, then Link SBA training could be valuable in case the pilot had to make a landing away at an airfield with SBA. At the end of the exercise the Instructor could discuss the result by examining the stylus trace with reference to the chart, after which the glass could be cleaned ready for the next exercise.

In WW2 great ingenuity was often used in the development of training aids, as exemplified by a modification carried out to the Link Trainer at an OTU where some 51 Squadron aircrew trained. A model electric train carrying an assembly of small electric bulbs ran around three walls of the room. As the Link was 'flown' in a circular pattern, the train moved and the lights simulated the apparent movement of the approach and runway lights so that night flying circuits could be practised. To achieve realism night vision simulation equipment was used. In addition to ground training in the Link, Pilots obtained experience with flying the Squadron aircraft in various exercises which included Cross Countries, Circuits and Bumps, Air Tests, SBA Training, Bomb Load Climbs, Radar Tests and Training, 'Bullseyes', Practice Bombing, Fighter Affiliation and Air to Sea Firing. When new Pilots arrived on the squadron it was the policy to let them fly as 'Second Dickie' with an experienced Pilot for at least one operation. New Pilots and crews on arrival at the squadron had to carry out at least one Bomb Load Climb to familiarise them with the problems of taking off with a full bomb load, acompanied by an experienced Pilot. The duration of the exercise was normally about two hours and could include experience for the Navigator in carrying out a radius of action circuit and using navigation equipment.

Airborne training exercises which were normally carried out between operations applied particularly to the less experienced crews and could be organised on either a Squadron or a Group basis. When detailed they had to be carried out just like an operation. Navigator John MacCoss reports on the hassle which occurred when an experienced crew got lumbered with being detailed for a Group exercise. The squadron had been stood down for a few days with some of the crews on leave but being an experienced crew the Pilot and Flight Engineer had been detailed as duty officers in the appropriate sections. The rest of the crew were not slow to take the opportunity for a trip to York and call in to their favourite restaurant, the Davey Hall, for a meal. They had almost finished eating when they received a phone message from the Flight Engineer that they had to return to Snaith immediately. They travelled back by the next available transport and reported to the Squadron Offices to be informed by their Skipper that they had been detailed, as one of two aircraft from 51 Squadron, for a Group 'Bullseye' exercise. As they were a very experienced crew, with six ops in the last nine days under their belt, they were flabbergasted at this sudden detail for a training excise. John's opinion was that the Skipper had volunteered for this exercise to get off admin. duties. Salt was rubbed in the wound when the exercise was cancelled at 2100 hrs. This produced a very disgruntled group of Sergeants and resulted in the sort of 'situation' between crew members which could occur from time to time.

NAVIGATORS

Members of the crew other than Pilots were the responsibility of leaders for the various aircrew sections, it being their task to keep their members up to scratch. Navigation was of prime importance which was why so much research effort was expended on developing electronic navigational aids. In addition to help from the Squadron Navigation Leader, aircrew could call upon the Station Navigation Officer (S/L Paul Jousse). He

TRAINING AND PRACTICE

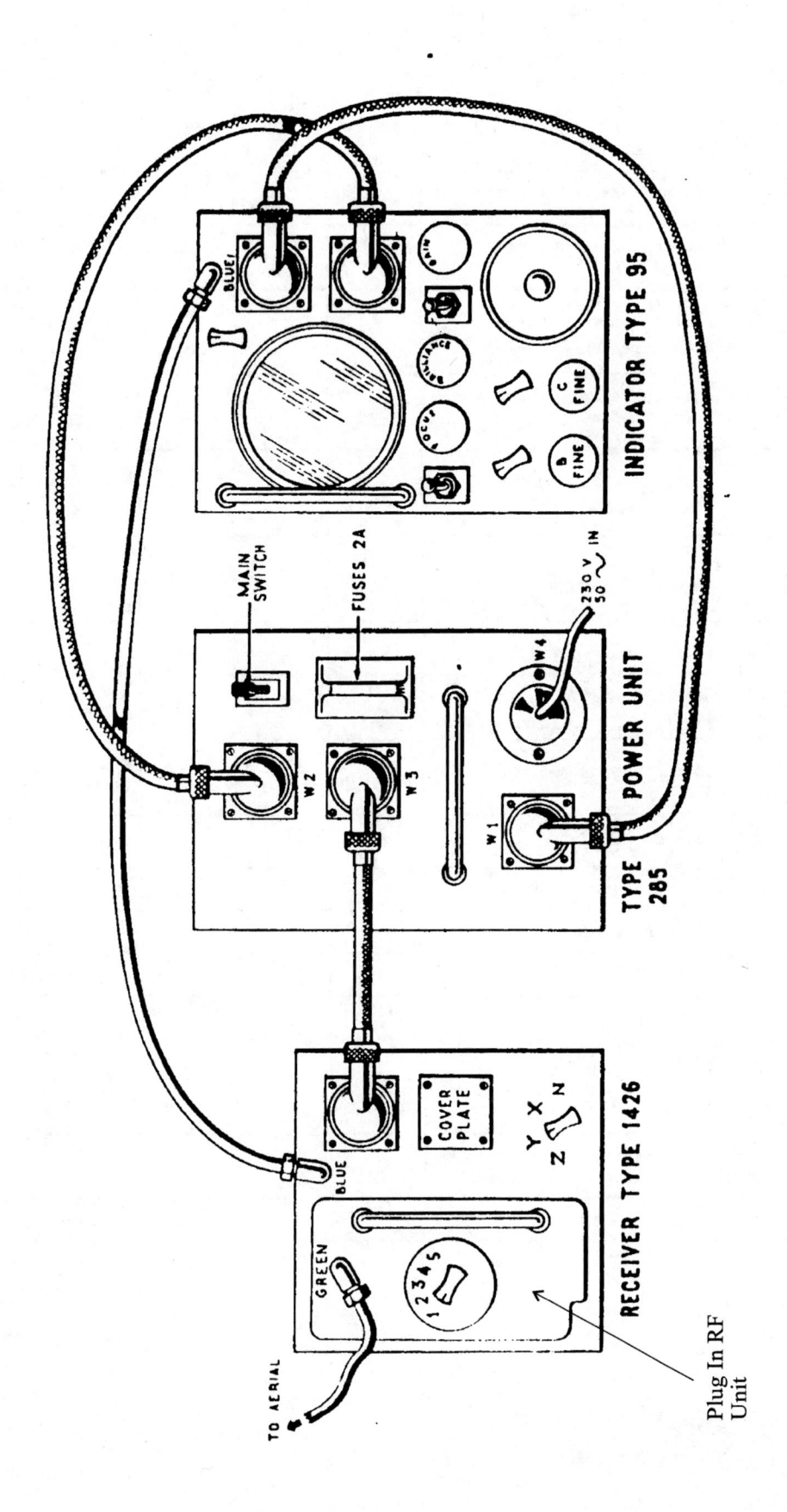

FIG 30 Mains Operated 'Gee' Set
Crown Copyright

TRAINING AND PRACTICE

AIDS	CONDITIONS UNDER WHICH POINTS ARE TO BE ALLOCATED	NUMBER	TOTAL	POINTS	POINTS
Jay & Lorenz Beams.	If heard and entered in log	—	—	2	—
	If heard and entered in log and used as P/L	—	—	5	—
A S T R O	Each shot taken and entered in log but NOT plotted			2	
	Each shot taken and entered in log and plotted	IIII	4	5	20
	Each Astro FIX from two or more shots	I	1	10	10
	BONUS of 50% for all Astro used on way to TARGET	I		50%	2½
L O O P S	Each bearing entered in log			1	
	Each bearing entered in log and plotted	IIIIIIIII IIII	13	2	26
	Each loop FIX from two or more loop bearings	II	2	3	6
W/V's	OUT First three	3	3	3	9
	Subsequent	3	3	5	15
	HOME First three	3	3	3	9
	Subsequent	1	1	5	5
Pinpoints	provided they are used	8	8	10	80
Drifts and Back Bearings	By Tail Gunner, drift recorder or bearings by Astro Compass	1	1	3	3
Other Fixes	e.g. Back bearings & Lorenz beam Loop line & Jay beam etc.etc.	—	—	3	—
Met.	Form 2330			20	20

TOTAL 205½

FIG 31 via Harry Keeling
Navigator's Assesment Form Employed In 1943

could provide advice, help in preparation of flight plans and supply training documents.

When the squadron arrived at Snaith to convert to Halifax aircraft the ex Whitley Navigators were unaccustomed to 'Gee'. This new Radar navigation aid had come into use by Bomber Command, being accurate to within 6 miles at a distance of 400 miles from the transmitters. The Germans developed a jamming system which meant it was really only usable for a limited distance but nevertheless it was a useful homing aid. Practice in the air was very important, but ground training could be a very useful and efficient method of reinforcing skills. At Snaith early in 1943 there were a couple of working 'Gee' sets in the Navigation Section with attachments to produce the effects of jamming. The purpose of these was to give the Navigators experience of the effects of jamming transmissions by the enemy, on the display on the Indicator Unit. After crossing the enemy coast 'Gee' became increasingly more difficult to use. The types of jamming experienced were CW, mod CW and railing, the latter being the most difficult to overcome. The early training sets were useful but there were limitations to the experience which could be gained from them, also the German jamming became more effective. The most effective jammers were installed at Feldberg and became operational in 1945. These fed misleading signals into the 'Gee' system.

F/Lt Harry Keeling, a very proficient Navigator joined the squadron in 1942, finishing his ops. with them in April 1943. He was then posted to 1658 HCU at Riccall as a Navigation Instructor. Because of his deep interest in navigation he realised the problems of teaching it and the use of modern navigation aids. Harry worked with another Navigation Officer named Bill Ould and a Canadian Sergeant who was a skilled Radar Mechanic, on the development of a 'Gee' simulator. Bill Ould was an Electrical Engineer in civilian life with experience in electronics, who unfortunately, later on in the war was killed in a flying accident whilst taking part in a course for Navigation 'Boffins'. The three men developed what was known as the Riccall 'Gee' Trainer, incorporating signal generators and special controls which enabled Instructors to produce any type of 'Gee' display they required on the CRT screen. This trainer became available for use at other 4 Group stations such as Snaith in conjunction with the mains powered 'Gee' equipment supplied for ground use (Fig 30). Type 24 and 25 'Gee' RF Units had 5 spot frequencies selected by switching but the Type 27 set was tuneable.

The Navigators had to learn to operate the 'Gee' sets as efficiently as possible in order to obtain the required fixes for a reliable DR plot and an accurate estimate of the wind vectors. Air Bombers who assisted their Navigators in operating the 'Gee' sets would also require practice. The following operations were carried out to obtain a fix with the 'Gee' Indicator Unit:

1) With the equipment switched on the gain control was adjusted for the correct level of pulse signal and the oscillator control adjusted to obtain stationary pulses.

2) The oscillator control was then used to move the double A (Master transmitter) pulses, i.e. pulse and ghost, to the left hand side of the bottom trace (See display A in Fig 15). 3 Then using B and C strobe coarse controls the fast time base

markers were moved near these B and C (Slave) pulses. With the strobe fine control the markers were moved onto the pulses which caused them to invert (See display A in Fig 15).

4) The strobe time base was selected with the time base switch

5) Then using B and C fine strobe controls the B and C pulses were lined up with the A pulses (See display B, Fig 15).

6) Putting the clearing switch in the down position the calibration pips were displayed. Readings relating to the delay times were read off from the B and C traces using this scale to obtain the decimal places of the coordinates.

7) With time base switch, main time base was selected to obtain the whole number of the coordinates.

8) Using the numbers obtained from the display the position lines on the 'Gee' chart could now be determined and a fix obtained.

Navigators and Air Bombers could go to the Radar Servicing Section for training in the use of the Type 27 unit which was plugged into the 'Gee' ground set shown in Fig 30. The Type 27 had a Muirhead precision drive for continuous tuning between 65 and 85 MHz. After checking that the aerial was connected and the aerial loading unit set to its appropriate stud the tuning technique could be practised with the Type 27 unit. The Muirhead tuning dial was set to the appropriate dial reading on the illuminated pointer, a calibration curve related dial position to frequency. The gain control on the indicator unit was then adjusted to give about a quarter inch of 'grass' on the main time base on the indicator unit display. The fine tuning unit was adjusted around the required frequency till the maximum signal was obtained, and it was important to ensure that the gain was not set too high. When the foregoing procedure had produced a satisfactory signal, fine tuning could be carried out with the tuning knob on the bottom left hand corner of the RF unit. On an operation the gain control could be used to compensate for reduced signal strength.

In early 1943 the Navigation Officer had a system for assessment of Navigators and one of the forms used is shown in Fig 31. At this stage astro navigation techniques were still being used by Navigators, who were expected to carry out astro fixes during an operation. The navigation systems listed in this form included 'Jay' beams. The story about this navigation aid is that it was instigated by Dr R V Jones in 1941 as a decoy for fact that the 'Gee' system was in operation. The German 'Knickerbein' system was copied by erecting stations emitting Lorenz type signals and since all the squadron's aircraft were fitted with SBA equipment these could be used as navigation aids. RAF aircrews were encouraged to use the beams in order to give them an air of authenticity, hence their inclusion in the Navigators assessment form. The name 'Jay' was chosen because it could sound like 'Gee' and if the Germans heard POWs talking about 'Gee' they might think they were refering to 'Jay'. This ruse did appear to work because squadron POWs were interrogated about the 'Jay' beams. In true RAF style both these aids received nicknames, the 'Gee' Indicator Unit was known as the 'Goon' box because it was implied that any fool could navigate using this equipment and the 'Jay' beams were called 'Jerry' beams.

As mentioned earlier in 1943, security aspects did not permit the Navigators to enter information in their log in such a manner as to allow it to be identified as appertaining to 'Gee'. These logs were handed in at the end of the operation and retained by the Navigation Officer, a separate assessment form was filled in as mentioned above. In 1944 there was a change in procedure in that assessment forms were not employed but log sheets were still handed in. The Station Navigation Officer or his deputy carried out an assessment of the Navigators performance by examination of the log. The log was rated on a 1 to 10 scale but it was very exceptional for a Navigator to receive a rating above 8. In addition to the foregoing rating the Navigation Officer included a written report on the log and handed it back to the Navigator. In the Navigator's log reproduced in Fig 42, Ken Staple was awarded a rating of 7 and the assessor's comments are shown on the last page.

The navigation aid which followed 'Gee' was H2S, initially it was only used by PFF, but towards the end of 1943 sufficient supplies of sets became available to start issuing them to main force aircraft. Since this equipment was independent of an external signal it was resistant to jamming and its effective operational range was unlimited. From January 1944 onwards when the squadron was being issued with the new Mk3 Halifax there were an increasing number of 51 Squadron aircraft fitted with this new navigation aid (Fig 32). Consequently the need for training Navigators in the use of this new navigation aid became important. In 1944 The risk of gas warfare had diminished and no more Decontamination centres were being installed at airfields. F/O Jim Gill was therefore able to obtained permission from 4 Group HQ to allocate the Gas Decontamination building for use as a home for radar ground training aids. Consequently a Type 54 H2S trainer was issued to Snaith and installed in the Training Room with a Navigation and Bombing set up which included the API, IFF and 'Fishpond', with Radar and Navigation Training Officers available to give assistance if required.

The H2S equipment initially issued to the squadron was based on a 10 cm. wavelength and the display on the cathode ray tube was known as a Plan Position Indicator since it gave a chart like representation. The rotating scanning aerial was displayed on the screen as a rotating line and in order to obtain a readable picture, phosphors giving a high persistance display were used in the tube. Varying ground targets gave different displays on the screen. Sea or inland waters scattered the incident radar waves so that very few were returned to the aircraft resulting in dark areas on the display. Land gave a better reflection than water, since only partial scatter occured so producing lighter areas on the screen which meant that coast lines could be detected. Built up areas produced the best radar returns, some buildings acting almost like corner reflectors giving a high reflection. To aid the Navigators, charts with expected radar returns were issued to them.

In the Type 54 trainer shown in Fig 33, a miniaturisation of the H2S radar transmission system was achieved by using ultrasonic waves in a

TRAINING AND PRACTICE

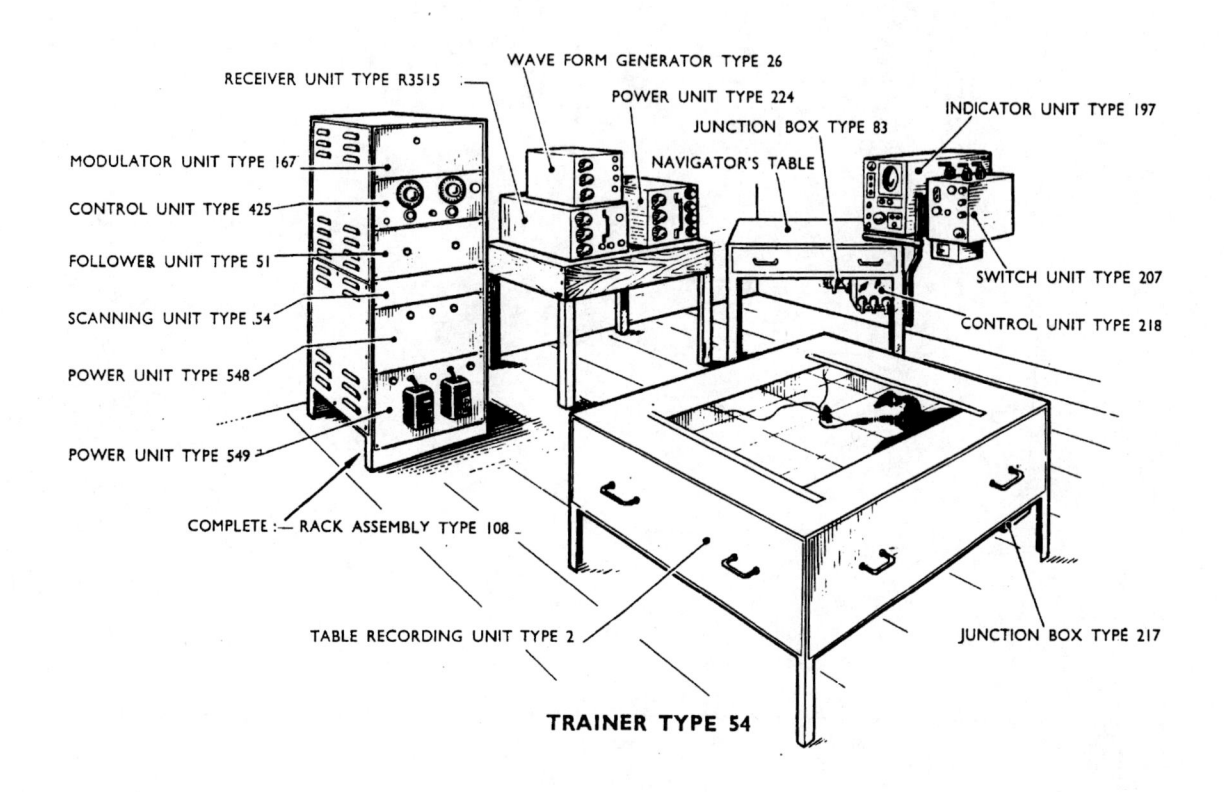

FIG 33
H2S Ground Training Equipment
Crown Copyright

TRAINING AND PRACTICE

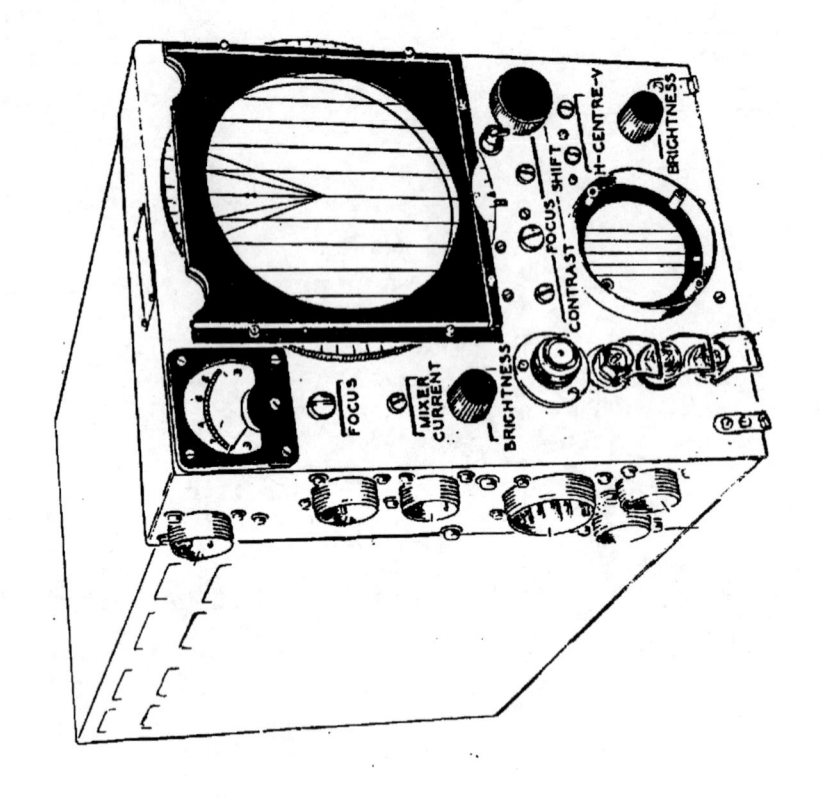

FIG 32 H2S Indicator Unit
Crown Copyright

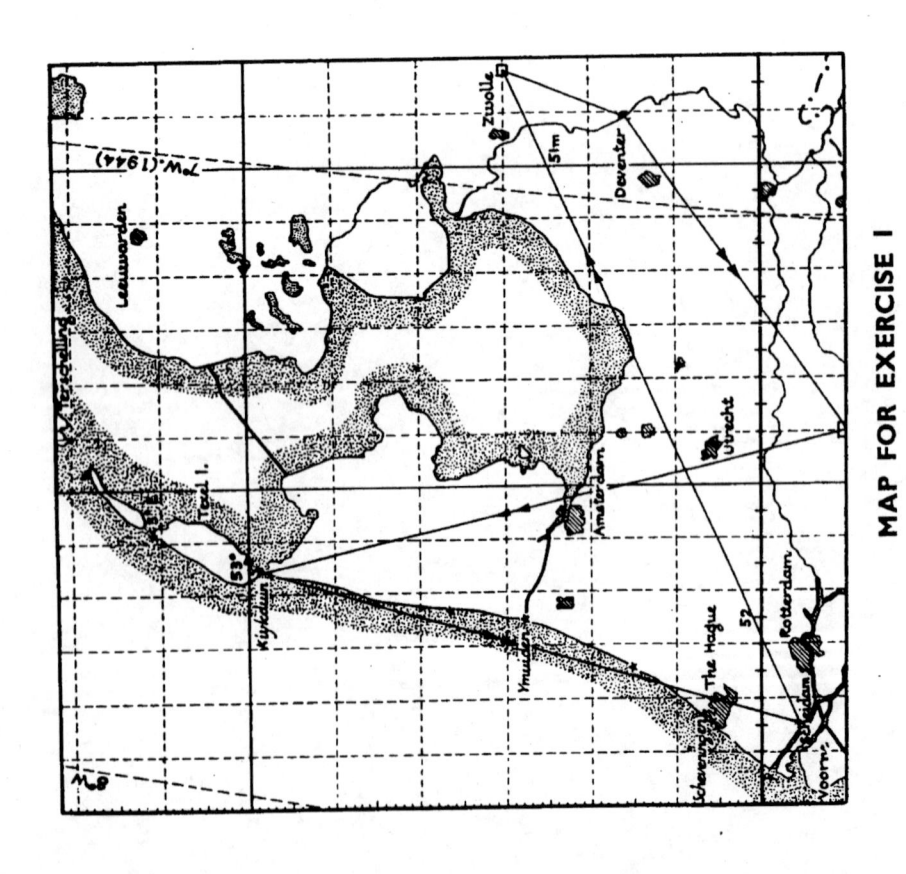

FIG 34 One of the Maps Used In Conjuction With H2S Trainer
Crown Copyright

water tank. Inside the tank was a 3ft square glass map representing an area of 12,000 sq miles with areas of the glass being either smooth, sandblasted or built up with sand, simulating the three types of display produced by seas or lakes, land areas and towns. In place of the H2S scanner a crystal transducer was employed, emitting a pulsed signal of normal PRF at 13.5 MHz frequency and scanning the glass map at the normal scan rate of 60 rpm.

The navigation of the crystal transducer which represented the aircraft was achieved by suspending the crystal from a carriage which was driven along rails in an EW direction, these rails then ran on another set of rails running in a NW direction so that movement in any direction could be achieved. By operating the trainer controls the Radar Instructor could navigate over the glass map and simulate air speed, course, wind speed and wind direction. Although the trainer's transducer was different to the aircraft scanner the presentations on the Switch Unit 207 and Indicator Unit 197 were similar to those received by an aircraft in flight. Hence the trainer could be flown like an aircraft and navigated by means of the PPI displays which were equivalent to the signals received in an aircraft at 21,000 ft.

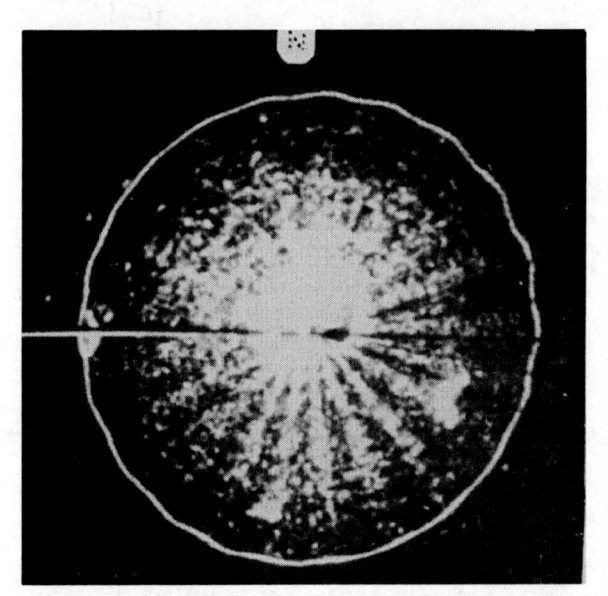

Photo 68 Photograph Of Display On H2S Trainer

On top of the tank was a perspex map corresponding to the glass map in the tank and a pen which was linked to the crystal tracked its movements on the map. Various maps were available for different exercises, one of these is shown in Fig 34 and the object of the exercise was to follow a given track on the map by using the display on the CRT to identify ground features, obtain fixes and carry out a DR plot. The Navigator and Bomb Aimer could work together on the exercise with the Bomb Aimer obtaining fixes and the Navigator carrying out the plot. If a permanent record of any of the displays was required this could be obtained by using a camera to photograph the the CRT screen (Photo).

Navigators could obtain airborne practice in cross country exercises and from about April 1944 special H2S cross countries were carried out in order to develop the Navigators skills in the use of H2S as a navigation aid.

AIR BOMBERS

When the crew of a squadron Halifax had gone through all the problems of getting their aircraft to the target it was most important to carry out an accurate bombing run to ensure the operation had been worthwhile. Therefore the task of the Bombing Leader was to ensure that his Air Bombers were well trained and highly proficient. It goes without saying that the Bombing Leader himself should be fully conversant with all the problems of bomb aiming and consequently Bombing Leaders were generally chosen from experienced Air Bombers often with a full tour of Ops already under their belts. To ensure that they were up-to-date with all the techniques of bomb aiming they could be sent on a Bombing Leader's Course at No 1 Air Armament School, Manby, Lincs.

At Snaith, to help him maintain the Air Bomber's skills the Bombing Leader had the use of an AML Bombing Trainer for Ground Training, which was housed in a tall building similar in appearance to the Gunnery Trainer located next to the Squadron Offices. This Bombing Trainer was developed by the Air Ministry Laboratories (AML) at Imperial College, London, and manufactured by Vickers as the Bygrave Bombing Teacher. The layout of the Bombing Trainer as shown in Fig 35 employed a photographic representation of 900 square miles of ground area reproduced on a glass plate. Any portion of the plate equivalent to 4 square miles at 8,000 feet could be projected onto a white screen on the floor of the darkened trainer building. The plate was on a frame controlled by two electric motors which traversed the plate for air and wind speed and rotated it for turning, hence giving the impression of the ground moving under an aircraft. The simulated height and air speed were fixed, but the Instructor could alter the wind speed and direction

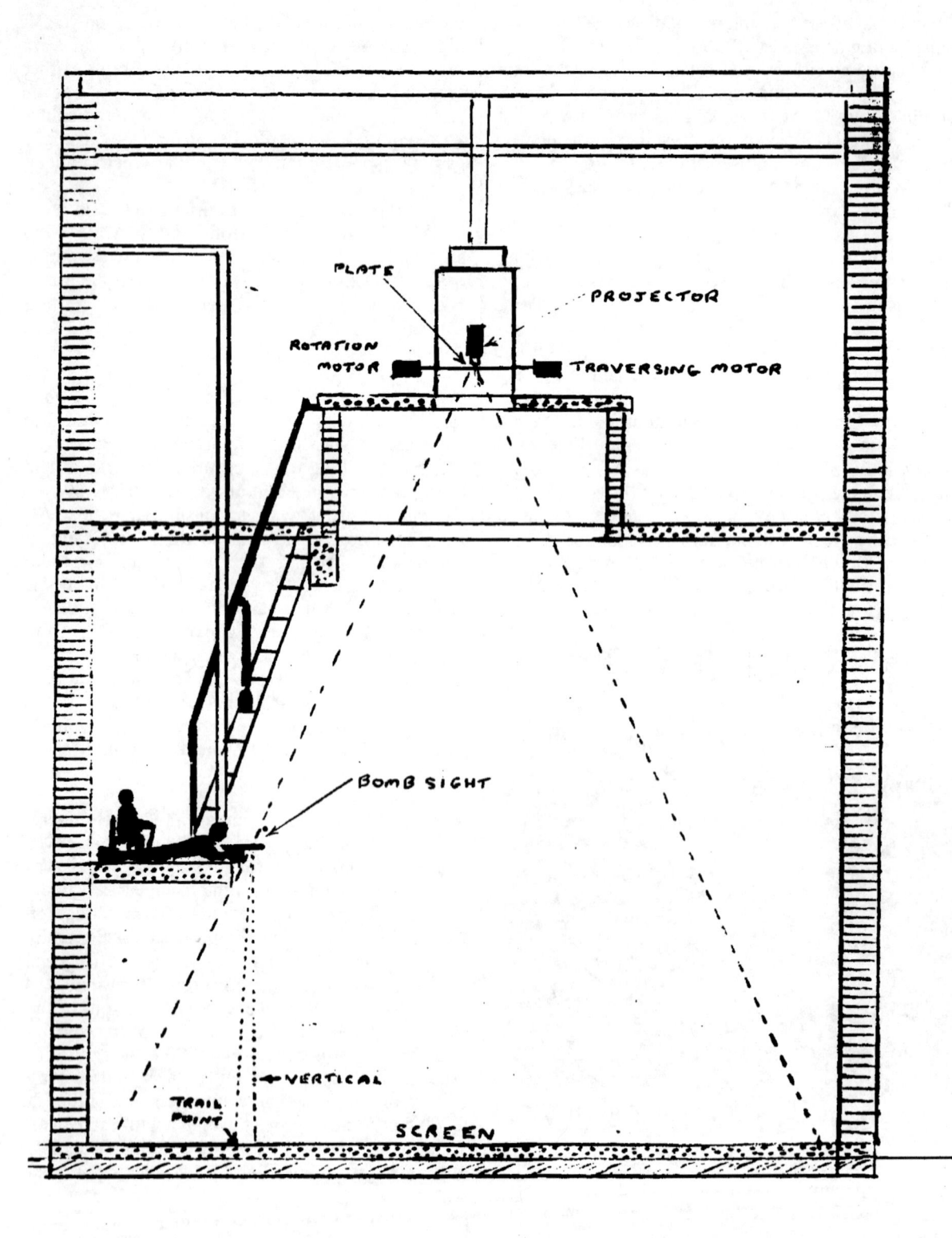

FIG 35
AML Bombing Simulator For Ground Training

for the exercises, so that this had to be allowed for by the Bomb Aimer.

Since a bomb falls down the trail line, a trail line datum was marked on the screen. The Bomb Aimer lined up the target in his bomb sight and pressed the bomb release button. The ground continued to travel under his sight, whilst a timing mechanism was taking account of the time of fall of the bomb. Therefore when the point was reached at which the bomb would have impacted with the ground, the timer stopped the ground movement. then any discrepancy between the position of the target on the screen and the trail point datum was the bombing error.

In addition to his bomb aiming duties an Air Bomber could assist a Navigator by operating 'Gee' and H2S sets. He would participate in some of the navigation training exercises and in particular operate the Radar Trainer in co-operation with the Navigator. It was important to remember that the 'Bombing Team' comprised Pilot, Navigator and Bomb Aimer. For bombing practice there were various ranges about the country where the Bomb Aimer could drop practice bombs, his performance being monitored by the Range Operators. Eight small 8 lb practice bombs were carried and released one at a time, these gave off a puff of smoke when landing so that the point of impact could be pin-pointed. The Bomb Aimer would record the point of impact on a chart. The nearest ranges to Snaith were Strenshall about 5 miles north of York, and Skipsea (6 miles south of Flamborough Head) which organised sea bombing and firing trials. The sea targets were rafts or smoke floats with an observation post on Flamborough Head. The Bombing Leader would keep a record of all his Air Bombers' performances in practice and on actual operations.

The Bombing Leader would maintain a close liaison with the Navigation Leader and the Photo Section on all matters connected with air bombing and with the Armament and Instruments Sections on the serviceability of, or problems with bomb sights and bombing equipment. He would need to liaise closely with the Operations Section to discuss bomb loads, their distribution and the bombing results as shown by bombing photos. The bombing photos would be pinned up by the Operations Section after an operation to demonstrate to the air crew the accuracy of their bombing.

The first Halifaxes to be delivered to the squadron were Mk IIs fitted with the Mk IX Course Setting Bomb Sight as used in the Whitleys, but in early 1943 the squadron changed over to the more advanced Mk XIV which was a continuously set vector sight as described in Chapter 8. The gyro in the sighting head could cope with 60 degree banks and 40 degree dives without toppling. It was designed to cope with problems of evasive action over the target since only 8 to 10 seconds of steady flight was necessary before dropping the bombs. The sighting head was automatically adjusted by the computer for the correct sighting angle with the impact point being indicated on the reflector plate. This bomb-sight had height limitations in that it was not suitable for use above 20,000 ft and below 1,000 ft.

When the Air Bomber looked at the reflector he saw the illuminated graticule projected by the collimator on to the glass and through it the target on the ground. The Bomb Aimer fed the manual settings into the computer and the automatic settings were applied continuously to cope with changes of the aircraft's attitude etc. The sighting angle and the drift angle on the sighting head were altered continuously by the flexible drive feed from the computer, wind vectors having been fed into the computer before the run up to the target. If all these settings were correct the target slowly moved parallel to the long illuminated graticule to meet the cross line, indicating to the Air Bomber his point of bomb release.

In early 1943, Miss Robson, a 'Boffin' from RAE Farnborough and a colleague, who had been involved in the development of the Mk X1V bomb-sight, came to the squadron to familiarise the Air Bombers and the Instrument personnel on its installation, maintenance and operation. She went on a number of air tests with the squadron and one of the recollections by squadron members was that she wore a fur coat when flying. She also visited other 4 Group squadrons but sadly was killed in a flying accident with 76 Squadron.

'Bulls Eyes' exercises which received their name from a target centre were carried out to improve a crew's skill in finding and bombing a target at night and could include night affiliation with anti-aircraft batteries and searchlights. These involved the aircraft flying to a 'Target area' which was not likely to be visited by enemy aircraft and carry out a simulation of a bombing operation by infra red photography. The aiming point was indicated by a light projector which transmitted a vertical cone of radiation through a filter producing an infra red beam invisible to the Bomb Aimer. This was detectable by infra red sensitive film in a modified

F24 camera which was used for the exercise. The light occulted at definite periods so that a dotted trace could be recorded on the film in the camera as the aircraft traversed the target.

The procedure for the exercise was to wind on three frames before the start. Then prior to the mock attack a Simulation of Bombing Chart was consulted so that for the height and speed at which the exercise was to be carried out the time of fall for a bomb could be calculated. These were set on the Type 35 control along with the terminal velocity setting on the computer. Before the run-in to the target, wind vectors would also be inserted.

When the Pilot approached the appointed target he would carry out a straight and level bombing run at the designated height and airspeed. With a bombing frame being exposed in the camera the Air Bomber lined up for the target on the sighting head and when the release point was reached pressed his 'Bomb Release' which would start the Type 35 control. At the end of the time interval on the control unit, at which point it was considered the bomb would have exploded, the shutter in the camera closed automatically, terminating the light trace. On returning from the exercise the film was developed and the end of the trace on the film gave the approximate position of the target at the moment of impact of the bomb. The distance between the end of the trace and a pin point on the film which indicated the point of impact of the bomb was measured. This distance was an indication of the bombing error.

AIR GUNNERS

The responsibility for co-ordinating the training of the Air Gunners was that of the Gunnery Leader who has been referred to as 'Boss of all the Turret Dwellers'. Techniques which were important to Air Gunners included gun sighting (a good Gunner could pepper a drogue at 400 yards), aircraft recognition, gun harmonisation, breeching up, and fighting control. The RAF issued black solid 1/72nd scale model aircraft for use in aircraft recognition training. These were hung up in the Gunnery Section along with aircraft recognition silhouettes, aircraft recognition being of prime importance since there were cases of Air Gunners firing on friendly aircraft. To improve a Gunner's skill in eradicating stoppages etc, a gun would be available for blindfolded stripping and re-assembling. At Snaith there was a Gunnery Range on the north side of the airfield to which aircraft could be towed for firing practice or harmonisation, if necessary. Clay pigeon shooting was also part of ground training and this took place on the airfield not far from the Gunnery Section, the purpose being to perfect rapid co-ordination of hand and eye.

For ground sighting practice there was a Gunnery Trainer near the Squadron Offices housed in a tall building similar to the Bombing Trainer Building. This training aid was one of those devised with the help of the NIIP (National Institute of Industrial Psychology) and was called the SFGT (Standard Free Gun Trainer). The trainer included a 20 ft hemispherical screen standing on its edge and resembling a Radar dish. On a steel framework in front of the screen was mounted an electrically operated aircraft gun turret with a light source to project a cross on to the screen. This indicated to the Instructor the point at which the Gunner in the turret was aiming his guns. The instructor operated an Aldis lamp to beam a spot of light on to the screen. The object of the exercise was for the trainee in the turret to follow the Aldis spot with his gun sight. To add realism films of attacking aircraft could be projected onto the screen and load speakers used to produce sound effects.

Airborne practice for Air Gunners was available at Skipsea Range where the gunners could participate in air to sea firing practice using smoke floats dropped on the sea, bullet splashes indicating point of impact. Another airborne training aid was a Fighter Affiliation exercise and when Gunnery Leaders such as Tom Bayfield required to set this up they would 'phone Hutton Cranswick Airfield, where No 16 Armament Practice Camp was located. They would supply a fighter aircraft, usually a Spitfire, from one of their resident squadrons. The fighter would try and manoeuvre behind the Bomber to get into an advantageous position whilst the Air Gunner would practice aiming his sights and giving the Pilot evasion instructions, in addition the Wireless Operator could gain experience with the use of Fighter Warning Radar. In order to assist the various Gunnery Leaders, 4 Group set up a 'Travelling Circus' which on 9 February 1944 visited 51 Squadron for a presentation involving several days of lectures on tactics, gunnery and aircraft recognition along with fighter affiliation practice.

WIRELESS OPERATORS

Wireless Operators were the responsibility of the Signals Leader, who would ensure that they were fully briefed in all signal procedures and Codes at a special briefing before an operation. If there were any changes in Signal procedures then the Wireless

TRAINING AND PRACTICE

Operator had to receive briefing on these. Changes which occurred between 1942 and 1945 included a modification of the phonetic alphabet and the adaption of the 'Q' code in place of the 'X' code. The purpose of these codes was to improve the efficiency of CW (ie Morse) transmissions by employing short code groups to signify standard terms, eg QFE interrogatory, means 'What is the barometric pressure at airfield level'. In 1943 when aircraft carried pigeons in special containers, Wireless Operators could be trained in handling them along with other crew members by the Pigeon Corporal, Jack Adams. (See photo 37).

When aircraft were fitted with Radar equipment for the purpose of warning the aircrew of the proximity of enemy aircraft these were the responsibility of the Wireless Operator. 'Boozer' equipment was installed in a few aircraft for a limited period but the equipment more widely used was called 'Audible Monica' and was being fitted to Squadron aircraft from June 1943 onwards. The first aircraft to be fitted out was MH-Q HR 838 and in order to assess its capabilities a 'Monica' proving flight was carried out by Sgt C Wilson's crew on June 9th. Fighter affiliation tactics were carried out by two fighter aircraft, namely a Spitfire approaching from astern and a Hurricane for making beam approaches with Air Gunners Louis Wooldridge and Les Sharpe observing the fighters. The purpose of this test was to establish the effective range and the angle of the cone of detection obtained with 'Monica'. The presence of a fighter was revealed in the intercom by an intermittent audio signal in the form of short or long bleeps ('dots' and 'dashes'). When the fighter was on the port side of the aircraft 'dots' were produced and when it moved to the starboard side these changed to 'daashes'. If the aircraft detected was dead astern then this was denoted by a steady note.

'Audible Monica' not being very popular was replaced by 'Visual Monica' but only a few 51 Squadron aircraft were fitted with this. With this equipment the Wireless Operators had to operate a modified ASV monitor, installed in their compartment, which indicated the presence of enemy aircraft, so airborne practices were set up to give them experience in evaluating the displays.

The ultimate night fighter warning device in 1945 was 'Fishpond' (see Fig 25 & 26). The indicator unit was located on the left hand side of the wireless operator's desk. The equipment received its code name because it was considered to be like looking at fish moving in a fish tank. The w/op received training on the use of this equipment so that he could identify hostile fighters by their size and movement.

FLIGHT ENGINEER

Flight Engineers were the responsibility of the Engineering Leader who would evaluate all the Flight Engineers' logs to check on their procedures and fuel consumptions. When the squadron changed from the Mark II Halifax with Merlin engines to the Mark III with Hercules engines, the Engineering Leader had to set up training sessions to brief the Flight Engineers on the new engine. The Engineers also had to be briefed on new equipment installed in the aircraft such as the nitrogen purge system for the fuel tanks.

In a bomb load climb, which was one of the training exercises for new crews, the Flight Engineer played an important part since engine performance could be critical in this exercise. The engine control procedure for a bomb load take-off was a follows:

At Take-off.

Engine revolutions 2,800 rpm with a boost pressure of +8 lbs, gills closed and supercharger 'M' gear engaged. Cylinder temperature not greater than 230 degrees C and oil temp over 15 degrees C.

Below 9,000 ft. Engine revolutions 2,400 rpm, +6 lbs boost (boost reduced before

engine revolutions lowered). Recommended indicated air speed 160 mph and maximum rate of climb 155. Cylinder temp, minimum 160 degrees C with a maximum of 270 degrees C. Oil temp 90 degrees C and 'M' gear in use below 9,000 ft.

Above 9,000 ft

Supercharger changed to 'S' gear when boost drops to +3 lbs. This keeps the flow of air to the carburettor constant since the air becomes thinner as the altitude increases.

One of the Air Publications used by Flight Engineers for training and reference.

```
        A.P.1719
         PILOT'S
           and
   FLIGHT ENGINEER'S
          NOTES
       HALIFAX III
```

ADMINISTERING THE STATION

THE SEVEN DEADLY SINS OF A.G's. No. 1.

Failing to Harmonize.

THE SEVEN DEADLY SINS OF W/OPS. No. 7.

Failure to acknowledge Recall Signal

FIG 37 & 38 'Tee Emm' Training Cartoons
Crown Copyright

PHYSICAL TRAINING INSTRUCTORS

One obvious task for the PTIs was the organisation of physical training for some sections before they started work. All ranks paraded in the long navy blue PT shorts which today would be viewed with great amusement. The PTIs included some well known personalities including Sgt Jackie Robinson a Manchester City goalkeeper and Cpl Arthur Ellis the referee who post war became famous because of his participation in the 'Its a Knockout' programme on the television. The PTIs were also responsible for some aspects of air crew training including Dinghy Drill, Swimming and Night Vision Training. They provided squash court facilities, the idea being that this sport could improve air crews' reactions. For Night Vision Training Physical Training personnel, including their officer P/O Mitchelson, went on a course at the Night Vision Training School at Leconfield. The PTIs organised training sessions for the air crews who donned special goggles to give the effect of darkness. Then they had to practice catching balls which were difficult to see with their restricted vision. (See photo No 27).

Since part of the journey to the target was over water there was always a possibility of landing in the sea. A Ditching Demonstration Room was set up next to the Navigation Section containing all the rescue equipment available to the air crew. To put into practice what was learnt in the Demonstration Room the PTIs would take the air crew to Cowick Reservoir for what could, in summer, be a pleasant way of spending an afternoon. Single seater 'K' Type dinghies and seven seater 'Q' type dinghies (with an overload capacity of two) were used. Air crew were trained how to enter a dinghy from the water. One difficulty they experienced was that their legs tended to go under the dinghy and become difficult to lift out of the water particularly with flying boots on. The layout of a 'Q' type dinghy which was drawn by an ex 51 Squadron Flight Engineer, the late Arthur Ashton, is shown in Fig 36. Details of the ditching procedure are given in Chapter 6. The PTIs were particularly elated when one of the crews they had trained managed to get back safely after ditching. Aircrew teams trained by the PTIs regularly gave demonstrations to the public in the local swimming baths.

AIRFIELD DEFENCE

After the Battle of Britain and the aborted German Invasion, ('Operation Sealion') Bomber Command became concerned about Airfield Defence and the RAF Regiment was formed, also Army Officers were appointed to RAF Stations to advise on Airfield Defence. From October 1943 onwards the Army Liaison Officer at Snaith was Lt.Col. C J M Riley of the Coldstream Guards and Bomber Command had an Army Liaison Officer, Lt. Col. Carrington, at its HQ to advise on military matters, including Airfield Defence. Since all ground personnel were expected to participate in defence commitments, Bomber Command required all Stations to organise what were known as 'Backers Up' Courses which involved training for members of the squadron in all aspects of Airfield Defence. This included practice on the Firing Range with rifles and Sten guns and the operation of twin Browning machine guns on a 'Motley Stalk' mounting, intended for Anti Aircraft Defence.

In order to assess the defence capabilities of the Station, a Defence Exercise was carried out on the 3/4 December 1943 when the 51 Division Battle School provided an attack force of 150 soldiers representing enemy paratroops. All the available personnel at Snaith took part in the exercise to defend the airfield, along with the help of the local Home Guard and 373 Searchlight Battery (RE), which was stationed at Pollington. The various

Photo 69 ex. Linton Memorial Room

Twin Brownings On Motley Stalk Mounting Used For Airfield Defence

ranks from Snaith participating in the exercise were issued with rifles, Sten guns or pistols but no ammunition. For exercises like this in order to simulate firing, a string of firecrackers was attached to the muzzle of the rifle. Each time the string was pulled, one of the fireworks exploded to represent the firing of a round. Some of the army used guns with blank cartridges. Having been organised into patrols the airmen took up defensive positions around the airfield along with their military colleagues, waiting for the attack which started at 2100 hrs from three different directions.

The attackers' objective was to simulate destruction of aircraft and damage to buildings, with adjudicators assessing the claims of both attackers and defenders. They reached some aircraft and stuck Swastikas on them so that the adjudicators recorded as having been destroyed but the attack did not surprise the defenders who were considered to have repulsed them. It was a very dark night and an interesting experience for the airfield defenders to suddenly encounter the 'enemy' creeping up on them with blackened faces. The exercise finished at 0300 hrs, the concensus being that the squadron had acquired very useful experience in night fighting and the organisation of defensive patrols. However the stations commanding officer was not very pleased since he was captured by the 'enemy'.

Chapter 10

MISHAPS, ACHIEVEMENTS AND ANECDOTES

MISHAPS

There is an old saying "Do you want the good news or the bad news". Lets look at the 'bad news' first namely the various mishaps, some of them very serious, which occurred at Snaith. One of the earliest mishaps took place on 6 February 1943 when a tragic road accident occurred. A Service bus had been used to take a number of personnel from Snaith for a joyful evening out at Pontefract, but on the way back to the station this joy suddenly turned to tragedy when the bus driven by AC1 Trevor Jones overturned when taking a bend near the Knottingley crossroads. The bus was so overcrowded that an appreciable number of casualties occurred. It contained 41 passengers, 15 of them standing, instead of the official maximum of 31 passengers. Seven people died and 29 required treatment at Knottingley Hospital. Because of the overcrowded conditions, suffocation was the cause of many of the casualties.

'Bug' in Bomb Selector

On the 13 February 1943 the aircraft were bombed up ready for an operation against Lorient and over on 'B' Flight the various air crew were standing round their aircraft having a last minute chat. The Bomb Aimer of Sgt Rawcliffe's crew told his skipper he was going to make a final check of the bomb circuitry and nipped into their aircraft, DT722, MH-M. After his checks he came out and stood with his crew who were talking to the crew from MH-V parked on the next dispersal. At approximately 1730 hours blue smoke was observed emerging from the bomb bay so the Bomb Aimer re-entered the aircraft to rescue the two pigeons and shouted to everyone to take cover since an explosion was likely as the fire was in the bomb bay. There were a couple of 'Erks' working on the wings of the aircraft who realising the danger they were in took running jumps off the wings at about 10 ft from the deck and fled for cover. The aircrews having, decided discretion was the better part of valour, headed for a nearby wooded area and lay flat on the grass.

Flying Control having been alerted, a convoy consisting of the Squadron CO, W/C 'Tom' Sawyer, in his 'Hillman' Utility, the Fire Crash Tender and an Ambulance, sped across the airfield. At the dispersal the C/O realised that the fire was uncontainable and gave instructions to abandon the aircraft. The fire raged out of control and an explosion occurred. The burnt out aircraft eventually collapsed in the middle. At approximately 18.00 hours a similar incident occurred on the other side of the airfield on 'A' Flight. The C/O therefore ordered the convoy to turn round and drive over to 'A' Flight, but unfortunately the Fire Tender Crew had difficulty in getting their vehicle to start.

Over on 'A' Flight, the Bomb Aimer had checked his equipment on MH-H, DT 724, a fairly new aircraft, Captained by P/O Rawlings, which was standing on the dispersal with its bomb doors open. Then on connecting up the batteries suddenly a pile of incendiaries fell on to the hard standing. Being nose heavy these incendiaries fell so that the nose hit the floor and ignited immediately. At first the Armourers tried to kick them out of the way but had to stop because they contained a percentage of 'X' type explosive incendiaries. Appreciating the danger of the situation Cpl Simms, the Armourer in charge of the team, warned everyone to evacuate. The Armourers ran about 60 yards and threw themselves into the nearest dugout. The aircraft's bomb load was 3 x 1000 lb HEs plus incendiaries, and one of the HE bombs went off scattering the remainder of the load onto the airfield. The 5 armourers hid in the dugout, peering out at the burning aircraft until the bomb exploded and one of them, Richard Carter, reported that he had a ringing in his ears due to the explosion for a long period afterwards. The aircraft continued to burn, eventually collapsing in the middle. A tail unit from the bomb which exploded went through the roof of an unoccupied bunk in one of the barrack huts and a large hole was blown in the dispersal. The squadron's operations were cancelled for that night. The nearby Army unit hearing the explosion, were fully alerted, thinking that a Luftwaffe air raid was in progress

The Squadron Electrical Engineering Officer was obviously very concerned about these mishaps and instructed the Electrical Section to carry out a full investigation. The aircraft involved were newly arrived on the Squadron and fitted with some American manufactured bomb controls which were found to contain drilling swarf produced during the manufacturing process. The effect of the swarf was to cause a short circuit in the Selector Unit so that when set on 'safe' it released the bombs prematurely. To overcome this all the Units on the Bomb Control Panels on new aircraft were examined for the possibility of short-circuiting due to swarf and no further incidents occurred.

The Bomb Dump Explosion

At about 1030 on Saturday morning 19 June 1943, F/Sgt Benfield, the NCO in charge of the bomb dump, received information on the bomb load required for the night's operation, this had to be prepared and delivered to the aircraft at their dispersals. The total bomb load comprised 38 x 1000 lb GP HE bombs fused for long delay, 38 x 1000 lb MC HE bombs tail fuse for a delay of 1.25 deconds, and 114 x 500 lb MC HE bombs tail fused with a delay of .025 seconds. The Station Armourers working in the bomb dump commenced preparing these bombs whilst the Squadron Armourers on the Flights carried out their daily inspections and got the aircraft ready to receive their bomb loads.

However, at 1320 hours these preparations were suddenly interrupted by a serious explosion in the Bomb Dump which was situated on the west side of the Airfield. Halifax JD 244 MH-K a new aircraft piloted by Sgt Fred Heathfield, which had just reached a dispersal after carrying out its first air test, was suddenly blown sideways by the blast. At the same time Halifax MH-D piloted by Sgt Foster, had just landed on Runway 213 and was taxiing along the peri. track when it was also knocked sideways by the explosion. A third aircraft just starting to land when the explosion occurred decided to overshoot and landed at Burn. A couple of ground crew tradesmen cycling to lunch along the peri. track were blown off their bikes, and the blast was even felt indoors as observed by Eileen a WAAF Pay Clerk, when a cup of tea she was carrying along the corridor in SHQ shook in her hand. Cpl Archie Spence an Airframe Fitter in charge of the Hydraulics section, situated in one of the workshops attached to the northern side of No 1 hangar, was glad his section was at lunch when the explosion occurred because all the windows of the workshop were blown in. The room was peppered with sharp glass splinters and anyone inside could have been seriously injured by the flying glass.

In the Sergeant's Mess the various NCO's, having had lunch, were standing around drinking and chatting when suddenly there was a tremendous explosion and the whole building rocked like a boat on water. Everyone made a dive for the floor as they thought they were being bombed by the Luftwaffe. When they had recovered from the shock all the occupants of the mess rushed outside and saw a huge column of smoke issuing from the bomb dump.

Fire broke out in the area where the incendiaries were being stored and further explosions occurred at intervals, the last one some twelve hours after the initial explosion, which could possibly have been caused by the delayed action bombs. Despite the loss of the Bomb Dump facilities the squadron was still required to carry out the Le Creusot operation, so it was necessary to bring in bombs from other Stations. RAF Riccall, the home of 1658 HCU, was willing to supply bombs and Armourers so all the Armourers on that Station were alerted to transport bombs to Snaith and help in fusing them. In view of the urgency some bombs were prepared by the armourers on the low loader vehicles during transportation to Snaith. Bombs were provided by Riccall and the Escrick Park bomb store. A temporary Bomb Dump was set up on the east side of the Airfield and Armourers from Snaith and Riccall sweated in the hot sun to prepare the bomb loads.

The next day at 0900 hours a recce. of the Bomb Dump was carried out by W/Cdr Rowlens an Air Ministry Bomb Disposal Officer and S/Ldr Apted C/O of 5131 Bomb Disposal Squadron stationed at Snaith. They reported that on the east side of the dump there were 22 x 1000 lb bombs in a fused condition, these could have been affected by the fires and explosions which could make them unsafe. Some of the bombs contained No 37 pistols, with a long delay time of anything up to a week, so on the advice of the Bomb Disposal Officers an area around the Bomb Dump was placed out of bounds to all RAF personnel and civilians. To enforce this action patrols were stationed at road junctions near the airfield to reduce traffic and the civil police were notified in

MISHAPS, ACHIEVEMENTS AND ANECDOTES

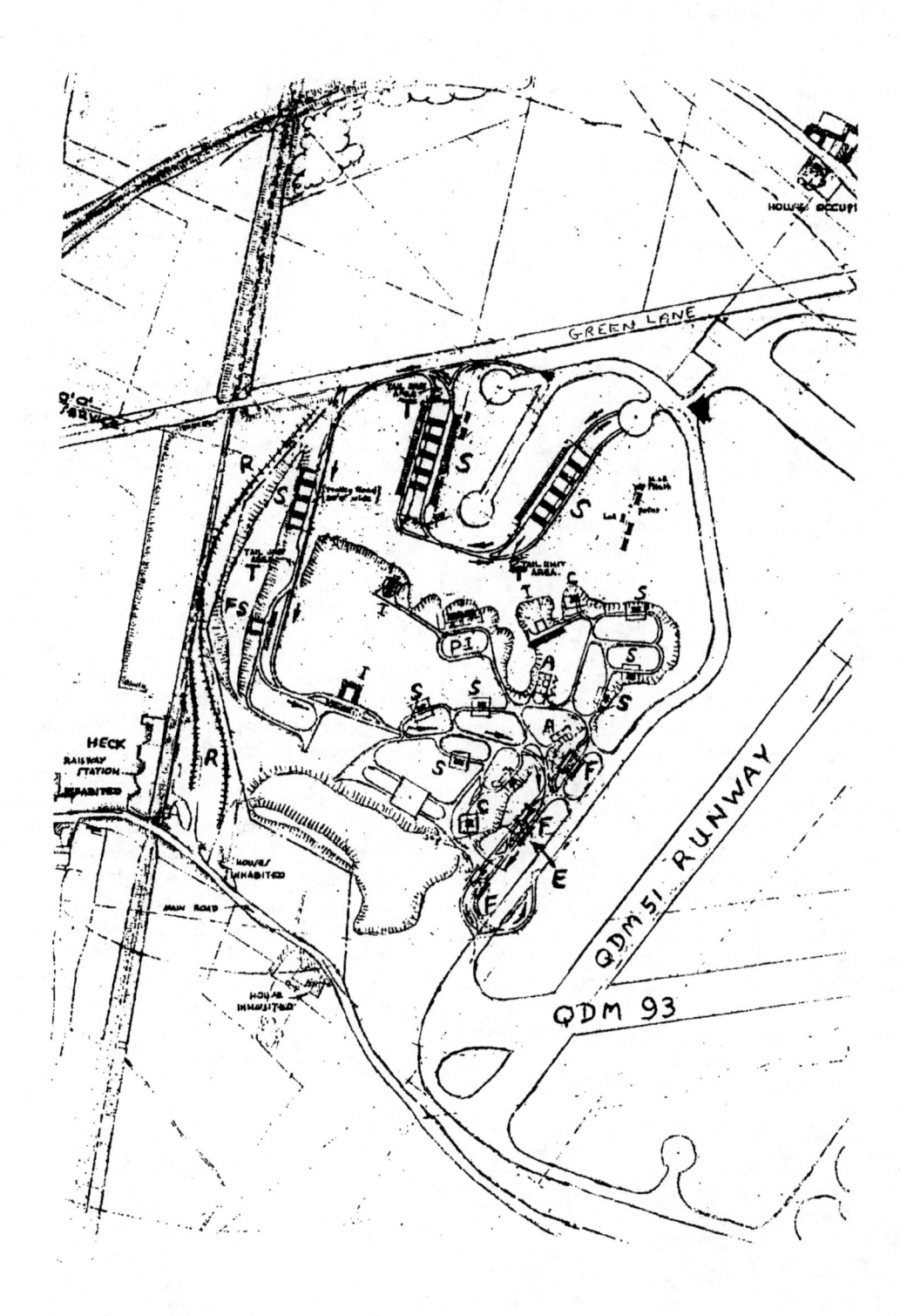

Map 15, Snaith Bomb Dump

C=Component stores
E=Site of explosion in 1943.
T=Tail unit areas.
Pl=Pyrotechnics and incendiaries store.
I=Incendiaries store

R=Railway sidings
S=Bomb stores.
A=Small arms amunition stores
FS=Fused and spare bombs
F=Fusing points

MISHAPS, ACHIEVEMENTS AND ANECDOTES

case the evacuation of civilians was necessary. The railway authorities (LNER) were also warned to close the main line to the North which ran alongside the Bomb Dump. The CO took off in a Tiger Moth aircraft to examine the Bomb Dump from the air and reported that he saw a number of bodies lying flat on the ground almost as if they were sunbathing in the hot June sun.

On the following Saturday, 26 June, a further recce. of the Bomb Dump was carried out by W/Cdr Rowlens and S/Ldr Apten and ten bodies were removed, one of which was unidentified. The ammunition in the Bomb Dump was disposed of and in some cases this was quite difficult since the concrete roof of the bomb shelter had been blown on top of it. This required jacking up in order to reach underneath the concrete for the ammunition and some of the bodies. There was a large crater in the middle of the Tarmac area with ammunition in the base of it so the Armourers involved in removing the ammunition has to scramble up the sides of the crater carrying the explosives.

On the 29 June a further examination of the Bomb Dump was carried out but no further bodies were discovered and consequently the sentries and the traffic restrictions were withdrawn and the LNER informed that the railway line was now safe. The funeral of the ten victims took place at Selby Abbey on 30 June 1943 after which the relatives were taken back to the Officers Mess at Snaith for a meal and Reception by the Station CO. Even after the Bumb Dump had been made safe, both Station and Squadron Armourers had to spend a month there clearing up, in between bombing up and other work, as a result of which a number of them were 'Mentioned in Dispatches'. Ultimately the Bomb Dump was redesigned and the necessary reconstruction work carried out as shown in Map 15.

Photo 70

Via N. Jackson L.R.P.S.

One of the gravestones at Selby for aimen killed in the bomb dump explosions

On 18th Feb 1943 'T' Tommy W7818, one of the original Mk II aircraft issued to the squadron, took off at 1850 hours Piloted by Sgt Haly and carrying two mines on board. There was an engine failure on take off and the Pilot closed the throttles as a result of which the aircraft crash landed and careered across the grass with its propellors churning up the grass. A degree of panic gripped some of the occupants of the Tower when they saw the aircraft heading in their direction but fortunately it stopped about 20 feet from the peri track near the Squadron Offices. The crew evacuated rapidly but left the engines running so the NCO I/C Maintenance in the hangar with another NCO entered the aircraft and switched them off. For this action he was awarded a medal. When the ground crew came to examine this aircraft they found a rather battered pigeon carrier containing a bird which was unharmed but a bit distressed.

Intruder raids by Luftwaffe long range night fighters were a problem for tired aircrews returning from a raid. One tactic of the Fernnachtjagd as they were called was to join a returning RAF squadron and attack the bombers during their landing approach, when they were most vunerable. When intruders were active the stations were warned by an Air Raid Warning Red signal. During these alerts the airfield lights were not switched on until Flying Control was sure there were no enemy aircraft in the circuit. One night an enemy Ju88 flew down the main runway and dropped a stick of bombs which missed the airfield and landed in a field to the North of Domestic Site No 1. There was an occasion when the airfield lights were switched off due to the presence of intruders, resulting in the squadron aircraft being diverted to another airfield. Unfortunately one of them was shot down by intruders at the alternative airfield.

ACHIEVEMENTS

There are a number of achievements at Snaith which are worth recording and one of these was a feather in the cap for the WAAFs whose support was greatly appreciated by the squadron. They were awarded the Sunderland Cup which was given

MISHAPS, ACHIEVEMENTS AND ANECDOTES

to the best WAAF section in Bomber Command. Air Commandant Lady R M E Welsh, Director of the WAAFs, accompanied by the AOC of 4 Group visited the station on 26th July to present the cup (see photo No 19). After a parade there was the presentation followed by a march past. Finally Lady Welsh visited various sections on the station in which WAAFs were employed. To celebrate the event the concert party put on a special show which was attended by Lady Welsh and all the other guests. A previous visit by a senior WAAF officer was on the 12th December 1943 when Group Officer Growger inspected a handicraft exhibition on the WAAF site. In view of the wartime shortages in the shops the WAAFs had produced a wide variety of toys as Christmas presents for children (see photo No 20).

There were other efficiency successes for the station. In August the M.T. Section was awarded the cup for the best M.T. Section in 4 Group for the second year running and placed fourth in the Bomber Command competition. In 1944 the station received an award for the best airman's dining hall in 4 Group.

Thanks to the support from the PTIs the station was very successful in various sports competitions. They won the 4 Group cups for the inter group rugby (photo 25) and hockey (photo 26) competitions and were runners up in football and netball. In addition the station received the AOCs trophy for the station gaining the most points in all sporting events.

ANECDOTES

FIG 50
'Butch'

'Butch'

One of the highlights for the squadron was the visit of that great man Air Chief Marshal Harris when he came to inspect the squadron. He attended the briefing for the Mont Lucon operation on the 15th Sept 1943 and give a pep talk to the aircrew whom he affectionately referred to as 'his old lags'. He made his presence particularly felt on the station in view of one of his comments. In common with many other Discip. Sections the one at Snaith was not adverse to a bit of 'Bull', so the stones lining the roads on the Technical Site were painted white, one of the jobs which could keep the 'Janker Wallahs' occupied. The discip. people could have been acting on the old RAF adage for raw recruits on arrival at a unit:-"If something moves salute it, if it doesn't move pick it up, if you can't pick it up paint it!" When Harris was walking around the station he noticed these white painted stones and commented to the Commanding Officer that they would make good aiming marks for intruder aircraft. As a consequence the white stones had to be darkened. Another VIP who visited the station was the Inspector General of the RAF, ACM Sir Ludlow Hewitt CBE KB CMG DFC, principal ADC to the King. He arrived by air on 27.6.44 accompanied by AVM Carr the AOC of 4 Group.

Pilot Michael Foster, who attended Harris's pep talk has supplied a very interesting anecdote about a dog called 'Butch', which was the nickname given to Harris.

*"The Bomber crews of No 51 Squadron knew him well, back in 1943. He was their self-appointed mascot, an evil smelling ragbag of a dog, nearer to a sheepdog than anything else, but he could do no wrong. The tastiest scraps from every Mess found their way into his ever-open mouth, and he always claimed a place on the most crowded crew-wagon going out to dispersal. After Ops. he was there to welcome those who returned - and to share in the early morning bacon and eggs. Butch never missed a Briefing, his attendance was as essential as that of the Met. Officer or of the Group Captain himself. He was good for morale, part of the intangible spirit of the squadron; hounded around, yet beloved by groundcrews and aircrews alike.
On one well-remembered occasion when Air Chief Marshal Sir Arthur Harris, after whom Butch had been*

167

irreverently but affectionately named, came to give the crews a pep talk, the dog's casual unconcern for all authority ensured his place in squadron history. As the great man entered the expectant Briefing oom and advanced towards the dais, Butch preceded him solemnly. Then, with superb timing, he lay down in his path and began to scratch himself with relish. Sir Arthur was forced to halt and, at some risk, to step over him. In the eyes of the squadron this was Butch's finest hour. He has no monument, he was not the kind of dog many people would have been proud (or even willing) to own. But he was part of the wartime squadron experience which those who lived through will not easily forget."

The 'Butch' cartoon was drawn by an ex 51 Squadron amateur cartoonist, W/Op. John J Jamieson, hence his signature 'J3'. When serving with the squadron he drew cartoons about life on the unit and on one occasion he produced a drawing which was a dig at the station CO. This was pinned up on the notice board in the Sergeant's mess, but after a couple of days it disappeared. John thought it may have been taken down because it was considered to be in bad taste and he might be hauled over the coals about it. But exactly the opposite was the case because it re-appeared on the notice board in the Officers Mess, where it remained for a period.

Animals at Snaith

In addition to the story about 'Butch' there are some other interesting animal anecdotes. One of the squadron fitters out on the flights who carried out poaching activities in civilian life became an unofficial 'Station Poacher' and used his talents to catch rabbits for the Officer's Mess. When the supply of wild rabbits diminished he augmented the supply by breeding rabbits in one of the air raid shelters on the airfield. F/Sgt Clayton the Maintenance NCO bought a pig in a pub to be fattened up for sale and sold a half share to the squadron WO. This pig was kept in the air raid shelter along with the rabbits and fed on swill from the airmens mess. In 1943 the station had a ram as a mascot which was kept in the building used for storing the pigeon carriers (photo 4). There is also the story about the Air Gunner who used to carry a poisonous snake in a basket with him when he went on operations. What he hoped to achieve with this is not clear.

Two of the WAAFs who worked in the Battery Charging Room mentioned in Chapter 8 were Agnes Jackson and Lorna Williamson. A cat on the WAAF site had kittens, but did not appear to be feeding them, so the WAAFs used to take them to the battery room to feed them. There was one occasion when a WAAF had not been able to deposit the kittens so she had to go on parade with them under her battledress blouse. When the NCO i/c the parade asked her what she had under her blouse 'she nearly had kittens'.

'The Morning After'

Most aircrew did not normally drink before an operation in order to keep a clear head. There was however one occasion when they were not able to keep to this resolution. 'Skip' Seymour the Intelligence Officer informed the crews one afternoon that they were being stood down because no operations were planned so the aircrews decided to celebrate by a night in the local pubs. Very early next morning they were surprised by a Tannoy call informing them of an urgent daylight operation. The ground crews and in particular the Armourers had to work flat out to get the 'Kites' ready and then came take off time. One Squadron Association aircrew member reported that he had never seen so many ropey take offs in his life, since a lot of the Pilots were still suffering from a night on the ale.

Jack Ripper's Accident.

Jack Ripper, a very competent Pilot, was the Captain of MH-U and consequently his colleagues were known as "Jack the Ripper's crew". He was appointed flight commander and hence issued with a motor cycle. One night about midnight after an evening in the mess he came riding into the Domestic Site on his motor cycle, and taking a wrong turn, drove straight into the Picket Hut. The Picket Post Orderly was on duty inside the hut but the sudden entry of the motor cycle so unnerved him that he jumped out of one of the windows. He then ran across to one of the huts to drag a couple of 'erks' out of bed to come and help him with the intruder. One of the 'erks' was Cpl Fitter Steve Brown, who walked back to the Picket Hut with the Orderly and found Jack Ripper lying on the Orderley's bed with this motor cycle beside him. The three men carried Jack back to his own room and then decided to remove the bike but found that the door was so narrow that they had to turn the handlebars and footrests round to get it out. How Jack managed to drive the bike through the narrow door opening remains a mystery to this day, and was a feat worthy of one of the leading stage magicians.

Hi-Jinks in the Mess.

Jim Gill who served at Snaith from 1943 to 1945 has a fund of anecdotes about activities in the Officer's Mess and an amusing one concerns the station CO Group Captain Fresson. In the Officer's Mess the only person allowed to wear a hat was the CO so there was a rack in the mess for officers to hang their hats, one peg being reserved for the CO. One evening the aircrew boys were engaged in a very boistrous and noisy activity in the mess ante room, which included throwing cushions around. For a joke Jim Gill took the CO's hat off its peg and having put it on popped his head round the ante room door, ordering the occupants to make less noise. All went quiet for a short period until they realised who it was, at which point they pelted Jim with cushions causing him to make a strategic withdrawal. A bit later on the CO himself had put his hat on and was preparing to leave the mess when he heard the noise in the ante room. He therefore opened the door, stepped into the ante room and ordered some quiet. The assembled company thought it was Jim again, so they greeted him with a volley of cushions and catcalls. Imagine the number of red faces when they realised it was the CO.

"Please Sir, can we have our prop back"

This is a request Flight Engineer Bill Powell could have made on behalf of his crew after an incident which occurred with one of the new Mk III Halifax aircraft delivered to the squadron. Mention has been made of the 'Bugs' in new aircraft and in this case they were instrumental in upsetting a Policeman in Goole.

In Jan 1944 a crew took up an aircraft for an air test, flying out over the North Sea but on the way back the 'Gremlins' took over and Sgt Bill Powell, who was monitoring the Flight Engineers, panel observed a sudden drop in oil pressure on the port inner engine. The engine started to emit ominous sounds which Bill described as 'coughs' and 'bangs' and still monitoring his instrument panel he noted a rapid increase in the cylinder head temperature. Consequently he switched the engine off after notifying the pilot and decided to feather the prop. Unfortunately an oil leak had developed in the D.H.Hydromatic feathering system so that he was unable to feather the propeller with the result that it started to windmill rapidly and the engine eventually caught fire. The Methyl Bromide fire extinguisher in the engine nacelle was operated which put the fire out. The Flight Engineer had been watching the windmilling prop with apprehension when it suddenly shot off the engine and flew backwards catching the tail fin in its travels down to earth. The aircraft was over Goole at the time and the prop landed in one of the streets of the town where it just missed a policeman, the draught knocking him off his bike. Back at base the offending 'kite' was put in the hands of the ground crew to rectify the offending 'Bugs'.

Upsetting the Medics

Mention has been made previously about life in the Station Sick Quarters. There was an occasion early in 1943 when when a fellow crew member of W/Op. John Jamieson went sick and had to go into a ward in SSQ. Naturally the crew went to visit him but the staff in SSQ were not very amenable to visits from aircrew members. They did not like all the laughing and joking that went on, which was intended to cheer their colleague up and aircrew were also accused of smuggling beer in. On leaving the invalid to carry out their operation they loudly informed him within the hearing of the nursing staff they would let him know as soon as they returned safely from the operation.

The operation went off without anything untoward happening but on returning to Snaith the Skipper was coming in for a landing when an unexpected very strong gust of wind suddenly caught the aircraft and blew it sideways to port. Having realised that he would have to abort his landing the Pilot made a turn to port in order to miss the Control Tower and Hangars, reporting "Overshoot" to the Tower. He overflew the area of the Technical Site where the Station Sick Quarters was located and rejoined the circuit for another landing.

It wasn't till next day that the crew were able to visit their sick colleague and when they trooped into the ward they found that their popularity rating amongst the medics was zero. The medical staff believed that on returning from the operation they had 'shot up' the Sick Quarters at a very low altitude in order to inform their crew member of their safe return. The claim was that some occupants of SSQ sought shelter under their beds, receiving a bigger fright from John Jamieson's aircraft than from the Luftwaffe.

The 'Ghost' Halifax.

For a raid on Nuremberg on 8/9 March 1943 Claude Wilson's crew along with the rest of the squadron was operating with a Mk II Halifax, BB240 MH-X, fitted with a 200 gallon overload tank in the bomb bay for the long haul into Germany. With this particular aircraft there was no mid upper turret installed, so the M.U. Air Gunner assisted the Pilot at take-off by operating the throttles. On the way to the target the Flight Engineer decided to switch on to the overload tanks, but as soon as he operated the appropriate feed cocks the engines started racing. On switching back to the wing tanks the engines went back to normal and he tried this transfer switching procedure several times assisted by A.G. Louis Wooldridge, who was an ex ground crew Rigger, without success. The two crew members then realised that the overload tank was empty because the effect of the engine drawing petrol from an empty tank was to produce less restriction to the flow of the fuel left in the pipes. This meant more fuel could be drawn in, thus increasing the speed of the engine. The required 200 gallons of petrol had not been supplied despite the entry in the Form 700. Fuel calculations by the Flight Engineer revealed that there was insufficient fuel to reach the target and return, so the skipper aborted the sortie and turned for home, flying back at an economical cruising speed.

The aircraft landed at West Malling, a Beaufighter night fighter base, with about 20 minutes supply of fuel left and joined another Halifax squadron which had been diverted because of fog. The other squadron's base had been notified of their aircraft's diversion but the MH-X aircraft was overlooked because there was an 'X' among the other squadrons aircraft. Snaith was not informed about its arrival and consequently it was reported as missing.

Next day MH-X flew back to Snaith and entered the circuit requesting permission to land. There was obviously confusion in Flying Control because some minutes elapsed before the R/T operator replied and numerous personnel were observed issuing from various buildings on the site to observe the circling aircraft. When permission to 'pancake' was given the skipper landed the aircraft and taxied towards its dispersal followed by a 'Flying Standard' utility vehicle. When the Pilot parked his aircraft in its dispersal and the crew had alighted, the vehicle pulled up nearby. 'Dinty' Moore the Flight Commander got out and on walking across to the newly returned crew his first comments were, "What happened to you", "where the hell have you been", "Dont you know you are all listed as missing". At this point the crew realised why there had been an audience to their landing. They thought they had seen a "Ghost".

As a follow up to this there was a heated exchange between Bomber Command and Fighter Command about lack of notification of the diversion of MH-X. An investigation into the missing petrol revealed that a tanker had been filling up the aircraft when he ran out of fuel. He filled in the Form 700 but promised to return with the missing fuel, but unfortunately he was diverted from his task by a senior NCO and consequently the extra fuel did not get delivered. This incident exemplifies the pressure on the various personnel concerned with preparing for operations. Nevertheless the airmen concerned were disciplined.

Problems with Firearms.

Dave Storey, an ex Navigator, jokingly remarked at a Reunion about being billeted in an air conditioned Nissen hut. His story is that at one period in 1944 ammunition for revolvers appeared to be freely available and aircrew used to lie in their beds and shoot the lights out with their revolvers. This resulted in the 'Air Conditioning' holes in the roof. Some aircrew were even more irresponsible, since one of the Flight Engineers pointed a revolver at an aircrew colleague without checking it was loaded and pulled the trigger. The result was that the unfortunate airman was shot through the lung. A Court of Inquiry was convened and the result was the withdrawal of ammunition and a strict control on its issue.

Dave also recounts a firearms incident which occured with a Flight Commander, S/Ldr Nick Simmonds. Nick an ex Guards officer was quite a character and a real buccaneering type. A photograph of him sat on a horse in full guards uniform always stood on his desk in 'C' Flight office. The issue of service revolvers to all aircrew took place shortly before the Leipzig opertion on 19/20.2.44 and many crewmen took them on operations with them. For the Leipzig raid Nick was flying with Johnny Morris's crew and whilst standing around on the dispersal for the usual hour before take off he drew his revolver and said "I wonder if this bloody thing works". Without further ado, having spotted, in the deep twighlight, a vague white blob through the hedge he aimed at it and fired off a couple of rounds. Next morning a very angry and indignant farmer called in at Station Headquarters demanding to know who had killed one of his sheep. Needless to say nobody claimed any knowledge of the incident.

'The Backwoodsman'

Keith Alderson's crew had an average age of 21 and were all NCO's except the rear Air Gunner. The 'Tail-end Charlie', P/O Myles Burns DFC, was the old man of the crew at the age of 45. According to his fellow Air Gunner, Don Nicolson DFC, DFM, he was quite a character, being a backwoodsman from Canada who had to shave off his beard to make himself look younger when he joined up. He was a first class marksman with his guns but was hopeless at aircraft recognition and at an OTU identified a twin engined Oxford as a single engined Harvard, hence lumbering the crew with an extra 7 days training. Being the first member of the crew to be commissioned his fellow crew members painted a large notice pointing towards the rear turret stating 'Officers this way only'.

Another anecdote about this crew concerns an occurrence on a raid to Dosseldorf. After being hit by flak the navigator's dividers went missing and could not find them anywhere. The were eventually discovered by Ted, the Wireless Operator, inside his T1154 transmitter. They were badly bent because a piece of the shrapnel entering the nose of the aircraft had scooped up the dividers and penetrated the case of the radio with them.

Visitors

There were visitors from other squadrons whilst 51 was at Snaith. On 27.4.44 the squadron members working on the airfield were surprised by an unusual engine sound which was the roar of the Napier Sabre engines powering the eighteen Hawker Typhoons of 226 Squadron which were coming in to land on the airfield. The rest of the squadron arrived by road, the total complement being 17 officers and 160 other ranks. This squadron being a member of 2nd TAF, was a mobile unit which had to travel around under its own steam and provide its own accommodation in the form of tents.

The purpose of this visit was for the squadron to practice ground attack and 'cab rank' tactics, whereby on behalf of the Army an Air Support Signals unit would ask the rocket firing Typhoons to attack ground targets such as tanks. There was a special range for 2nd TAF rocket firing practice at Goswick in Northumberland. By contrast to 51 Squadron who were night birds, during their stay at Snaith 226 Squadron used to take off early in the morning for daily exercises. They often took advantage of the hump in the main runway to assist their take-off. This squadron only stayed for a short period, moving in May to Needs Oar Point in order to prepare for 'Operation Overlord'. Another interesting visit was on the 29th Oct 1944 when the airfield became very crowded with the Lancasters of 57 and 630 Squadrons which had been diverted to Snaith.

'The Jinx Bed'

In F/O Les Clark's billet in early 1944 there was a tradition that new-comers occupied the beds nearest the door and the longest serving members had the beds nearest to the stove. Consequently when anyone went missing there was a tradition of changing beds to move nearer the fire. One bed nearest to the fire had the reputation of being a 'Jinx Bed' and its occupants were likely to 'get the chop'. Les Clark told his sister that it was his turn to move into the 'Jinx Bed' and she should be prepared for the worst. Unfortunately his premonition came true since he was killed with S/Ldr Eno on the Stuttgart raid of 15/16.3.44.

Entertainments

A wartime organisation called ENSA, which provided entertainment for the forces, visited Snaith in Oct 1943 to put on a show in the Corporal's Mess. This show was not a great success the general concensus amongst the audience being that it lived up to ENSA's joke nickname 'Every Night Something Awful'. Although to be fair to the dancers they were operating on a very cramped stage. The worst act was the comedian who was filthy rather than funny, he went down like a lead balloon and disgusted most of the airmen since there were WAAFs present.

A very professional show arrived on the 5.1.44, this was 'Randalls Scandals' headed by the famous comedian Frank Randall who will be remembered for his facial expressions when he performed without his false teeth. Our Canadian colleagues from 6 Group in northern Yorkshire provided a concert party called the 'Tarmacs' on 23.2.45. This was an excellent show and one item which went down well was three Canadians who dressed up as the Andrew Sisters and mimed to their records. One of Ralph Reader's RAF "Gang Show" teams came to the the unit. Many post-war stars who were unknown during the war started their careers with the RAF 'Gang Shows' and these included Tony Hancock, Peter Sellers, and Dick Emery. The well known camp fire choruses of 'Ging Gang Goolie' and 'Crest of a Wave' were very nostalgic to many ex Scouts serving with the squadron. The show was a continuity of action with laughs, guffaws and the

MISHAPS, ACHIEVEMENTS AND ANECDOTES

MENU

Dinner.

Cream of Tomato and Lentil Soup.

Roast Turkey.
Sausage Stuffing.   Boiled Ham.
Roast and Creamed Potatoes.
Brussel Sprouts.
Tinned Peas.

Christmas Pudding and Sauce

Biscuits and Cheese.

Fruit, Beer, Minerals and Cigarettes.

Tea.

Bread and Butter and Jam.
Cold Ham, Beef and Pickles.
Mince Pies.
Fruit Cake.

Programme of Entertainments.

December 24th.
Grand Carnival Dance.
Prizes, Competitions, etc.
R.A.F Riccall Band.

December 25th. 15.00 Hrs.
Free Show at Station Cinema
(Limited to Corporals and other Ranks)
"Keep 'Em Flying."
18.30 Hrs.
Social Evening.
Whist Drive.   Games.   Cabaret.
Prizes.

December 27th. 19.45 Hrs.
Concert by the Band of the
Royal Household Cavalry.

December 31st.
Grand New Year's Eve Dance.
20.00 – 00.30 Hrs.
Royal Household Cavalry Band.

FIG 45 Menu & Entertainment Programme For Christmas 1943

MISHAPS, ACHIEVEMENTS AND ANECDOTES

various signs of enjoyment emitted by the audience.

However we must not forget that the station had organised its own concert party composed of volunteers with talent and one wing of the Airmens Mess was converted into a concert hall. An American aircrew officer named Tex McQuiston (Photo 24) played the guitar but unfortunately he was lost during a raid on Aachen. The station band (Photo 22) which played for the concert party was a six piece ensemble which had the support of F/O Jim Gill, who arranged for one of his Sergeants to paint the music stands whilst he personally took care of the financial arrangements for the purchase of instruments. A rather amusing situation occurred during the first performance by the concert party because dress suits were hired for one of the numbers but no shoes were available so they had to wear RAF boots on the stage.

A theatre company came to the station to present a play, one of the leading roles being played by that well known actor Alistair Sim. Some of the personnel on the station who were interested in acting got together to form an Amateur Dramatic Society and their first production in 1945 was the play 'Outward Bound'.

A more serious type of acting took place at Snaith, because midway through the war something must have prompted the Air Ministry to consider seriously the possibility of having to drop gas bombs. As a consequence they decided to produce a Training and Propaganda film, with the result that in 1943 a Film Crew from the Crown Film Unit arrived at Snaith and selected a team of Armourers, led by Cpl Roy Lister, to act as 'film stars'. Dummy gas bombs arrived at Snaith and the team of Armourers had to don gas masks, Wellington boots and full gas protection equipment to demonstrate the bombing up procedure. The bombs were loaded into SBCs, three to a container, and winched up into the bomb bays, the action being filmed by cameras located inside and outside the aircraft. Inside the aircraft a camera was installed to photograph through one of the inspection covers over the bomb bay and when bombing up was completed the aircraft took off to carry out a dummy drop at a bombing range north of York. A camera above the bomb bay photographed the drop.

In 1944 a NAAFI club was opened and to mark the event a special party was held. Senior NCO's and Officers were invited but during the evening some of the aircrew sergeants got out of hand with their boisterous activities. A radiogram was donated to the club, but there was only one record. This was the South Rampart Street Parade by Bob Crosby, but on occasions it was supplemented by the 'erks' providing their own records.

Christmas Cheer.

Operations at Snaith and all ground support responsibilities, including the important maintenance activities, did not cease during the festive season. Nevertheless every endeavour was made to celebrate Christmas in true British style despite the limitations imposed by operational constraints and war-time shortages. Christmas lunches were provided in the various messes and in line with service tradition, in the Airmen's mess the other ranks were served by the Officers. In 1943 a printed menu was provided for the lunch together with a list of the entertainments planned (fig 45), and the NAAFI sold economy size Snaith Christmas cards (fig 51).

National Savings Week

The week commencing 12 May 1944 was a very busy one for the station. A National Savings Campaign was organised by the Station Savings Committee, the target being £ 2,000. Activities were arranged so that something took place every day. The station sports took place on the 13th (Photo 23), this was marred somewhat by rain in the afternoon, but was followed in the evening by a dance on the WAAF site. On the 14th a parade of all ranks with small arms took place when there was an address by the station CO Group Captain N H Fresson DFC. Afterwards he took the salute at a

FIG 51
Economy Sized Snaith Christmas Card

MISHAPS, ACHIEVEMENTS AND ANECDOTES

march past and in the evening a performance was given by the concert party. On the 16th the new station library was opened with a repeat performance by the concert party in the evening with all the proceeds going to the Red Cross POW fund, which helped to provide food parcels for the RAF 'Kriegies' including 51 Squadron members. The finale on the 18th was a visit by the AOC of 4 Group to present the station with the RAF Yorkshire Hockey Cup, followed by an evening performance by the station band.

Local Hostelries

For off duty haunts there were numerous hostelries convenient for the personnel at Snaith. The nearest ones were in Pollington Village, one of which was the George and Dragon and mine host, Mr Sidebottom, had a daughter Kitty who was a WAAF stationed at Snaith and married to one of the LACs. The other village pub was the Kings Head known to the aircrew as 'His Majesties Loaf' with Bill and Lottie Bateman as proprietors. This pub was very popular, since the lads from the squadron were entertained well and good meals were provided by Lottie. Other pubs in the vicinity were the Bay Horse and New Inn at Heck, Horse and Jockey at Whitley Bridge and the Four Horse Shoes over the canal bridge at Balne. Pilot Des Byrne regularly played the piano at the latter pub, aircrew being discouraged from the common practice of pouring beer inside the instrument to 'lubricate' the keys.

For those who didn't require alcoholic beverages there was the YMCA canteen in Pollington Village officially opened by the Princess Royal. This was located in the Bethesda Chapel and manned by lady volunteers, who provided refreshments, food and various games. 'Ma's Cafe', (Ma being a Mrs Shaw), which was located on the East side of the airfield just north of the army camp, was a popular rendezvous. This was a transport cafe where hungry airmen could buy mugs of tea and bacon sandwiches. The village Post Office was owned by LAC Freddie Bateman who was stationed at Snaith and living out. Marie Jackson who worked there found it to be a very busy place whilst 51 Squadron was stationed at Snaith, with airmen banking their pay, but frequently having to draw it out before the next pay day. Aircrew, including those from the Commonwealth, would regularly send telegrams home telling their loved ones they were safe. Sadly on one occasion an Australian crew all sent telegrams home saying they were safe only to go missing that same night.

'Two of the Few'

In 1943, as mentioned earlier, not many Skippers completed a full tour of operations with all or part of their crew and two of these crews are mentioned below. Doug Wilson's crew took part in the squadron's first operations from Snaith and the crew comprised:

Pilot Sgt C.R.Wilson
Navigator Sgt P.Finnett
Bomb Aimer Sgt R.Airey
Flight Engineer Sgt P.K.Anger
Wireless Operator Sgt D.Hall
Mid Upper Gunner Sgt L.P. Wooldridge
Rear Gunner Sgt L.Sharp

A few of the crew's experiences have been reported in other chapters, some of which W/O Louis Wooldridge DFC supplied from his unpublished book, 'Day Squire-Knight Flier'. Louis served a second tour of ops with 578 Squadron at Snaith's satellite Burn. This crew finished their tour of operations with the Wuppertal raid on the 29/30.5.1943. The Pilot, F/Lt Claude Wilson, like many other 51 Squadron aircrew went into Transport Command after the war but unfortunately he was killed in a crash whilst engaged in route flying. Along with Navigator P.Finnett he took over a Stirling Mk V, transporting ex POWs, from the crew which had flown it from the Far East. After taking off from the Staging Post at Castel Benito the engines cut out at 700 ft with the result that the aircraft crashed killing everyone on board.

When Pilot Johnny Morris and his Navigator Dave Storey completed a tour of ops they were the last of the original members of one of the longest serving 1943 crews at Snaith, having operated for nearly eleven months. Their first operation was the Krefeld raid in June 1943, which has been dealt with in detail in earlier chapters, and by December they had become a veteran crew. The squadron then decided to use them as an example of longevity by spacing out their operations, thus being able to boost the moral of 'sprog' crews by demonstrating that it was possible for a crew to operate for a long period.

The initial crew was:
Pilot Sgt John Morris
Navigator Sgt Dave Storey
Bomb Aimer P/O Jim Bingham
Wireless Operator P/O Arthur Hebblethwaite
Flight Engineer Sgt Jock Russell

Rear Gunner Sgt Paddy Boyd
Mid Upper Gunner Sgt Paddy Flynn

During the tour Paddy Boyd was lost on his third trip, with another crew, being replaced by Allan Massey. Paddy Flynn left the crew in mid summer to join a Wellington squadron and was replaced by a Canadian, Bob Kennedy. Arthur Hebblethwaite was promoted to squadron Wireless Leader his replacement being W/O Sparks (an apt name for a W/Op) who was commonly known as 'Sparky'. He was a very experienced operator on his second tour. Jim Bingham, whom Dave Storey considered to be one of the coolest most unflappable customers he had ever met, developed lung trouble and was taken off operations. This may have been due to the fact that he used to move around the aircraft at altitude without using the portable oxygen bottles.

On the final trip to Lille on the 9/10.4.1944, John Morris and Dave Storey were the only two members of the original crew left, being screened after this operation.

Louis Patrick Wooldridge DFC, from one of the foregoing crews, supplied a poem which he has dedicated to the members of 51 Squadron. This has been adapted from an original poem 'Knights of the Air' contained in his aforementioned unpublished book.

51 SQUADRON-KNIGHTS OF THE AIR

Amid the night sky, studded with stars bright to fair.
Sometimes graced by a brilliant silvery moon,-at other times bare
Borne upon outstretched wings of wings of speed.
51's 'Knights of the Air'.
Upon their Whitley and Halifax metallic steeds.
Like their counterparts, the bold Knights of Old.
Rode out to give battle.
Not with Shield and Lance.
But to the accompaniment of cannon and machine gunfire rattle.
The fortunate few returning, albeit covered in surrounds of glory.
Whilst alas, the unfortunate many, by fate's decree-their frames so bloody gory.
Thus all ye persons of the peacetime future who dare.
To visit Snaith airfield, hangars and messes and find them converted, or in disrepair.
Listen intently, and give imaginative thought to to what it once had been.

And it is possible, that once again the events of those years.
May yet again unfold and and be seen.
Allowing perhaps to be heard, o'er the faint eerie sounds of cannon and machine gun rattle .
The ghostly echoes of aero engines, mingling with the voices of 51's 'Knights of the Air'.
As they once more fly the skies in spectral battle.

FIG 49

Nose Art

In the foregoing poem Louis Wooldridge refers to 51 Squadron's 'Knights of the Air'. Rather like knights of old, many of the squadron's aircrew displayed a form of heraldry on their 'steeds'. These light hearted displays produced with the help of their ground crews were called Nose Art. An NCO in the photographic section used his civilian talents to paint many of these works of art on a portion of aircraft fabric. This was then bonded to the skin of a Halifax by the ground crew in charge of the aircraft. The design for 'D' Dopey, HR981, which was the aircraft flown by the crew mentioned in the poem 'Memories' reproduced at the end of this chapter, is shown in Fig 49. In Fig 52 there is a selection of photographs showing the Nose Art displayed on some of the squadron aircraft in 1944.

Halifax Dirge.

A.V.Nicolson DFM supplied the following 51 Squadron Halifax dirge, sung to the tune of the well known pub song 'Nellie Dean'.

MISHAPS, ACHIEVEMENTS AND ANECDOTES

'W' Winsome WAAF

'T' Tiger

'E' Expensive Babe

'F' Flying Fox

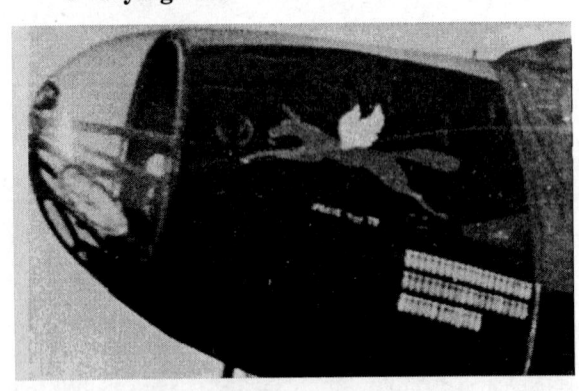

FIG 52
Nose Art On Squadron Aircraft

176

So your flying 'Hali Threes' - NEVER MIND!
So you need a nimble brain   - NEVER MIND!
It's four Hercules -
No more Merlins if you please,
It is speedy (with a breeze) - NEVER MIND!
It is faster than a 'Lib'   - NEVER MIND!
and goes faster than a 'Lanc' - NEVER MIND!
Its a 'greaser' every time,
flies in hail, rain and shine,
Safer than a train   - NEVER MIND!
It is not a seventeen   - NEVER MIND!
and flies slower than a 'Beau'- NEVER MIND!
It will bring us back from Hell
and will do us very well'
It's an 'HP' Blooming Belle - NEVER MIND!
It is better than a 'Fort'   - NEVER MIND!
A Stirling (ad lib)   - NEVER MIND!
It's a bomber with a mission
and there'll be no intermission,
It will 'win the bloody war'! - NEVER MIND!

The final anecdote is a copy of a poem provided by Navigator Rex Payne which was written by a fellow crew member and personifies life at Snaith. The author of the poem, mid-upper Air Gunner Joe Grudzein, dedicated it to Mac's (W J MacPherson) crew.

MEMORIES

It is just dusk, the sun has set
And as I walk the grass feels wet
Carrying with me my parachute gear,
And all equipment airmen wear.

Across the dispersal to my kite
To that mass of four-engined might -
With pride to look on that comrade of strife
In whom so often I trust my life.

Here come the rest of my crew
The best bunch of chaps I ever knew
Tony, Dinty, Rex, Ralph, Silvo and Mac
Laughing and joking at some funny crack.

They greet me with a rib about my guns
Though they'll never hit anything but Huns
And I, poor A.G. that I am,
Take all derision like a lamb.

Take off time draws near
Somehow my stomach feels queer,
As the engines rev up with a din
Its time to get in, there's a war we must win
And so we take off and leave our old 'drome,
That place in past months we've learnt to call home,
The Skipper spurs onwards his steed of war
Which responds with a din not heard before.

And as we circle to gain height
Our aircraft seems eager to enter the fight
While in our hearts we can't help but wonder
As the engines strike up their symphony of thunder
If we'll see again this beautiful land
With a friendly ever welcoming hand.

But gritting our teeth with determination
We set course again for our destination
And as we fly through a land of clouds
We forget about death and her dark shrouds
And only remember there's a job to be done
If this bloody war is ever to be won.

So braving flak, fighter and searchlight beams
We try and make possible those hopeful dreams
Of coming days of love and peace
When wars and gory massacres cease
And people will live to a ripe old age
And read life's book to its very last page.
                                    Gunner Joe.

There is now little left in the locality to tell people of the presence of 51 Squadron in 1942-45. Apart from a few Hangars and buildings on what was the technical site there is a memorial in Pollington Church. This comprises a brass plate presented by the Crispin Society to Pollington Village on behalf of 51 Squadron for services rendered during the war. The plaque is accompanied by a painting of a Halifax. The main squadron memorial is located at Selby Abbey.

MISHAPS, ACHIEVEMENTS AND ANECDOTES

Many of those who served at Snaith are members of the Squadron Association and attend the annual reunion weekend at Wyton which includes an Association Dinner on Saturday evening and a church service on Sunday morning. It therefore seems apt to finish with a Grace for the Squadron supplied by S/Ldr Ken Dean and composed by his friend Canon Jack Armstrong.

Whitley, Halifax and Nimrod too,
These are the planes that fifty one flew,
War's great loss and sacrifice vast,
Before you brought us peace at last,
Now in thanks that we survive,
Lord bless the meal that you provide,
In your service be our guide,
And keep our loved ones by your side,

APPENDIX A

51 SQUADRON AIRCRAFT LOSSES

SERIAL No \ DATE \ CODE LETTER \ CAPTAIN \ CAUSE OF LOSS.

1943
DT483 \ 9.Jan \ MH-F \ Sgt R.A.Banks-Martin \ FTR Mining
DT506 \ 16/17.Jan \ MH-D \ Sgt S T Brett \ Ex Lorient, u/c collapsed landing at Pocklington as aircraft ran on to soft ground.
DT581 \ 21/22.Jan \ MH-Y \ P/O Gatliffe \ Crashed at Hoarside Moor, Yorks ex Gardening ops "Nectarine 3".
DT705 \ 27/28 Jan \ MH-S \ Sgt F H Barrett \ FTR Dusseldorf.
DT721 \ 27/28 Jan \ MH-J \ W/O L O Weakly \ ditto
W1185 \ 29/30 Jan \ MH-V \ F/Sgt W A O Whitworth \ During an air test at 1120 hrs, on landing at Burn was baulked on first attempt, on 2nd approach hit ground with port outer on fire and swung off runway onto railway hut, 1 civilian killed and 3 injured. A/c caught fire.
DT722 \ 13.Feb \ MH-M \ Sgt J Rawcliffe \ Incendiaries fell out on dispersal, a/c burnt out.
DT724 \ 13.Feb \ MH-H \ P/O Rawlings \ Ditto
W7818 \ 18.Feb \ MH-T \ Sgt E P H Haly \ E/F on T/O at 18.50 hrs. Pilot thought all engines overspeeding, so he closed the throttles, aircraft crashed in front of Control Tower with mines onboard.
DT648 \ 1/2 Mar \ MH-K \ —————— \ Crashed on landing at Snaith after engine fire.
BB223 \ 1/2 Mar \ MH-C \ F/O J D W Stenhouse \ FTR Berlin
W7861 \ 3/4 Mar \ MH-B \ F/Sgt J M Johnson \ FTR Hamburg
DT567 \ 7/8 Mar \ MH-F \ P/O A L Holmes \ FTR Mining
BB244 \ 29/30 Mar \ MH-Q \ P/O R G Harris \ FTR Berlin
DT666 \ 3/4 April \ MH-T \ Sgt C R Wilson \ Aircraft caught fire whilst in landing circuit and crashed at Shortland's Farm.
DT738 \ 3/4 April \ MH-D \ Sgt J Rawcliffe \ FTR Essen
DT686 \ 4/5 April \ MH-N \ F/O Emery \ FTR Keil
DT670 \ 16/17 April \ MH-C \ Write-off ex ops.
DT690 \ 16/17 April \ MH-A* \ Sgt J E McCrea \ FTR Pilsen
DT561 \ 16/17 April \ MH-K \ Sgt E W Cox \ FTR Pilsen
HR784 \ 16/17 April \ —— \ F/Sgt R H Stewart \ FTR Pilsen
HR729 \ 16/17 April \ MH-R \ W/O J G Edwards \ FTR Pilsen
—— \ 16/17 April \ —— \ Sgt D M Inch \ FTR Pilsen
DT628 \ 20/21 April \ MH-B \ Sgt B T Brett \ FTR Stettin
HR787 \ 26/27 April \ —— \ Sgt C M Brigden \ FTR Duisburg
HR778 \ 26/27 April \ —— \ Sgt G Fisher \ FTR Duisburg
HR733 \ 30 Ap.1 Mar \ —— \ Sgt D R Wilson \ FTR Essen
DT729 \ 3 May \ MH-R \ Sgt N F Owen \ Crashed near Lindholme after engine fire.
DT637 \ 13/14 May \ —— \ Sgt D W Thompson \ Force landed near Riccall after port inner engine failure.
DT645 \ 12/13 May \ MH-B* \ Sgt D C Smith \ FTR Duisburg
DT685 \ 12/13 May \ MH-A \ Sgt N E Jones \ FTR Duisburg
HR786 \ 12/13 May \ MH-J \ P/O G W Locksmith \ FTR Duisburg
JB806 \ 12/13 May \ MH-J \ Sgt B Brown \ FTR Duisburg
HR790 \ 13/14 May \ —— \ P/O C W H Byres \ FTR Bochum

51 Squadron Aircraft Losses

DT526 \ 13/14 May \ MH-V \ F/Lt R D Johnstone \ FTR Bochum
HR842 \ 23/24 May \ —— \ Sgt J W G Parker \ FTR Dortmund
HR844 \ 23/24 May \ —— \ Sgt R R Mascall \ FTR Dortmund
HR835 \ 23/24 May \ —— \ Sgt L A Wright \ FTR Dortmund
HR836 \ 23/24 May \ —— \ F/O J E Rigby \ FTR Dortmund
JB792 \ 23/24 May \ —— \ P/O A D Andrews \ Crashed at Woolfox Lodge, due to hydraulic failure.
HR747 \ 25/26 May \ —— \ P/O R J Cribb \ Crashed at Snaith ex ops Dusseldorf
HR853 \ 25/26 May \ —— \ Sgt W P Davies \ Force landed at Doncaster ex ops Dusseldorf
HR789 \ 27/28 May \ MH-Z \ P/O A P B Wilson \ FTR Essen
HR750 \ 27/28 May \ MH-W \ W/O R Beeston \ FTR Essen
HR788 \ 11/12 June \ —— \ F/Sgt J J Anderson \ FTR Dusseldorf
HR852 \ 11/12 June \ MH-D \ F/Sgt K J S Harvey \ FTR Dusseldorf
DT742 \ 11/12 June \ MH-Y \ F/Sgt Collins \ Returning from ops shot down by convoy and ditched off Norfolk coast.
DT568 \ 12/13 June \ MH-F \ Sgt Chambers \ Crashed in Holland ex Bochum operation
JD244 \ 21/22 June \ MH-K \ Sgt F Heathfield \ FTR Krefeld
JD251 \ 22/23 June \ —— \ Sgt R.H.Elliott \ FTR Mulheim
JD250 \ 24/25 June \ MH-R \ F/O J M Mckenzie \ FTR Wuppertal
HR731 \ 25/26 June \ MH-C \ Sgt A Osmond \ FTR Gelsenkirchen
JD261 \ 25/26 June \ —— \ Sgt D H V Davis \ FTR Gelsenkirchen
HR839 \ 28/29 June\ LK-L \ P/O J P Tay \ FTR Cologne
DT513 \ 28/28 June \ MH-N \ Sgt D W Sigournay \ FTR Cologne
JD262 \ 3/4 July \ MH-J \ Sgt J S Garnham \ FTR Cologne
HR843 \ 9/10 July \ MH-A \ Sgt J Foulston \ Crashed at Gatwick ex Gelsenkirchen
HR940 \ 24/25 July \ —— \ Sgt W J Murray \ Shot down by Ju88 near Sonderborg on a Hamburg raid.
HR934 \ 25/26 July \ —— \ F/O J S Cole \ FTR Essen
HR749 \ 25/25 July \ HR-J \ Sgt E J Jones \ FTR Essen
JD309 \ 29/30 July \ —— \ Sgt E Fletcher \ Shot down by night fighter on Hamburg raid.
HR859 \ 2/3 Aug \ —— \ W/O E R Sklarchuk \ Shot down by night fighter on Hamburg raid.
HR783 \ 6 Aug \ —— \ P/O C A Lambert DFM \ Crashed at Escrick, York after engine fire (See Chapter 6).
HR981 \ 10/11 Aug \ MH-D \ W T Macpherson \ After force landing crashed into farmhouse, see Chapter 6.
HR838 \ 10/11 Aug \ MH-Q \ W/O R E Leeper \ FTR Nuremburg
JD125 \ 12/13 Aug \ —— \ P/O C A H Silvester \ FTR Milan.
HR951 \ 19 Aug \ —— \ ——————- \ Swung on landing at Snaith and u/c collapsed.
HR936 \ 23/24 Aug \ MH-J \ P/O R J Cribb \ FTR Berlin
HR869 \ 27/28 Aug \ MH-Z \ F/L T R Dobson \FTR Nuremburg
HR931 \ 31 Aug.1 Sep \ MH-F \ P/O L R Cates \ FTR Berlin
JN902 \ 31 Aug.1 Sep \ —— \ Sgt S C Turner \ FTR Berlin
JD263 \ 5/6 Sept \ —— \ F/Sgt W J King \ FTR Mannheim
JN901 \ 22/23 Sept \ —— \ F/O J Pohe \ FTR Hannover
JN900 \ 27/28 Sept \ —— \ P/O F J Bishop \ u/c collapsed on landing at Ridgewell, returning from a Hanover raid.
JN924 \ 2/3 Oct \ MH-D (MH-H) \ F/O D J Cheal \ DBR after mining operation.
LW287 \ 2/3 Oct \ —— \ Sgt J E Nixon \ FTR after mining operation.
HR728 \ 3/4 Oct \ LK-D \ F/L W Irwin \ FTR Kassel
LW287 \ 4 Oct \ MH-C \ Sgt J E Nixon RAAF \ FTR Mining
HR727 \ 4/5 Oct \ MH-V \ Sgt E Fenning \ Crashed at Ashop Moor on return from Franfurt.
JN885 \ 8/9 Oct \ MH-A \ F/Sgt A W James \ FTR Hannover
JD253 \ 8/9 Oct \ LK-A (LK-E) \ Sgt K Chislett \ FTR Hannover
HR870 \ 18 Oct \ MH-H \ ——————— \ Crashed on take off at Snaith
JN920 \ 22/23 Oct \ LK-L \ Sgt C E Hall RCAF \ FTR Kassel
HR950 \ 19/20 Nov \ MH-S (MH-X) \ F/Sgt M C Cutcheon \ FTR Leverkusen

HR726 \ 22/23 Nov \ MH-B (LK-B) \ W/C C L Wright \ FTR Berlin
LW286 \ 22/23 Nov \ LK-H \ P/O H F Farley \ FTR Berlin, crashed in the sea, 7 killed.
HR732 \ 3/4 Dec \ MH-Y \ P/O A Salvage \ FTR Leipzig.
HR782 \ 3/4 Dec \ MH-R (MH-A) \ ——————— \ FTR Leipzig.
JN922 \ 5 Dec \ MH-Z \ F/Lt McCreanor \ On air test forced to land on one wheel.
JN923 \ 20 Dec \ MH-F \ F/Lt T.S.Blyth \ Damaged by incendiaries during practice bombing.
HR948 \ 20/21 Dec \ MH-W \ F/Lt A Burchett \ FTR Frankfurt.
JD123 \ 20/21 Dec \ MH-S \ Sgt H H Sherer DFM \ FTR Frankfurt.
HR868 \ 20/21 Dec \ MH-B \ F/O McKew \ Crashed ex Franfurt operation.
JD264 \ 29/30 Dec \ MH-H (MH-U) \ F/Sgt A.R.Baird \ FTR Berlin.
1944
LV779 \ 21/22 Jan \ MH-L \ P/O Bruce \ FTR Magdeburg.
LV775 \ 21/22 Jan \ MH-G \ McKenzie \ FTR Magdeburg.
LV774 \ 21/22 Jan \ MH-B \ F/O J A Price \ FTR Magdeburg.
LW468 \ 21/22 Jan \ LK— \ ——————— \ 51 Sqdn a/c operating for 578. Ditched off Flamborough Head ex Magdeburg.
LW466 \ 28/29 Jan \ MH-H \ F/Sgt T J Griffin \ FTR Berlin.
LW481 \ 19/20 Feb \ MH-X \ P/O T Carder \ FTR Leipzig
LV778 \ 24/25 Feb \ C6-D (MH-T) \ P/O D Jackson \ FTR Schweinfurt.
LW497 \ 15/16 Mar \ MH-W \ S/Ldr Eno \ FTR Stuttgart.
HX330 \ 15/16 Mar \ MH-V \ F/Lt A.K.D.Fell \ FTR Stuttgart.
LK750 \ 18/19 Mar \ MH-Y \ Sgt C R Seaman \ FTR Frankfurt.
LW679 \ 22/23 Mar \ MH-R \ ——————— \ Crash landed at Snaith when flaps failed.
LW539 \ 24/25 Mar \ MH-H \ F/O G.McPherson \ FTR Berlin.
MZ507 \ 24/25 Mar \ MH-P* \ F/Lt R Curtiss \ FTR Berlin.
LW671 \ 26/27 Mar \ MH-K \ Sgt A J Weaver \ Crash landed at Bury St Edmunds.
LV777 \ 30/31 Mar \ MH-F \ S/Ldr F P Hill \ FTR Nuremburg.
LV822 \ 30/31 Mar \ MH-Z \ F/Sgt E Wilkins \ FTR Nuremburg.
LV857 \ 30/31 Mar \ MH-H \ Sgt J P G Binder \ FTR Nuremburg.
LW537 \ 30/31 Mar \ MH-C \ F/Sgt N M Stembridge \ FTR Nuremburg.
LW544 \ 30/31 Mar \ MH-Q \ F/Sgt G C Brougham \ FTR Nuremburg.
LW579 \ 30/31 Mar \ MH-V (C6-E) \ P/O J Brookes \ Crashed at Stokenchurch, Oxford ex Nuremburg.
LV880 \ 10/11 April \ MH-E \ F/Sgt M H Hall \ FTR Tergnier.
LW522 \ 10/11 April \ MH-J \ Sgt C Shackleton \ FTR Tergnier.
HX350 \ 10/11 April \ MH-Y (MH-U) \ F/Sgt A Sarjantson \ FTR Tergnier.
LW578 \ 22/23 April \ C6-F \ Sgt Malling \ u/c collapsed on landing.
MZ566 \ 22/23 April \ MH-Y \ F/Lt D L Sedgwick \ FTR Dusseldorf.
MZ565 \ 27/28 April \ MH-O \ F/Sgt J P O'Neill BEM \ FTR Montzen.
LV783 \ 27/28 April \ MH-Z (MH-R) \ Sgt P Keenan \ FTR Montzen.
LW479 \ 27/28 April \ MH-E \ F/Lt L Rothwell DFC \ FTR Montzen.
MZ593 \ 1/2 May \ MH-Z \ F/Sgt G R French \ FTR Malines.
LK835 \ 22 May \MH-U\Sgt A.S. Jones \ Crashed near Monmouth.
LK885 \ 24/25 May \ MH-Z \ P/O W C Lawson \ FTR Aachen.
LV784 \ 24/25 May \ MH-S (LK-K) \ F/Sgt G B Hyndman \ FTR Aachen.
LW498 \ 24/25 May \ MH-T (C6-T) (MH-Z) \ F/Lt C McQuiston (USA) \ FTR Aachen.
LW364 \ 8/9 June \ MH-B (MH-K) \ F/Sgt J C Davies \ Crashed at Holme on Spalding Moor ex ops against Chateadun.
MZ643 \ 12/13 June \ MH-Z \ F/Sgt G E Smith \ Returned but DBR after bombing communications target at Amiens.
LV782 \ 30 Ju/1 July \ MH-T \ Sgt J R A Cooke \ FTR
LV862 \ 6 July \ MH-K \ F/Sgt R P Hampson \ Abandoned ex ops.
MZ581 \ 20/21 July \ C6-C \ F/O H A Jowett \ Collided over Bottrop, crash landed in UK.

51 Squadron Aircraft Losses

MZ821 \ 20/21 July \ MH-H \ P/O R P Hampson \ FTR Bottrop.
LW546 \ 6 Aug \ MH-R (C6-L) \ F/Lt G Brown \ FTR Hazebrouck.
LW588 \ 11/12 Aug \ MH-O (MH-S) \ W/O R A Garrett \ FTR Somain
MZ349 \ 12 Aug \ MH-U \ F/O T B Compton \ FTR Braunschweig.
LW538 \ 18/19 Aug \ MH-N \ F/O W P Quan \ FTR Sterkrade.
LW362 \ 25 Aug \ —— \ ———————— \ Crashed on landing.
MZ758 \ 3 Sept \ MH-V \ W/O K O Potts \ Belly landed near Strubby airfield after returning from operation against airfield in Holland.
MZ319 \ 11 Sept \ MH-B \ F/O J R R Preston \ FTR attack on Nordstern plant at Gelsenkirchen.
MZ624 \ 11 Sept \ MH-N \ F/O L C Ainsley \ Crash landed on return from Nordstern due to flak damage.
MZ916 \ 11 Sept \ MH-O \ P/O K.P.Cross \ FTR from daylight raid on Nordstern.
LV865 \ 17 Sept \ MH-Y \ F/O B M Twilley \ Crashed on take-off at Snaith.
MZ972 \ 24 Sept \ MH-O \ F/O J N Bischoff \ FTR Calais.
MZ870 \ 1 Oct \ —— \ P/O D Dixon \ Crashed at Snaith.
MZ343 \ 6 Oct \ MH-T \ F/Lt R D Bell \ FTR Sterkrade.
NP933 \ 7 Oct \ MH-M \ F/O C T Collyer \ FTR Kleve.
NR128 \ 27 Oct \ MH-S \ P/O Tomms RAAF \ Overshot landing at Snaith.
LL612 \ 25 Oct \ MH-A \ F/O Comer \ Crashed at Snaith ex ops.
LV819 \ 4/5 Nov \ C6-F \ F/Sgt E G Stevens \ Cat. E ex ops Bochum.
LW177 \ 4/5 Nov \ MH-N \ F/O A G N Reay \ FTR Bochum.
MZ933 \ 4/5 Nov \ MH-W \ F/Sgt L Berry \ FTR Bochum.
LK844 \ 14 Nov \ MH-M \ F/Sgt G W R Millard \ Crashed near Tingley, Leeds on a training flight.
NR241 \ 18 Nov \ MH-A \ W/O T Bruce \ Collided in circuit with a 578 Squadron aircraft, ex op Munster.
NR129 \ 21 Nov \ —— \ ——————— \ FTR Sterkrade operation after colliding with another aircraft
NP934 \ 17/18 Dec \ —— \ P/O B M Twilly \ FTR Duisburg.
NR248 \ 17/18 Dec \ MH-A \ W/O W A Bates \ FTR Duisburg.
1945
MZ918 \ 5/6 Jan \ MH-U \ P/O E G Stevens \ FTR Hannover.
LV952 \ 5/6 Jan \ MH-F \ P/O A Leach \ FTR Hannover.
MZ767 \ 5/6 Jan \ MH-D \ F/O G I Hodgson \ FTR Hannover.
MZ811 \ 6/7 Jan \ MH-X \ F/O S J Brown \ FTR Hannover.
LW461 \ 16 Jan \ MH-D \ F/O J D Brayshaw \ FTR Magdeburg.
MZ794 \ 28/29 Jan \ MH-T \ ——————— \ Crash landed in France, ex Stuttgart, after flak damage and fire in starboard inner
MZ487 \ 2/3 Feb \ MH-Z \ F/Lt W Arnold \ FTR Wanne Eickle.
MZ765 \ 17 Feb \ MH-E \ F/O Longman \ Crashed at Manning Heath, Essex ex ops.
MZ451 \ 2 Mar \ MH-F \ F/O F S Eastwell \ FTR Koln.
NP932 \ 14\15 Mar \ MH-J \ P/O S E Chopping \ Crash landed at Snaith ex ops.
MZ348 \ 21 Mar \ MH-D \ F/O J E Paradise \ FTR Rheine.

Code letters in brackets indicate an earlier registration.

Appendix B

HALIFAX AIRCRAFT SERVING WITH 51 SQUADRON

(Excluding aircraft listed in Appendix A)

SERIAL No \ CODE \ MARK \ T/F TO

W1212 MH-U   B11 T/F to 1654 HCU
W1224 MH-E&A B11 to 466/51Sqn/1656 HCU
W7772 MH-S&O B11 T/F to 10 Sqdn.
W7860 MH-W   B11 T/F to 1668 HCU.
BB240 MH-X   B11 T/F to 1652 HCU.
BB241 MH-S   B11 T/F to 1652 HCU.

BB253 ——   B11 T/F to 1658 HCU.
DT580 MH-Z   B11 T/F to 78 Sqdn.
DT582 MH-X   B11 T/F to 1666 HCU.
DT584 MH-J   B11 T/F to 1666 HCU.
DT614 MH-H   B11 T/F to 1658 HCU.
DT626 ——   B11 T/F to 1658 HCU.
DT638 MH-C*   B11 T/F to 158 Sqdn.
DT671 MH-S   B11 T/F to 1652 HCU.
DT693 MH-B&F B11 T/F to 1661 HCU.
DT730 MH-A*   B11 T/F to 77 Sqdn.
HR711 ——   B11 T/F to 102 Sqdn.
HR716 MH-S   B11 T/F to 102 Sqdn.
HR730 ——   B11 T/F to 102 Sqdn.
HR755 ——   B11 T/F to 78 Sqdn.
HR834 MH-V&Q B11 T/F to 102 Sqdn.
HR858 ——   B11 T/F to 78 Sqdn.
HR868 MH-B   B11 T/F to 1656 HCU.
HR930 ——   B11 T/F to 1662 HCU.
HR935 LK-J   B11 T/F to 77 Sqdn.
HR939 MR-R   B11 T/F to 1652 HCU.
HR946 MH-T   B11 T/F to 77 Sqdn.
HR947 MH-K   B11 T/F to 102 Sqdn.
HR949 MH-E   B11 T/F to 77 Sqdn.
HR952 MH-X   B11 T/F to 10 Sqdn.
HX228 ——   B11 T/F to 1658 HCU.
HX237 ——   B111 T/F to 466 Sqdn.
HX241 MH-J   B111 T/F to 78 Sqdn.
HX355 ——   B111 T/F to 78 Sqdn.
JD118 LK-K   B11 T/F to 78 Sqdn.
JD153 ——   B11 T/F to 1658 HCU.
JD248 MH-S   B11 T/F to 78 Sqdn.

JD252 MH-T   B11 T/F to 78 Sqdn.
JD266 LK-C   B11 T/F to 1659 HCU.
JD299 LK-F   B11 T/F to 1663 HCU.
JD300 MH-Y   B11 T/F to 78 Sqdn.
JD302 ——   B11 T/F to 102 Sqdn.
JD308 ——   B11 T/F to 1652 HCU.
JD310 ——   B11 T/F to 78 Sqdn.
JD311 MH-L   B11 T/F to 102 Sqdn.
JD461 LK-E   B11 T/F to 102 Sqdn.
JN883 LK-A   B11 T/F to 10 Sqdn. JN887 ——
B11 T/F to 78 Sqdn.
JN891 ——   B11 T/F to 102 Sqdn.
JN899 LK-K   B11 T/F to 10 Sqdn.
JN906 MH-D   B11 T/F to 78 Sqdn.
JN917 MH-W   B11 T/F to 10 Sqdn.
JN919 MH-B   B11 T/F to 78 Sqdn.
LK748 ——   B111 T/F to 1658 HCU.
LK751 ——   B111 T/F to 1663 HCU.
LK753 MH-B   B111 T/F to 10 Sqdn.
LK756 MH-J   B111 T/F to 578 Sqdn.
LK812 MH-E   B111 T/F to 10 Sqdn.
LK827 ——   B111 T/F to 10 Sqdn.
LK830 —   B111 SOC 31-12-46
LK843 ——   B111 T/F to 578/51Sqdn/SOC.
LK845 ——   B111 T/F to 431 Sqdn.
LK846 ——   B111 T/F to 578 Sqdn.
LL270 ——   BV   T/F to 644 Sqdn.
LL328 ——   BV   T/F to 644 Sqdn.
LL331 ——   BV   T/F to 644 Sqdn.
LV784 MH-K   B111 T/F to 578 Sqdn.
LV815 ——   B111 T/F to 578 Sqdn.
LV817 ——   B111 T/F to 78 Sqdn.
LV818 ——   B111 T/F to 35 Sqdn.
LV820 ——   B111 T/F to 578 Sqdn.
LV832 MH-P & X B111 SOC 31-12-46.
LV876 ——   B111 SOC 20-8-46.
LV937 MH-E   B111 SOC, Over 100 ops.
LW194 ——   B111 SOC 29-11-46.
LW227 ——   B11 T/F to 102 Sqdn.
LW289 MH-U&J B11 T/F to 10 Sqdn.
LW291 ——   B11 T/F to 78 Sqdn.
LW299 MH-B   B11 T/F to 102 Sqdn.
LW348 LK-X   B111 T/F to 578 Sqdn.
LW442 MH-Q   B111 T/F to 187 Sqdn.
LW445 MH-Z   B111 T/F to 1658 HCU.
LW465 ——   B111 T/F to 578 Sqdn.
LW469 LK-A   B111 T/F to 578 Sqdn.
LW470 ——   B111 T/F to 158 Sqdn.
LW471 MH-D   B111 T/F to 578 Sqdn.
LW472 MH-H   B111 T/F to 578 Sqdn.
LW473 MH-E   B111 T/F to 578 Sqdn.
LW474 MH-B   B111 T/F to 578 Sqdn.

Halifax Aircraft Serving With 51 Squadron

LW475 MH-E B111 T/F to 578 Sqdn.
LW478 —— B111 T/F to 578 Sqdn.
LW480 MH-A B111 T/F to 347 Sqdn.
LW495 MH-C B111 T/F to 578 Sqdn.
LW496 C6-A B111 T/F to 578 Sqdn.
MH-S
LW503 —— B111 T/F to 578 Sqdn.
LW504 C6-E&D B111 T/F to 347 Sqdn.
& MH-Q
LW508 LK-Y B111 T/F to 578 Sqdn.
LW521 —— B111 T/F to 466 Sqdn.
LW538 MH-N&T B111 T/F to 578 Sqdn.
LW539 MH-N&H B111 T/F to 578 Sqdn.
LW540 —— B111 T/F to 578 Sqdn.
LW541 MH-Y B111 T/F to 347 Sqdn.
C6-J
LW542 —— B111 T/F to 578 Sqdn.
LW543 MH-R B111 T/F to 578 Sqdn.
LW545 MH-K B111 T/F to 10 Sqdn.
C6-D
LW553 —— B111 T/F to 578 Sqdn.
LW556 —— B111 T/F to 1665 HCU.
LW557 —— B111 T/F to 578 Sqdn.
LW642 MH-L B111 T/F to 347 Sqdn.
LW677 C6-B B111 T/F to 158 Sqdn.
LW689 —— B111 T/F to 434 Sqdn.
MZ401 —— B111 T/F to 462 Sqdn.
MZ402 —— B111 T/F to 462 Sqdn.
MZ465 MH-Y B111 SOC 3-9-45
MZ484 —— BIII SOC 21-12-46.
MZ485 —— BIII SOC 24-2-47.
MZ535 —— B111 T/F to 1658 HCU.
MZ563 —— B111 T/F to 578 Sqdn.
MZ571 —— B111 T/F to 347 Sqdn.
MZ634 MH-U B111 T/F to 1658 HCU.
MZ635 —— B111 T/F to 347 Sqdn.
MZ689 —— B111 T/F to 77 Sqdn.
MZ708 —— B111 T/F to 77 Sqdn.
MZ743 —— B111 T/F to 77 Sqdn.
MZ754 MH-U B111 SOC 8-1-47.
MZ766 MH-B&Z B111 SOC 19-10-46.
MZ771 —— B111 SOC 13-7 45.
MZ790 —— B111 SOC 29-6-45.
MZ820 —— B111 SOC 17-10-45.
MZ851 —— B111 SOC 5-7-45.
MZ868 —— B111 SOC 29-11-46.
MZ897 —— B111 SOC 18-9-46.
MZ917 MH-R B111 T/F to 158 Sqdn.
MZ934 MH-P B111 SOC 14-3-47.
MZ938 —— B111 SOC 24-7-45.
MZ972 —— B111 T/F to 298 Sqdn.
MZ974 MH-N B111 SOC 28-8-46.

MZ988 —— BV11 SOC 28-8-45.
NA123 —— BV11 SOC 27-8-45.
NA150 MH-N BV11 SOC 14-10-45.
NA196 MH-N BV11 T/F to EANS.
NA200 —— BV11 SOC 14-3-47.
NA493 —— B111 T/F to H.Page.
NA496 MH-L B111 T/F to 187 Sqdn.
NA525 —— B111 SOC 27-11-45.
NA529 —— B111 T/F to 578 Sqdn.
NA625 —— B111 T/F to 187 Sqdn.
NA626 —— B111 SOC 15-8-47.
NP962 MH-V B111 SOC 28-1-47.
NP963 MH-R B111 SOC 12-2-47.
NP972 —— B111 SOC 30-9-44.
NP974 —— B111 SOC 1652 HCU.
NR142 MH-S B111 SOC 31-1-47.
NR202 —— B111 SOC 15-8-47.
NR254 MH-A B111 T/F to Leconfield.
NR255 —— B111 T/F SOC 6-12-45.
PN184 MH-Q B111 T/F to 640 Sqdn.
RG445 —— B111 SOC 20-3-47.
RG446 MH-U B111 Converted to 5339M

T/F means Transferred

SOC means Struck of Charge

APPENDIX C

51 SQUADRON OPERATIONS BETWEEN JAN 1943 AND MAY 1945

Target \ Date \ No of aircraft \ Report

'NECTARINES' 2 \ 9.1.43 \ 16 a/c \ Minelaying
LORIENT \ 14/15.1.43 \ 5 a/c \ Lorient docks, U boat base, PFF marking accurate but bombing 'wild'.
LORIENT \ 15/16.1.43 \ 7 a/c \ Lorient docks, bombing more accurate than in previous operation.
BERLIN \ 17/18.1.43 \ 2 a/c \ No important damage, night fighters able to find bomber stream.
'NECTARINES' 3 \ 21/22.1.43 \ 3 a/c \ Minelaying
LORIENT \ 23/24.1.43 \ 10 a/c \ Lorient docks, good visibility, successful bombing.
DUSSELDORF \ Population 530,000. Transport centre and steel production facilities.
Operation \ 27/28.1.43 \ 4 a/c \ First use of 'Oboe' ground markers by PFF. Bombing well concentrated.
COLOGNE \ Docks and Marshalling yards. An important transport target.
Operation \ 2/3.2.43 \ 3 a/c \ Cloud cover, TIs dropped by 'Oboe' Mosquitoes and heavy bombers with H2S. Widespread damage, and a military airfield hit.
HAMBURG \ 3/4.2.43 \ 8 a/c \ Very bad weather with icing conditions. Bombing scattered.
TURIN \ 4/5.2.43 \ 5 a/c \ Raid produced very heavy and widespread damage.
LORIENT \ 7/8.2.43 \ 9 a/c \ Submarine pens at Lorient, PFF marking good, devastating attack.
WILEMSHAVEN \ 11/12.2.43 \ 2 a/c \ Squadron flew over cloud most of the way. Target also covered by cloud, so PFF employed sky markers. Widespread damage in Naval dockyard.
LORIENT \ 13/14.2.43 \ Heaviest attack on this target, considerable damage done.
COLOGNE \ 14/15.2.43 \ 9 a/c \ Sky marking by PFF. Raid was a limited success.
LORIENT \ 16/17.2.43 \ 11 a/c \ Lorient had now suffered severe damage.
WILEMSHAVEN \ Naval town, submarine construction yards.
Operation \ 18/19.2.43 \ 8 a/c \ Good visibility and accurate marking but the bombing was inaccurate.
'NECTARINES' 3 \ 18/19.2.43 \ 2 a/c \ Minelaying.
WILEMSHAVEN \ 19/20.2.43 \ 13 a/c \ Most bombs missed target, faulty marking blamed.
NUREMBERG \ Second largest town in Bavaria and "Spiritual Centre" of the Nazi movement. A round trip was over 1,000 miles long.
Operation \ 25/26.2.43 \ 13 a/c \ Weather conditions bad so PFF marking late. Bombs fell to north of aiming point.
'NECTARINES' \ 26/27.2.43 \ 2 a/c \ Minelaying in the Frisians.
COLOGNE \ 26/27.2.43 \ 9 a/c \ Only a quarter of the main force hit the target, most bombs south west of aiming point.
St NAZAIRE \ 28.2 & 1.3.43 \ 17 a/c \ U Boat base, wide spread destruction caused.
BERLIN \ 1/2.3.43 \ 10 a/c \ PFF had difficulty with H2S marking, widespread damage. This was the night when the Germans captured an H2S set from a shot down aircraft.
GARDENING \ 2/3.3.43 \ 2 a/c \ Minelaying.
HAMBURG \ 3/4.3.43 \ 12 a/c \ Faulty marking due to misreading H2S, hence wrong target bombed.

BATTLE OF THE RUHR

The Ruhr was an important strategic target vital to German war production. It contained numerous Engineering Works, Steel Production Plants and Coal Mines. There was an efficient system of railways and canals to carry the products produced to any part of Europe.
ESSEN \ Population 670.000. Very important industrial centre. Contained the Krupps Works which was the largest engineering plant in the Ruhr, involved in war production including shells, bombs, torpedoes, armoured vehicles, engine components and the manufacture of locomotives vital to the German transport system. There were also the Goldschmidt AG chemical and metal works and a synthetic aviation fuel production plant.

51 Squadron Operations Between Jan 1943 And May 1945

Operation \ 5/6.3.43 \ 12 a/c \ Opening raid in the Battle of the Ruhr. First of a series of successful raids on Essen. Unusually clear weather conditions. Good marking, squadron in first of three waves. 160 acres of destruction.
'NECTARINES' \ 7/8.3.43 \ 1 a/c \ Minelaying in Dutch Frisian islands.
NUREMBERG \ 8/9.3.43 \ 13 a/c \ Target beyond 'Oboe' range so visual and H2S marking used which was wide spread. Many bombs well away from aiming point.
MUNICH \ Largest town in Bavaria.
Operation \ 9/10.3.43 \ 5 a/c \ Bombing concentrated to west of aiming point. Much industrial damage. Locomotive works damaged.
STUTTGART \ Over 500 miles distant from UK. Difficult target to find since it was located in a series of deep valleys, the problem of identification being compounded by poor visibility. Precision engineering centre also containing the Bosch factory which was an important strategic target.
Operation \ 11/12.3.43 \ 10 a/c \ PFF marked the target but main force aircraft were late in arriving so many bombs dropped away from town. First use of dummy TIs by the Germans.
ESSEN \ 12/13.3.43 \ 8 a/c \ Clear weather over target. Successful raid due to good 'Oboe' marking. 27% of Krupps factory damaged as a result of this and the previous raid
ST NAZAIRE \ 22/23.3.43 \ 10 a/c \ Naval target. Attack concentrated on port area.
DUISBURG \ Ruhr target. Population 440,000. Coal, steel production and transport centre.
Operation \ 26/27.3.43 \ 11 a/c \ No 'Oboe' marking so bombing scattered.
BERLIN \ 27/28.3.43 \ 12 a/c \ PFF marking incorrect so bombing widespread.
ST NAZAIRE \ 28/29.3.43 \ 7 a/c \ 'Oboe' marked raid on port.
BERLIN \ 29/30.3.43 \ 2 a/c \ Raid carried out in bad weather, bombing well to south of aiming point.
ESSEN \ 3/4.4.43 \ 15 a/c \ Third attack by the squadron on this target. Increased AA defences. Clear sky over target, bombing accurate. Some local serious damage to workshops. This was an important achievement adding to the damage caused to Munich and Berlin railway workshops in previous raids since there was a shortage of locomotives caused by Fighter Command shooting them up
KIEL \ Naval town, principal base of the German fleet.
Operation \ 4/5.4.43 \ 14 a/c \ Weather conditions caused marking problems, so only few bombs on target.
DUISBURG \ 8/9.4.43 \ 5 a/c \ Bad weather again spoilt marking so bombing scattered.
FRANFURT \ 10/11.4.43 \ 12 a/c \ First operation against this target from Snaith. Raid was a failure due to complete cloud cover and consequent poor marking.
STUTTGART \ 14/15.4.43 \ 15 a/c \ Good marking but bombs falling short.
PILSEN \ 16/17.4.43 \ 17 a/c \ Bombers missed the main target, the Skoda armament factory.
MANNHEIM \ Second in size to Duisburg as an inland port. Important I.G.Farben chemical plant located in suburb of Ludwigshaven on the west bank of the Rhine.
Operation \ 16/17.4.43 \ 1 a/c \ Successful raid due to accurate PFF marking.
STETTIN \ Longer trip than Berlin, over 1250 miles round trip. Largest seaport in the Baltic acting as a port for Berlin. Important transport centre since an appreciable amount of strategic raw materials came through Stettin from Scandinavia.
Operation \ 20/21.4.43 \ 12 a/c \ See Chapter 7 for personal report.
DUISBURG \ 26/27.4.43 \ 14 a/c \ Accurate marking but raid only partially successful.
'GARDENING' \ 27/28.4.43 \ 4 a/c \ Part of a large minelaying operation by 160 aircraft.
'GARDENING' \ 28/29.4.43 \ 9 a/c \ Denmark area. Large number of aircraft involved in minelaying operations.
ESSEN \ 30.4/1.5.43 \ 11 a/c \ Good sky marking by 'Oboe', appreciable damage to city.
DORTMUND \ Ruhr target. Population 550,000. Contained Hoesch A.G.and Vereinigte Stahlwerke A.G. engineering works ranking in importance with Krupps.
Operation \ 4/5.5.43 \ 10 a/c \ First heavy raid on this target, severe damage caused, aided by accurate marking.
DUISBURG \ 12/13.5.43 \ 18 a/c \ Another 'Battle of the Ruhr' raid with excellent PFF marking producing severe damage.
BOCHUM \ Ruhr target. Population 634,000. Coal and iron production centre.
Operation \ 13/14.5.43 \ 14 a/c \ Due to decoys many bombs missed the target.
DORTMUND \ 23/24.5.43 \ 19 a/c \ Heaviest raid so far in the 'Battle of the Ruhr'. Good marking and clear weather resulted in a successful raid.
DUSSELDORF \ 25/26.5.43 \ 15 a/c \ This raid was not very successful due to marking difficulties caused by the weather.

ESSEN \ 27/28.5.43 \ 12 a/c \ Sky marking used and bombing scattered.
WUPPERTAL \ Ruhr target. Population 411,000. A Chemical Industry centre. It comprised a continuous built up area alongside the river.
Operation \ 29/30.5.43 \ 13 a/c \ This was one of the successful raids of the Ruhr campaign, with severe damage being caused.
DUSSELDORF \ 11/12.6.43 \ 20 a/c \ This was a fairly successful raid with extensive damage produced.
BOCHUM \ 12/13.6.43 \ 16 a/c \ Target covered by cloud but accurate marking resulted in a successful raid.
LE CREUSOT \ 19/20.6.43 \ 20 a/c \ The target was the Schneider et Cie armament works and a steelworks. The bombers came in at different heights
KREFELD \ Ruhr target. Population 170,000. Contained a number of large steel works including production of special steels. Also a textile industry.
Operation \ 21/22.6.43 \ 18 a/c \ Described in detail in Chapters 3 & 6.
MULHEIM \ 22/23.6.43 \ 15 a/c \ Accurate bombing resulting in severe damage.
WUPPERTAL \ 24/25.6.43 \ 16 a/c \ Accurate marking, successful attack on area of target not previously bombed.
GELSENKIRCHEN \ Ruhr target. Population 323,000. Coal mining area. Gas, coke and synthetic petroleum production facilities.
Operation \ 25/26.6.43 \ 11 a/c \ Target covered by cloud, poor marking, raid on this oil target not very successful.
COLOGNE \ 28/29.6.43 \ 16 a/c \ Successful raid, severe damage.
COLOGNE \ 3/4.7.43 \ 14 a/c \ A second sucessful raid.
GELSENKIRCHEN \ 9/10.7.43 \ 16 a/c \ Poor marking and light damage.
AACHEN \ 13/14.7.43 \ 20 a/c \ Good visibility over target, severe damage caused by incendiaries.

END OF THE BATTLE OF THE RUHR.

MONTBELIARD \ 15/16.7.43 \ 17 a/c \ A 4 Group raid on the Peugot factory which did not receive many hits.

One measurable effect of the bombing campaign on German industrial production could be the coal production figures. In 1942 the annual German coal production reached a high of 547 million tons, but by 1944 this had been reduced to 404 million tons. Then by 1945 it had reached a low of 164 million tons per year.

`BATTLE OF HAMBURG'

HAMBURG \ Second largest city in Germany and its and its greatest port. Population 1,800,000. Contained Blohm and Voss and Deutsche Werft A.G. shipyards, engineering works and armament factories. Also there were manufacturing facilities for chemicals, explosives, and poison gases and large warehouses for storing consumables.

Operation \ 24/25.7.43 \ 24 A/C \ This was the first operation in the `Battle of Hamburg', see Chapter 7.
ESSEN \ 25/26.7.43 \ 19 a/c \ This was a night off for Hamburg, but no rest for the squadron. Successful raid, Krupps works damaged.
HAMBURG \ 27/28.7.43 \ 20 a/c \ See Chapter 7.
HAMBURG \ 29/30.7.43 \ 22 a/c \ See Chapter 7.
REMSCHEID \ 30/31.7.43 \ 19 a/c \ Acurate marking resulted in a successful raid.
HAMBURG \ 2/3.8.43 \ 21 a/c \ See Chapter 7.
MANNHEIM \ 9/10.8.43 \ 16 a/c \ Poor marking resulted in scattered bombing, but appreciable widespread damage.
NUREMBURG \ 10/11.8.43 \ 20 a/c \ Reasonably successful raid.
MILAN \ 12/13.8.43 \ 19 a/c \ An Italian target, raid considered successful. Alfa Romeo works was one of the targets. See post-op notes in Chapter 6.
PEENEMUNDE \ 17/18.8.43 \ 24 a/c \ See Chapter 7 for details of `Operation Hydra'
LEVERKUSEN \ 22/23.8.43 \ 19 a/c \ The main target was the I.G.Farben chemical works but because of scattered bombing due to poor marking the aiming point was missed.

`BATTLE OF BERLIN'

BERLIN \ Distant target with a round trip of over 1,200 miles. As well as its political significance as the capitol of Germany it was of strategic importance. Important transport centre and inland port linked to various parts of Germany by canals and waterways. Contained Tempelhof locomotive workshops.

51 Squadron Operations Between Jan 1943 And May 1945

Operation \ 23/24.8.43 \ 27 a/c \ First raid in the 'Battle of Berlin' campaign. Moderately successful raid marred by high losses amongst the Halifax squadrons.
NUREMBURG \ 27/28.8.43 \ 21 a/c \ H2S marking. Bombing scattered on outskirts.
MUNCHEN GLADBACH-RHEYDT \ Ruhr target. Population 130,000. Textile centre.
Operation \ 30/31.8.43 \ 20 a/c \ Good marking and very concentrated bombing.
BERLIN \ 31.8/1.9.43 \ 21 a/c \ Unsuccessful raid, again with high losses amongst the Halifax squadrons.
'GARDENING' \ 2/3.9.43 \ 6 a/c \ Minelaying.
MANNHEIM-LUDWIGSHAFEN \ 5/6.9.43 \ 21 a/c \ Cloud free target along with successful marking resulted in severe destruction.
MUNICH \ 6/7.9.43 \ 16 a/c \ Scattered bombing due to aiming problems.
MONTLUCON \ 15/16.9.43 \ 18 a/c \ The target was the Dunlop Rubber factory which was hit thanks to accurate marking.
MONDANE \ 16/17.9.43 \ 16 a/c \ This raid on important railway yards was not very successful.
HANNOVER \ 22/23.9.43 \ 24 a/c \ Faulty forecast winds resulted in bombing being concentrated away from aiming point.
MANNHEIM \ 23/24.9.43 \ 20 a/c \ Concentrated bombing around the aiming point.
HANNOVER \ 27/28.9.43 \ 23 a/c \ Faulty forecast winds again meant bombs dropped well away from the aiming point.
BOCHUM \ 29/30.9.43 \ 12 a/c \ Accurate and concentrated bombing.
'GARDENING' \ 2/3.10.43 \ 8 a/c \ Minelaying.
KASSEL \ 3/4.10.43 \ 22 a/c \ Bombs fell mainly on suburbs and outskirts.
FRANFURT \ 4/5.10.43 \ 20 a/c \ This raid produced extensive destruction of parts of the city.
HANNOVER \ 8/9.10.43 \ 21 a/c \ Accurate marking with concentrated bombing. Night fighters very active.
KASSEL \ 22/23.10.43 \ 21 a/c \ Devastating firestorm with a large number of casualties. Aircraft factories seriously damaged.
DUSSELDORF \ 3/4.11.43 \ 22 a/c \ Extensive damage produced.
CANNES \ 11/12.11.43 \ 20 a/c \ This mainly Halifax raid on railway workshops was very innaccurate.
MANNHEIM-LUDWIGSHAFEN \ 18/19.11.43 \ 19 a/c \ This was a diversionary raid for a Berlin operation, but due to attacks from fighters the losses were greater than amongst the aircraft involved in the main operation.
LEVERKUSEN \ 19/20.11.43 \ 19 a/c \ Bad weather produced scattered bombing but it helped the RAF by grounding the night fighters and reducing losses.
BERLIN \ 22/23.11.43 \ 18 a/c \ This was the most effective and concentrated of the Berlin raids. The night fighters were grounded by bad weather, which reduced casualties.
FRANKFURT \ 25/26.11.43 \ 15 a/c \ This was a mainly Halifax raid and the bombing was scattered.
STUTTGART \ 26/27.11.43 \ This mainly Halifax raid was a diversion for the main Berlin raid and withdrew many of the nightfighters.
LEIPZIG \ 3/4.12.43 \ 16 a/c \ The most successful raid on Leipzig during the war. Junker's aircraft factory damaged.
MOON PERIOD \ 4.12 to 10.12.43 \ 51 Squadron was stood down for 7 days.
CANCELLED OPERATIONS \ Raids on 1.12 and 11.12.43 cancelled late in the evening after a briefing had been carried out.
FRANFURT \ 20/21.12.43 \ 16 a/c \ The Germans predicted the track the bombers would take, so the night fighters produced high losses.
BERLIN \ 29/30.12.43 \ 23 a/c \ A diversionary approach route confused the defenders and this along with bad weather reduced the losses. Attack was concentrated on sky markers.
BERLIN \ 20/21.1.44 \ 51 Sqdn. 11 a/c, 578 Squdn. 6 a/c \ First joint raid by the 2 squadrons at Snaith after formation of 578 Squadron from 'C' Flight of 51 Squadron.
MAGDEBURG \ 21/22.1.44 \ 51 Sqdn. 11 a/c, 578 Sqdn 6 a/c \ Fighters engaged the bombers early on, losses high, in particular amongst the Halifax contingent. Bombs dropped well away from the target area.
BERLIN \ 25.1 and 27.1.44 \ Both raids cancelled after briefing.
BERLIN \ 28/29.1.44 \ 51 Sqdn. 11a/c & 578 Sqdn 9 a/c \ Cloud over target, bad weather reduced fighter interception but Halifax squadrons had higher percentage losses than Lancaster squadrons.
BERLIN \ 30/31.1.44 \ 51 Sqdn. 8 a/c, 578 Sqdn 13 a/c, last operation of 578 Sqdn at Snaith. Concentrated attack, losses high.
BERLIN \ 15/16.2.44 \ 16 a/c \ Heaviest raid on Berlin. Diversionary tactics appeared to reduce losses.

LEIPZIG \ 19/20.2.44 \ 16 a/c \ Night fighters harried the bomber stream most of the way causing high losses in the Halifax contingent. This resulted in the withdrawal of Halifax 11s & Vs from operations over Germany.
STUTTGART \ 20/21.2.44 \ 12 a/c \ Bombs scattered. Diversionary operations resulted in low losses.
SCHWEINFURT \ 24/25.2.44 \ 16 a/c \ Attack in two waves 2 hours apart. Highest loss in first wave. Target ball bearing factories.
AUGSBERG \ 25/26.2.44 \ 8 a/c \ First major raid on this target carried out in two waves which reduced casualties. Successful attack in clear weather.
STUTTGART \ 1/2.3.44 \ 14 a/c \ Heavy cloud affected the marking and reduced night fighter activity. Very low losses.
TRAPPES \ 6/7.3.44 \ 15 a/c \ Squadrons first pre-invasion strategic operation against a railway target produced a lot of damage.
LE MANS \ 7/8.3.44 \ 11 a/c \ A mainly Halifax raid on another railway target.
LE MANS \ 13/14.3.44 \ 19 a/c \ Halifax raid on a railway station, engines and rolling stock.
STUTTGART \ 15/16.3.44 \ 20 a/c \ Bombs fell short of target.
FRANKFURT \ 18/19.3.44 \ 20 a/c \ Accurate marking resulted in heavy damage. Losses lower than average.
FRANKFURT \ 22/23.3.44 \ 18 a/c \ Another successful raid but higher losses than previous raid.
BERLIN \ 24/25.3.44 \ 17 a/c \ Last raid in the Battle of Berlin campaign. Bomber stream scattered because of strong winds. Very high losses.
AULNOYE \ 25.3.44 \ 2 a/c \ Railway target, bombing very innacurate due to poor marking.
ESSEN \ 26/27.3.44 \ 18 a/c \ Successful raid with low losses.
NUREMBERG \ 30/31.3.44 \ 18 a/c \ Very traumatic experience for the squadron following on from the end of the Battle of Berlin campaign. See Chapter 7.

STRATEGIC BOMBING CAMPAIGN SEE MAP 12

ST GHISLAIN \ 1/2.4.44 \ 10 a/c \ Railway yards and loco sheds damaged.
LILLE\9/10.4.44\ target Lille\Delivrance Goods Station 72% of goods wagons destroyed.
TERGNIER\10/11.4.44\ Successful raid on railway yards.
TERGNIER \ 18/19.4.44 \ 16 a/c \ Halifax raid on railway target.
OTTIGNIES \ 20/21.4.44 \ 14 a/c \ Railway yards severely damaged by a predominantly Halifax raid.
DUSSELDORF \ 22/23.4.44 \ 13 a/c \ Raid into Germany again. High losses mainly due to night fighters.
KARLSRUHE \ Population 190,000. Transport centre for conveying Ruhr coal to Italian war industries.
Operation \ 24/25.4.44 \ 14 a/c \ Strong wind and cloud over target spoilt marking and reduced the success of the raid.
VILLENEUVE-ST- GEORGE \ 26/27.4.44 \ Important railway yards near Paris. Target successfully bombed.
ESSEN \ 26/27.4.44 \ 9 a/c \ The other part of the Squadron took part in a successful attack on this German target.
MONTZEN \ 27/28.4.44 \ 18 a/c \ A Halifax raid on these railway targets was intercepted by fighters with 10% losses.
MALINES \ 1.5.44 \ 10 a/c \ Marshalling yards attacked and loco sheds damaged.
MANTES-LA-JOLIE \ 6.5.44 \ 12 a/c \ Stores depots and loco sheds damaged.
MORSALINES \ 8/9.5.44 \ 13 a/c \ Heavy batteries in Pas de Calais area attacked as part of the 'spoof' raids. Direct hits on gun positions.
LENS \ 10/11.5.44 \ Successful attack on railway yard.
COLLEIN BEAUMONT \ 11/12.5.44 \ 10 a/c \ Heavy gun positions attacked.
HASSELT \ 12/13.5.44 \ This Halifax raid on railway yards was not very successful.
ORLEANS \ 22/23.5.44 \ 24 a/c \ Halifax raid damaged marshalling yards and workshops.
AACHEN \ 24/25.5.44 \ 18 a/c \ These marshalling yards were an important link in railway system between France and Germany. See Map 12.
COLLEIN BEAUMONT \ 24/25.5.44 \ Heavy gun positions which PFF found difficult to mark.
BOURG LEOPOLD \ 27/28.5.44 \ 24 a/c \ This was a military establishment and the PFF TIs were very accurately dropped so severe damage resulted.
TRAPPES \ 31.5/1.6.44 \ 20 a/c \ Successful attack on marshalling yards.
FERME D'URVILLE \ 1/2.6.44 \ 10 a/c \ Important German radio monitoring station in the invasion area.
HERQUELINGUE \ 4/5.6.44 \ Coastal batteries in Pas de Calais, one of the deception targets.
MONT FLEURY \ 5/6.6.44 \ 23 a/c \ 'D' Day target. See Chapter 7.

51 Squadron Operations Between Jan 1943 And May 1945

CHATEAUDUN \ 6/7.6.44 \ 29 a/c \ 29 a/c \ One of the railway communication targets behind the Normandy battle area bombed at the request of General Montgomery.
ALENCON \ 8/9.6.44 \ 25 a/c \ Railway communications target to prevent German reinforcements from reaching the Normandy beach head.
AIRFIELD \ 9/10.6.44 \ 24 a/c \
MASSEY-PALAISEAU \ 11/12.6.44 \ 25 a/c \ Successful raid on a railway target. See report in Chapter 8 on accurate bombing by F/Sgt Alderson's aircraft.
AMIENS \ 12/13.6.44 \ 30 a/c \ Railway target.
DOUAI \ 14/15.6.44 \ 19 a/c \ Railway target.
FOUILLARD \ 15/16.6.44 \ 19 a/c \ Ammunition dump.
ST MARTIN L'HORTIER \ 17/18.6.44 \ 17 a/c \ Railway target.
SIRACOURT \ 22.6.44 \ 23 a/c \ Squadron's first daylight operation. Target was a 'V' weapons site and storage area which was accurately bombed.
OISEMONT \ 23/24.6.44 \ 24 a/c \ V1 Site. Master bomber transmissions jammed.
LE GRAND ROSSIGNOL \ 24.6.44 \ 23 a/c \ V1 site accurately bombed.
MIMOYECQUES MARQUISE \ 27.6.44 \ 25 a/c \ Daylight raid on V3 supergun site. Bombing conditions good, two large explosions observed.
WIZERNES \ 28.6.44 \ 24 a/c \ Daylight raid on 'V' weapons construction site near St Aumer, France.
VILLERS BBOCAGE \ 30.6.44 \ 24 a/c \ See Chapter 7.
ST MARTIN L'HORTIER \ 4.7.44 \ 22 A/C \ Daylight raid on flying bomb site. Target covered by cloud.
CROIXDALLE \ 6.7.44 \ V weapons site.
LES CATELIERE \ 9.7.44 \ 26 a/c \ Daylight raid on flying bomb launch site. Target covered by cloud.
THIVERNEY \ 12.7.44 \ 20 a/c \ Storage dump for 'V' weapons. Target covered by cloud.
NUCOURT \ 15/16.7.44 \ 20 a/c \ Accurate night attack on flying bomb supply dump.
BOIS DE LA HAIE \ 17.7.44 \ 9 a/c \ Flying bomb sites.
CAEN \ 18.7.44 \ 21/a/c \ 'Operation Goodwood' see Chapter 7.
VAIRES \ 18.7.44 \ 6 a/c \ Halifax operation against railway yards.
BOTTROP \ Ruhr target. Population 86,000. Important industries Rheinische Stahlwerk and oil refineries.
Operation \ 20/21.7.44 \   \Target synthetic oil refinery.   Northern part badly damaged.
KIEL \ 23/24.7.44 \ The first major raid on a German city for two months. An elaborate deception combined with radio countermeasures and a surprise return to a German city confused the nightfighters. The result was a low loss of 0.6% of the bomber force.
STUTTGART \ 24/25.7.44 \ Heavy raid produced severe damage.
FORET DE NIEPPE \ 28/29.7.44 \ Military stores dump in the forest.
TRACEY-BOCAGE AREA \ 30.7.44 \ 4 a/c \ Army support operation. Due to cloud and acting on Master Bomber's instructions not all the aircraft bombed the target.
ANDERBEK \ 1.8.44 \ 26 a/c \ Daylight raid on a flying bomb construction works. Poor weather conditions meant some aircraft could not bomb.
FORET DE NIEPPE \ 3.8.44 \ 10 a/c \ 'V' weapon launching site attacked in in good visibility. Accurate bombing.
BOIS DE CASSAN \ 4.8.44 \ 18 a/c \ Daylight raid on flying bomb storage site.
FORET DE NIEPPE \ 5.8.44 \ 28 a/c \ Daylight raid on flying bomb storage site in good bombing conditions.
HAZEBROUCK \ 6.8.44 \ 21 a/c \ Daylight raid on marshalling yards.
'OPERATION TOTALISE' (MAY-SUR-ORNE) \ 7.8.44 \ 22 a/c \ See Chapter 7.
FORET DE NORMAL \ 9.8.44 \ 25 a/c \ Fuel storage dump.
SOMAIN \ 11.8.44 \ 25 a/c \ Railway marshalling yards.
FORET DE NIEPPE\3.8.44\Daylight raid on 'V' weapon site. Clear visibility produced good bombing results.
BRUNSWICK\12/13.8.44\ Experimental raid without path finder marking to determine accuracy obtained when using H2S to locate target. Some crews bombed wrong towns due to misreading radar returns. Highloss of aircraft.
'OPERATION TRACTABLE' \ 14.8.44 \ 9 a/c \ See Chapter 7.
TIRLEMONT \ 15.8.44 \ 25 a/c \ Luftwaffe night fighter airfield
KIEL \ 16/17.8.44 \ 10 a/c \ Severe damage inflicted on docks, shipbuilding facilities and ships in the harbour.
STERKRADE \ 18/19.8.44 \ Synthetic oil plant in the ruhr severely damaged.
PONT ASBAGNOL \ 25/26.8.44 \ 21 a/c \ Target heavy anti-aircraft gun position south of Brest. Accurate bombing.

HOMBERG \ 27.8.44 \ The target was the Rhenpreussen synthetic oil refinery at Meerbeck. First major daylight raid into Germany from Snaith. 'Oboe' marking. Intense flak.
LUMBRES \ 31.8.44 \ 20 a/c \ Daylight raid on V2 rocket site near St Omer, N France.
VENLO \ 3.9.44 \ 19 a/c \ Attack on Luftwaffe airfield in Holland.
ALYIS LE HAVRE \ 10.9.44 \ 24 A/C \ German strong point.
GELSENKIRCHEN \ 11.9.44 \ 24 a/c \ Daylight raid on Nordstern synthetic oil plant. Bombing hampered by a smoke screen.
WILEMSHAVEN \ 14.9.44 \ 15 A/C \ Aircraft recalled whilst over the North Sea.
BOULOGNE\17.9.44\Daylight attack on German troop positions. Garrison surrendered shortly afterwards.
MUNSTER\12.9.44\First raid on this target since June 1943. severe fire damage.
KIEL\15/16.9.44\Highly concentrated raid.
CALAIS \ 20.9.44 \ Operation cancelled.
DUSSELDORF \ 23/24.9.44 \ 24 a/c \ Docks and factories bombed.
CALAIS\25.9.44\Daylight attack on German defensive positions. Due to low cloud on 33% of aircarft bombed.
CALAIS \ 27.9.44 \ 11 a/c \ Operation against German troop positions.
COLOGNE\28.9.44\Enermous damage to target including power stations, Railway & harbour installations.
BOTTROP \ 30.9.44 \ 15 a/c \ Oil plant target.Aircraft had difficulty in finding target.
STERKRADE \ 6.10.44 \ 24 a/c \ Daylight raid on oil plant in clear conditions resulting in accurate bombing.
KLEVE \ 7.10.44 \ 28 a/c \ Daylight army support raid, to hold up German reinforcements.
BOCHUM \ 9/10.10.44 \ 17 a/c \ Target covered with cloud, raid not very successful since bombing scattered.
DUISBURG \ 14.10.44 \ 18 a/c \ This raid was part of 'Operation Hurricane' which was a joint effort with 8th USAAF Bomber Command to demonstrate to the enemy that the Allies had aerial superiority. The enemy flak defences were overwhelmed by the magnitude of the attack which involved 1,013 RAF bombers with fighter escort.
WILEMSHAVEN \ 15/16.10.44 \ 19 a/c \ Target suffered severe damage.
HANNOVER \ 21/22.10.44 \ 18 a/c \ Aircraft recalled because of deteriorating weather over England.
ESSEN \ 23/24.10.44 \ 23 a/c \ Heaviest raid of the war on this target. Bomb load mainly HEs.
ESSEN \ 25.10.44 \ 22 a/c \ Daylight raid. Cloud cover over target so sky marking used. Severe damage to Krupps steel works.
COLOGNE \ 28.10.44 \ 17 a/c \
COLOGNE \ 30/31.10.44 \ 20 a/c \ Cloud cover so sky markers used. Large tonnage of HEs dropped.
COLOGNE \ 31.10/1.11.44 \ 13 a/c \ Cloud covered target marked by 'Oboe'.
DUSSELDORF \ 2/3.11.44 \ 19 a/c \ Very heavy raid.
BOCHUM \ 4/5.11.44 \ 20 a/c \ Successful raid producing heavy damage.
GELSENKIRCHEN \ 6.11.44 \ 20 a/c \ Target Nordstern synthetic oil plant.
JULICH \ 16.11.44 \ 23 a/c \ Daylight raid in support of American army advance.
MUNSTER \ 18.11.44 \ 21 a/c \ Daylight raid but bombing not very concentrated.
STERKRADE \ 21/22.11.44 \ 22 a/c \ Target a synthetic oil refinery.
ESSEN \ 28/29.11.44 \ 26 a/c \ Another attack on Essen causing considerable damage to the industrial area and Krupps armament works.
DUISBURG \ 30.11/1.12.44 \ 30 a/c \ Target obscured by cloud and bombing not concentrated.
HAGEN \ 2/3.12.44 \ 21 a/c \ Successful raid since a lot of industrial targets were damaged.
SOEST \ 5/6.11.44 \ 18 a/c \ Successful raid on an important railway installation.
OSNABRUCK \ 6/7.12.44 \ 22 a/c \ Factories and railway yards damaged. The squadron aircraft LV937 achieved its 100th operation on this raid.
ESSEN \ 12/13.12.44 \ 19 a/c \ Early night raid causing appreciable damage to an already well bombed target.
DUISBURG \ 17/18.12.44 \ 20 a/c \ Appreciable damage.
BINGEN \ 22/23.12.44 \ 10 a/c \ Accurate attack on railway marshalling yards.
OPLADEN \ 27/28.12.44 \ 23 a/c \ Attack on Kalk-nord marshalling yards.
LUDWIGSHAVEN \ 2/3.12.44 \ 23 a/c \ Accurate bombing, the main target being the I.G.Farben chemical works.
HANNOVER \ 5/6.1.45 \ 21 a/c \ First heavy raid on this target which the squadron had participated in since October 1943.
SAARBRUCKEN \ 13/14.1.45 \ Effective raid on a railway yard.
DULMEN \ 14/15.1.45 \ 20 a/c \ See report in Chapter 7.

51 Squadron Operations Between Jan 1943 And May 1945

MAGDEBURG \ 16/17.1.45 \ 18 a/c \ Successful area raid.
STUTTGART \ 28/29.1.45 \ 19 a/c \ Target Zuffenhauser aero engine and jet engine plant.
WANNE EICKEL \ 2/3.2.45 \ 20 a/c \ Target synthetic oil plant.
GOCH \ 7/8.2.45 \ 20 a/c\ Support operation for advance of British XXX Corps. Some aircraft came below cloud base but could not bomb because smoke obliterated target.
GELSENKIRCHEN\4/5.2.45\Target Nordstern synthetic oil plant. Most bombs missed target.
CHEMNITZ \ 14/15.2.45 \ 12 a/c \ Raid took place in two phases, three hours apart.
WESSEL \ 17.2.45 \ 15 a/c \ Master Bomber aborted raid after only a few Halifax aircraft had bombed.
DUSSELDORF \ 20/21.2.45 \ 11 a/c \ Bombing caused cessation of oil production at Rhenania Ossag refinery.
WORMS \ 21/22.2.45 \ 14 a/c \ First raid on this target.
ESSEN \ 23.2.45 \ 12 a/c \ Daylight raid on cloud covered target.
KAMEN \ 24.2.45 \ 14 a/c \ 'Oboe' assisted daylight raid on synthetic oil plant.
MAINZ \ 27.2.45 \ 15 a/c \ Successful 'Oboe' assisted raid
COLOGNE\2/3.3.45\Highly destructive raid, shortly before capture by American Army.
KAMEN\3/4.3.45\Successful raid. Production ceased at Bergkamen sythetic oli plant.
CHEMNITZ \ 5/6.3.45 \ 15 a/c \ 'Operation Thunderclap'.
HEMMINGSTEDT \ 7/8.3.45 \ 13 a/c \ Target, Deutches Erdoel oil plant.
HAMBURG \ 8/9.3.45 \ 12 a/c \ Target U Boat construction yards.
ESSEN \ 11.3.45 \ 14 a/c \ Accurate raid on cloud covered target assisted by 'Oboe' marking.
DORTMUND \ 12.3.45 \ 16 a/c \ Cloud covered target.
WUPPERTAL/BARMEN \ 13.3.45 \ 16 a/c \ Daylight raid on cloud covered target.
HOMBERG \ 14/15.3.45 \ 9 a/c \ Army support raid to restrict movement of German troops.
WITTEN \ 18/19.3.45 \ 19 a/c \ Raid carried out in good visibility, large amount of damage.
RECKLINGHAUSEN \ 20.3.45 \ 15 a/c \ Daylight raid on marshalling yards.
RHEINE \ 21.3.45 \ 15 a/c \ Target railway yards.
STERKRADE \ 24.3.45 \ 26 a/c \ Very successful daylight raid on railway yards.
OSNABRUCK \ 25.3.45 \ 18 a/c \ Daylight raid which produced extensive damage.
HARBURG \ 4/5.4.45 \ 20 a/c \ Severe damage to Rhenia oil plant.
TRAVEMUNDE \ 8/9.4.45 \ 22 a/c \ Diversionary raid for main raid on Hamburg.
BAYREUTH \ 11.4.45 \ 20 a/c \ Daylight raid on railway target as diversion from main raid on Nuremberg.
KIEL \ 13/14.4.45 \ 20 a/c \ Halifax raid on U Boat shipyards.
SQUADRON REDUCED TO 2 FLIGHTS \ 15.4.45 \
HELIGOLAND \ 18.4.45 \ 20 a/c \ Last raid from Snaith by 51Squadron. Targets naval base and airfield.
SQUADRON MOVED TO LECONFIELD \ 20.4.45 \
WANGEROOGE \ 25.4.45 \ 18 a/c \ Last raid carried out by squadron now operating from Leconfield. Target, coastal batteries controlling approaches to Bremen and Wilemshaven.

VICTORY IN EUROPE 8th MAY 1945.

APPENDIX D

ROLL OF HONOUR

Casualties which occured whilst the squadron was serving at Snaith.

(See end of list for abbreviations)

NAME	RANK	DATE	A/C OR INCIDENT
Adams K E C	Sgt	18.08.44	LW538
Adams L R	Sgt	30.03.44	LV822
Adams R H	W/O	30.03.44	LV777
Adams S G	Sgt	04.04.43	DT686
Ainsworth S	Sgt	03.12.43	HR782
Aitken A	Sgt	27.05.43	HR789
Albone A R	Sgt	19.02.44	LW481
Allan A	W/O	05.01.45	MZ767
Allen C M	Sgt	30.06.44	LV782
Ambrose B J	F/Sgt	04.11.44	LW177
Anderson J J	F/Sgt	11.06.43	HR788
Anderson P N	F/Sgt	18.08.44	LW538
Andrew A S	Sgt	08.10.43	JD253
Andrews H	Sgt	14.03.45	NP932
Andrews W	Sgt	24.06.43	JD250
Annis L	Sgt	16.01.45	LW461
Arbon F J	Sgt	01.05.44	MZ593
Arbon H G	F/O	04.11.44	LW177
Armstrong Y A	F/Sgt	21.03.45	MZ348
Arnold W R	F/Lt	02.02.45	MZ487
Atkinson J J	Sgt	16.01.45	LW461
Atkinson L N	F/Sgt	24.02.44	LV778
Audley D J	Sgt	29.07.43	JD309
Austin F H	Sgt	04.04.43	DT686
Austin G F	Sgt	02.10.43	LW287
Austin W T	Sgt	08.10.43	JD253
Avery C	Sgt	01.03.43	BB223
Axtell D	F/Sgt	16.04.43	HR784
Bailey C	Sgt	08.10.43	JD253
Baker F J	P/O	03.12.43	HR732
Baldry C N	Sgt	21.01.44	?
Baldwin L H	Sgt	18.03.44	LK750
Ball L W	F/Sgt	20.12.43	JD123
Bankes-Martin R A	Sgt	09.01.43	DT483
Baptist R	Sgt	06.08.44	LW546
Barker D	Sgt	29.04.43	JD309
Barnard J A	Sgt	03.03.43	W7861
Baron E H	F/O	18.12.44	NP934
Barrett F H	Sgt	27.01.43	DT705

Barrie A	Sgt	20.04.43	DT628
Barron H	Sgt	30.06.44	LV782
Barton J G	Sgt	25.06.43	HR730
Bates W.A.	W/O	17.12.44	NR248
Baston	Sgt	12.06.44	NA294
Beachump A	Sgt	01.03.43	BB223
Beare E S	Sgt	21.07.44	MZ821
Beech S P	Sgt	24.05.44	LK885
Bell K T	F/O	02.02.45	MZ487
Bell R D	F/Lt	06.10.44	MZ343
Bell W A	F/O	21.07.44	MZ821
Benfield V H	F/Sgt	19.06.43	B.D.E.
Bennett G H	Sgt	22.10.43	JN920
Bennett J H	Sgt	05.09.43	JD263
Berry H E	Sgt	18.12.44	NR248
Berry L	F/Sgt	04.11.44	MZ933
Bidwell J	Sgt	18.11.44	NR241
Biddle F J	Sgt	11.06.43	HR788
Binder J P G	Sgt	30.03.44	LV857
Bird H	Sgt	14.03.43	NP932
Bischoff J N	F/O	24.09.44	MZ972
Bishop A T	Sgt	03.07.43	JD262
Bishop P W	Sgt	24.05.44	LV784
Black A M	Sgt	23.05.43	HR836
Blackburn E A	F/Sgt	08.06.44	LW364
Blackie W	Sgt	24.06.43	JD250
Blake P R J	Sgt	12.05.43	DT685
Blundell P	Sgt	25.06.43	HR730
Bonner S	Sgt	28.06.43	DT513
Boulton A W T	Sgt	05.01.45	MZ767
Bowen W G	Sgt	05.01.45	LV952
Bowling H	F/O	30.03.44	LW544
Bowthorpe D F	Sgt	24.03.44	LW539
Boyce J S	Sgt	26.04.43	HR778
Boyd R V	Sgt	28.06.43	DT513
Boyes W H	Sgt	08.10.43	JD253
Bradley A A A	F/O	12.08.44	MZ349
Bradshaw A J	Sgt	30.03.44	LV822
Bramwell C A	F/Sgt	08.06.44	LW364
Brandon A	Sgt	22.11.43	HR726
Brandon A G	F/O	07.10.44	NA933
Branscombe J	Sgt	03.04.43	DT738
Brawn H	F/Sgt	11.08.44	LW588
Bray L R	Sgt	16.04.43	DT561
Brear J	Sgt	30.03.44	LV857
Brett B T	Sgt	20.04.43	DT628
Briffett S J	Sgt	16.04.43	DT561
Brigden C M	Sgt	26.04.43	HR787
Briggs H A	Sgt	30.04.43	HR733
Brisbane W C	F/O	16.04.43	HR729
Brodie A E	Sgt	11.06.43	HR788
Brondgeest L J	W/O	31.08.43	HR931
Brooks G E	F/Lt	12.04.45	O.A.S.
Brooks J	P/O	30.03.44	LW579
Brookes J H	Sgt	27.01.43	DT705
Brougham G C	F/Sgt	30.03.43	LW544
Brown A	Sgt	25.05.43	HR853

Brown E G	Sgt	12.05.43	DT685
Brown F C	Sgt	27.04.44	LV783
Brown G	F/Lt	06.08.44	LW546
Brown G H	Sgt	08.10.43	JN885
Brown J F	Sgt	24.02.44	LV778
Brown W	Sgt	23.05.43	HR835
Bruce T	W/O	18.11.44	NR241
Buchanan J G	Sgt	13.11.43	O.A.S.
Buckingham E M	F/Sgt	30.03.44	LV777
Bucknall J G	Sgt	21.01.44	LV774
Bunn S J	F/O	06.01.45	MZ811
Bunting B A	Sgt	12.05.43	DT645
Burchett A	F/Lt	20.12.43	HR948
Burgum R E	Sgt	27.04.44	MZ565
Burrows D E	F/Sgt	04.11.44	MZ933
Burt R C	Sgt	16.04.43	DT561
Burton W	F/Sgt	05.01.45	LV952
Busby S	Sgt	25.05.43	HR853
Butler W C	Sgt	28.06.43	HR839
Cameron D J	F/Sgt	27.08.43	HR869
Cameron S	Sgt	28.01.44	LW466
Campbell A	Sgt	21.01.43	DT581
Campbell A	Sgt	03.03.43	W7861
Cantle A B	F/Sgt	04.11.44	MZ933
Canty F A	Sgt	28.01.44	LW466
Carmichael J A L	F/Sgt	24.02.44	LV778
Carrington G C	F/Sgt	27.08.43	HR869
Carter L T	Sgt	21.11.44	NR129
Cartwright J E	Sgt	18.08.44	LW538
Cassini C W	F/O	18.12.44	NP934
Cates L R	P/O	31.08.43	HR931
Cattrall P R	Sgt	15.03.44	HX330
Cawthorne J T	Sgt	05.09.43	JD263
Chaplin R	W/O	27.04.44	MZ565
Chapman G W	F/Lt	21.11.44	NR129
Chambers W J	Sgt	25.05.43	HR853
Chester J H	P/O	18.11.44	NR241
Chislett K	Sgt	08.10.43	JD243
Chittock I L	Sgt	24.05.44	LV784
Chittock W V	Sgt	26.04.43	HR787
Chopping S E	P/O	14.03.45	NP932
Christie C	Sgt	18.04.44	LW522
Churchill D A	Sgt	30.03.44	LW579
Clark J D	Sgt	21.11.44	NR129
Clark W G	F/Sgt	27.04.44	LW479
Clarke L F	P/O	15.03.44	LW497
Claxton R	Sgt	01.05.44	MZ593
Clements R F	F/O	16.04.43	?
Cockbaine M W	F/Sgt	21.11.44	NR129
Cogdell C N V	Sgt	12.05.43	HR786
Colangelo W	Sgt	01.03.43	BB223
Cole J S	F/O	25.07.43	HR934
Coleman S H	F/O	06.08.44	LW546
Collas C	F/Sgt	18.11.44	NR241
Colley R J	Sgt	24.02.44	LV778
Collyer C T	F/O	07.10.44	NP933

Connell T S	Sgt	30.03.44	LW579
Conner J G	F/O	02.10.43	LW287
Cook R G	Sgt	02.08.44	MZ767
Cooke J R A	Sgt	30.06.44	LV782
Cookson J	F/O	23.05.43	HR835
Cope J F	Sgt	08.06.44	LW364
Cordery T S	Sgt	18.11.44	NR241
Corps A G	Sgt	03.05.43	DT729
Coscriff B P	F/O	21.07.44	MZ581
Costello J J	Sgt	03.07.43	JD262
Cotton E J	Sgt	27.05.43	HR789
Coughlin L	Sgt	27.04.44	LV783
Cousin H	Sgt	24.07.43	HR940
Cousin J R	AC2	19.06.43	B.D.E
Cowan R J A	Sgt	09.01.43	DT483
Cowie J C	Sgt	22.10.43	JN920
Cowling A F	P/O	06.08.44	LW546
Cox E W	Sgt	16.04.43	DT561
Craig W H	P/O	20.12.43	JD123
Crofts R	Sgt	08.10.43	JN885
Crowther J	Sgt	25.07.43	HR749
Cumber J S	Sgt	11.08.44	LW588
Cummings A P	F/O	30.03.44	LV777
Cunningham A F	F/O	06.10.44	MZ343
Curtiss R	F/Lt	24.03.44	MZ507
Dadds K	F/Sgt	30.03.44	LV777
Daragon J A	Sgt	27.01.43	DT731
Dards E P	Sgt	16.04.43	?
Darvall J H J	Sgt	20.12.43	JD123
Davies C	Sgt	03.03.43	W7861
Davies J C	P/O	08.6.44	LW364
Davies J S	F/Sgt	14.03.45	NP932
Davies W P	Sgt	25.05.43	HR853
Davis D H V	F/O	25.06.43	JD261
Davis F	Sgt	08.10.43	JN885
Davis I C	F/Sgt	03.12.43	HR732
Dawkins J J	F/O	03.10.43	HR728
Debben R E	Sgt	03.07.43	JD262
Dempster D	Sgt	20.12.43	JD123
Dennis T R	Sgt	15.03.44	HX330
Dixon J	Sgt	03.10.43	HR728
Dobson T R	F/Lt	27.08.43	HR869
Donkin E W	F/Sgt	06.08.44	LW546
Dormon R E	F/Sgt	07.03.43	DT567
Dowling V J	P/O	29.03.43	BB244
Duckworth N	Sgt	15.03.44	HX330
Duncan J B	Sgt	01.03.43	BB223
Dunkley R H	Sgt	17.09.44	LV865
Dyer E	Sgt	22.11.43	LW286
Eastwell F S	F/O	02.03.45	MZ451
Edwards A J	Sgt	25.07.43	HR934
Edwards J G	W/O	16.04.43	HR729
Edwards J L	Sgt	23.05.43	HR835
Edwards R J	Sgt	03.12.43	HR732
Elliot J H	F/Sgt	14.03.45	NP932

Name	Rank	Date	Aircraft
Elliot R H	Sgt	22.06.43	JD251
Emerson J	Sgt	25.06.43	HR730
Emery A	F/O	04.04.43	DT686
Eno L H	S/Ldr	15.03.44	LW497
Entwistle D	F/Sgt	21.01.44	LV774
Everitt J O	Sgt	15.03.44	LW497
Evans G E	Sgt	11.06.43	HR788
Evans H J	Sgt	06.08.43	HR783
Fairmaner A W	Sgt	25.06.43	JD261
Farley H F	P/O	22.11.43	LW286
Farrar D W	Sgt	02.02.45	MZ489
Fell A K D	F/Lt	15.03.44	HX330
Fenner R C	Sgt	28.01.45	MZ794
Fenning E	Sgt	04.10.43	HR727
Findley W	Sgt	08.10.43	JD253
Fisher G	Sgt	26.04.43	HR778
Fitchett A J	P/O	24.06.43	JD250
Fleming R A	Sgt	24.07.43	HR940
Flemming W	Sgt	04.04.43	DT686
Fletcher A	F/O	21.04.44	LV775
Fletcher A	Sgt	29.07.43	JD309
Ford D C	Sgt	24.07.43	HR940
Fortin G	F/Sgt	04.10.43	HR727
Francis E D	Sgt	19.06.43	B.D.E.
Franklin R F J	Sgt	18.08.44	LW538
Freeman H G	Sgt	23.05.43	HR836
French G R	F/Sgt	01.05.44	MZ593
Garnham J S	Sgt	03.07.43	JD262
Garrett R A	W/O	11.08.44	LW588
Gartland J	Sgt	07.10.44	NP933
Gibbs H J	Sgt	23.05.43	HR836
Gilchrist W J	Sgt	18.04.44	LW522
Glass S	Sgt	30.03.44	LW579
Glassmane D	Sgt	11.06.43	HR788
Glover E A	F/Sgt	18.03.44	LK750
Glover R H	P/O	20.04.43	DT628
Goddard H	Sgt	12.05.43	DT685
Godfrey S.H	Sgt	22.11.43	LW286
Goldstein D	Sgt	08.10.43	JD253
Gordon J F	Sgt	03.10.43	HR728
Goskirk J D	Sgt	30.03.44	LW537
Gosnav W A	Sgt	24.05.44	LK885
Gott A	F/Sgt	20.12.43	HR948
Green B F K	Sgt	26.04.43	HR787
Green T H	F/O	23.05.43	HR836
Greenhorn W	Sgt	03.05.43	DT729
Greenwood B F	P/O	21.03.45	MZ348
Griffin T J	F/Sgt	28.01.44	LW466
Griffith W D	Sgt	26.04.43	HR787
Griffiths D	Sgt	03.08.43	HR859
Griffiths J E L	Sgt	09.01.43	DT483
Gregory J	Sgt	12.08.44	MZ349
Grose K P	P/O	11.09.44	MZ916
Grozier T E	Sgt	20.12.43	HR868
Grundy J A	F/Lt	03.10.43	HR728

Roll OF Honour

Name	Rank	Date	Code
Guley H R R	Sgt	03.08.43	HR859
Gunn R F	Sgt	21.03.45	MZ348
Gunning E C	Sgt	04.11.44	MZ933
Guy R K	Sgt	03.04.43	DT738
Guy W A	F/Sgt	30.03.44	LV857
Gwynn H J C	Sgt	28.01.44	LW466
Hadlow D	Sgt	08.10.43	JN885
Hall C E	Sgt	22.10.43	JN920
Hall H M	F/Sgt	10.04.44	LV880
Hall R	Sgt	18.12.44	NP934
Hamilton W W B	Sgt	03.12.43	HR732
Hammett L	Sgt	28.01.44	LW466
Hammond L J	Sgt	27.01.43	DT721
Hampson M	F/Sgt	03.12.43	HR732
Hampson R P	P/O	21.07.44	MZ821
Hanson H	Cpl	07.02.43	K.B.C.
Harding A R	Sgt	07.03.43	DT567
Hardwick H	Sgt	06.01.45	MZ811
Harris J J	Sgt	06.10.44	MZ343
Harris R G	P/O	29.03.43	BB244
Harris L G	F/Sgt	11.08.43	HR838
Harthill J C	Sgt	25.02.44	LV778
Hartley C T	F/O	10.04.44	LV880
Harvey C E	Sgt	15.03.44	HX330
Harvey O S	Sgt	22.04.44	MZ566
Hastie E H	Sgt	27.04.44	LV783
Hauber D	F/Sgt	13.01.45	MZ465
Hawes A A	Sgt	25.06.43	JD261
Hawes F	Sgt	22.06.43	JD251
Hawkins S	Sgt	26.04.43	HR778
Hayden T P	Sgt	16.04.43	?
Healey W L	Sgt	06.08.44	LW546
Helliwell A R	Sgt	11.06.43	HR788
Hendry A J	P/O	12.05.43	HR786
Hendry J	Sgt	20.12.43	JD123
Heptonstall A	F/Sgt	29.03.43	BB244
Hepworth R	Sgt	24.03.44	MZ507
Hetterley H O	F/O	22.11.43	LW286
Hewitt R W A	Sgt	30.04.43	HR733
Hickmott E	Sgt	08.10.43	JN885
Hilderbrand H W	W/O	18.12.44	NP934
Hill F P	S/Ldr	30.03.44	LV777
Hill J	Sgt	14.11.44	LK844
Hilton J	Sgt	08.06.44	LW364
Hissette A	W/O	16.01.45	LW461
Hitchen R C	Sgt	18.12.44	NP934
Hobbs F	F/Sgt	30.03.43	LV777
Hobkirk K S	Sgt	12.05.43	DT685
Hockley P D	Sgt	18.11.44	NR241
Hodgson G I	F/O	05.01.45	MZ767
Holden R	F/Sgt	18.12.44	NP934
Holding W	Sgt	26.04.43	HR787
Holmes A L	P/O	07.03.43	DT567
Houlston J L R	P/O	28.06.43	HR839
Hovell D J	P/O	14.03.45	NP932
Howarth A	Sgt	03.04.43	DT686

Howe A	Sgt	01.03.43	BB223
Howse D G	P/O	25.06.43	JD261
Huddy L W A	Sgt	25.07.43	HR749
Huggan B	Sgt	25.06.43	HR731
Hughes R	Sgt	11.09.44	MZ319
Hunt C O V	Sgt	11.08.44	LW588
Hunter L	Sgt	11.09.44	MZ319
Hutchings M L	Sgt	12.06.43	DT568
Hutchinson J	Sgt	04.11.44	LW177
Hyndman G B	F/Sgt	24.05.44	LV784
Iliff J M	Sgt	27.01.43	DT705
Inch D M	Sgt	16.04.43	?
Irwin W	F/Lt	03.10.43	HR728
Jackson D	P/O	24.02.44	LV778
Jackson F	Sgt	03.08.43	HR859
Jackson T J	Sgt	20.12.43	JD123
Jacobs J A C	Sgt	13.05.43	HR790
James A J	AC1	07.02.43	K.B.C.
James A W	F/Sgt	08.10.43	JN885
James B H	Sgt	26.04.43	HR778
James W K	F/O	30.03.43	LV822
Johns D L	F/Sgt	16.01.45	?
Johnson A	Sgt	24.05.44	LW498
Johnson C A	F/O	24.06.43	JD250
Johnson C M	Sgt	06.08.43	HR783
Johnson J M	F/Sgt	03.03.43	W7861
Jones E F	F/Sgt	06.08.44	LW546
Jones E J	Sgt	25.07.43	HR749
Jones H B	Sgt	18.12.44	NP934
Jones J	Sgt	23.05.43	HR835
Jones J A	Sgt	18.12.44	NR248
Jones L J	Sgt	24.09.44	MZ972
Jones N E	Sgt	12.05.43	DT685
Jowett H A	F/O	21.07.44	MZ581
Joyce N	Sgt	24.09.44	MZ972
Jukes A E	Sgt	30.06.44	LV782
Kasher F	Sgt	30.03.44	LV857
Keenan P	Sgt	27.04.44	LV783
Kelly R F	Sgt	30.03.44	LW579
Kemp D W	Sgt	27.08.43	HR869
Kempson K K	F/Sgt	18.08.44	LW538
Kendrick W P	Sgt	14.11.44	LK844
Kennedy D W	Sgt	18.04.44	LW522
Kennedy S W	Sgt	22.06.43	JD251
Kent E	Sgt	28.06.43	DT513
Kent E C	Sgt	02.10.43	LW287
Kenyon J	Sgt	22.04.44	MZ566
Kewell J S	Sgt	02.02.45	MZ487
Kinder W R	Sgt	27.04.44	MZ565
Kinernan E F	Sgt	12.05.43	DT645
King C L	Sgt	12.05.43	DT645
King W J	F/Sgt	05.09.43	JD263
Kinnear G P	F/O	22.04.44	MZ566
Kitchen A D	Sgt	16.04.43	HR729

Roll OF Honour

Name	Rank	Date	Code
Knight F M	Sgt	03.04.43	DT666
Knight R F	Sgt	03.07.43	JD262
Lambert C A	P/O	06.08.43	HR783
Lanaghan J	P/O	21.01.44	LV774
Langford F G	F/Sgt	24.02.44	LV778
Lancaster E L	F/Sgt	16.04.43	?
Lane E	Sgt	04.10.43	HR727
Laroche R E	Sgt	27.04.44	MZ565
Latchford P	Sgt	18.04.44	LW522
Lauder F J	Sgt	03.05.43	DT729
Lawson W C	P/O	24.05.44	LK885
Leach A	P/O	05.01.45	LV952
Leeper R E	W/O	11.08.43	HR838
Leslie D B	Sgt	31.08.43	JN902
Lester A T	Sgt	21.01.44	?
Lewis A O	Sgt	16.04.43	HR729
Lewis J V	Sgt	22.10.43	JN920
Lewis N E	Sgt	21.11.44	NR129
Lheame A H	Sgt	11.08.44	LW588
Liptrott E J	Sgt	31.08.43	JN902
Livermore R E	Sgt	24.07.43	HR940
Locksmith G W	P/O	12.05.43	HR786
Longbottom F	Sgt	06.10.44	NZ343
Longley C N	Sgt	30.04.43	HR733
Lowe R A E	F/O	21.07.44	MZ581
Luff G	Sgt	11.06.43	HR788
Lyster R F	Sgt	20.04.43	DT638
Macphedran G C	Sgt	25.05.43	MR853
Maines F R	P/O	28.06.43	DT513
Marlow G E	F/Sgt	21.01.44	LV775
Marshall J B	F/O	30.03.44	LV822
Martin D B	Sgt	20.04.43	DT628
Martin M A	Sgt	28.01.44	LW466
Mastin J M	Sgt	27.05.43	MR789
Massir de G O M Turville	P/O	12.05.43	HR786
Mathews C J	Sgt	22.06.43	JD251
Matthews W H	Sgt	06.10.44	MZ343
Maughan H F	Sgt	27.08.43	HR869
Maxwell J F	Sgt	04.11.44	LW177
McAleese P J	Sgt	07.03.43	DT567
McBriar W R	P/O	16.04.43	HR784
McCardle F G	Sgt	16.04.43	BT561
McCarthy M G	Sgt	18.04.44	HX350
McClean D	Sgt	02.10.43	LW287
McCormack D P	F/Sgt	30.03.44	LW579
McDonald G	Sgt	04.04.43	DT686
McFarlane A D	Sgt	25.06.43	JD261
McGlynn J	Sgt	27.04.44	LW479
McGregor A A	Sgt	27.08.43	HR869
McKean R P	P/O	27.04.44	LV783
McKensie A L	P/O	21.01.44	LV775
McKenzie J M	F/O	24.06.43	JD250
McLaren E C	Sgt	18.08.44	LW538
McLaren R A	Sgt	16.04.43	DT561

200

McLaughlin T	Sgt	24.07.43	HR940
McQuater J	Sgt	27.04.44	LW479
McQuiston C	F/Lt	24.05.44	LW498
Meering E	Sgt	06.10.44	MZ343
Meeson W G	F/O	18.04.44	HX350
Menary B H	Sgt	30.03.44	LV857
Merricks K	Sgt	27.08.43	HR869
Merrigan W J	Sgt	12.05.43	DT645
Merritt J J	Sgt	03.04.43	DT666
Midgley E R	P/O	12.06.43	DT568
Midlane A L	F/Sgt	15.03.45	?
Millard G W R	F/Sgt	14.11.44	LK844
Milne G	Sgt	20.12.43	HR948
Miluken D W	F/Sgt	03.12.43	HR732
Minmouth M W	F/Lt	11.11.43	O.A.S.
Minton J D	Sgt	23.05.43	HR835
Mitchell W I G	LAC	09.08.44	O.A.S.
Mohr M J S	F/O	06.10.44	MZ343
Monk E J P	Sgt	30.03.44	LV857
Morse A L	Sgt	25.06.43	HR730
Mortimer C C	Sgt	03.08.43	HR859
Moyniham F H	F/O	22.11.43	LW286
Muddiman A A	F/Sgt	16.01.45	LW461
Mullins N A	Sgt	24.05.44	LW498
Mumford H G	F/Sgt	14.03.45	NP932
Mumme R M	Sgt	16.04.43	?
Murdoch R E	Sgt	24.06.43	JD250
Murphy T L	Sgt	22.04.44	MZ566
Murray A	F/Sgt	08.06.44	LW364
Murray K D	Sgt	31.08.43	HR931
Murray W J	Sgt	24.07.43	HR940
Nash H D	Sgt	18.04.44	HX350
Neal R	Sgt	03.08.43	HR859
Neale P	Sgt	05.01.45	LV952
Negrich T	F/O	30.06.44	LV777
Nelson C S	Sgt	02.10.43	LW287
Nelson R	Sgt	05.09.43	JD263
Nesbitt E J	Sgt	12.05.43	DT645
Newman C	Sgt	23.05.43	HR835
Newstead F L	F/O	30.03.44	LV777
Newton W R	Sgt	22.06.43	JD251
Nicholl J	Sgt	30.03.44	LV822
Nixon J E	Sgt	02.10.43	LW287
Noble A	LAC	27.04.45	O.A.S.
Noble G B	Sgt	07.02.43	K.B.C.
Noble J L	Sgt	12.05.43	HR786
O'Donnell A C	AC2	19.06.43	B.D.E.
O'Dowda J F	W/O	15.03.44	LW497
Ollinger J J	W/O	21.07.44	MZ821
O'Neill J P	F/Sgt	27.04.44	MZ565
Osborn J B	F/Sgt	10.04.44	LV880
Osborne C J	Sgt	09.01.43	DT483
Osman E A	Sgt	11.08.44	LW588
Osmond A	Sgt	25.06.43	HR730
Osmond W	Sgt	02.02.45	MZ487

Roll OF Honour

Name	Rank	Date	Aircraft
O'Sullivan J	Sgt	21.04.44	LV774
Owen N F	Sgt	03.05.43	DT729
Oxenburg J	Sgt	01.05.44	MZ593
Page C M	Sgt	27.01.43	DT705
Page L G	F/Sgt	24.09.44	MZ972
Paradise J E	F/O	21.03.45	MZ348
Parker E	Sgt	22.10.43	JN920
Parker J W G	Sgt	23.05.43	?
Parker R H G	Sgt	30.03.44	LW537
Parkin C E	P/O	25.07.43	HR934
Parsons J	Sgt	05.09.43	JD263
Partridge C A	Sgt	27.03.43	?
Payton A W	Sgt	14.11.44	LK844
Pearson I C	Sgt	03.03.43	W7861
Peck G J W	Sgt	10.04.44	LV880
Peel L F	F/Sgt	30.03.44	LW544
Perkins H	Sgt	30.06.44	LV782
Peters G C	Sgt	26.04.43	HR787
Pheloung C E	Sgt	03.04.43	DT666
Pierce E W	Sgt	28.06.43	DT513
Plested J G	F/Sgt	24.09.44	MZ972
Pohe J	F/O	22.09.43	JN901
Pollitt W	Sgt	07.10.44	NP933
Pond A L W	Sgt	26.04.43	HR778
Pople L A	Sgt	07.10.44	NP933
Popplewell E H	F/O	16.01.45	LW461
Porter A G	Sgt	24.05.44	LV784
Porter E D	F/O	08.10.43	JN885
Porter W A	W/O	21.11.44	NR129
Poston W	W/O	02.02.45	MZ487
Powell J E	AC2	19.06.43	B.D.E.
Preece W J	F/Sgt	08.10.43	JN885
Preston J R R	F/O	11.09.44	MZ319
Price J A	F/O	21.01.44	LV774
Pritchard A R	Sgt	05.01.45	MZ918
Pronger G B	F/O	21.04.44	LV774
Pyne W E	Sgt	22.11.43	MR726
Quan W P	F/O	18.04.44	LW538
Radley K M	F/Sgt	30.03.44	LW544
Ralstone D B	Sgt	03.04.43	DT738
Ramshaw J G	Sgt	07.03.43	DT567
Rawcliffe J	Sgt	03.04.43	DT738
Rawlings	P/O	06.04.43	HCU
Ray H	Sgt	16.04.43	HR729
Readman J L	Sgt	26.04.43	HR778
Reay H G N	F/O	04.11.44	LW177
Redshaw A C	Sgt	28.06.43	HR839
Reed D M	Sgt	29.03.43	BB244
Reed W	Sgt	25.07.43	HR749
Rees W	LAC	06.08.43	HR783
Reid D H	Sgt	16.04.43	HR784
Rich P C W	Sgt	12.05.43	DT685
Richards J	F/Sgt	03.04.43	DT738
Richards T W	F/Sgt	06.01.45	MZ811

Richardson C A	Sgt	25.05.43	DT853
Richardson W G	Sgt	03.04.43	DT738
Rigby J E	F/O	13.05.43	HR790
Riley H	Sgt	16.04.43	DT578
Ritchie J B	Sgt	25.07.43	HR749
Roberts A	Sgt	12.06.43	DT568
Roberts E W	F/Sgt	09.01.43	DT483
Roberts G E	Sgt	16.04.43	HR729
Roberts H A	Sgt	12.05.43	HR786
Roberts J	Sgt	25.06.43	JD261
Roberts L G	Sgt	18.12.44	NR248
Robertson J M	Sgt	24.05.44	LV784
Robinson T C	F/O	16.04.43	HR784
Rochester A E	Sgt	13.05.43	HR790
Rogers W A	F/O	16.04.43	DT561
Rohrer F R	P/O	24.04.44	LV778
Rorison J	Sgt	25.06.43	HR730
Rothwell L	F/Lt	27.04.44	LW479
Royal E W	Sgt	11.08.44	LW588
Rudge H	LAC	19.06.43	B.D.E.
Rudkin B A G	F/Sgt	09.01.43	DT483
Runciman I B	F/Sgt	04.11.44	LW177
Saines K E D	Sgt	14.11.44	LK844
Salad J	Sgt	03.05.43	DT729
Salvage A J	P/O	03.12.43	HR732
Sarginson J	P/O	25.07.43	HR934
Sarjantson A	F/Sgt	18.04.44	HX350
Scheffler R S	F/Sgt	18.04.44	HX350
Scott J		24.03.44	MZ507
Seamah C R	Sgt	18.03.44	LK750
Sedgwick D L	F/Lt	22.04.44	MZ566
Sees R G C	Sgt	26.04.43	HR787
Sewell P R	F/O	24.05.44	LV784
Shackleton C	Sgt	18.04.44	LW522
Sharp R	F/Sgt	15.03.44	HX330
Sherer H H	Sgt	20.12.43	JD123
Sherrington S V	Sgt	29.07.43	JD309
Short B	Sgt	04.10.43	HR727
Shortland P	Sgt	20.04.43	DT628
Sigournay D W	Sgt	28.06.43	DT513
Silvester C A H	P/O	10.08.43	HR781
Simpson A F	F/Sgt	02.10.43	LW287
Simpson A F	Sgt	14.11.44	LK844
Sitch R S	Sgt	22.10.43	JN920
Sklarchuk E R	W/O	03.08.43	HR859
Smith A	Sgt	28.06.43	HR839
Smith D C	Sgt	12.05.43	DT645
Smith D J	Sgt	27.05.43	HR789
Smith H	LAC	19.06.43	B.D.E.
Smith H A	Sgt	09.01.43	DT483
Smith J A	Sgt	18.04.44	HX350
Smith J C	Sgt	18.11.44	NR241
Smith R S	Sgt	29.07.43	JD309
Smollan D	AC1	07.02.43	K.B.C.
Smyth J S	P/O	25.07.43	HR934
Snell R	Sgt	17.06.44	O.A.S.

Snow A G	Sgt	03.03.43	W7861
Soloman T C	Sgt	21.01.44	LV775
Spencer H P	Sgt	30.04.43	HR737
Spragg V T	Sgt	14.11.44	LK844
Spratt W S	Sgt	05.01.45	MZ918
Spreckley P G	Sgt	11.06.43	DT742
Springett A B	Sgt	22.11.43	LW286
Spur A	Sgt	22.11.43	HR726
Squibbs F	Sgt	04.10.43	HR727
Stacey W H	Sgt	26.04.43	HR778
Standfield E	F/Sgt	07.10.44	NP933
Staple J S	Sgt	05.01.45	LV952
Steer G	Sgt	13.05.43	HR780
Stembridge M M	F/Sgt	30.03.44	LW537
Stenhouse J D W	F/O	01.03.43	BB223
Stevens A W	Sgt	12.06.43	DT568
Stevens E G	P/O	05.01.45	MZ918
Stevenson R W	Sgt	24.06.43	JD250
Stewart R H	F/Sgt	16.04.43	HR784
Stiefel P G	F/Sgt	24.09.44	MZ972
Stringer C	Sgt	13.05.43	HR790
Stubbs S M	AC1	19.06.43	B.D.E.
Suffolk J D	Sgt	18.11.44	NR241
Sumner T L	Sgt	18.11.44	NR241
Tarrant H	Sgt	03.12.32	HR782
Tay J P	P/O	28.06.43	HR839
Taylor A L	Sgt	24.03.44	MZ509
Taylor F	F/Sgt	18.04.44	LW522
Taylor J M	Sgt	29.03.43	BB244
Taylor L A	Sgt	25.07.43	HR934
Taylor R M	LAC	19.06.43	B.D.E.
Telgam E	Sgt	03.08.43	HR859
Thomas J H	Sgt	27.04.44	LV783
Thomas R	Sgt	18.12.44	NR248
Thompson D	Sgt	04.11.44	LW177
Thompson F	Sgt	12.05.43	DT645
Thompson F H	Sgt	16.04.43	HR784
Thompson G C	Sgt	25.07.43	HR934
Thompson H B	F/Sgt	15.03.44	LW497
Thompson S I	Sgt	22.04.44	MZ566
Thorn R	Sgt	22.11.43	HR726
Toft C	Sgt	21.07.44	MZ821
Tomalin H F	F/O	15.03.43	HX330
Tombe G	Sgt	07.03.43	DT567
Tremain J T	Sgt	07.02.43	K.B.C.
Trott A	F/O	12.06.43	DT568
Tunstall E T	F/O	12.08.44	MZ349
Tunstall R	Sgt	12.05.43	HR786
Turner S C	Sgt	31.08.43	JN902
Twilley B M	P/O	18.12.44	NP934
Ulrich J E	P/O	07.03.43	DT567
Uppington B S	P/O	15.03.44	LW497
Vandy C	Sgt	20.04.43	DT628
Vann D	F/Sgt	21.07.44	MZ821

Veal J K B	Sgt	04.04.43	DT686
Ventham J A	Sgt	03.05.43	DT729
Vidal A	F/Sgt	28.06.43	HR839
Wallace W C	Sgt	25 07.43	HR749
Wallis E V	Sgt	21.11.44	NR129
Walsh B T	Sgt	24.07.43	HR940
Walters L	F/O	16.04.43	HR729
Waring C G	Sgt	20.04.43	DT628
Warren G A	Sgt	06.08.43	HR783
Warwick P V	F/Sgt	24.05.44	LV784
Watkins C	Sgt	29.07.43	JD309
Watkinson R	F/O	03.10.43	HR728
Watson A B	F/Sgt	24.09.44	MZ972
Watson D L	Sgt	21.07.44	MZ821
Watson E	Sgt	06.08.43	HR783
Watson J	Sgt	31.08.43	HR931
Watson W	P/O	03.10.43	HR728
Waye W C	W/O	30.06.44	LV782
Weakley L O	W/O	27.01.43	DT721
Webb J	F/Sgt	17.02.45	MZ765
West G W	Sgt	30.03.44	LW579
White A	Sgt	27.04.44	MZ565
White S	Sgt	27.04.44	MZ565
Whitehead J E	Sgt	22.11.43	LW286
Whitehouse S H	Sgt	13.01.45	MZ465
Whitmore J R	Sgt	05.01.45	MZ918
Whittock W F A	Sgt	21.01.44	LV775
Whyte G E	F/Sgt	21.01.43	DT581
Widdowson T	F/O	20.12.43	HR948
Wilkins E	F/Sgt	30.03.43	LV822
Wilkins J A	P/O	06.08.43	HR783
Williams A H	F/Sgt	30.03.44	LW544
Williams G	Sgt	14.03.45	NP932
Williams H	F/Sgt	30.03.44	LW544
Williams N	Sgt	04.11.44	MZ933
Williams N S	Sgt	22.10.43	JN920
Williams R A B	P/O	01.03.43	BB223
Williams W	F/O	21.01.44	?
Willson W V	Sgt	24.03.44	MZ507
Wilson A P B	P/O	27.05.43	HR789
Wilson D R	Sgt	30.04.43	HR733
Wilson L A	F/O	05.01.45	LV952
Wilson R H	F/Sgt	30.03.44	LV857
Wilson R V S	Sgt	06.01.45	MZ811
Winning T H G	F/Lt	17.02.45	MZ765
Wood K R	Sgt	25.06.43	JD261
Wood M	Sgt	28.06.43	DT513
Wood S	Sgt	12.06.43	DT568
Woods R F	W/O	28.01.44	LW466
Woolhouse S	W/O	03.10.43	HR728
Woosnam W	Sgt	04.04.43	DT686
Worden A C	Sgt	25.05.43	HR853
Worral R	Sgt	29.07.43	JD309
Worthington T W	Sgt	18.12.44	NR248
Wright C L	W/Cdr	22.11.43	HR726
Wright H	Sgt	11.09.44	MZ319

Wright L A	Sgt	23.05.43	HR835
Wyness L H	Sgt	30.03.44	LV822
Yearsley J H	Sgt	05.01.45	MZ918
York L B	Sgt	25.07.43	HR749
Yorke E O D	F/Sgt	18.04.44	LW522
Young J P	Sgt	29.07.43	?
Zapfe M E	Sgt	23.03.43	HR836

ABBREVIATIONS
A/C   = Serial No of Aircraft involved, see Appendices A and C for details of operation and loss.
K.B.C. =   Knottingley bus crash, see Chapter 10.
B.D.E. =   Bomb dump explosion, see Chapter 10.
D.A.S =   Died on active service.
H.C.U. =   Heavy Conversion Unit

P/O Rawlings was killed whilst instructing at an HCU after completing a tour of operations with 51 Squadron. He was flying with a crew under instruction when the aircraft crashed due to a failure of retaining bolts causing a wing to drop off

APPENDIX E

COMMANDERS AND AWARDS

Officers Commanding 51 Squadron at Snaith and Dates of Appointments

Wg/Cdr A.V.Sawyer   8 Oct 1942
Wg/Cdr A.D.Franks   28 Apr 1943
Wg/Cdr D.S.S.Wilkerson   14 Nov 1943
Wg/Cdr R.C.Ayling   1 Feb 1944
Wg/Cdr C.W.M.Ling   1 Apr 1944
Wg/Cdr H.A.R.Holford   8 Nov 1944
Wg/Cdr E.F.E.Barnard   30 Apr 1945

Group Captain D.C. Thompson 1942
Group Captain S.H.C. Gray OBE 1943
Group Captain R.B. Jordan DFC July 1943
Group Captain N.H. Fresson DFC Dec 1943
Group Captain B.D. Sellick DSO Feb 1945

Awards:

Figures which have been quoted for the number of awards gained by 51 Squadron members during World War 2 are as follows:

4 Distinguished Service Orders
1 Bar to the above
237 Distinguished Flying Crosses
3 Bars to the above
1 Military Cross
144 Distinguished Flying Medals
2 Air Force Crosses
Air Force Medals also awarded
2 Conspicuous Gallantry Medals

Mentioned In Despatches citations were awarded to an appreciable number of Ground Crew personnel.

BIBLIOGRAPHY

Air Bombardment, AM Sir Robert Saundby.

The Bomber Offensive, Anthony Vernier.

The Bomber Command War Diaries, Martin Middlebrook.

Bomber Aircraft, Alfred Price.

Confound and Destroy, Martin Streetly.

Night Bombing, Hector Hawton.

Most Secret War, R.V.Jones.

Pathfinder, AVM D.C.T.Bennett.

The Right of the Line, John Terraine.

Watch Opened, R.V.Radford.

51 Squadron Camouflage and Markings, Andrew Thomas,

P405 Scale Aircraft Modelling Aug. 1992.

51 Squadron Operational Record Books, PRO Kew.

Aircraft Record Cards, Air Historical Branch MOD.

GLOSSARY

GLOSSARY

AG - Air Gunner
AI - Air Borne Interception Radar
AM - Air Ministry or Air Marshal
AOC - Air Officer Commanding
AP - Air Publication
API - Air Position Indicator
ASI - Air speed Indicator
ASR - Air Sea Rescue
AUW - All up weight
AMO Air Ministry Orders

BAT - Beam Approach Training
Best Blue - No 1 uniform
BFP - Blind Flying Panel
Blower - Telephone
Bods - Personnel
Boffin - Scientist
Boozer - Rear warning radar.

Cat 'E' - Aircraft written off
CGM - Conspicuous Gallantry Medal.
Chance Light - Landmark Beacon
Chiefy - Flight Sergeant
CO - Commanding Officer
Corkscrew - Evasive action

Darky - Emergency call.
DBR - Damaged beyond repair
DCO - Duty carried out
DF - Direction Finding
DFC - Distinguished Flying Cross
DFM - Distinguished Flying Medal
Ditch - Force landing in the sea
DNCO - Duty not carried out
DR - Deduced or Dead Reckoning
DRC - Distant Reading Compass
DRO - Daily Routine Orders
DREM - Colloquial name for lighting system at Snaith

E/F - Engine fire

EMR - Electro Magnetic Release mechanism.
ENSA - Entertainments National Service Association
'Erks' - Ground crew airmen
ETA - Estimated time of arrival
EWS - Emergency Water Supply

Fag - Cigarette
FFI - Freedom from infection
Fishpond - Night fighter detection device
Flak - German Anti-Aircraft (Flieger Abwehr Kanone)
F/O - Flying Officer
FTR - Failed to return
Fug - Germany radio equipment
'Gardening' - Mine laying
GCI - Ground controlled interception
Get the chop - Fail to return from an operation
Gee - Radar navigation aid
George - Automatic pilot
Goodwood - Maximum effort
Grass - Interference on radar
Gremlins - Mythical spirit blamed for aircraft faults.

HF - High Frequency
Halibag - Halifax aircraft
Happy Valley - Ruhr
HCU - Heavy Conversion Unit
HE - High Explosive
H Hour - Start time for operation
H2S - Ground scanning radar.

IFF - Indentification Friend or Foe
Intruders - German night fighters over UK
IO - Intelligence Officer
I/O Intelligence/Operations

JG - German fighter squadron

Kite - Aircraft
KRR - Kings Rules and Regulations

Lichtenstein - German AI radar
Line shoot - Boast or exaggerate

Mandrel - Radio jamming device
MC - Military Cross
MF - Medium Frequency

Glossary

Monica - Night fighter warning device
MU - Maintenance Unit
M/U AG - Mid upper Air Gunner

NAAFI - Navy Army and Air Force Institute
Naxos - German device to home in on H2S
Nickels - Propaganda leaflets
No Ball - V Weapon sites
NJG - German night fighter squadron

Oboe - Ground controlled radar bombing aid
Oppo - Close friend
OR - Other Ranks, non commissioned ranks
Overlord - Code for Normandy invasion

PFF - Path Finder Force
POR - Personnel Occurrence Report
POW - Prisoner of War
PPI - Radar Plan Position Indicator
Pundit - Flashing landmark beacon

RDF - Original code name for Radar.
Rookie - Raw recruit
RPG - Rounds Per Gun.
R/T - Radio Telephony (Voice communication)

Schrage Musik - German upward firing cannon
Screening - Rest from operations
Sgt - Sergeant
Ski site - V1 weapon site
Skipper - Captain of aircraft
SMO - Station Medical Officer
SNCO - Senior NCO
SP - Service Police
Sprog - Inexperienced airman
SN2 - German AI radar

Tannoy - Amplification system
Tinsel - Jamming system
TI - Target Indicator
TOT - Time over Target
T.Stoff - V1 hydrogen peroxide

U/S - Unserviceable

V Weapon - Vergeltung, revenge weapon
Vegetables - Mines
VHF - Very High Frequency

Wads - Slang for NAAFI cakes.
Wanganui - PFF cloud marking
Wasserman - German early warning radar
Wilde Sau - Free ranging night fighters
Wop/AG - Wireless Operator / Air Gunner.
Wurzburg - Early warning radar

'Y' Form - Intelligence report to Group HQ

Zahme Sau - GCI controlled night fighters